MW00378976

Car Crashes without Cars

Acting with Technology
Bonnie Nardi, Victor Kaptelinin, and Kirsten Foot, editors

Car Crashes without Cars

Lessons about Simulation Technology and Organizational Change from Automotive Design

Paul M. Leonardi

The MIT Press
Cambridge, Massachusetts
London, England

MIT Press books may be purchased at special quantity discounts for business or sales promotional use. For information, please email special_sales@mitpress.mit.edu or write to Special Sales Department, The MIT Press, 55 Hayward Street, Cambridge, MA 02142.

Set in Stone Sans and Stone Serif by Toppan Best-set Premedia Limited. Printed and bound in the United States of America.

Library of Congress Cataloging-in-Publication Data

Leonardi, Paul M., 1979–
Car crashes without cars : lessons about simulation technology and organizational change from automotive design / Paul M. Leonardi.
    p. cm. — (Acting with technology)
Includes bibliographical references and index.
ISBN 978-0-262-01784-8 (hardcover : alk. paper)
1. Automobiles—Design and construction—Data processing. 2. Automobiles—Computer simulation. 3. Technology—Social aspects. I. Title.
TL240.L426 2012
629.28'26—dc23
2012002756

10 9 8 7 6 5 4 3 2 1

for Rodda and Amelia

Contents

Acknowledgments

This book provides an ethnographic account of people's work. People love to talk about their work. In fact, most ethnographers joke that the hard part is not getting people to talk about what they do; it's getting them to shut up! To get people to talk candidly about their experiences, I promised them anonymity. For this reason, I have disguised the names of the individuals I observed and interviewed. This precludes me from thanking them personally here. Nevertheless, my sincerest thanks go out to all the people who taught me about their work. I am also indebted to the terrific engineers at Autoworks (a pseudonym) who warmly welcomed a young researcher. I truly appreciate the assistance and support they provided me in navigating around Autoworks' obstacles.

Steve Barley and Diane Bailey also made this book possible. I learned everything I know about ethnography and the study of technology and work from them. I am lucky to have trained with such masters of the craft. I will always be grateful for the tips they provided as I encountered problems in the field, the encouragement they gave me to pursue my research interests, and the constant friendship they have shown me over the years. Many colleagues at Stanford, including Bob Sutton, Pam Hinds, Woody Powell, Carlos Rodriguez-Lluesma, Tsedal Neeley, and Ingrid Erickson and many colleagues at Northwestern, including Noshir Contractor, Pablo Boczkowski, Eszter Hargittai, Bob Hariman, Dan O'Keefe, and Barbara O'Keefe, also offered very helpful comments on the ideas that found their way onto these pages. Bonnie Nardi, Victor Kaptelinin, and Kristen Foot, the editors of the Acting with Technology series, and Margy Avery and Katie Persons at the MIT Press also worked tremendously hard to make this book possible. I am appreciative of their help. Generous financial support for this research was provided by a grant from the National Science Foundation (ITR 0427173).

On a more personal note, I probably could not have finished writing this book (or maybe I would have finished it faster) had my sisters,

Marianne and Karen, not called constantly to check on my progress. I thank them for their support. I owe my parents, Dan and Vicki, a tremendous debt of gratitude even though they would say I don't. They have always believed in me. Always. Finally, I thank my wife, Rodda, for all her support. I thank her for traveling with me while I collected the data reported herein. I thank her for giving me the gifts of friendship, love, patience, and Amelia while I was writing.

Earlier versions of some of the material in chapter 2 appeared in my 2009 article "Crossing the Implementation Line: The Mutual Constitution of Technology and Organizing Across Development and Use Activities" (*Communication Theory* 19, no. 3: 277–310); portions of that material are included herein with permission from the International Communication Association and John Wiley & Sons.

Earlier versions of some of the material in chapters 2 and 8 appeared in my 2011 article "When Flexible Routines Meet Flexible Technologies: Affordance, Constraint, and the Imbrication of Human and Material Agencies" (*MIS Quarterly* 35, no. 1: 147–167; portions of that material are included herein with permission from the Management Information Systems Research Center at the University of Minnesota's Carlson School of Management.

Earlier versions of some of the material in chapters 4 and 5 appeared in my 2011 article "Innovation Blindness: Culture, Frames, and Cross-Boundary Problem Construction in the Development of New Technology Concepts" (*Organization Science* 22, no. 2: 347–369); portions of that material are included herein with permission from the Institute of Operations Research and the Management Sciences.

Earlier versions of some of the material in chapter 6 appeared in my 2009 article "Why Do People Reject New Technologies and Stymie Organizational Changes of Which They Are in Favor? Exploring Misalignments Between Social Interactions and Materiality" (*Human Communication Research* 35, no. 3: 407–441; portions of that material are included herein with permission from the International Communication Association and John Wiley & Sons.

1 Perceptions of Inevitability

In August of 2005, a team of experienced technology developers at Autoworks—the pseudonym that will be used here for a major American automaker[1]—filed into a dark conference room for yet another meeting with consultants from a young and eager software startup firm. In the past two years, Autoworks' team of developers had met with representatives from the startup at least two dozen times to discuss the specifications for Crash-Lab, a computer-based simulation technology that was supposed to "revolutionize product design work at Autoworks." Looking at the faces of the consultants from the startup, one could see they were excited to be there. Helping to build a mathematically sophisticated computer-based simulation tool for a major automobile company was not only good work; it also helped to raise the company's profile in the industry. The developers from Autoworks looked less than overjoyed. This particular startup was the third vendor with which Autoworks had contracted in a ten-year period to bring CrashLab to the engineering-analysis community. Patience was running thin at various levels of the Autoworks hierarchy. One of the company's senior directors asked "Where is the damn technology? Why is it taking so long? They've been working on this thing for almost ten years and we still haven't been able to use it in our vehicle design work." The developers from Autoworks were well aware of these concerns and also felt the increasing pressure of a diminishing budget in a company that tightened its purse strings with every new quarterly announcement of falling sales.

Just after 7 a.m., a discussion of several problems that had surfaced in a recent round of CrashLab's user testing began. The lead consultant from the startup took copious notes as two of Autoworks' developers recounted the bugs they had found as they tried to replicate the actions an engineering analyst would take as she interacted with the technology. In response to one of these problems, a young consultant from the startup made what would seem, from the outside, to be a simple suggestion:

We could probably fix this problem pretty easily if we didn't constrain the location where engineers put their section cuts. I mean a section cut is just a cross-sectional view of the part where engineers measure the energy produced in a crash, right? So, if they want to make those section cuts in other places it's not that much of a change. I think we should be able to accommodate it easily and get it taken care of. Would that work for you guys?

The room fell silent. The developers from Autoworks looked at each other, surprised that the young consultant would propose something that, to them, seemed preposterous. Martin Yuen, one of the senior technology developers from Autoworks, leaned back in his chair and answered coolly:

There's no way we can change the location like you suggest. We just can't do it. We have to define a specific process of making section cuts. CrashLab is about making sure everyone works the same way. That's what it's supposed to do; it's not up to us; it's just what this technology is supposed to do. That's just the next logical step in the sequence of where we've been with technologies. We can't argue with that. We'll just have to find another way around this issue because that procedure will stay intact. That's just the way it is.

Six months later, Suresh, an engineering analyst at Autoworks who was responsible for conducting computer-based simulations of frontal-impact crash tests, sat down at his workstation and opened a software application that had been in development at the company for about ten years. Suresh hoped that CrashLab would help him prepare his simulation model for a series of tests. He had taken a three days of training on how to use the technology when it had first come out, and he recalled that the instructor demonstrated how, with no more than a few mouse clicks, one could automatically set up section cuts and then use them to determine the energies produced at the sections indicated in the model. The idea of using a technology that would perform this tiresome procedure automatically was very appealing to Suresh. He opened CrashLab, pulled out a reference guide that had been given to him during his training, and went to work.

After nearly an hour, Suresh leaned back in his chair with a frustrated look on his face. He stared at his monitor for a few minutes, then began to flip hurriedly through the training manual. "I've really run up against a wall," he said disappointedly. He scratched his head, stood up, and walked over to the desk of a colleague, Andrew. This exchange ensued:

Suresh Hey, I've got kind of a weird question.
Andrew Yeah, what's up?
Suresh I've been trying to use CrashLab to set up my section cuts. You see, I'm having some issues with correlating my model, so I want to put

some section cuts in the rear bumper just to see what's going on. But every time I try to do it, it's like the program won't let me.

Andrew Why are you doing that? That's not what it's for. CrashLab's only for setting up the barrier [into which the vehicle will crash in the simulation]. That's all it's good for. You can't really use it for section cuts. I'm surprised you tried. Everyone I've talked to says just use it to set up your barriers. It works great for that. It's not a tool for section cuts. That's just the way it is.

That's just the way it is. Isn't it? Life is full of choices that appear to be delimited by forces outside our control. Plans to take a walk are canceled because a rainstorm suddenly sweeps in. That's just the way it is. Your conversation with a good friend is cut short because your cell phone's battery runs out. That's just the way it is. Your flight is delayed five hours because a technician detected a problem with the landing gear and a part has to be flown in from another state. That's just the way it is. Or is it?

Although we often don't give such occurrences a second thought, the tautology that things are the way they are because that's the way they are quickly breaks down under even the weakest scrutiny. It's easy to take a walk in the rain if you have an umbrella, a cell phone can be plugged into a charger, and delays in flights can be avoided if the airline keeps replacement parts in stock at airports. Sure, things could be different if only we would envision the alternatives and act on them. But why is that often so difficult to do? And why do we think that doing so is outside of our control?

Few choices in life seem to be as limiting as those concerning our encounters with technology. The fan over my stove either blows very hard or hardly blows at all. I can't choose a speed in the middle. The email program I use at work allows me only to send and receive messages; I can't use it for video conferencing. Perhaps it is because technology is often viewed as somewhat magical, or because it is too scientific and complex to understand, that every day many millions of people—even well-trained and highly intelligent technology developers and engineers at Autoworks— say "That's just the way it is."[2] But just as there are umbrellas, cell phone chargers, and spare airplane parts, there is always the possibility that the technologies we use and the way we use them could be different.[3]

Questions concerning technological change pervaded the work of historians, social scientists, economists and technologists for the better part of the twentieth century. Today, in what is often hailed as "the information age," such questions seem increasingly important not only for academics but for people everywhere. Engineers at Autoworks, for example, are asking these important questions: Why must this new technology constrain the analysts' liberty to choose where to put section cuts? Why should this technology be used only for positioning barriers? The questions are good ones, but sometimes the simplest answer is the hardest to understand: That's just the way it is.

Perceptions of the inevitability of cultural change caused by a deterministic technology are already well accepted by societies around the world. Some scholars argue that ideas about technological inevitability run rampant in popular discourse in Western industrialized nations (Leitner 2002; Wyatt 2008). Langdon Winner (1998, p. 62), for example, suggests that people may actually wish to treat technology-driven effects as if they were inevitable because such a conceptualization provides cognitive relief for fears of an uncertain future:

Why, then, do predictions of a technological inevitability now have such strong popular appeal?...What ordinary folks derive from these future visions is the comfort of believing that the future has already been scripted and that (if they scramble fast enough) they can find agreeable parts in the drama.

In a complementary thesis, the historian Merritt Roe Smith (1994b) claims that many people believe in technological inevitability because they liken technology to progress. In the Western world, Smith traces such thinking to the Enlightenment project. In non-Western, non-industrialized nations, following the "inevitable" logic of technology may be a compelling sentiment because it promises that such countries will be able to "advance" in much the same way as the Western world.

Although we might expect to encounter perceptions of the inevitability of particular kinds of technological change in people not among the technologically elite, we might not expect engineers and technicians—who have a hand in designing the technologies we use—to succumb to thinking that certain changes have to be a particular way and that's the way it is. But detailed studies of engineering and technical work show that even people with technical acumen sometimes develop a fatalistic belief that technologies have to be built in certain ways, and that certain changes resulting from their use are indeed inevitable. "As we read and listen to what designers and technology commentators have to say," the anthropologists Bonnie Nardi and Vicki O'Day (1999, p. 17) observe, "we are struck by how often technological development is characterized as *inevitable*. We are concerned about the ascendance of a rhetoric of inevitability that limits our thinking about how we should shape the use of technology in our society." In the years since Nardi and O'Day offered this poignant observation, there has been little evidence to suggest that perceptions of inevitability are on the decline. In fact, I have argued elsewhere that such perceptions seem to be on the rise in engineering and technical communities (Leonardi 2008; Leonardi and Jackson 2009). Perceptions of technological inevitability are problematic because if even the creators of our technologies think they have little influence on the tools they build, then as a society we run the risk of losing our ability to affect the kinds of changes that will make our work, and the organizations within which that work happens, better.

This book grapples with the strange reality that managers who are responsible for designing formal and informal organizational structures and engineers who explicitly design and redesign advanced computational technologies often come to believe that particular kinds of change are inevitable. To account for this strangeness, I advance a simple thesis: People come to see particular changes as inevitable because routine work dynamics obscure the processes through which those changes were decided upon. A consequence of this obscurity is that the technologies we develop and use and the organizations in which we develop and use them *appear* to evolve in fairly straightforward ways such that when those managers and engineers reach the next choice point, they reflect on the apparent inevitability of the changes that have occurred previously and use those perceptions of inevitability to justify their current decisions.

The growing tendency to see the relationship between technological change and organizational change as coevolutionary, although quite admirable in its intentions, makes it difficult to explain perceptions of inevitability because it treats computer-based technologies as artifacts that exist independent of the organizations in which they are developed and used. Drawing on recent theorizing about the role of "sociomateriality" in organizational life, I suggest that organizations and technologies are made up of the same basic building blocks: human and material agencies.

Human agency is typically defined as the ability to form and realize goals (Emirbayer and Mische 1998; Giddens 1984). For example, a person may ask a question because she wants a response, or may use a word-processing program because she wants to produce a report. Both are empirically observable examples of enacted human agency. A human-agency perspective suggests that people's work is not determined by the technologies they employ. As Wanda Orlikowski (2000, p. 412) has written, people "have the option, at any moment and within existing conditions and materials, to 'choose to do otherwise' with the technology at hand." Studies show that human agents, even when faced with the most apparently constraining technologies, can exercise their discretion to shape how those technologies affect their work (Boudreau and Robey 2005). People often enact their human agency in response to technology's material agency (defined as the capacity for nonhuman entities to act on their own, apart from human intervention). As nonhuman entities, technologies exercise agency through their performativity (Pickering 1995)—in other words, through the things they do that users cannot completely or directly control. For example, a compiler translates text from a source computer language into a target language without input from its user, and a finite element solver calculates nodal displacements in a mathematical model and renders the results of this analysis into a three-dimensional animation without human intervention.

Although human and material agencies are both capacities for action, they differ with respect to intentionality. Andrew Pickering (2001) offers a concise and useful empirical definition of human and material agencies that illustrate this difference. For Pickering, human agency is the exercise of forming and realizing one's goals. Thus, the practice of forming goals and attempting to realize them is a concrete operationalization of human agency. Material agency, by contrast, is devoid of intention. Artifacts don't act to realize their own goals, because they have no goals of their own making. In other words, "machine artifacts have no inherent intentionality, independent of their being harnessed to or offering possibilities to humans" (Taylor, Groleau, Heaton, and Van Every 2001, p. 137). Thus, material agency is operationalized as the actions taken by a technology without immediate or direct instigation by humans. Thus, even though human and material agencies may be equally important in shaping practice, they do so in qualitatively different ways.

James Taylor and his colleagues provide a useful language for reconciling the constructivist notion of human agency with the idea that technological artifacts can have a material agency of their own.[4] They argue that although human and material agencies both influence people's actions, their influence is disproportionate, because human agency always has a "head status" while material agency has a "complement status":

It is not that Agent$_1$ (some human) had purposes and Agent$_2$ (tool) does not (they both incorporate purposes, and both have a history that is grounded in previous mediations), but that we generally attribute head status to the human agent and complement status to the tool. In this way, the human subjectivity is given recognition even as the subject's agency (the capability of acting) is constituted objectively, as an actor in mediated communication with others. In this sense, Giddens is right: Intentionality is a product of reflexive interpretation. However, he fails to see the implications of his own principle. That to which we accord intentionality becomes, ipso facto, an agent—individual or not. (Taylor et al. 2001, p. 71)

By treating the relationship between human and material agencies in this way, Taylor et al. are able to incorporate the recognition that technologies have a material agency that transcends changes in context into constructivist approaches to technology development and use while still giving primacy to the people who design and use them.[5] The ability to do this rests on the use of a metaphor of *imbrication*.

The word 'imbrication' is not complex academic jargon; its origins are both humble and practical. The verb 'imbricate' is derived from names of roof tiles used in ancient Roman and Greek architecture. Tegulae and imbrices were interlocking tiles used to waterproof a roof. The tegula was a plain flat tile laid on the roof; the imbrex was a semi-cylindrical tile laid over the joints between the tegulae. The interlocking pattern of tegulae and imbrices divided the roof into an equal number of channels. Rainwater flowed off the row of ridges made by the imbrices and down over the surfaces of the tegulae, dropping into a gutter. The imagery of tiling suggests that different types of tiles are arranged in an interlocking sequence that produces a visible pattern. A roof couldn't be composed solely of tegulae nor imbrices—the differences between the tiles in shape, weight, and position prove essential for providing the conditions for interdependence that form a solid structure. Human and material agencies, though both capabilities for action, differ, phenomenologically with respect to intention. Thus, I argue that, like the tegula and the imbrex, they have distinct contours, and that through their imbrication they come to form an integrated organizational structure.[6]

By drawing on this metaphor, we see that organizing is a process through which multiple individual human agencies (hereafter, "social agency" to indicate that multiple people are forming coordinated intentions) are imbricated with the material agency of technological artifacts. The major implication of a perspective that examines the imbrication of social and material agencies is that it allows us to move past a metaphor of coevolution and recognize that the act of developing and using technologies is a constitutive feature of the organizing process. By focusing on sociomaterial imbrication processes, I aim to convince the readers of this book that not only can we arrive at better explanations of why workplace change unfolds as it does, but we can also explain why people come to think that those changes had to occur as they did.

When we view organizing as a process of sociomaterial imbrication, we also begin to recognize the inherent flexibility of computer-based technologies. As material agencies enable people to do new things in new ways, people change their goals and consequently bring changes to the technologies with which they work. The consequence of this recognition is that the vaunted "moment of implementation"—the moment in which a technology's development is over and its use begins—becomes, at best, a passing street sign on the highway of sociomaterial imbrication and, at worst, a red herring for scholars and managers who are compelled to think that certain technological or organizational changes are inevitable.

From Road to Lab to Math

Using the framework discussed above as a guide, I examine the process of sociomaterial imbrication through a detailed ethnographic study of the development, implementation, and use of an advanced computer-based simulation technology called CrashLab at Autoworks. People known as *crashworthiness-engineering analysts* design the structures of the vehicles we drive. They make decisions about how the frame should look, what steel it should be made from, and how thick that steel should be. They also make decisions about how well the structure of the vehicle fares in a collision. It may surprise you to learn that crashworthiness analysts think that a good-faring vehicle is one that is quite deformed after a crash—deformed in a very specific way. A well-deformed vehicle is one whose frame and body absorbed the energy of the collision so that it wasn't transferred into the occupant compartment, where it would have caused the driver and the passengers to collide with the certain areas of the vehicle's interior. Crashworthiness is one of the most heavily regulated areas of automotive engineering. All automakers must certify that their vehicles meet minimum requirements outlined by the U.S. Federal Motor Vehicle Safety Standards (FMVSS). The National Highway Traffic Safety Administration (NHTSA), the regulatory body that sets FMVSS requirements, has a great deal of influence on regulations that affect how automobiles are built; so does the Insurance Institute for Highway Safety (IIHS), a nonprofit research and communications organization funded by auto insurers. Crashworthiness engineering affects the lives of people all over the world, even those who don't drive, because most countries have regulations for how a vehicle's structures should deform in the event of a collision with a pedestrian.

As anyone with an Internet connection or access to newspapers knows, the last few years have been rough on the global auto industry. Since the late 1990s, automakers' profits declined steadily as the costs of engineering and manufacturing vehicles have skyrocketed. Amid these cost increases, worldwide vehicle sales have fallen precipitously since the events of September 11, 2001 and the resulting global wars. In 2009, two of the world's largest automakers (General Motors and Chrysler) declared bankruptcy, Japanese automakers posted some of their largest financial losses in history, and overall consumer demand for vehicles fell to levels not seen since before World War II.[7] Not surprisingly, automakers have been looking for ways to cut costs and return to profitability. Though the expenses passed on to consumers from executive compensation and employee health care commitments have garnered much attention in the popular media, industry insiders suggest that design and engineering are among the most expensive costs in the development of vehicles. In fact, the best estimates suggest that nearly 30 percent of the cost of a consumer vehicle can be traced to engineering and testing.[8]

Today, in the midst of a severe financial crisis, leaders of the global auto industry, and of American automakers in particular, are placing a tremendous amount of faith in the ability of computer-based simulation technologies to reduce engineering costs by revolutionizing the way automotive engineering is done. Such appeals to the potential of computer-based simulation technologies to dramatically reduce costs are the culmination of a decade-long campaign among automakers that the Society of Automotive Engineers (SAE) calls "road to lab to math."[9] As Nigel Gale (2005), Vice-President of Automotive Performance Research at the Southwest Research Institute, suggests, "road to lab to math" summarizes an industry-wide belief that the engineering analysis is evolving away from expensive road and laboratory tests and toward cost-efficient mathematically intensive computer-based simulations. One Autoworks executive characterized "road to lab to math" as "basically the idea that you want to be as advanced on the evolutionary scale of engineering as possible." He continued: "Math [meaning mathematics-based computer simulation] is the next logical step in the process over testing on the road and in the lab. Math is much more cost effective because you don't have to build pre-production vehicles and then waste them. We've got to get out in front of the technology so it doesn't leave us behind. We have to live and breathe math. When we do that, we can pass the savings on to the consumer."

Commentators suggest that the pressure exerted by the current economic crisis, in combination with an already popular belief in the effectiveness of math-based simulation analyses for reducing engineering costs, will encourage American automakers to strengthen their commitments to purchasing and using simulation technologies. Indeed, despite the economic downturn, companies that produce computer-based simulation and other automation technologies for the auto industry reported record profits in 2008,[10] one of the worst years on record for the auto industry as a whole.

Of all the automotive development functions that rely on math-based simulation technologies to reduce cost, none does so more than crashworthiness engineering. Today's crashworthiness analysts run both physical hardware tests (e.g., tests in which pre-production vehicles are crashed into walls) and math-based computer simulations (virtual tests of vehicles crashing into walls). Through the late 1990s, math-based simulations were used in a decidedly reactive fashion; they verified the results of physical crash tests already conducted. But because the cost of a pre-production vehicle crash test is normally more than $650,000, and because usually more than twenty crash tests are conducted before a vehicle goes into production, managers have been very interested in having math-based simulations supplant physical testing to the greatest possible extent. Since the early 2000s, most automakers have invested large sums of money in giving math-based simulation a more proactive role in crashworthiness analysis. In fact, Autoworks and other major automakers, even while downsizing their workforces in every other area, continue to hire engineering analysts who conduct computer-based simulations of vehicular crashes. So strong is the belief among company executives and industry analysts that computer-based simulation will revolutionize the way vehicles are designed that managers today use the results of simulation technologies almost exclusively to *predict* what will happen in a real crash. Better prediction is good for auto companies. In the short term, it makes for fewer physical tests in which vehicles are crashed into walls. In the medium term, it offers the hope of faster vehicle design. And in the long term, it brings hopes of cheaper and safer vehicles.

Simulation Technologies and the Scientific Culture of Prediction

Prediction is an integral part of the human experience. Although cultures vary greatly across the globe and societies have changed significantly over time, prediction of the future is a universal human practice. In early societies, people attempted to predict the future by interpreting dreams, by reading the stars, or by taking hallucinogens. Shamans, prophets, and spiritual guides held positions of high status, often serving as advisors to political leaders and powerful families. The methods by which we predict the future today are different, but our desire to know what will come remains much the same as it was for our ancestors.

In today's industrial and post-industrial societies, the authority to predict the future is often bestowed on scientists and engineers. Armed with mathematical models of biological, mechanical, electronic, and human systems, scientists and engineers plug their equations into advanced computer technologies to simulate the dynamics of a physical system. Once they are satisfied that the base-line simulation correlates well with the behaviors of that system, they perturb the model in some specified way and let the computer determine how its behavior will change. The results of these simulations are increasingly used to make predictions about the movement of financial markets (MacKenzie 2006), medical epidemics (Homer and Hirsch 2006), population growth (Billari and Prskawetz 2003), climate change (Lahsen 2005), earthquakes (Sims 1999), and, of course, automotive design.

There are always markets for accurate predictions, and those markets have not changed much throughout history. Individuals want accurate predictions of the future so they can improve their own lives; businesses want accurate predictions so they can remain profitable; political leaders want accurate predictions so they can make policy decisions that will increase the safety and prosperity of their constituents. Although we still rely on many of the methods our ancestors used to predict the direction of their personal lives, business managers have made a decisive shift in the past 30 years to the nearly exclusive use of mathematical models and computer-based simulation.

Recently, researchers have begun to turn their attention toward how computer-based simulations are used in the creation of facts and the prediction of the future (Lahsen 2005; Sundberg 2009; Yearly 1999). Steven Yearly's early work (e.g., Yearly 1999) focused on the public's (that is, non-experts') responses to computer-based simulations. He found that people's assessment of the trustworthiness of policy makers, their confidence in their own technical knowledge, and their evaluation of the social assumptions that underlay the model overrode the immediate "face credibility" of the computer-based simulation's realistic-looking predictions. However, Myanna Lahsen (2005) and Mikaela Sundberg (2009), who observed climate scientists using much more sophisticated computer-based simulations than those studied by Yearly, found that the scientists who created the computer-based simulations (and, presumably, understood well the assumptions they embodied) were among the people least critical of the predictions those models made. As Lahsen (2005, p. 917) suggests, the results of simulations were "seductive" to scientist and modelers whose "careers and identities become intertwined with, and partly dependent on, the quality of their models, to the point that they sometimes may be tempted to deny it when their models diverge from reality." As simulation technologies become more advanced and are capable of more closely approximating mathematically the behavior of physical phenomena, the very scientists and engineers who use them may come to believe that the simulated dynamics they are observing are as "real" as, or "more real" than, the physical systems they represent. What researchers don't often explore, however, is that there are many ways to use simulation technologies. Different uses of them can produce very different predictions, and those different uses are scripted, to an important degree, by the organizational processes out of which they are born.

Technologies have long been argued to alter the form and function of workplace organizations. For about 50 years research has consistently shown that introducing a new information technology into an established organizational context brings about changes in structure and work practice; however, there has been considerable debate over how and why such changes actually occur. Today few studies make baldly deterministic claims about the relationship between technology and organizational form and function. Instead, the commonly held notion is that organizations and technology use coevolve. Existing organizational structures shape how new technologies are used. New technologies, to the extent that they provide new capabilities, can change formal and informal organizational structures. (Formal structures typically refer to different departments—e.g., Research and Development vs. Marketing—and different positions—e.g., vice-president vs. account executive. Informal structures refer to the networks of interaction through which work gets done in organizations—who seeks advice from whom, and who controls access to specific resources.)

Although we know a great deal about how technologies become integrated into work practices, a less explored aspect of technology's role concerns what I have called elsewhere the *informational capabilities* enabled by the new technologies, such as computer-based simulations (Leonardi 2007). Simulation technologies are distinct from other types of computer-based technologies because they provide the capability to *create new information* that the organization didn't previously have and that was extremely difficult or impossible to generate by other means. Reviews of the literature on computer-based technologies and organizational change show that most extant studies have treated computer-based simulation technologies (if they have studied them at all) in much the same way as conventional mechanical or communication-based technologies, drawing explicit comparisons between them in theory building. (See Dewett and Jones 2001 and Rice and Gattiker 2001.) The shortcomings of such an approach are that the role of information in organizational change is often undertheorized and that computer-based simulation technologies are treated as if they were just "technologies" like any other.

Research has shown that information often plays an important role in defining the contours of an organization's formal and informal social structures. Many early organizational researchers, carrying the banner of "structural contingency theory," recognized the importance of information in shaping organizational form. James Thompson (1967), Jay Galbraith (1973), and Michael Tushman and David Nadler (1978) all viewed the organization as an information-processing entity and argued that the most appropriate form for an organization's formal structure was the one that most closely matched its information-processing requirements. More recent research has worked to explain how information affects the patterns of interaction through which formal and informal organizing are actually accomplished (Davidson 2006; Volkoff, Strong, and Elmes 2007). This more recent research is based on a performative theory of organizing, such as the one advanced by the social psychologist and management researcher Karl Weick (1979, p. 88):

> The word *organization* is a noun and it is also a myth. If you look for an organization you won't find it. What you will find is that there are events, linked together, that transpire within concrete walls and these sequences, their pathways, their timing, are the forms we erroneously make into substances when we talk about an organization. . . . Most things in organizations are actually relationships, variables tied together in a systematic fashion. Events therefore depend on the strength of these ties, the direction of influence, the time it takes for information in the form of differences to move around the circuits.

Weick's view, which allies with many other contemporary sociological perspectives on organizing,[11] treats organizing as a process. Communication plays a central role in the constitution of those things we call organizations. And information is what often flows through communication channels. The organizational theorists Martha Feldman and James March (1981) argued that individuals in organizations often acquire information (even if it serves no immediate purpose) in order to signal to others that they have knowledge about certain processes. This means that when there is no reliable alternative for assessing a decision maker's knowledge, visible aspects of information-gathering and information-storage practices are used as implicit measures of a person's ability to make an informed decision. The implication is that certain individuals come to have more power in the decision-making process as a result of others' perceptions of their information-acquiring practices.

Information is a valuable commodity in organizations because the possession of it or the lack of it can change social structure by positioning those who have information as powerful and those who lack information as less powerful. Richard Daft and Karl Weick (1984) suggest that acquiring information is an important antecedent to organizational change because organizations must routinely collect or scan for information in order to make the decisions that will, either directly or inadvertently, initiate formal and informal structural shifts. The research suggests that if new technologies (such as computer-based simulations) provide new information that wasn't previously available, workers may take it upon themselves to change their consultation habits and their work practices, thereby altering the informal structure of work (Burkhardt and Brass 1990; Robey and Sahay 1996). The research also suggests that if a new technology has the potential to provide new information that managers will be able to use in making decisions, those managers may decide to reconfigure the formal structure of the organization so as to make the delivery of such information more reliable and routine.

Taken together, this research on the coevolution of technology and organizing suggests that scientists and engineers who use computer-based simulation technologies to build mathematical models will use those technologies in ways that coincide with existing organizational structures (Boland, Lyytinen, and Yoo 2007; Dodgson, Gann, and Salter 2007). To the extent that use of the technologies provides new and important information, changes in formal or informal organizational structural may occur; those changes will then lead to changes in how the simulations are used. Such a theoretical stance is certainly accurate, but it fails to offer much specific insight into why certain changes might take place.

Computer-based simulation technologies can provide new information about physical systems and, in so doing, help people who use their results to make predictions about the future. But just because simulation technologies can provide new information, there is no guarantee that people will use the information or that they will believe it. It is not surprising that early simulations, which used numerical outputs or the movement of crude shapes to describe the behavior of physical systems, weren't always convincing to the uninitiated. In the semiotic language of the philosopher Charles Sanders Peirce (1932), these simulations produced representations that were merely *symbolic*. According to Peirce, symbolic representations stand in for objects by virtue of some general association and not because of any likeness between the symbol and the object. On a flow chart of a production process, for example, a rectangle may represent a machine, but the machine itself may not be rectangular at all. We come to understand that the rectangle represents the machine because a legend on the flow chart tells us so, or because it is standard practice in a given industry to represent machines by rectangles, or because we are able to infer from the relationship of the rectangle to other symbols on the process flow chart that the rectangle must represent a machine. Because the symbol lacks all the required details of the object, such as its size and shape, one couldn't build a replica of an object by using its symbol as a plan. The rectangle, for example, provides no clues as to the appearance and design of the machine.

Today, with advances in computer-based simulation technology, iconic (as opposed to symbolic) representations of physical systems are becoming more common. In Peirce's terms, iconic representations stand in for an object through their similarity to the object; they are a likeness or a facsimile of it. Thus, the icon, unlike the symbol, carries with it some sense of the shape of the object it represents. Icons are familiar to all computer users: We delete files by placing them in a "trash bin" icon; we get a hard copy by clicking the "printer" icon. These icons are simplistic; others are much more sophisticated. For example, scientists in chemistry and physics now employ interactive computer graphics that yield intricate iconic representations of molecular structures (Francoeur and Segal 2004).

Because viewers can easily index features of the representations to features of the object or system for which they stand, iconic representations are immediately recognizable in a way that symbolic representations are not. Further, as my colleagues and I have shown, iconic representations lower the perceived barriers to understanding and comprehension because they allow the observer to make visual comparisons between objects and their representations without having to learn specified cultural language (numbers) or conventions (interpreting symbols) to do so (Sheppard 2005). Consequently, observers of iconic representations may feel that they can use their knowledge of the physical world to evaluate the validity of the simulation, thus ensuring that the "evidence" for prediction is solid. In this way, visualization may exaggerate the tendency toward "consensus validation" (e.g., using the models to support widely held beliefs as opposed to thoroughly interrogating the data on which they are built) that William Dutton and Kenneth Kraemer (1985) observed in early non-visualization-capable computer models. Researchers studying occupations as diverse as automotive engineering (Thomke 2003), urban planning (Ben-Joseph, Ishii, Underkoffler, Piper, and Yeung 2001), and atmospheric research (Sheppard 2005) are quite hopeful that the visualization (iconic representation) capabilities embedded in new computer-based simulation technologies will help managers to use the results of simulations more frequently in their decision making.

Although the visualization capabilities of simulation technologies may encourage a "seeing is believing" attitude (Rohrer 2000), visualizations only render the behavior of the mathematics underneath them. And, as was discussed above, those mathematical equations are social products that are shaped and shaped by the organizations in which they are produced. Thus, although the move toward iconic representations may have changed how data are presented and may give people who aren't scientists and engineers the confidence to use simulation technologies for decision-making purposes, in most cases the "evidence" itself hasn't changed.

For these reasons, it is critically important to understand how occupations such as crashworthiness engineering develop and employ advanced computer-based simulations. If engineers develop and use new simulation technologies, if the development and the use of these technologies change the process of organizing in important ways, if the changes that result are viewed as inevitable, and if the perceptions of inevitability bring even more changes, it behooves us to understand the process of sociomaterial imbrication well. That is the goal of this book.

Structure of the Book

I begin chapter 2 by drawing on existing social constructivist approaches to technology development and use, which advocate a coevolutionary view of technological and organizational change. I argue that this coevolutionary approach sows the seeds for an explanation of the mutual constitution of technology and organizing, but that it is not useful for explaining how and why particular technological or organizational changes occur and under what conditions those changes come to be seen as inevitable because it fails to recognize that both technologies and organizations are made of the same basic building blocks: social and material agencies. To overcome this omission, I build a perspective on sociomaterial imbrication. In chapter 3, I describe the context of this study by providing an overview of crashworthiness-analysis work specifically and of Autoworks more generally. Crashworthiness-analysis work is very technical. Consequently, informants use quite a bit of jargon when engaging in and describing their work. Also, complex product development organizations such as Autoworks have so many divisions, departments, and groups that it is sometimes hard to keep them all straight. The glossary may help the reader to keep track of the technical and organizational terms used in the book.

I begin the journey into Autoworks in chapter 4 by describing how individuals from four divisions within the company—the Safety Division, the Global Technology Production Division ("Techpro"), the Information Systems and Services Division ("Infoserv"), and the Research and Development Division ("R&D")—were engaged in an effort to move math-based analysis into a more central role in the process of designing a vehicle. In chapter 4 I discuss how engineers in these various organizations didn't identify problems to be solved and develop technologies to solve them; instead, I document how, even though informants commented that the technology development process was straightforward, comparing across these four divisions reveals that the decision was hardly so simple. I suggest that problem development preempts technology development. In fact, for those involved in developing problems, technologies seem to present themselves just as easily or as surely as if they were meant to be there all along.

In chapter 5, I detail how the Safety Division, the Global Technology Production Division, the Information Systems and Services Division, and the Research and Development Division eventually reconciled their differences to produce a sophisticated computer-based simulation technology called CrashLab. As one manager noted, CrashLab was an "organizing technology." What he meant was that the technology would revolutionize crashworthiness analysis by reorganizing engineers' patterns of consultation and, consequently, their decision-making practice. This chapter focuses on explaining how these varying interests became aligned so as to produce a functional technology for the automation of model setup and model analysis. Specifically, articulation among the four organizations involved three processes. In the first process, *conceptual integration*, members of each organization worked to come to a loose mutual understanding about the purpose of CrashLab. Techpro, Infoserv, R&D, and Safety each faced independent pressures that made it difficult to fully take over the project and promote their own vision of what standardization truly meant. Some of the organizations had the technical capability to decide what constituted "standard work," but (because of impending vehicle development deadlines) didn't have the time to take the reins. Other organizations had the time (they didn't work directly on vehicle programs), but they didn't have the expertise or authority to determine what "standards" to use to "standardize" work. To mitigate this problem, a new organization—the Best Practice Evaluation Department ("Bestpra"), which sat outside regular program-related work but had expertise in the domain of crashworthiness analysis—was created. Thus, a substantial organizational change was necessary to continue the development of CrashLab.

In chapter 6, I explore how engineers formed interpretations about the new technology in the course of their work. Specifically, crashworthiness-engineering analysts working in two different groups, which I call the Piston Group and the Strut Group, interpreted CrashLab in different ways, largely because of their exposure to different framing strategies employed by managers and implementers. That analysts in the Piston Group were inundated with a "discourse of efficiency" while analysts in the Strut Group were not was due partly to chance and partly to the structure of the development process. More managers from the Piston Group were closely involved with the Focus Group (including its chair) than managers from the Strut Group. Thus, managers from the Piston Group had an inside source of information about CrashLab's indented functionality. Because only the results of negotiations were presented at the Focus Group meetings, most managers in the Piston Group weren't aware that the goal of "speed" had been established primarily by Techpro. Analysts in the Strut Group were inundated with another framing strategy—one constructed by trainers at Autoworks' center and by managers who lacked inside knowledge about what CrashLab was "supposed to do" for crashworthiness engineering. To make up for this lack of information, the trainers and managers from whom most members of the Strut Group initially learned about CrashLab constructed a broad "discourse of inevitability" that attempted to make sweeping generalizations about the changes CrashLab would bring to crashworthiness work while lacking any real knowledge of what those changes might be. Confronted with a group of engineers who were justifiably agitated at the prospect of having to learn a new technology and who tried to project their anxiety on the people who told them about CrashLab, trainers and managers hedged. When Strut Group analysts blamed managers for the fact that they would have to learn to use a new technology, those managers attempted to shift the blame away from them and place it on the technology.

In chapter 7, I show how analysts in the Piston Group and analysts in the Strut Group appropriated CrashLab's features very differently in their routine work. Analysts in both groups initially appropriated CrashLab's features in widely divergent ways, experimenting to see what CrashLab could do and how it could be used in their work. This pattern of use was not what CrashLab's developers intended. Members of R&D and Techpro wanted analysts to use CrashLab's features in the order in which they were presented to the user, and to use all of them. In fact, CrashLab's developers believed that for standardization and automation of the work to take place, CrashLab had to be used in this way. But analysts adopted different patterns of appropriation. After a major vehicle deadline, the work of analysts in both groups became more intense, and engineers could no longer afford to "experiment" with CrashLab's features. Because analysts in the Piston Group had developed an interpretation of CrashLab as an inefficient preprocessor, they saw little reason to keep using it under increased time pressures. Analysts in the Strut Group, on the other hand, who also didn't have time to continue their experimentation, now began to appropriate CrashLab's features in line with their interpretation of it as a tool for setting up models. Appropriating CrashLab's features in a convergent way allowed analysts in the Strut Group to develop a critical mass of users who were using CrashLab to do the work of setting up models. Because CrashLab's automation routines were executing many of the tasks that analysts had previously had to do by hand, the engineers now had more time available to consult one another on matters related to model analysis. The analysts in the Piston Group, who never converged on a common appropriation of CrashLab's capabilities, failed to achieve a critical mass of users and thus weren't able to use CrashLab's features to change the way they worked.

In chapter 8, I integrate the findings of the four preceding empirical chapters to consider how the social and material aspects of work became imbricated. Analysts, developers, managers, and implementers consistently made choices about how they would orient toward a new technology and how they would shape their work in its presence. Such choices, however, carry constraints resulting from choices made previously and delimit an actor's perception that the choice is indeed his to make. Consequently, even people who explicitly worked to design and develop a new technology tended to believe that they had little to do with either technological change or organizational change. I suggest that these findings can help us to reconsider the role that technology plays in work. Importantly, I argue that developing, implementing, and using a technology are all parts of the process of organizing, and that attempts to build a distinction between technology and organizing will inadvertently lead researchers toward deterministic explanations of change. I end by discussing the implications of a theory of sociomaterial imbrication for future studies of technological and organizational change and for the development, the implementation, and the use of technology in organizations.

2 Between Technological and Organizational Change

Virtually all social scientific research on technology and organization—whether by promoting or denying it—owes some intellectual debt to technologically deterministic thinking. Early studies adopted deterministic perspectives to provide causal explanations of technological and organizational change, and recent researchers have worked hard to empirically falsify the logic of technological determinism. Generally, the determinist's thesis is underwritten by two guiding propositions. The first suggests that technological change occurs independent of human action. The second argues that organizational change is caused by the introduction of a new technology into an established social system. Since the early 1970s, researchers in several disciplines have consistently defined these twin propositions in similar ways. Consider the following definitions, spanning four decades of interest in technologically deterministic explanations of change:

Understood in its strongest sense, technological determinism stands or falls on two hypotheses: (1) that the technical base of a society is the fundamental conditions affecting all patterns of social existence, and (2) that changes in technology are the single most important source of change in society. (Winner 1977, p. 76)

The first part of technological determinism is that technical change is in some sense *autonomous*, 'outside of society,' literally or metaphorically. The second part is that technical change *causes* social changes. (MacKenzie and Wajcman 1985, pp. 4–5)

(1) The nature of technologies and the direction of change are unproblematic or pre-determined (perhaps subject to an inner 'technical logic' or economic imperative and (2) Technology has necessary and determinate 'impacts' upon work, upon economic life and upon society as a whole: technological change thus produces social and organizational change. (Williams and Edge 1996, p. 868)

Generally, technological determinism is represented by either one of two beliefs. . . . The first is the belief that technological development follows a trajectory that is intrinsic to the technology itself. Technology "advances," with newer artifacts replacing the old, on a progressive course. Denying technological advance is to intervene socially—which in this context means prejudicially—and to work against the natural order of the world. The second is the belief that technologies act upon the social world in predictable, inevitable ways. (Leonardi and Jackson 2004, p. 674)

Technological determinism is a simple and elegant idea. As Michael L. Smith (1994a, p. 34) observes, it is also "heartbreaking in its simplicity." We are surrounded by explanations of social changes inspired by what Winner (1977) calls "technological animism"—the notion that technologies are acting agents in the world and can "make" us do some things or "prohibit" us from doing other things.

Another reason for determinism's appeal is that in some senses it cannot be refuted. The media theorists Harold Innis (1951), Marshall McLuhan (1964), and Walter Ong (1982) postulated technologically deterministic accounts of social change at a macrosocial level. Those writers weren't concerned with the technology's effects on people's everyday lives. They were concerned with how technological development changes our entire way of thinking and being in the world. For that reason, they don't acknowledge many radical technological transformations. They do, however, acknowledge the shift from orality to literacy, and perhaps the shift from literacy to electronic communication.[1] These technological changes have brought such fundamental social transformations that, determinists suggest, it will not be possible even to comprehend the nature of the changes until the epoch has passed. With such sweeping arguments at such macro levels, the theory of technological determinism is formulated in such a way that it is difficult to deny, because to do so would require empirical evidence that can't be collected in our lifetimes.

Indeed, when examined at a macrosocial level of analysis (i.e., with organizations or society at large as the unit of analysis) new technologies do appear to have uniform effects on the social world. In fact, whether it is society at large or just a single organization that is treated as a macrosocial object, the theory looks similar. For example, the anthropologist Leslie White (1949, p. 338) argues that, when one is looking at society in general, "technology is the independent variable, the social system the dependent variable," and "social systems are therefore determined by systems of technology; as the latter changes, so does the former." The sociologist Charles Perrow (1967, p. 195) makes a familiar claim about the relationship between technology and organizations, arguing that a macrosocial perspective "treats technology as an independent variable and structure—the arrangements among people for getting work done—as an independent variable." Deterministic outcomes appear quite natural and even predictable when examined at the level of social structure. Because most theories of macrosocial change aim to explain alterations in social structure over extended temporal periods (sometimes epochs), they often focus on the moments or events to which particular outcomes can be traced. Because in many cases exogenous shocks to a social system come in the form of new technologies, historians and macrosociologists often posit a causal relationship between technology and changes in a social structure. As Wiebe Bijker (1995a) notes, however, the problem with tracing outcomes retrospectively to crucial technological junctures is that investigators always suffer the temptation to blind themselves to the distortions that linear descriptions inevitably require.

The preferred antidote to this problem across a range of disciplines has been to examine the relationship between technology and society at the microsocial level, with the interaction as the unit of analysis. From this vantage point, the relationship between technological and social change appears to be in much greater flux. Implementation is an inherently political process in which technologies rarely seem to cause any immediate social transformations and are oftentimes resisted or subverted by those who incorporate them into their work. For that reason, it becomes increasingly difficult to conflate technological and social change as macrosocial theorists often do.[2] From a social constructivist perspective this socio-technical relationship appears anything but orderly:

> The relationship between technological and social change is fundamentally indeterminate. The designers and promoters of a technology cannot completely predict or control its final uses. There are always unintended consequences and unanticipated possibilities. (Wajcman 1995, p. 199)

In this logic, no changes are "inevitable" or predetermined; instead, changes arise through the coevolution of technological and social factors. Cause and effect are hard to untangle.

In the view of some, these microsocial and macrosocial perspectives on technology and social change are not naturally antagonistic. Instead, they can coexist peacefully at different levels of analysis (Heilbroner 1967; Misa 2003). Michael Tushman and colleagues (Anderson and Tushman 1990; Tushman and Anderson 1986) provide a compelling case for such reasoning. They argue that radical technologies emerge from the negotiations and political concessions of entrepreneurs, designers, engineers, and others. Surely the design of a technology and the features it comes to embody are the results of social practice. However, once a technology becomes an industry standard (a dominant design) it is difficult to dislodge. The logic derived from such a perspective is that technologies and the social world around them coevolve, and that "this process of coevolution is characterized by periods of social construction and periods of technological determinism" (Rosenkopf and Tushman 1994, p. 404).

The peaceful coexistence of deterministic and voluntaristic theories of technological and social change depends, as Bruce Bimber (1990) suggests, on the variant of technological determinism that is being used to explain the nature of such changes. Bimber argues that of the three definitions of determinism identifiable in writings on technology and society, the most pervasive and by far the most wide-reaching account is that of "logical sequence," or what he later calls "nomological" (Bimber 1994). Such an account holds that society evolves along a fixed and predetermined path, regardless of human intervention, and that the path is itself given by the incremental logic of technology. In a nomological account of technological determinism, technological and social change don't vary by level of analysis, as Rosenkopf and Tushman might suggest. Instead, even those micro-level actions are given over to the logic of science and technological change. This nomological view of technological determinism—surely the most compelling and most parsimonious view (Misa 1994; Ramos Alvarez 1999)—is frequently discussed in broader social discourse about technological and social change Also, the four definitions of technological determinism presented earlier define the phenomena in question from this nomological vantage point. The idea represented in these definitions is that at no point in its contact with technology is humanity free from the force of determinism. When developing a technology, individuals are held accountable by the "scientific" advance of their disciplines and thus are compelled to design the next "logical" and "inevitable" tool. Likewise, when people interact with a technology in the context of their work, they are given over to those logics embedded in the technology and guided purposefully through predetermined social change.

For microsocial theorists who believe that macrosocial phenomena such as societies, cultures, and organizations are nothing but the outcomes of human activity, nomological deterministic thinking is in fundamental opposition to their ontological principles. Because conceptualizations of the relationship between technological and social change are imbued with deterministic thinking in popular culture, and even in many positivist academic communities, the burden of proof that things are otherwise falls on the shoulders of the challenger.

Since the mid 1980s, two separate social constructivist research programs have worked to establish the empirical invalidity of technological determinism. Both have been concerned with debunking the notion of technological "impact" - that technologies are independent variables and organizations are the dependent variables. Each program, however, has worked to dethrone deterministic thinking by approaching one of determinism's two propositions at the near exclusion of the other.

Developing New Technologies

The social constructivist program of research on the development of new technologies, which is associated with the work of sociologists of technology and which has theoretical roots in the sociology of scientific knowledge, has attempted to deal with the notion of "impact" by focusing not on "impacts" themselves but on the technologies that are said to "cause" those "impacts."[3] The logic is that if technology has "impacts," those "impacts" aren't natural processes; rather, they are preconfigured by those who are involved in the development of the technology. To this end, Donald MacKenzie and Judy Wajcman (1985, p. 8) write:

Our focus—and where our criticism of technological determinism would centre—is on the assumption that technological change is autonomous, "outside" of the society in which it takes place. Our question is, what shapes the technology in the first place, before it has "effects?" Particularly, what role does society play in shaping technology?

Clearly this approach takes direct aim at determinism's first proposition: that technological change follows some property intrinsic to the material features of the artifact. To fight this first proposition, researchers in this program have suggested that technological *development* always occurs within a socio-political context in which actors negotiate and use persuasive techniques to guide the evolution of a technology's material features. Thus, researchers have linked technological change to activities associated with a technology's development.

Interest in fighting determinism's first proposition can be traced to the 1980s, when researchers began to speak out against popular notions of innovation that suggested an abstract model of linear development. In other words, researchers often proposed that the development of a new technology followed a strict innovation process that was largely devoid of human intervention.[4] As Robin Williams and David Edge (1996) suggest, sociologists of technology began to directly criticize the models of linear innovation that were popular in academic communities (particularly economics) and were prevalent in British government and industry in the 1970s and the early 1980s precisely because they viewed particular paths of technological change as "inevitable" and as impervious to competing interests.

In criticizing determinism, sociologists of technology drew on a number of ideas that had been generated in the sociology of scientific knowledge. David Bloor (1973), for example, argued that sociologists investigating the causes of scientific beliefs should be impartial to their truth or falsity and should attempt to explain them symmetrically. In other words, both knowledge that is taken to be true and knowledge that is taken to be false are susceptible to socio-cultural explanation, and that these explanations should be given equal consideration. Within the sociology of scientific knowledge, all knowledge is treated as a social construction—facts are constructed through social processes rather than "natural" processes (Knorr Cetina 1981; Latour and Woolgar 1979).

As Wiebe Bijker, Thomas Hughes, and Trevor Pinch (1987b) point out, constructivist studies of knowledge making and a renewal of interest in the study of technological development led to the beginning of a new research program on the social construction of technology development. Within this constructivist program scholars have distinguish three related attempts to fight against the first of determinism's two propositions regarding the nature of technological and social change: the SCOT (social construction of technology) approach, the actor-network approach, and the systems approach.[5]

Pinch and Bijker offered the initial formulation of the SCOT approach in 1984. In their critique of deterministic models of evolutionary change, Pinch and Bijker (1984) proposed an alternative theory that explains how social practices shape the development of new technologies. The processes of "variation and selection" are the social practices constructing technological development that the authors wish to elaborate. The SCOT approach attempts to explain how these processes work by making several assumptions about the relationship between technology and society (Jackson, Poole, and Kuhn 2002). The first is that the features of a technology aren't determined by a natural technological evolution, but instead the result from the social and cultural practices that designers carry with them. The process of design is not arbitrary, or determined by previous generations of the technology; rather, it is active in seeking to serve the interests of some over others. The second main assumption is that technological artifacts are unstable and never complete. All technological developments are subject to change. Although a designer may build an artifact to accomplish a certain purpose, the ways in which various parties conceive of its use can shape further development of the artifact. As an example of this position,

Pinch and Bijker cite the development of the safety bicycle at the turn of the twentieth century as an example of an artifact's continually changing as different groups used it for different purposes. Pinch and Bijker trace the development of the bicycle from the "high-wheeler" to the "safety bicycle."

A second constructivist approach to technology development—Actor-Network theory (ANT)—emerged from the work of Bruno Latour (1987), Michel Callon (1986), and John Law (1987) at roughly the same time that the foundation of the SCOT approach was being laid. Working sometimes separately and sometimes together, Latour, Callon, and Law criticized Pinch and Bijker's SCOT approach for making arbitrary distinctions between the social and the technological. ANT's main proposition is that the split between technology and society is artificial. To reconcile these two entities, ANT focuses on multiple networks composed of (human and non-human) actors who share the same ontological status. In other words there is no distinction between the social and the technical. Neutrons, scallops, people, and organizations are all treated as similar semantic components capable of influencing an actor network. While still seeking to explain how the process of technological development unfolds, ANT's supporters argue that a social constructivist theory of technology must take into account the status of the actors involved throughout the process of a technology's development and the study of the "social" not as the characteristics of any one individual but rather as a distinct network in which heterogeneous relationships constitute different actors (Kaghan and Bowker 2001).

The third constructivist approach to technology development—systems theory, developed by Thomas Hughes (1983, 1986, 1987)—is also interested in how technologies gain their meaning over time. Joining ANT in criticizing SCOT for being too concerned with independent artifacts, it proposes that artifacts should be understood as elements in a system of corresponding elements. For Hughes, a system is a set of organizations, rules, artifacts, and procedures that co-create and reinforce one another. Hughes argues that an artifact is created and perpetuated through a system in which various parties have interests in a technology's development. The notion of "system" in this theory is distinct from the ANT notion of "network" because a system "has an environment—a remaining outside—that a network does not" (Hughes 1986, p. 290). Once a technology has been developed and has achieved closure, it can culminate in a technological system of its own, other elements in the system helping to keep the artifact in the forefront of the developmental process—"they have a mass of technical and organizational components; they possess direction, or goals; and they display a rate of growth suggesting velocity" (Hughes 1987, p. 76).

Using New Technologies

Social constructivist studies of technology use, associated with the work of organizational theorists and drawing their theoretical insights from a variety of sources (including symbolic interactionism, ethnomethodology, and structuration theory), have worked to describe technological "impact" by focusing on the recipient organization rather than on the formation of the technologies that do the "impacting." The logic of this approach is quite simple: If technologies have "impacts," those impacts are mediated by the systems of meaning and interpretation into which the technologies are introduced. This approach places determinism's second proposition—that technologies affect organizations in predictable ways—squarely in its sights. It suggests that organizational changes aren't prefigured by a technology's material features, but rather are enacted while people are physically engaged in the *use* of a technology. By focusing on the power of human agency to create and change social orders, researchers in this program have linked organizational change to the ways people use the features of a new technology.

Social constructivist studies of technology use were taken up primarily by organizational and information-systems researchers who responded to the early work of organizational contingency theorists, who themselves strongly advocated a perspective on the relationship between technology and organizing that expanded determinism's second proposition. Contingency theory proposes that there is no single organizational structure that is effective for all organizations (Perrow 1970). Because organizations are protean, membership can change continually, along with organizational strategy, purpose, size, new ideas, and new technologies. In effect, organizational structure and form are contingent upon factors not inherent to the organization—factors that are products of the external environment. From the perspective of contingency theory, the relationship between an organization and its external environment is unidirectional. Environmental factors, such as new technologies, have the power to alter the structure of an organization, but the relationship doesn't work in reverse. Paul Lawrence and Jay Lorsch (1969, p. 10) offer an explanation of the nature of this relationship: "A machine cannot alter its gear train, an animal cannot develop an extra leg, but an organization can and does do analogous things." Because organizations are dynamic structures operating in a certain space and time, they are susceptible to outside influence. Pursuant to this logic, contingency theory explains that organizational systems have the property of interdependence of parts, insomuch as a change in one part affects the structure of the organization. Technology is thus an external, environmental factor upon which organizational structure can be contingent. In the worldview of this perspective, technology is static and unchanging whereas organizations are dynamic and capable of adjusting their boundaries.

Among the first researchers to take seriously the study of technology and organizations from a the perspective of contingency theory were Joan Woodward (1958), James Thompson (1967), and Charles Perrow (1967). They suggest that the social system of an organization is compelled to adapt itself to the demands of its "core technology," defined as a system for turning inputs into outputs and thus not necessarily implying a technological artifact in the form of hardware or software.[6] From the perspective of contingency theory, changes in a core technology resulting from internal or external innovation bring about direct changes in the structure of an organization and the work that people perform daily. The causal arrow moves from technology to organization, causing "necessary" and "determinant" impacts. Therefore, contingency theorists argue that a perceptive manager, considering the type of technology at the organization's core and the demands of the organization's external environment, should be able to structure the organization along any series of continua (i.e., centralization/decentralization, independence/interdependence, or authority/autonomy) so as to optimize its performance (Blau, Falbe, McKinley, and Tracy 1976; Hickson, Pugh, and Pheysey 1969).

Dissatisfaction with these stances and the contradictory outcomes they suggest has led researchers to a more balanced view of the relationship between technologies and the organizations into which they are introduced (Robey and Boudreau 1999). The broad program of social constructivist research on technology use attempts to dislodge determinism's second proposition by carefully describing the interaction of technology's material properties with the social contours of the organization in which it is used. Generally speaking, we can distinguish three broad theoretical attempts at this goal: social influence approaches, structuration approaches, and role-based approaches. These approaches all acknowledge that technological artifacts have material "properties that transcend the experience of individuals and particular settings" (Orlikowski 2000, p. 408). Of interest to this broad research program is how those properties become interpreted, understood, used, and reinforced by their interactions with features of the social system in which they are implemented. The consistent finding, which is reproduced across these approaches, is that social context buffers the effects the technology has on the organization.

In their attempt to explain how individuals' perceptions of new technologies are formed, Janet Fulk, Charles Steinfield, Joseph Schmitz, and J. Gerard Power (1987) developed a model of technology use that draws on the insights of social information processing theory. Their model proposes that perceptions of the objectivity, saliency, and rationality of a newly implemented technology are formed "to a substantial degree by the attitudes, statements, and behaviors of coworkers" (ibid., p. 537). It highlights the fact that individuals choose to use a new technology on the basis of how their perceptions of the technology are influenced by social processes. Social influence models focus primarily on the adoption of a new technology. Since organizational implementation of a new technology doesn't necessarily mean that individuals will readily adopt it (Lewis, Agarwal, and Sambamurthy 2003), the empirical focus should be on the process by which perceptions occasion common behaviors toward the technology. Most social influence studies work to uncover how such perceptions correlate with technology use. Accordingly, the dependent variable of primary interest is the use of a new technology, normally measured either as a nominal or an ordinal variable. Consequently, the studies are more concerned with whether a new technology is used at all than with how it is used. The insight that a technology is socially constructed through processes of social influence that encourage users' perceptions to grow common has been important in explaining why technology implementation efforts are sometimes successful and sometimes not.

Since about 1990, a second approach to constructivist studies of technology and organization has employed Anthony Giddens' (1984) structuration theory to explore the links between new technological artifacts and the social contexts into which they are introduced (DeSanctis and Poole 1994; Orlikowski 2000). Structuration models generally focus directly on how members of an organization use a technology in ways that align its features with their existing work practices.[7] The basic premise of this approach is that uses of a technology are constitutive of macrosocial structures, such as organizational form. This means that, as people use the features of a new technology, and by association reproduce or change their work practices in the presence of the artifact's constraints and affordances, they are either reproducing or changing the structure of their organization. In other words, because actions are constitutive of organizational structure, the action of using a new technology can be seen as a structural property of organizing.

Two streams of research using structuration models can be distinguished. First, Adaptive Structuration Theory (AST) has evolved primarily from the work of Marshall Scott Poole and Gerardine DeSanctis (DeSanctis and Poole 1994; Poole and DeSanctis 1990). The premise underlying this perspective is that certain structures for use are built into a technology and that individuals who encounter those structures appropriate them in ways that are consistent with existing organizational and group requirements. AST aims to take seriously the interactions between the deep structures that constitute technological artifacts, organizations, and work groups. Researchers using AST take norms for interaction to be the modality by which structuration is accomplished. Not coincidentally, the types of technologies studied are ones in which specific norms for interaction are "designed in." Group decision support systems and online collaboration tools, for example, are specifically designed to promote certain idealized interaction patterns (e.g., Gopal and Prasad 2000; Poole and DeSanctis 1990). The second stream has evolved primarily from Wanda Orlikowski's (1992) "duality of technology" model. As defined by Orlikowski (2000, p. 407), research in this stream "starts with human action and examines how it enacts emergent structures through recurrent interaction with the technology at hand." Accordingly, the majority of studies follow a two-step process. First, they seek to uncover the ways in which users "call forth" specific features of a technology by using them repeatedly in social practice. Second, they explore how those newly constituted features change individuals' work practices within the organization. Researchers in this stream begin their examination of the construction process by examining individuals' situated and recurrent work practices. Sedimented in these work practices are organizational objectives (Orlikowski 1992), templates for interaction (Orlikowski 1996), and conceptualizations of solutions to relevant organizational problems (Boudreau and Robey 2005). Thus, each time a micro-level work practice is enacted, particular features of the macro-level organizational structure are reproduced (Orlikowski 2000). As particular structures of technology use are enacted, the work practices through which they are created change slightly (Vaast and Walsham 2005). Over time, gradual changes in work practices produce alterations in the social structure of which they are constitutive. Thus, numerous small improvisations in the appropriations of a technology result in changes of the macro-level organizational structure that become sedimented once again in new work practices.

Another set of studies conceptualizes technology use as a process that occurs through the alignment of technological structures with existing social structures. Typically these social structures are represented as the "roles" and "role-relations" that are enacted in the everyday context of work. This perspective lifts its gaze from the micro-level practices of use represented in the structuration models and makes a meso-level examination of how newly implemented technologies influence and are influenced by individuals' interactions around the new technology. Newly implemented technologies serve as "occasions" for triggering structural changes, rather than as determinants of them (Barley 1986). In this way, technology implementation is socially constructed as certain exogenous social forces set the conditions for how the technology will affect the organization of work. Role-based approaches to the study of the implementation of new technologies have focused on the relationships between members who are fulfilling different roles (Barley 1990a; Black, Carlile, and Repenning 2004), on the creation of new roles as a consequence of the change effort (Edmondson, Bohmer, and Pisano 2001; Robey and Sahay 1996), and on the adaptation of existing roles to accommodate the physical demands of the new technology (Zuboff 1988). In short, this approach doesn't simply describe the norms for interaction; it traces the evolution of actual patterns of interaction. By focusing so heavily on social interaction, however, such research largely overlooks the micro-level practices of technology use that structuration models capture. In this approach, such social processes are taken for granted and are assumed to influence interactions among individuals, although such influences aren't shown directly.

Unintended Theoretical Consequences of the Implementation Line

As the foregoing discussion illustrates, researchers attempting to show that technological change is a socially constructed microsocial process have generated a number of mechanisms to explain how technologies are developed. Importantly, mechanisms such as negotiation, closure, inscription, and momentum all indicate that the social processes surrounding a technology's development eventually come to an end. Because each of these mechanisms enables technological change, the implication of their gradual dissipation is that technological change is seen to end once development activities cease. For such researchers, implementation marks a natural closing point for investigations of technological change. That is, those who posit social constructivist accounts of technological change rarely develop a sophisticated notion of why, and sometimes don't even notice that, the technology has a new life in the organization into which it is introduced. As Mackay and colleagues (2000, p. 749) note, "it is striking that much constructivist research on technology assumes that once an artifact has left the bench or the factory, its form and meaning have solidified and the story is complete."

Conversely, researchers attempting to show how technology use is socially constructed have begun their empirical examinations only after a technology has already been implemented. Thus, in this perspective the physical features of a technological artifact are considered stable and unproblematic. The perceptions, uses, and interactions that individuals generate in response to that technology, however, are seen to evolve and change over time.[8] Because perceptions, uses, and interactions (which are constitutive features of the organizing process) are shown to evolve in response to a non-changing technology, we are left with a view that organizational change is confined to contexts in which technologies are used. Robert Thomas (1992, p. 443) states the case plainly:

Even the most sensitive accounts of the adjustment occasioned by technological change (e.g. Barley 1986) begin *after* the new equipment or machines arrive on the scene. Largely missing is an attempt to explain or even to describe the problems or perceived pressures which lead organizations to change technologies in the first place.

What we begin to see by looking at how the various programs have dealt with the problem of determinism is that they have separated themselves from each other by the construction and perpetuation of what I will call an *implementation line*. 'Implementation' is a common term. In its most recognized form, the verb 'implement' means "to put into practice."[9] Such a definition suggests that there is some "thing" that will be put into practice. What this "thing" actually is doesn't come under scrutiny in such a definition, nor does the "practice" into which it is put. Thus, there is an implicit distinction between "things" and "practice." With these two domains conceptually established, implementation is neatly viewed as the "putting together" of these hitherto separate spaces: There exists no space between them, only the "moment" in which they are combined. We can then say that the *development* and the *use* of a technology are, in most present-day conceptualizations, separated by an implementation line. This line demarcates these two phases of interaction between the material and the social, indicating the end of the development phase and the beginning of use phase. It would not be much of a leap to suggest that it is the implementation line that separates the reflected propositions of technological determinism. On the one side of the line, technology is developing according to its own internal logic. On the other side of the line, it affects organizational practice in orderly ways.

The implementation line is an arbitrary division between theories of technological and theories of organizational change. In other words, linking technological change to technology development activities and organizational change to technology-use activities leaves us with the notion that technological change ends once a technology is implemented and that organizational change begins there. This view is perpetuated empirically because sociologists of technology (e.g., Kranakis 2004; Rodgers 1996) have traditionally examined developmental activities at the exclusion of use activities whereas organizational researchers (e.g., Barley 1986; Vaast and Walsham 2005) have done the opposite. In the absence of any explication in either program of how development activities might continue while a technology is being used, or how use activities might lead to further technology development, the implementation line becomes not only an empirical divide separating studies of technology development from technology use but also a theoretical divide separating ideas about technological change from ideas about organizational change. We can then say that in present-day conceptualizations technological change occurs during *development* activities and organizational change occurs during *use* activities. Thus, technological and organizational changes are often depicted as non-overlapping, temporally sequenced events separated by an implementation line.

The notion of an implementation line suggests a point of finality. When it reaches the "moment" of implementation, a technology is for all intents and purpose "done." It can then be "thrown over the wall" to manufacturing and "transferred" to the user community. Both notions imply movement—that a technology is "crossing" the implementation line. Both also imply fidelity—that the same object that was "thrown" will be caught on the other side and the same object that is "transferred" will be received on the other end. In such a frame, problems that occur when a new technology crosses the implementation line (e.g., problems due to lack of fidelity of use) are attributable to "distortions" or "noise" in the communication environment.[10] In other words, the problem is not with the technology, but rather with the environment.

The concept of the "black box" described by both research programs illustrates and reinforces the notion of an implementation line between the development and use spaces in which technology and organizations interact. As Winner (1993, p. 365) suggests,

The term *black box* in both technical and social parlance is a device or system that, for convenience, is described solely in terms of its inputs and outputs. One need not understand anything about what goes on inside such black boxes. One simply brackets them as instruments that perform certain valuable functions.

The social constructivist position argues that uncovering what goes into black boxes is important in order to untangle the relationships between technological and organizational change. Researchers in the development space are immensely curious about black boxes. Williams and Edge (1996) suggest that the broad array of researchers who oppose deterministic critiques of the development of new technologies are united by an insistence that the black box of technology must be opened to allow the socio-economic patterns embedded in both the content of technologies and the process of innovation to be exposed and analyzed. Bijker (1995b, p. 256) similarly argues that the goal of constructivist research into the development of new technologies is to "pry open the black box of technology and to monitor the evolution of socio-technical systems." Accordingly, studies of technology development begin with a technology that is already a black box and then work backward to open it up. In other words, they often begin by taking a technology that is essentially "done" and tracing its evolution to uncover the social practices that led to the choice and stabilization of various technological features. The goal is not necessarily to show how a technology becomes closed, but rather to show that technology, in general, is not really a black box at all—there is no mystery or magic; there are only negotiations among interested actors, which become obscured and forgotten over time.[11] The history of a technology can thus be re-read not as a history of linear evolution, but as an alternation of variations and selections (Pinch and Bijker 1984). It should come as no surprise that the overwhelming majority of development studies are constructed by retrospective histories of change in the technological and social orders.[12]

Researchers in the use space are also concerned with the same black boxes. Their inquiry, however, recognizes that a technology enters an organizational context as a black box, and that, in order to understand how a technology changes an organization, we must open the black box up to demonstrate that it has no meaningful existence outside the context of use. As Orlikowski (2000, p. 412) suggests, "technologies are thus never fully stabilized or 'complete,' even though we may choose to treat them as fixed, black boxes for a period of time." This is because people can and do often use one technology in radically different ways. The finer point to be taken from this suggestion is that the functionality of a technology doesn't exist outside of a situated context of use. In other words, our expectations of what features a technology has, what those features are good for, how they should be used, and how they will change the way we work—all of which we draw from the culture in which we encounter the technology—buffer our perceptions of the material elements, those elements of the technology that don't change across contexts of use. As Michele Jackson (1996) notes, the act of identifying or perceiving a technology is part of that technology. This is also Orlikowski's point that it is less beneficial to view technologies as black boxes or collections of static and stable elements than to view them as "technologies-in-practice," since a technology and its functionality will be instantiated differently in each new situation in which it is engaged. For this reason, studies of technology use also begin with a closed black box. But instead of tracing its history backward they trace it forward, opening it up to reveal that, although the actual physical features of the technology have stopped evolving, the uses to which those features are put and the outcomes those uses create have not.[13]

Conceptualizing development as ending with a black box and use as beginning with one means that the implementation line becomes an important empirical and disciplinary divide. This means that for development researchers technological change is conceptualized to occur *before* the implementation line, and therefore is of empirical or theoretical interest only before that line. Conversely, for use researchers any interest in the implementation process begins only *after* the implementation line.

The disciplinary and empirical divide created and reinforced by the implementation line unintentionally separates the space of technology development from that of technology use. The implication is that the corresponding technological and organizational changes occurring in one space will not have implications for the technological and organizational changes in the other. Recent empirical work suggests that respecting an artificial implementation line is empirically inaccurate. Researchers frequently report that changes in organizing affect how technologies are developed (Mackay, Carne, Beynon-Davies, and Tudhope 2000; Poole and DeSanctis 2004)—i.e., organizational change happens during the process of technology development—and that implementers and users of technologies contribute to technological change (Pollock 2005; Yates 2005)—i.e., technological change happens during the process of technology use.

Despite such insights, allowing the implementation line to continue to separate studies of technology development from studies of technology use leaves us with an "incomplete" account of the relationship between technological and organizational change. The major problem that arises when analyses of technology development are separated from analyses of technology use is that even the most careful social constructivist studies must continue to hold that technologies and organizations are separate analytic phenomena. The reason they must hold this position is illustrated by figures 2.1 and 2.2. The upper panel in each of these figures shows a microsocial constructivist analysis of technology and social change. As the figures illustrate, the organizational and the technological change in direct response to one another. Determinism is denied in favor of coevolution. All any constructivist researcher would have to do to make the case for a coevolutionary relationship between organizational and technological changes would be to fill in the boxes of the upper panel in either figure 2.1 or figure 2.2 with the specific changes identified in their field work. Researchers of technology development would continue to fill in those boxes until the "moment" at which the technology (now with its functionality firmly inscribed in technical features) was implemented, and we could then end our exercise.

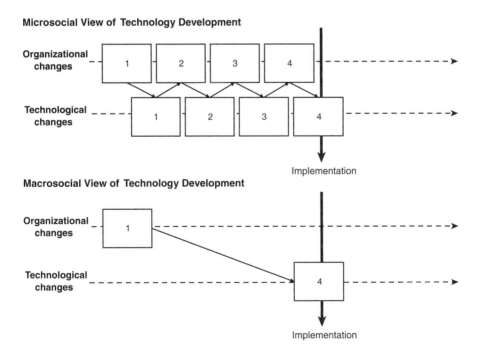

Figure 2.1
Images of coevolution from social constructivist perspective on technology development.

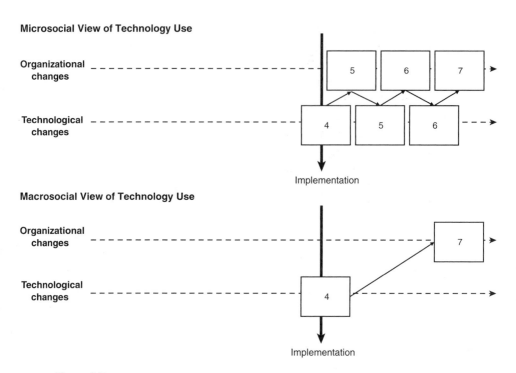

Figure 2.2
Images of coevolution from social constructivist perspective on technology use.

However, using the implementation line as an artificial point at which to end the inquiry creates two problems. First, it forces us to end our analysis by filling in a "technological change" box rather than an "organizational change" box, thereby promoting a view that the technological change is "complete" once implementation has taken place. Second, to move from mere description of our findings to a more general theory of the middle range we must begin to abstract away from the minutia of microsocial practice. Such abstraction, which all theorizing requires, focuses our attention on beginning and end points. With all of the thick description of the coevolutionary relationship between organizational and technological changes hidden within a macrosocial account, we are left, as Louis Bourgeois (1984, p. 590) suggests, with deterministic explanations:

As one abstracts away from the individual towards the collectivity, one runs the risk of personifying the collectivity; and even if that trap is avoided, one has defined away the individual as the prime influencer of organized activity. With the individual lost to the aggregate, the explanation of the behavior of organizations in terms of "causal textures" . . . "natural selection" . . . or other abstract "forces" becomes plausible.

In this respect, a macrosocial view of technology development processes with an "organizational" starting point and a "technological" end point leads us to the belief that the form and function of the technology was socially determined.

It would be inaccurate to suggest (as does the lower panel in figure 2.1) that the organizational change in box 1 determined the technological change in box 4. In the absence of the microsocial details intervening between these two changes, we are left to draw such a conclusion. As Stephen Barley and I have suggested, substituting technological determinism for social determinism doesn't help us to avoid the trap of casual inference (Leonardi and Barley 2008). Using the arbitrary implementation line as an empirical and disciplinary divide leads social constructivist researchers who study implementation into a similar trap. In a study of "technologically induced" organizational change, the research design (identify a technology and watch whether or not it changes the social interactions that constitute a work system) necessarily directs researchers to make causal claims when they abstract away from the microsocial changes to construct generalizable theory. For example, a technology-implementation process could be read at a microsocial level as a series of coevolutionary organizational and technological changes. (See upper panel of figure 2.2.) However, when we abstract away from these microsocial findings we are left with a "technological" (box 4) starting point and an "organizational" (box 7) end point. (See lower panel of figure 2.2.) Thus, we can reasonably draw the conclusion that technologies do induce social change within organizations, even if this is not always a neat and tidy process.

Consequently, if researchers continue to respect an artificial implementation line separating technology development activities and technology use activities, we will always be left to draw two complementary conclusions as we abstract away from the particularities of our data: (1) that technologies and organizations are distinct empirical phenomena and (2) that organizational change determines technological change during a technology's development whereas technological change determines organizational change during a technology's use. The first idea is a corollary of the second because, in order for the organizational to "determine" the technological, organizations and technology have to be empirically distinct. In short, adopting a traditional social constructivist approach would force us to conclude that organizing is a social phenomenon whereas technology is a material phenomenon. Consequently, by constructing an artificial implementation line, students of technology and organizing inadvertently support the metaphor of "impact" that they work so hard to deny.

Imbrication of Social and Material Agencies

One way to avoid inadvertent slippage from microsocial demonstrations of coevolution to macrosocial generalizations of impact would be to deny any separation of technology from organizing. To be sure, if no separation exists between the two, one cannot impact the other—impact is defined, after all, as one thing colliding against another. To deny their separation is not to say that technologies and organizing are identical phenomena, or even different phenomena of the same order; rather, it is to say that organizing is a process that is accomplished through the development and the use of technologies. Nearly 30 years of insights from the heretofore-distinct social constructivist programs of research into technology development and technology use suggest that development or use of a technology always takes place within the confines of the actions of organizing. Technologies enable and constrain the social, communicative activities that allow organizing to happen, and those communicative activities shape technologies and their use.

I have suggested that a primary reason that a distinction between the ideas of technology and organizing exists at all is that scholars have fashioned their programs of research by creating artificial starting and stopping points (such as implementation) that enforce arbitrary distinctions between what might count as a technology and what might count as organizing. Although social constructivist researchers rejected the deterministic components of their studies, it seems fair to say that social constructivist researchers of both stripes accepted the contingency theorists' bifurcation between the concepts of technology and organization. While attempting to explain the change processes they observed in manufacturing settings, contingency theorists decided to call some aspects of a production system "technology" and other aspects of the production system "organizational structure," and then to seek correlations between the two. Interestingly enough, what was taken to be technology and what was taken to be structure varied from author to author. (See Barley 1988b.) More than half a century later, most scholars who look at work settings continue to divide things into these two categories.

Orlikowski has proposed an alternative way for constructivist researchers to explore the dynamic of work contexts. Rather than specify some aspects of work as technological and others as organizational, she urges researchers to view organizing as a process that is "sociomaterial" in nature. "Such an alternative view," Orlikowski suggests,

asserts that materiality is integral to organizing, positing that the social and the material are *constitutively entangled* in everyday life. A position of constitutive entanglement does not privilege either humans or technology (in one-way interactions), nor does it link them through a form of mutual reciprocation (in two-way interactions). Instead, the social and the material are considered to be inextricably related—there is no social that is not also material, and no material that is not also social. (2007, p. 1437)

This emerging sociomaterial approach makes two important conceptual moves. First, it recognizes that technologies are as much social as they are material: The material properties of technologies are configured through social relations and used in social contexts. Second, it recognizes that technologies themselves are constitutive features of the organizing process, not orthogonal to it. "Notions of mutuality or reciprocity," Orlikowski elaborates,

presume the influence of distinct interacting entities on each other, but presuppose some *a priori* independence of these entities from each other. Thus, for example, we have tended to speak of humans and technology as mutually shaping each other, recognizing that each is changed by its interaction with the other, but maintaining, nevertheless, their ontological separation. In contrast, the notion of constitutive entanglement presumes that there are no independently existing entities with inherent characteristics. (ibid., p. 1438)

In short, an approach that treats organizing as a sociomaterial process avoids the tendency to slip into images of impact because it denies any separation of technology from organizing.

Within this emerging perspective, two arguments have been made about how to study the relationship between the social and the material. The first argument, made by Orlikowski and Scott (2008), suggests that researchers should refrain from treating activities of technology development and technology use as "special cases" of the organizing process and instead should examine what the material characteristics of a technology do once they have become "constitutively entangled" in all aspects of organizational life. Orlikowski and Scott urge researchers to move away from studying development, implementation, and initial use and instead to study technologies already incorporated in people's routine practice. The second argument is one that I and my colleague Stephen Barley have made (Leonardi and Barley 2008, 2010). We suggest that, in contrast to

Orlikowski and Scott's insistence that scholars should move away from studies of the development, implementation, and use of technology, engagement in such activities marks a time when an existing sociomaterial fabric is disturbed, offering researchers an opportunity to "see" more clearly how the social and the material become constitutively entangled. To "see" in this way, we argue that, instead of weaving the social and the material together conceptually, researchers should begin unraveling them empirically in order to study how each contributes to the whole. At the very least, this means that, in addition to studying social processes, researchers should pay attention to what a technology lets developers, implementers, and users do, to what it doesn't let them do, and to the workarounds that people develop.

Though both approaches to the study of organizing as a sociomaterial process are important and necessary for explaining the dynamics of workplace change, I follow the latter approach in this book. I do so because I believe that it is in explaining *how* the social and the material become (in Orlikowski's words) "constitutively entangled" that we can not only account more precisely for how the process of organizing unfolds but also explain why people come to believe that particular changes were somehow predestined or inevitable. To do so, I draw on the metaphor of imbrication I introduced in chapter 1.

James Taylor (2001), Saskia Sassen (2002), Claudio Ciborra (2006), and others have recently begun to characterize the interweaving of social and material agencies as a process of imbrication. Again, to imbricate means to arrange distinct elements in overlapping patterns so that they function interdependently. Three visual examples of imbrication—of tiles on roofs, rocks in riverbeds, and bricks in walls—are presented in figure 2.3. Each of these examples provides imagery that is useful for describing the metaphor of imbrication and for suggesting why it may be valuable for examining organizing as a sociomaterial process.

Geologies use the notion of imbrication to describe the orientation of rocks in fluvial settlements (Rust 1972; White 1952). Researchers have observed that patterns of rock imbrication along the bottom or the sides of a riverbed can explain subtle local changes in the direction of a river over time. As Kauffman and Ritter (1981, p. 299) describe,

Flattened cobbles[14] can be observed to lie on one another in an imbricated pattern on modern river bottoms, with the plane that includes the long and intermediate axes inclined in an upcurrent direction. Inferences concerning direction of transport have commonly been made by using such imbrication orientations for consolidated rocks.

Figure 2.3
Images of imbrication in roofs, riverbeds, and brick walls.

By examining patterns of rock imbrication, geologists can determine how a river flowed in the past. As more and more rocks overlap in recognizable patterns along the sides and the bottoms of riverbeds, these patterns of imbrication can also shape the future direction of a river by altering the direction of the current's flow (Millane, Weri, and Smart 2006). Thus, the movement of a river shapes the way in which rocks are imbricated, and those patterns of imbrication shape the continued flow of the river. In keeping with the metaphor, we might envision the process of organizing as a moving river. The process of organizing imbricates social and material agencies. As further imbrication occurs, overlapped and interlocked patterns place restrictions on where the organization can move and thus come to shape its contours. As Taylor et al. (2001, p. 92) suggest, "Imbricated structures are resistant to change. That is the natural strength of this form of organizing—but also its weakness." But change is not impossible. Just as an overflow of water in a river can upset existing patterns of rock imbrication along its shore, new policies or strategies within an organization may reconfigure existing patterns of social and material agencies (Sassen 2002). Thus, the second principle that we can extract from the imbrication metaphor would suggest that the current imbrication of social and material agencies shapes and is shaped by previous imbrications.

Load-bearing masonry structures are normally made of two or more layers of bricks, with the bricks running horizontally (called *stretchers*) bound together with the bricks running perpendicular to the wall (*headers*).[15] This imbricated pattern of headers and stretchers is referred to as the *bond*. Once the imbrication pattern of a bond begins, it is very hard for a bricklayer to change it. Patterns of imbrication that have come before (e.g., how a row of bricks was laid at the base of a wall) affect imbrications that will come later (e.g., how the how the bond is patterned at the top of the wall). Although the patterning of a brick wall is surely path dependent, the placement of one brick doesn't "cause" a particular placement of the next brick. The metaphor of imbrication implies a gradual process of interrelation, in contrast with the image of causality provided by metaphors of impact. In fact, the metaphor of imbrication should drive researchers away from attempting to identify the causal nature of a structure—of a brick wall or an organization—because once a pattern of imbrication begins, there is no way of knowing what is cause and what is effect:

From either the top or bottom row of bricks, it is possible to read the tiling of a wall as a right-handed or a left-handed sequencing. Either way, the wall now becomes interpretable as a parallel adjunction of imbrications, each overlaid on the previous (think about how you would lay bricks to construct a wall). The problem is that the theoretical choice of a left-handed versus a right-handed orientation is arbitrary... There is no "right" way to read the tiling strategy. (Taylor 2001, p. 282)

Thus, in the realm of agency relations it would be of little utility to ask whether social agency caused material agency or, for that matter, to say that they caused each other. The reason for this is, as Taylor suggests, that starting and stopping points are read into the process of organizing by the researcher. In other words, constructing images like those presented in figures 2.1 and 2.2 requires the *a priori* idea that "implementation" is an important moment in the organizing process. This idea compels the researcher to see (depending upon whether he or she is interested in technology development or in technology use) that the moment of implementation is either an end point or a beginning point; indeed, this is Taylor's point about researchers' choosing "a left-handed versus a right-handed orientation" to "read a tiling strategy." If we were to remove the idea that implementation is particularly important and instead treat it as just another moment in the process of organizing, there would be no beginning point, no end point, and consequently no impact.

The coevolutionary imagery provided by social constructivist research suggests that people's patterns of communication and social interaction change and are changed by the development and the use of a technology. For this reason, figures 2.1 and 2.2 show two separate tracks of coevolutionary changes, one organizational and the other technological. Although most constructivist researchers eschew notions of technological determinism, they do tend (as figures 2.1 and 2.2 imply) to empirically operationalize organizations as patterns of social interaction (see Barley and Kunda 2001) and technologies as collections of symbol and material entities (see Orlikowski 2000). In other words, social agency exists in patterns of communication and material agency in a technology's material features.

But if constructivist research consistently shows that communication patterns shape and are inscribed in the features of a technology, if people's patterns of communication call forth the use of particular features of a technology, and if the use of features of a technology, in turn, can reconfigure communication patterns, it seems odd to claim that communication patterns and technology's features are ontologically different, even if they are empirically distinct. For this reason, I suggest that, if one were to look at communication patterns and technology features under a microscope, one would find that both communication patterns and technology features are made up of the same basic building blocks: social and material agencies.[16] Although we may make the ontological claim that communication patterns and technology features are indistinguishable phenomena because both are constituted by social and material agencies, we must be mindful that the ways in which those agencies are woven together produce empirically distinct types of infrastructures.[17] Latour (2005, p. 53) defines infrastructures (which he calls "figurations") as the processes by which agencies take on observable properties:

If you mention an agency you have to provide the account of its action, and to do so you need to make more or less explicit . . . its observable traces. . . . If agency is one thing, its figuration is another. What is doing the acting is always provided in the account with some flesh and features that make them have some form or shape.

Thus, sometimes social and material agencies interweave in ways that create or change communication patterns, and at other times they weave together in ways that produce or alter technology features.

There are several ways in which the metaphor of imbrication is useful for explaining the interweaving of social and material agencies

First, imbrication suggests that social and material agencies are effectual at producing outcomes (e.g., communication patterns or technology features) only when they are joined together, but that their interdependence doesn't betray their distinct characters. The notion of imbrication allows for maintaining the distinction between social and material agencies with respect to intentionality while still recognizing their synergistic interaction. The metaphor of imbrication is distinct from Latour's (1993, 1999) notion of the *hybridicity* between the social and the material. Latour argues that social and material agencies are indistinguishable (they are hybrids) and that action has no point of origin. In other words, either people or technologies can begin changes in sequences of action.[18] By keeping the distinction between social and material agencies, the imbrication metaphor asserts a slightly different relationship: People have agency and technologies have agency, but ultimately people decide how they will respond to a technology. As François Cooren (2004, p. 377) suggests, "To say that nonhumans *do things* does not mean that human contributions are passed over. . . . Humans can appropriate what nonhumans do."

Second, because the metaphor of imbrication sensitizes us to the production of durable patterns, it reminds us that all interactions between social and material agencies produce organizational residue. When social and material agencies imbricate to produce communication patterns or technology features, those figurations have staying power. Routine patterns of communication persist in the absence of their creators, as do technology features. As the people within the organization continue to enact communication patterns and use technology features, they become, in Susan Leigh Star and Karen Ruhleder's (1996) term, "infrastructure." That is, they provide the context and the means for organizing to happen, but they are taken for granted as natural relations. The imbrications that produce communication patterns and technology features become "black-boxed" such that we no longer actively question why they are there or what they are good for. As organizational infrastructure, Taylor and his colleagues suggest that imbrications are only ever, to use the philosopher Martin Heidegger's (1959) distinction, "ready-to-hand" (*zuhanden*), as opposed to "present-at-hand" (*vorhanden*). That is, the capabilities that social and material agencies create as they interweave with one another become proceduralized and are eventually forgotten. As long as social and material agencies are imbricated in ways that allow people to get their work done, the structures they create are transparent and always "ready-to-hand" as opposed to actively and reflexively drawn upon in every day action ("present-at-hand"). Thus, the products of earlier imbrications (e.g., a pattern of communication or a technology feature) lay the groundwork for continued organizing in that they provide communicative norms and technological capabilities that people can use to structure their actions.

With this recognition, the imbrication metaphor provides a third benefit to theory: It enables theorists to explain accumulation over time without resorting to deterministic language. To bridge the gap between the extreme poles of determinism and voluntarism, researchers must better explain how the accumulation of past changes bears on present changes. Imbrication implies accumulation in the sense that the overlap of social and material agencies is not replicated in the same way over time and doesn't necessarily have inertial tendencies, but that the way imbrication occurs at time 1 will influence the way it occurs at time 2.

Construction of Affordances and Constraints as Catalysts for Imbrication

The preceding discussion used the metaphor of imbrication as a way of recognizing that social and material agencies are distinct phenomena but that they are fundamentally interdependent, that past imbrications accumulate to help explain (though certainly not to predict) how social and material agencies will become conjoined in the future, and that members of the organization actively work together, within the framework established by previous imbrications, to reconcile their goals (social agency) with the things that a technology can or can't do (material agency).

As was outlined above, social and material agencies are the basic common building blocks of communication patterns and technology features. Changes in communicative patterns or technology features then require new imbrications of social and material agencies. Yet if a person has the option of changing how or with whom she communicates and the option of changing how a technology operates, how does she decide which option to exercise? To answer this question, I propose that we must consider the differential ways in which social and material agencies can become imbricated. To do so, I turn to a theory of affordances that provides a vocabulary useful for theorizing the imbrication of social and material agencies.

In an effort to explain how animals perceive their environments, the perceptual psychologist James Gibson suggested that surfaces and objects offered certain "affordances" for action:

If a terrestrial surface is nearly horizontal . . . nearly flat . . . sufficiently extended . . . and if its substance is rigid . . . then the surface *affords* support. . . . It is stand-on-able, permitting an upright posture for quadrupeds and bipeds. . . . Note that the four properties listed—horizontal, flat, extended, and rigid—would be *physical* properties of a surface if they were measured with scales and standard units used in physics. As an affordance of support for a species of animal, however, they have to be measured *relative to the animal*. They are unique for that animal. They are not just abstract physical properties. (1986, p. 127)

In Gibson's formulation, people don't interact with an object before or without perceiving what the object is good for. As Gibson suggests, the physical (or material) properties of artifacts exist apart from the people who use them, but artifacts are infused with meaning "relative to the posture and behavior of the animal being considered" (ibid., pp. 127–128). The concept of affordance is useful in explaining why social and material agencies become imbricated: Technologies have material properties, but those material properties afford different possibilities for action based on the contexts in which they are used. Although the material properties of a technology are common to each person who encounters them, the affordances of that artifact are not. Affordances are unique to the particular ways in which an actor perceives materiality. To this end, Gibson offers a perceptual explanation of the relationship between materiality and affordances:

The psychologists assume that objects are composed of their qualities . . . color, texture, composition, size shape and features of shape, mass, elasticity, rigidity, and mobility. . . . But I now suggest that what we perceive when we look at objects are their affordances, not their qualities. We can discriminate the dimensions of difference if required to do so in an experiment, but what the object affords us is what we normally pay attention to. (ibid., p. 134)

Because materiality can provide multiple affordances, it is possible that one artifact can produce multiple outcomes.

Gibson's work has been most notably applied to discussions of technology by Donald Norman (1990, 1999), who argues that good designers purposefully build affordances into a technology to suggest how its features should be used. Norman seems to suggest that affordances are intrinsic properties of artifacts and that the role of design is to make affordances easily perceptible to would-be users:

Affordances provide strong clues for the use of their materials. Plates are for pushing. Knobs are for turning. Slots are for inserting things into. Balls are for throwing or bouncing. When affordances are taken advantage of, the user knows what to do just by looking: no picture, label, or instruction is required. (1990, p. 9)

For Norman, affordances are "designed-in" properties of artifacts. The goal of an affordance is to signal to the user what the technology can do and how it is to do that thing. To do this, designers must make affordances easy to perceive: "The designer cares more about what actions the user perceives to be possible than what is true." (1999, p. 39) Users are important to Norman inasmuch as they can identify a technology's affordances; however, they don't create affordances. Instead, affordances are created strategically by the designer (if the designer is good at his or her job). In this formulation, Norman's argument differs from Gibson's in that Norman claims that affordances don't change across different contexts of use but rather are always there waiting to be perceived.

The sociologist Ian Hutchby (2001) seeks a middle ground between the earlier conceptualizations by emphasizing the relational character of affordances. In his view, affordances aren't exclusively properties of people or of artifacts; they are constituted in relationships between people and the materiality of the things with which they come in contact. In this formulation, materiality exists separate from people, but affordances and constraints don't. Because people come to materiality with diverse goals, they perceive a technology as affording distinct possibilities for action. For Hutchby, the affordances of an artifact can change across contexts even though its materiality doesn't. Similarly, people may perceive that a technology offers no affordances for action, perceiving instead that it constraints their ability to achieve their goals.

Lynne Markus and Mark Silver (2008, p. 620) suggest that "in terms of the relational concept of affordances . . . properties of objects are seen as necessary but not sufficient conditions [for changes in action]," and that "because action is goal-oriented, it is neither required nor appropriate to describe objects and affordances in a reductionist fashion." To emphasize that affordances arise when a person interprets a technology through his or her goals for action, Markus and Silver define affordances as "the possibilities for goal-oriented action afforded to specific user groups by technical objects" (ibid., p. 622). Because affordances are relational, existing between people and an artifact's materiality, artifacts can be used in many ways and can have various effects on the organization of work (Fayard and Weeks 2007; Zammutto, Griffith, Majchrzak, Dougherty, and Faraj 2007).

According to the relational view, we might argue that affordances and constraints are constructed in the space between social agencies and material agencies. People's goals are formulated, to an important degree, by their perceptions of what an organization or a technology can or can't do, just as those perceptions are shaped by people's goals. For this reason, I argue that as people attempt to reconcile their own goals with a technology's materiality they actively construct perceptual affordances and constraints. Depending on whether they perceive that a technology affords or constrains their ability to achieve their goals, they make choices about how they will imbricate social and material agencies. Acting on the perceived affordances of a technology can then lead users to realize new intentions that could be achieved by using these material features. The different ways in which social and material agencies are imbricated result in distinct outputs—either a new communication pattern (or patterns) or a new technology feature (or features).

As an illustration of this point, consider the following example, which is extremely basic for descriptive purposes: Coordinators in a not-for-profit community organization have recently begun to disseminate reports to community members that summarize the organization's service activities. This "news-dissemination routine" (a communicative pattern) is heavily reliant on the use of a word-processing technology that coordinators can use to create the summary. The word-processing technology is configured (by virtue of its features) to act in particular ways (material agency), and the capabilities that it provides are what led the coordinators to envision creating the newsletter in the first place. The news-dissemination routine is enabled by the functionality of the word-processing technology (material agency) that allows coordinators to create a summary document and the goal of disseminating information to community members (social agency), which was partially formulated by the acquisition of the technology. Figure 2.4 depicts this routine with one circle (M_1) representing material agency and another circle (S_1) representing social agency.

As the coordinators use the word-processing technology and its output, they decide that they would like to be able to turn their boring text document into a visually appealing, well-formatted newsletter. They attempt to use their current word-processing technology to do so, but they discover there is no easy way to format the text as they would like to format it or to draw diagrams. In the space between the technology's existing material agency (its ability to render text, but not to manipulate its placement or draw diagrams around it) and their goal of producing a visually appealing newsletter, the coordinators construct a perception that the

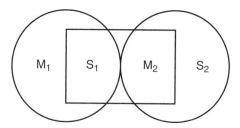

Figure 2.4

Imbrication of social and material agencies produces communication patterns and technologies. Circles represent figuration of agencies as communication patterns; square represents figuration of agencies as technology. Communication patterns and technologies are constituted by different imbrications of the same basic agencies.

technology they currently use constrains their social agency.[19] What do they do? They could decide not to create a newsletter. They also could change their communication patterns, perhaps altering the process of information dissemination so as to communicate the information verbally and thus not need a newsletter. But if the word-processing program is flexible for example, if it is designed to be easily redesigned, or if the coordinators have the skills to change the code that underlies its functionality, or if they have access to people who can make changes to the code for them), they may decide to change the materiality of the technology to meet their goals. Thus, the construction of the technology's constraint arose between the material agency of the existing word-processing program (M_1) and the consultants' collective goal (S_1) of creating a newsletter. To overcome this constraint, the coordinators changed the technology by giving it features that allow people to make digitized drawings. In so doing, they gave the technology new material agency (M_2)—the program now contains a feature that allows people to make digitized drawings. A social agency approach would treat the goal that created the technology's new features (S_1) and the material agency that the technology now has by virtue of those new features (M_2) as constitutive features of the technology (Boudreau and Robey 2005; Orlikowski 2000). Thus, the technology is represented in figure 2.4 by a box around S_1 and M_2.

What we begin to see when examining figure 2.4 is that the imbrication of an existing material agency with a new social agency (*material → social*) constitutes a pattern of communication. This imbrication produces the perception of both a capability and a constraint. To overcome the constraint, the consultants change the functionality of the technology, thereby giving it a new material agency. Consequently, the imbrication of an existing social agency with a new material agency (*social → material*) brings changes to a technology at some level. The coordinators may begin to use the newly changed features of the word-processing application (M_2) to produce digitized drawings and, in so doing, begin to construct a perception that these capabilities could afford them the possibility of expanding the readership of their newsletter because of the entertainment value provided by attractive graphics. Consequently, they begin to form a new goal: that the readership of their newsletter should expand (S_2). To achieve this goal, however, the group must reorganize itself by changing communication patterns. Some members must specialize in drawing, others in writing copy, and others in laying out the newsletter to include both text and images. The imbrication of this existing material agency with a new social agency (*material → social*) results in changes in the news-dissemination routine (e.g., specialization occurs, and people increase or decrease their consultations with one another on the basis of their newfound specialties).

As figure 2.4 illustrates, the perception of constraints produces a sequence of imbrication that changes technology features, whereas the perception of affordances produces a sequence of imbrication that changes communication patterns. Further, a new agency (social or material) doesn't just imbricate with an existing agency; rather, it is interwoven with an entire history of imbrications that came before it. Here one might consider that the tiler of a roof doesn't just imbricate a new imbrex with one existing tegula—she imbricates an imbrex with the entire history of imbrex-tegula relations that came before it and that history influences, to an important degree, where and how she can place the newest tile. Thus, although people can make choices about how they imbricate social and material agencies, the accumulation of choices that were made before their decision affect the types of imbrications they can make insomuch as they shape their perceptions of affordances and constraints.

When we look at an imbricated system of social and material agencies, such as the one idealized in figure 2.4, we can begin to see how fundamentally related changes in communication patterns are to changes in technology features because they contain the same building blocks, some of which are shared in common. Of course, where one begins reading the chain of imbrications (whether from a material-agency starting point or from a social agency starting point) is somewhat arbitrary, and the chain of imbrications certainly stretches out in either direction. In other words, it is arbitrary to look for a beginning point or an end point (e.g., implementation) in an imbricated system. Instead, the researcher should be more interested in explaining how imbrication occurs, and in how earlier sequences of imbrication affect future actions.

The examples provided above, though entirely hypothetical, begin to illustrate how imbrication looks, how it might occur, and why different types of imbrications of social and material agencies may produce various figurations and changes in communication patterns or technology features. To move this emerging framework of imbrication from the hypothetical to the empirical, I will now turn to data collected in an ethnographic study at Autoworks.

3 Crashworthiness Analysis at Autoworks

The framework laid out in chapter 2 suggests several important consider-ations for the ethnographic study of mutually constitutive technological and organizational change. First, understanding the social construction process surrounding any technology means collecting data on the events that occur during development, implementation, and use of the technol-ogy. Focusing on one set of activities to the exclusion of another would lead to only a partial understanding of how technologies and organizations change one another. Second, the researcher must be able to track the "relevant social groups" involved in the processes of change within each community, how those groups negotiate and come to agreement on the "workings" of the technology, how the technology reaches a point of "stabilization" (that is, how it seems to solve certain problems), and how that particular view of what the technology does gains momentum within a community. Third, researchers must recognize that the mechanisms by which the processes of technology development, implementation, and use are socially constructed are embedded in a larger organizational context. This context conditions those relevant social groups' perceptions of the technology, the work practices that give the technology its functional meaning, and the patterns of interaction that link together various indi-viduals within and among groups. Finally, the framework sketched above suggests that, although the processes of development, implementation, and use may sometimes exist in certain temporal sequencing, there is often tremendous overlap. Thus, developmental activities often occur in what we traditionally call the *usage space*, and vice versa.

Taken together, these four requirements suggest that the context of study in which it would be easiest to capture the relationship between technological and organizational change would be at an organization involved in developing, implementing, and using a new technology. In addition, the requirements suggest that the technology under study should be one being designed with a specific use in mind, or with certain ideas about how it will change the organization in which it will eventually be used. There are many examples of technologies that are developed with little intention as to their use. (See, e.g., Shane 2000.) Although social construction processes certainly also operate with such technologies, it would be difficult to understand the interplay between activities of development, implementation, and use if the designer had no intentions for the technology's use. In addition, the functionality of the technology must be flexible enough to allow for variation in how individuals use it. Therefore, it is important to find an architecture that is flexible, or a technology that can be diversely implemented. A comparative sample of users is also useful in understanding similarities and differences in the ways users interact with a given technology. The most effective studies of technology employ comparative designs that examine user communities in "parallel," because such designs allow researchers to generalize findings across similar social settings (Barley 1990b). Concordantly, the organizations in which the technology is implemented must be similar enough to warrant a comparative analysis, but diverse enough in social and cultural practices to reveal differences in how the technology is used.

The case of the development and implementation of CrashLab at Autoworks meets these criteria and provides a unique opportunity to understand how imbrications of social and material agencies shape the organizing process. In this chapter, I provide an overview of crashworthiness-engineering work, a preview of the technology that would eventually become CrashLab, and a partial explanation of how work and technology fit into the large organizational structure of Autoworks.

The Work

Most of Autoworks' engineering workforce is located in the midwestern United States, so it is there that I focused my data-collection efforts. The engineers at Autoworks' engineering center in Motorville, Michigan are responsible for the design and evaluation of a broad portfolio of vehicles the company sells throughout the world. Broadly, engineering efforts at the technical center are divided into two general specialties. The first specialty consists of a group of individuals known as design engineers (DEs). Design engineers are typically responsible for a particular vehicle part or assembly of parts (e.g., a brake booster or a bumper assembly) from conception through manufacturing. They work in a world of computer-aided drafting (CAD). Their jobs are quite similar to those of other engineers who use CAD, such as those studied by Bucciarelli (1994) and Henderson (1999). Design engineers attend numerous meetings with specialists and managers from all over Autoworks to determine the requirements for their parts. They then draft their parts in CAD, make sure that they are manufacturable, work with vendors to provide material specifications, and test the parts rigorously to make sure they meet a number of performance requirements.

In the crucial final step (testing), the design engineers work closely with Autoworks' crashworthiness analysts (hereafter referred to simply as analysts). Analysts are responsible for validating and testing the parts as they are assembled into complete vehicles. A design engineer designs his or her part using CAD software and assigns it vehicle coordinates (on a three-dimensional grid) that indicate the part's location in the vehicle. Using the vehicle coordinates, analysts assemble the parts they receive from design engineers into a fully integrated model that contains all the parts of a vehicle (over 30,000, on average), as well as the connections between them. Thus, the analysts are the first engineers to see how all the parts in a vehicle fit together and behave with one another. They are then responsible for testing the performance of the assembled vehicle on a number of different parameters, including crashworthiness, noise and vibration, aerodynamics, heat transfer, and cooling. To complete these performance tests in a virtual environment, analysts use computer-aided engineering (CAE) tools.[1] These software tools differ from CAD tools in that they are used for analysis rather than for design. That is, CAE tools use complex mathematical equations to determine the state (mechanical, thermal, magnetic, etc.) of parts, subsystems, or an entire vehicle. CAE tools employ a geometry definition created in a CAD program as a starting point, and typically utilize some form of finite element analysis (FEA) as the means of testing performance.

To understand the importance of finite element analyses in the work of crashworthiness analysts requires a bit of history. As early as the mid 1960s, automotive engineers began developing simple lumped-parameter models to test vehicle dynamics. A lumped-parameter model simply describes the functional relationships between a system's inputs and outputs, without explaining the particular function of each parameter in the system. Instead, the functions of the parameters are lumped together, with the goal of rendering an acceptable output. For this reason, lumped-parameter models are sometimes called "black-box models." "Lumped" parameter values are determined using an averaging technique (e.g., area weighting) to improve their ability to account for spatial variation. In the context of vehicle

structural analysis, lumped-parameter models represent a method of sub-
dividing a vehicle's primary structural entities into non-deforming zones
that can be measured in a laboratory by static crush methods.

Although these early models were novel, they weren't very accurate,
because they relied on a good amount of mathematical approximation
from experimental data. Because laboratory testing had only recently
advanced to a point where safety engineers understood how energy was
distributed in an impact, and because testing technologies capable of capturing these data had just emerged, many questions about the sequence of
events that occurred during a collision had to be answered before more
accurate models could be built. In the late 1960s, Autoworks launched an
ambitious study using high-speed motion cameras to determine the "collision sequence" of an impact—in other words, how parts moved and
interacted with one another (what safety engineers call "stacking up").[2] In
addition to high-speed photography, a more common method engineers
used to determine a collision sequence was to place the test vehicle in a
large press (such as those used by auto wreckers) and slowly crush it millimeter by millimeter, recording the forces along the way. These forces were
then used in mathematical models.

A potential solution to the many limitations of lumped-parameter
models was surfacing in the aerospace industry in the early 1970s. This
technique was FEA. Engineers in the aerospace industry used FEA was to
determine the spatial distribution of phenomena such as stress, heat, displacement, vibration, acoustic waves, and magnetic fields on airplane
wings and fuselages.[3] Rather than treat an entire object or collection of
objects as a black box, as the lumped-parameter model did, FEA decom-
posed an object into a large (though finite) number of much smaller
objects, called *elements*. In the term 'finite element analysis', the word
'finite' refers both to the countable number of elements generated and to
the separation of the technique from the infinitesimal elements used in
calculus (Hughes 2000). The elements are considered connected at defined
nodes (corner and mid-segment points), and the entire connected system
composes a defined structure referred to as a *mesh*. (See figure 3.1.) This
mesh is programmed to contain the material and structural properties that
define how the structure will react to certain loading conditions. These
material and structural properties are normally related in a stiffness matrix,
which defines the deformation patterns of the materials used to build
automobiles (such as steel, plastic, and foam) in relation to the shape
(normally called the "geometry") of the structure the materials constitute.
The model is then populated with a separate series of equations represent-

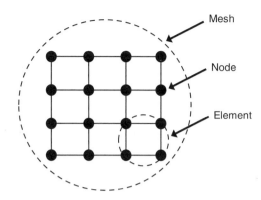

Figure 3.1
Relationship among nodes, elements, and mesh in finite element analysis.

ing boundary conditions—for example, the load that will be placed on the structure in a certain type of test, the velocity at which the vehicle is traveling, and the angle of travel. This entire system of equations is represented mathematically as a very large matrix consisting of complex differential equations or integral expressions, with the unknowns (in the case of crash-safety analysis, usually displacements) solved at the nodes.[4] Because FEA calculates parameters at each node, it is much more accurate than the lumped-parameter model.

Finite-element models require far more computing power than lumped-parameter models. Application of FEA to automotive design became possible with the advent of fast time-sharing computers. The earliest computers used in the auto industry had to be fast enough to run the FE code that solved the differential equations in the models. Time-sharing computers such as the Teletype Model 33 and the Houston Instruments DP-1 were among the earliest models used in the auto industry for finite element analysis. These computers made possible early FE code, which was developed in the mid 1960s in the aerospace industry with the help of government funding. Most development centered not only on the generation of large-scale structural codes, such as the structural analysis and matrix interpretive system (SAMIS) code and the NASA structural analysis (NASTRAN) code,[5] but also on the creation of sophisticated numerical methods for solving large sets of linear and nonlinear simultaneous equations.[6] Because early computers were slow, most FE equations could be solved only for quasi-static crush conditions.

Up until the mid 1970s, most automakers experimented with FEA to analyze crash safety in their R&D labs but didn't regularly use the models in routine engineering work. Most early FE solvers rendered the output in two dimensions, which made it difficult for engineers to visually determine whether the model behaved similarly to the test vehicle and hence whether it had a high degree of correlation. However, the advantages of FE models over lumped-parameter models started becoming clear to automakers by the mid 1970s, when several articles in *SAE Transactions* reported the favorable results of experiments performed on FE models at GM, Ford, and Chrysler. (See, e.g., Davis 1974; Peterson 1971; Wotiz 1974.) Around the same time, the Lawrence Livermore National Laboratory released a new FE code called DYNA3D, which, when processed on a Control Data CDC-7600 supercomputer, allowed the user to render the FE code in three dimensions and compute results for dynamic analyses. These two innovations were eagerly welcomed by safety engineers, who could now run a full set of analyses that mirrored the physical crash tests conducted in safety laboratories at proving grounds. Engineers could now also visually assess the results of a simulation in enough detail so the results could be compared against the outcomes of physical tests. DYNA3D was so well received by automakers and aeronautical engineers that two years later Livermore Lab completely rewrote the FE code so it could be processed on a high-speed Cray-1 computer and released a new version that was 50 times as fast as its predecessor. These innovations in computing power and code made FE models much more tractable for everyday engineering use and offered the potential to reduce the number of expensive crash tests automakers had to conduct to meet NHTSA certification. These developments effectively brought this new technology out of R&D labs into the production environment.

In the late 1970s, the cost of purchasing and installing supercomputers on which the FE code could be solved and implementing individual computer workstations for safety engineers to pre-process and post-process their finite-element models became a major concern for automakers. Solving FE code required several supercomputers, but implementing the individual workstations was even more costly. To take advantage of the analytic capabilities offered by finite element analysis, automakers had to figure out a way to organize the work to reduce the need for crash tests without incurring large computer and engineering costs.

To deal with the issue of cost, automakers created a new category of engineers that would be responsible for building and analyzing simulations to predict vehicle performance in a number of areas. These engineers would work closely with design engineers at the automakers' engineering centers and with safety engineers at the proving grounds, serving as an interface between the two worlds. The new engineers would receive architectural drawings of parts from various design engineers, convert the CAD drawings into FE models, integrate the parts to build a full vehicle model (typically consisting of more than 30,000 parts), and then run prospective tests in an effort to predict energy distribution during a crash. Because their primary responsibility would be to build and analyze FE models, the new engineers' need to interact with test engineers at the proving grounds was expected to be limited to a few times a month. In addition, locating the new engineers at the engineering centers would afford automakers maximum utilization of the supercomputers, which could be used for other engineering functions. And if the companies limited model building and analysis activities to a smaller group of engineers, they wouldn't have to purchase as many workstations.

In the late 1970s, automakers evaluated these three options for restructuring their engineering disciplines to use the capabilities of FEA in analyzing crashworthiness. In an article in *SAE Transactions*, two Ford engineers offered recommendations for restructuring an organization to best exploit the capabilities of FE methods and advocated the creation of a CAE department that would build and analyze models constructed by design engineers in Ford's various automotive divisions:

The critical question is how to organize a large company to use most effectively the technical skills available. . . . In many cases [a centralized] approach is to be preferred from the standpoint of effective utilization of manpower, minimal training, and the development of technical proficiency. It also offers the financial means to support a terminal-based computer system, computer graphics, and related software development. When properly managed, a centralized activity offers an efficient use of human and financial resources. (Carl and Hamaan 1974, pp. 16–18)

By the early 1980s, American automakers had established CAE centers—much like the ones Carl and Hamaan recommended—in which engineers performed computational analyses of a number of different performance criteria for vehicle dynamics, including crashworthiness, noise and vibration, ride and handling, aerodynamics and thermal, and HVAC (heating, ventilation, and air-conditioning). Many of these new performance engineers (analysts), who specialized in one particular area (such as HVAC analysis), held bachelor's or advanced degrees in the engineering subdiscipline in which they worked (for example, structural engineering).

Engineering analysts' work in the new CAE sectors required close interaction with both design engineers at the engineering center and safety test engineers at the proving grounds. Analysts were responsible for assembling the numerous CAD files for parts created by design engi ʾeers into a full-vehicle FE model and running simulations of the model to determine whether the vehicle would meet NHTSA's FMVSS regulations. If a model didn't meet the minimum criteria, analysts would redesign the parts (i.e., change their shape or the gauge of the steel used to build them) and iterate through various analyses until they met the minimum requirements for government certification. The analysts would then submit their analysis to design engineers, who would determine whether or not the design changes proposed were feasible from a number of different standpoints (shape, cost, weight restrictions, and manufacturability) and then revise the part accordingly. Once sufficient iteration had taken place between analysts and design engineers to suggest a vehicle with a particular design would meet FMVSS requirements, the vehicle was built and then tested at the proving grounds using impact sleds and electric linear motors. Then analysts would then work with safety test engineers at the proving grounds to verify the accuracy of their simulations by confirming them with physical tests. If the results of a physical test didn't match those of a simulations, analysts worked to change parameters in their FE models (such as algorithms for the material properties or the placement of accelerometers) to correlate their simulations with the results of the physical tests. This meant that the numbers obtained from accelerations and intrusions, as well as the physical deformation of the parts, had to look identical in the physical test and the simulation. (See figure 3.2.) Correlating the physical test and the simulation not only helped explain the factors affecting the test at hand; it also helped analysts to increase their knowledge of finite-element methods and to create better simulations, which enabled them to more accurately predict the crashworthiness of the vehicles they would test in the future.

Test
(full vehicle)

Simulation
(from FE model)

Figure 3.2
Correlation between a frontal-impact test and a frontal-impact simulation.

In combination with the computer revolution of the 1980s, the decision to develop a cadre of engineers to run vehicle crash simulations using FE models dramatically strengthened the power of FE models to help predict vehicle safety and to reduce the number of physical tests automakers had to conduct. The increased fidelity of math models allowed analysts to conduct more iterations for each crash scenario and, as a result, to optimize a design rather than merely meeting the FMVSS requirement. According to Stefan Thomke (1998), since the mid 1990s simulations from FE models have consistently led to an increase in problem-solving cycles in the field of crash-safety engineering while reducing the cost of design iterations. Thomke also found that this increased capacity to iterate through diverse experiments with novel possibilities enabled crash-safety engineers to learn more than they could learn with conventional physical prototypes, and therefore to design better vehicles.

As automakers steadily increased vehicle safety—thanks in large part to the technological and organizational changes in the engineering field that enabled the use of mathematically based simulations in vehicle testing during the 1980s and the 1990s—the federal government's attitude toward the crash problem began to change. For the first time since the 1966 regulations were passed, automakers were outpacing NHTSA in crash-safety innovation and were consistently designing their vehicles not just to meet the FMVSS requirements but to exceed them. Several judicial decisions in the mid 1970s and the early 1980s opposed NHTSA's mandatory performance standards when the agency lacked data to illustrate logical goals auto manufacturers could actually meet (Mashaw and Harfst 1990, pp. 87–104).

In an attempt to reposition itself as an effective consumer-advocacy group, NHTSA launched a new venture, the New Car Assessment Program (NCAP), to began its own crash testing of vehicles with the 1979–1980 model year. As publicized, the goal of the program was to provide customers with a set of performance metrics to indicate how well a vehicle fared in a crash. NHTSA began recording the values of frontal-impact tests and the relationship of those values to established injury-assessment references. The NCAP tests were based on FMVSS regulation 208, "Occupant Crash Protection"—except that the frontal NCAP test was conducted at 35 miles per hour instead of the 30 miles per hour required by the regulation. Initially, NHTSA was slow to disseminate this information to consumers.

By the year 2000, automakers' interactions with vehicle safety regulation had changed substantially. Automakers no longer designed vehicles to meet FMVSS requirements; instead, they consistently set objectives for vehicle programs with the goal of receiving a particular rating from consumer testing agencies. As a result, the tests administered by consumer agencies began to have an important effect on the structural design of vehicles. Most automakers considered the various tests conducted in the markets around the world in which they sold their automobiles as "driving load cases for vehicle design." (The term 'load case' refers simply to the way in which a load—that is, a force resulting from a collision—is applied to a vehicle's structure. For an example of common non-overlapping load cases, see figure 3.3.) In essence, the increasing number of crash tests conducted and publicized by consumer agencies, consumers' increasing interest in purchasing safe vehicles, and advances in mathematical simulation methods that made meeting and exceeding test requirements practical and financially feasible led to a more balanced approach to the accident problem. The public began to accept that automakers couldn't be blamed for every motor-vehicle death and that they were indeed working hard to improve the safety of their vehicles while simultaneously keeping prices down, and that people had a responsibility to practice safe driving and to make informed decisions about which vehicles to purchase.

The Technology

In an attempt to reduce the time and effort it took analysts to set up and analyze an FE model and to standardize the assumptions engineers used throughout the process, technology developers in Autoworks' R&D Division began development a new technology called CrashLab. As we will see, CrashLab has a long and complicated relationship with several communities within Autoworks. CrashLab is an FEA tool used for pre-processing the finite-element models (that is, setting up the mesh models in ways that can be analyzed by a solver to produce desired results) that safety and crashworthiness analysts use to predict how a vehicle's structure will respond in a crash, and for post-processing (how the results obtained from the computational analysis can be extracted and filtered so as to have predictive power). The idea for CrashLab emerged from Autoworks' R&D Division in 1994. After nearly ten years of development work, CrashLab was made available to analysts in September of 2004. The interface and the computational algorithms used by the tool are created by a vendor, Dynamic Software, that produces a commercial pre-processing tool called DynamicMesh. DynamicMesh uses a graphical interface to represent thousands of equations in the design and analysis of automobile subsystem components. The interface has a flexible design that users can configure in a variety of ways. In short, CrashLab was designed by Autoworks and

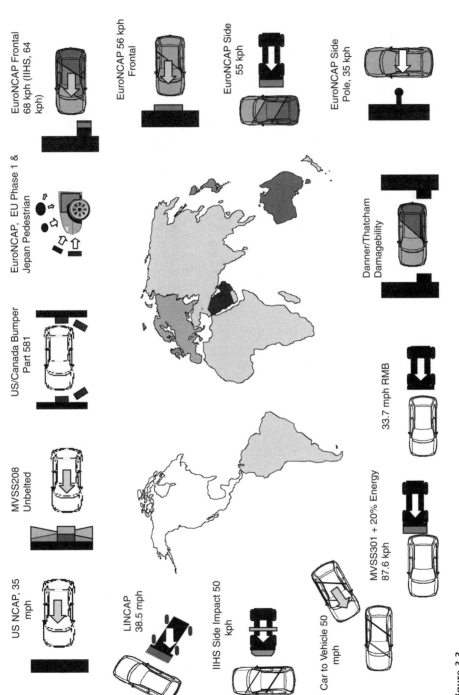

Figure 3.3
Geographic distribution of common load case evaluation.

built by Dynamic Software. CrashLab therefore meets the first two conditions for research within the framework presented above.

In addition to developing, implementing, and using CrashLab, Autoworks also satisfies the criteria established for a robust research site for observing technological and organizational change. In order to develop CrashLab, no fewer than four of Autoworks' departments had to coordinate their efforts over a ten-year period. To effectively implement it, three more had to join the effort. And to use it, three additional departments were enrolled in the process. Thus, there were ample opportunities to assess the negotiations that occurred within and across various communities at Autoworks involved in the technological and organizational changes inspired by CrashLab. The reader should keep in mind that the objective of the study was to understand how it was that an organization such as Autoworks would come to build a technology such as CrashLab, and how CrashLab would come to change that very organization.

The Organization

Autoworks is one of the largest automakers in the world, selling more than 9 million vehicles a year and employing more than 300,000 people worldwide. To accurately depict the development, implementation, and use of CrashLab over a ten-year period, I had to gain entry into many different divisions within Autoworks. Many of the divisions within the organization are larger than some entire independent auto companies. My initial entrée into the company was through the Research and Development Division, as part of a larger study on the changing nature of engineering work.[7] During the summer of 2004, I met several engineers in the R&D Division who told me about CrashLab. The technology sounded interesting: It was a new concept for automating engineering work using advanced computational algorithms, it was developed through the coordination of a number of different organizations at Autoworks, it was heralded as a technology that would help "revolutionize" crashworthiness work, and it was in the final stages of development. After some preliminary interviews with and observations of users, I determined that CrashLab would be an ideal subject of study for my research on the relationship between technological and organizational change. The biggest bet I had to make was on whether or not CrashLab's implementation would coincide with when I arranged to perform my data collection. This was a relatively risky gamble, since Crash-Lab had been in the works for nearly ten years and still hadn't been fully implemented in the Safety Division. However, because CrashLab was explicitly intended to change engineering work, and because Autoworks provided a natural laboratory in which to track CrashLab's development and observe its use, the gamble seemed worth taking.

Figure 3.4 presents a very abbreviated version of Autoworks' organization chart, with the names of most positions and departments disguised to protect the company's confidentiality and with only those divisions, departments, and groups whose members became informants in the study represented. Thus, many divisions, departments, and groups that are important to the development and distribution of vehicles, including styling, manufacturing, sales, and marketing, are not included.

Nearly all of the engineering work performed on vehicles that will be sold in the consumer market (called either "vehicle program work" or "product development work") takes place within the Global Product Development Organization. This group is divided into a number of specialties, including Global Design, Global Integration, and Global Engineering Process. In both the design functions and the integration functions, engineers work directly on production vehicles—vehicles that will be sold in the consumer market. Both of these divisions are further divided into different functional areas. Within the Global Design Organization, functions are determined by vehicle subsystem. For example, there is a body group, a power-train group, and a chassis group. Each of these areas is further divided into "vehicle platforms" (also called "vehicle architectures"). A vehicle platform is a common set of subsystem components upon which different programs are built. A vehicle program is roughly analogous to a consumer model. For example, Toyota produces several models—the Toyota Camry, the Toyota Highlander, the Lexus ES, and the Lexus RX—that share a common platform. In other words, structurally the vehicles are roughly the same, though their bodies and interiors are noticeably different.

The Global Integration Organization is structured in the same manner. However, in the GIO the integration engineers don't draft subsystems in CAD, as their counterparts in the Global Design Organization do. Instead, they analyze the performance of the subsystems as they are integrated to create complete vehicles. Engineers within Autoworks often refer to the departments that perform integration work as "crashworthiness-analysis groups." I use this nomenclature often throughout the book. Among the crashworthiness-analysis divisions are the Safety Division (the focus of this study), Noise and Vibration, Vehicle Dynamics, Aero/Thermal, and HVAC. The Safety Division is split into departments, the Car Department and the Truck Department, which follow the same systems and processes; in 2004, when I began my study at Autoworks, both of these departments were located at the company's engineering center in Motorville, Michigan. When I began my study, the Car Department and the Truck Department

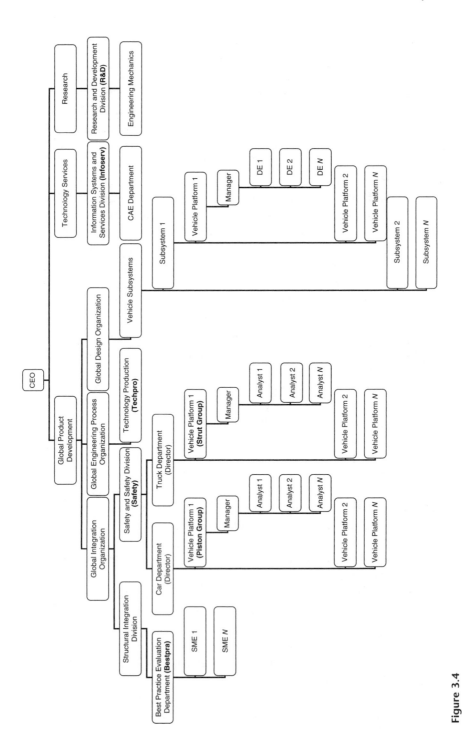

Figure 3.4
A simplified chart of the formal organization of work at Autoworks.

consisted of 66 and 59 analysts, respectively, who performed CAE work.[8] Within these departments, work is divided into vehicle platforms, just as it is in the Global Design Organization. Each vehicle platform group is staffed by a number of analysts (15 to 17 on average) who work on load case analyses for all the programs based on that particular platform.

Also within the larger Global Integration Organization, the Structural Integration Division, a crucial pre-production player in the process, runs Autoworks' Advanced Vehicle Development Center, which justifies the feasibility (from a performance standpoint) of a vehicle's design before. The Best Practice Evaluation Department, a relative newcomer to the company's structure, is organized as a subunit of the larger Structural Integration Division.

Global Engineering Process, the last pre-production functional area in the Global Product Development Organization, is responsible for developing new technologies and workflows for the Global Design Organization and the Global Integration Organization. Within this area, the Techpro Department is staffed with engineers who work to develop technologies for the crashworthiness-analysis groups.

Two other areas were important to CrashLab's development, neither of which was directly involved in product development work at Autoworks. First, the Information Systems and Services Division, which falls under Technology Services, is responsible for implementing the user-end and infrastructure technologies employed at Autoworks in both engineering and business operations. Finally, Research is home to Autoworks' R&D Division. Like most industrial R&D ventures, Autoworks' R&D Division is a research-focused laboratory aimed at developing new technologies—in this case, with the goal of helping engineers build better vehicles.

The names of each of all these groups have been disguised to protect the confidentiality of Autoworks. Throughout the book, I refer to specific actors who reappear throughout the narrative. Only actors who make multiple appearances are given names, which, of course, are pseudonyms. Those who appear only once are referred to simply by job description.

Becoming an Insider at Autoworks

I arrived at Autoworks for the first time in July of 2004 and spent nearly two months observing the work of analysts in the Safety Division. During this initial stint of data collection, I uncovered two pivotal events in

CrashLab's history, one of which had occurred more than nine years earlier and one of which would occur a year later. In June of 1995, a researcher from Autoworks' R&D lab made the first formal presentation of his idea for a technology that would later come to be CrashLab. This presentation is a seminal moment in the story—one I will mention again—because it was the impetus for a series of activities in development that would not crystallize into a fully functional technology until another important event in September of 2004. As summer came to a close, CrashLab was scheduled to be implemented in the Safety Division. These two events serve as important guide points for my study. I knew if I wanted to understand how CrashLab was developed, I had to go back to sometime before 1995 and follow its development through to September of 2004. In addition, if I wanted to understand how CrashLab was being used, September of 2005 would be an important month. Although these two time periods loosely demarcated boundaries in which I would focus my attention, they posed different challenges. Most of the activity integral to CrashLab's development had already occurred; thus, I would only be able to collect retrospective data about the processes that unfolded. By contrast, analysts hadn't yet used CrashLab in their work, so I would have to wait until September of the following year to observe in real time how analysts interpreted CrashLab, how they used it, and whether or not it changed the way they worked. As a consequence, I had to employ a number of different techniques to collect data that would allow me to understand the relationship between technological and organizational change.

CrashLab Development Activities

As Thomas (1994) points out, the processes of most major technological developments occur over of many years. In the case of CrashLab, tracing the pre-conditions for its development required going back more than ten years. Certainly real-time observation was neither feasible nor possible for such action. However, because over the years Autoworks' employee retention rate was high, the vast majority of the individuals involved in CrashLab's development were still with the company. Thus, I was able to conduct in-depth interviews with informants and, in the process, to gain access to archived data on the technology's development.

Interview Data

I began the interview process by identifying informants through the "snowball" method, conducting interviews with informants I knew were involved in CrashLab's development and, through these interviews, acquiring the names of others who were also involved. Autoworks maintained a very detailed and accurate database of employee contact information, and I was able to use the database to track down informants even if they had moved into new positions in the company. In a few cases, people involved in the development of CrashLab had left the company. However, in all but one instance I was able to track down those informants through informants still employed at Autoworks. Using this snowball method, I interviewed members of five different groups within Autoworks: Research and Development (R&D), the Information Systems and Services Division (Infoserv), the Global Technology Production Division (Techpro), the Safety Division, and the Best Practice Evaluation Department (Bestpra). In addition, I conducted interviews with informants at three technology suppliers that contributed to building CrashLab at various times: Link Software, Element Software, and Dynamic Software. I also conducted several interviews with other individuals who weren't members of any of the previously mentioned Autoworks groups or outside organizations, such as Autoworks senior managers, consultants from other supplier firms, and professors at nearby universities. Table 3.1 summarizes the interviews I conducted with each group and the number of informants interviewed. I conducted 58 interviews regarding the development of CrashLab with 36 informants.

In each interview, I aimed to solicit from informants their recollections of events surrounding the development of CrashLab and their interpretations of why certain things occurred. I began each interview by asking informants general questions about their employment experience at Autoworks (if applicable), the role of their particular group in the vehicle development process, and the nature of their work. I then asked more specific questions about the development of CrashLab and about changes that occurred in the organization of work at Autoworks. I hoped to uncover some more objective material, such as the composition of the teams involved in CrashLab's development, the fees paid to contracting organizations for their services, and the timing of certain events. To overcome information-recall bias, I asked multiple participants the same questions on multiple occasions (when they were interviewed more than once) to triangulate as best I could. In addition to gathering these more objective data, I was also interested in understanding informants' subjective interpretations of the events that unfolded during CrashLab's development, their feelings about how CrashLab evolved, and their hopes for the new technology.

Table 3.1
Summary of interviews regarding the development of CrashLab.

	Group interviewed								
	R&D	Infoserv	Techpro	Safety	Bestpra	Link	Element	Dynamic	Other	Total
Number of interviews	12	6	11	14	5	2	1	2	5	58
Number of informants	7	4	6	9	3	2	1	2	5	36

Specifically, the goal of interviewing was to solicit objective information about the development process as well as informants' subjective interpretations of the process. To do this, I followed the advice of Lindlof (1995, p. 172) and constructed the interview questions in ways that would achieve five interdependent goals: to clarify the meanings of common concepts and opinions, to distinguish the decisive elements of an expressed opinion, to determine what influenced a person to form an opinion or act in a certain way, to classify complex attitude patterns, and to understand the interpretations that people attribute to their motivations to act. Each interview was recorded on a digital audio recorder with the informant's permission. Interviews lasted from 45 to 180 minutes. Only two informants requested that I not transcribe their interviews, and in both of those cases I took thorough notes during each interview. With the digital recorder running, I was free to take notes about interesting things informants mentioned, issues they raised that I hadn't considered, the names of additional people with whom I should talk, and questions that remained unanswered. Before each interview, I reviewed the notes I had made during previous interviews to determine which questions were still unanswered and which issues I wanted to seek alternative interpretations of. I then used this information to construct specific questions for the next interview. All the interviews captured on audio were later transcribed verbatim and used as raw data for analysis.

Archival Data

During interviews, many respondents referenced documents, email, and presentations that were generated during the course of CrashLab's development. At the end of each interview, I asked informants if I could borrow and copy the archival data to which they referred. In almost all cases, they agreed. There were several times when informants couldn't locate the material they referenced. However, whenever that occurred I followed up a few days later via phone and email to see if I could procure the documents. My success rate was quite high. As was expected, upon reviewing the documents I encountered references to other documentation. I would then go back to the informants to try to track down the additional material. As I reviewed the archival data, additional questions about the development process surfaced; I was able to raise those questions in subsequent interviews.

Through this iterative process, I collected more than 2,200 pages of documentation pertaining to the development of CrashLab, including user specifications, white papers, vendor contracts, personal emails, and slide presentations. These data demonstrated the rhetoric and the persuasive processes employed by various groups as they formulated objectives for CrashLab and uncovered various problems the technology should solve. Moreover, the material demonstrates how certain issues were brought to the foreground and highly contested, then disappeared or came to be considered less important. I also gathered organization charts and briefings describing the structure and hierarchy at Autoworks at different times between 1995 and 2005 so I could correlate informants' accounts of organizational changes with formal alterations in Autoworks' organizational structure.

I divided my periods of observation at Autoworks into four phases. The first phase was a year before CrashLab was implemented, between July and August of 2004. The second phase was between August and November of 2004. This time, I arrived at Autoworks some three weeks before CrashLab officially launched, and I remained there for 13 more weeks to observe analysts as they made their initial interpretations of the technology and first used it. I then returned for a third visit between March and April of 2006. This visit began 26 weeks after CrashLab was implemented. Finally, I returned to Autoworks for five more weeks between July and August of 2006, nearly a year after CrashLab was implemented. Over a two-year period, I spent a total of just over nine months collecting data on site at Autoworks' engineering center in Motorville, Michigan.

During my time there, in addition to collecting retrospective data on CrashLab's trajectory of development between 1995 and 2004, I also conducted real-time observations of three separate but related activities: the work of crashworthiness analysts before CrashLab was implemented; the activities of developers, trainers, and managers during the implementation process; and the work of analysts after CrashLab was implemented. During each of my four visits, I utilized five primary data sources: observations of informants at work, artifacts informants produced or used in their work, interviews conducted with informants about their work, sociometric surveys distributed to informants, and logs kept by informants to track their use of CrashLab. I outline each of these data sources in the pages that follow. Table 3.2 summarizes the data that were collected through these first three methods during my four visits to Autoworks.

Observing Analysts

Research has repeatedly shown that people have difficulty articulating what work they do and how they do it (Collins 1974; Dreyfus and Dreyfus

Table 3.2
Summary of data collected before, during, and after implementation of CrashLab.

	Phase 1: July–Aug. 2004	Phase 2: Aug.–Nov. 2005	Phase 3: March–April 2006	Phase 4: July–Aug. 2006	Total
Work of analysts before CrashLab (general observations in Car Department and Truck Department)					
Observations	10				10
Artifacts	78				78
Interviews	7	42[a]			49
Implementation activities					
Observations		14			14
Artifacts		4			4
Interviews	3	6			9
Work of analysts after CrashLab (Piston Group)					
Observations		34	18	12	64
Artifacts		136	72	55	263
Interviews			19	4	23
Work of analysts after CrashLab (Strut Group)					
Observations		32	17	11	60
Artifacts		182	67	59	308
Interviews			16	3	19
Other interviews					
Managers	2	4	2	3	11
Design engineers		3		2	5
Vice-president		1			1

a. Nineteen informants from the Piston Group, seventeen from the Strut Group, and four miscellaneous informants

1986; Orr 1996). Therefore, although interviews are useful for uncovering attitudes and beliefs about work and for eliciting histories of organizational and technological change, direct observation is necessary to capture actual work practices and people's interactions with technology. In observing the analysts in the Safety Division, I aimed to compile a complete record of all the actions they took to build and analyze prospective FE models (with or without the use of CrashLab), to correlate those models with the results of retrospective physical crash tests, and to make recommendations for improving vehicle performance in various impact conditions. It quickly became clear that in order to carry out these activities analysts had to spend a lot of time interacting with fellow analysts and with the design engineers who created the CAD data that analysts used to build FE models. Analysts also spent a lot of time alone at their computers working with various pre-processing and post-processing applications. I therefore needed to capture the broad range of performance engineers' solo and group interactions. To do so effectively and in detail, I typically observed analysts for between three and five hours at a time. Each session was spent observing one analyst as the primary informant. Each analyst who participated in this study was independently observed for at least three sessions. After ten or so hours with each informant, I was able to clearly understand how the engineer worked and why he or she worked that way. In all, I spent a little more than 500 hours observing analysts at Autoworks.

I captured the activities that occurred during each session of observation in a number of ways. I sat behind the informants at their desks while they worked, and I followed them when they went to meetings and to talk to colleagues. I accompanied the engineers to the proving grounds in Test-ville, Michigan, to watch physical crash tests; I also went with them to vehicle teardowns, where they were able to inspect the state of the parts after a physical test.[9] During all these activities, I took notes on my small laptop computer, documenting the types of activities the engineers con-ducted, why they conducted them, and with whom or what they inter-acted. I also recorded all my observations on a digital audio recorder. Using audio recordings allowed me to document the engineers' conversations and capture their personal thoughts on different matters, which I encour-aged them to vocalize as they worked. I also let the audio recorder run when engineers were working silently at their computers. All the audio recordings were transcribed verbatim. I later integrated the audio transcrip-tions with my field notes. By using the digital time stamp on the audio recorder in conjunction with time notations I made in my field notes (I recorded the time in five-minute increments), I was able to document how long informants spent on particular tasks. The combined records of obser-vation (field notes and corresponding dialog) for one session were nor-mally between 20 and 30 pages of single-spaced text.

I arrived at Autoworks for the first time in July of 2004 and stayed through the end of August (phase 1). During this time, I conducted obser-vations of analysts in both the Car Department and the Truck Department. The purpose of these early observations was to gain a detailed understand-ing of how engineers worked before CrashLab was implemented so I would have a basis from which to measure whether or not their work changed after implementation. Thus, I adopted a pre-implementation and post-implementation design recommended by researchers in technology innovation (Barley 1990b; Van de Ven and Rogers 1988). During July and August of 2004, I conducted ten observations of analysts in the Safety Division.

Many researchers have suggested that, because technologies can be and often are used in multiple and conflicting ways across communities of users, having a point of comparison for user communities is beneficial for understanding how technological and organizational change unfolds (Barley 1990b; Edmondson et al. 2001; Robey and Sahay 1996). Barley (1990b) suggests that for this reason studies of technology use should employ a parallel form of analysis so that uses of the technology within two distinct socio-cultural contexts can be examined. Following this logic, I chose to limit my study to two different groups of CrashLab users when I returned to Autoworks in August of 2006 (phase 2). Three criteria guided me in choosing these groups.

First, because I was interested in whether and how CrashLab would change the organization of work, it was important to focus my observations on groups of users that represented a recognizable (both by the informants themselves and by outsiders) and intact social system. The various vehicle platform groups within the larger Car and Truck departments were an ideal choice. Each vehicle platform was a fully insulated social system whose members worked interactively to evaluate the crashworthiness of the programs based on that platform. In addition, analysts were officially assigned to one (and only one) vehicle platform—they attended weekly staff meetings with other assigned to only that platform. Moreover, an average of 15 to 17 analysts were assigned to each platform —a manageable number that made it possible to conduct observations of nearly all of the groups' members, and to solicit survey and log data from them.

Second, because I was interested in determining whether the effects of CrashLab on the organization of work were similar or different across two distinct social systems, it was important to reduce the number of variables that could affect the technology's outcome. Analysts working on the vehicle platforms in the Car Department and the Truck Department work in nearly identical ways. Both groups work for the same company (reducing variability in cultural and institutional influences), perform the same kind of work (reducing variability in task-based influences), and consist of individuals with a similar makeup in terms of ethnicity, gender, age, experience, education, and tenure at Autoworks (reducing variability in demographic influences). In addition, the groups are isolated enough from one another—both geographically and socially—that it was unlikely that one group's experiences with the CrashLab would, through word of mouth, affect the experiences of the other group. Finally and perhaps most important, my interviews with CrashLab developers demonstrated that a good number of managers and analysts from the Car Department were involved in selecting CrashLab's features and therefore had intimate knowledge of the technology's function and purpose; similar actors in the Truck Department were mostly unaware of and certainly uninvolved in CrashLab's development. Thus, because research shows that individuals who are involved in the development of an innovation are more likely to question it and change it (Rice and Rogers 1980; Thomas 1994), I had a hunch that this difference in involvement might somehow come to influence how CrashLab was used in each of these groups. In short, by choosing to focus my observation on analysts working on one vehicle platform in the Car Department and one in the Strut Group, I had a natural laboratory in which to show that, if CrashLab did bring about changes in the organization of work that were common to both groups, those changes would have to be attributed to the technology itself. However, if CrashLab brought about changes to only one of the groups, then, because the groups were so similar (in all the ways described above), the changes would have to be attributed to some outside factor that influenced analysts in each group to use the technology differently.

A third factor in my choice to observe one vehicle platform in the Car and Truck departments was that analysts in the Safety Division typically began work on a program based on a vehicle platform after the architecture passed a benchmark known as vehicle program initiation (VPI). Once the VPI stage was complete, there were, depending on the program, more than 100 weeks until the vehicle program was launched into regular production, or it began rolling off the assembly line onto dealer floors. Because Crash-Lab allowed analysts to build and analyze math models, managers and developers reasoned that it would result in the most change in the engineers' work when a particular program was still flexible enough to be redesigned and reconfigured using the results from the crashworthiness engineers' performance analyses. Typically, this period during which analysts could still radically affect the vehicle's design lasted from the VPI stage until the structure vehicle engineering release (SVER). This meant that analysts had, on average, a little over a year during which their analyses could dramatically affect the structure of the vehicle. This was the most intense period of model setup and analysis during a program's development cycle. After this stage, structural inertia by way of invested capital in manufacturing equipment and the like made it cost prohibitive to revise a vehicle's design radically. Quite fortunately, I found two vehicle-platform teams, one from the Car Department and one from the Truck Department, that were on roughly the same track. Both teams had just completed the VPI stage two weeks before CrashLab was implemented. Consequently, I knew I had slightly longer than one year during which analysts might, if they chose to, use CrashLab frequently. The vehicle platform in the Car Department consisted of 19 analysts, and the vehicle platform in the Truck Department consisted of 17 analysts. In the interest of simplification, and to eliminate confusion, I refer to these two vehicle platform teams respectively with the not-so-clever names "the Piston Group" and "the Strut Group" throughout the remainder of the book. I conducted 64 observations of analysts in the Piston Group and 60 observations of analysts in the Strut Group after CrashLab was implemented.

Observing the Implementation Process

Before and immediately after CrashLab was implemented, I observed a number of different events at which CrashLab was discussed, debated, and "pitched" to the users. These events included training sessions; developer, staff, managers, and process improvement meetings; and formal and informal conferences at which developers, trainers, implementers, and managers introduced CrashLab to analysts who were unfamiliar with the new technology. Twelve of these events were dedicated explicitly to discussing CrashLab; another twelve were events (most of them at Autoworks) at which CrashLab happened to be discussed. Table 6.1 in chapter 6 provides details about all 24 of these events. As I observed these events, I let my digital audio recorder capture the dialog, and I simply wrote down who was speaking. Later, after the audio recordings were transcribed, I integrated my notes about who was speaking and anything important that occurred with the transcripts of dialog.

Artifacts
The work of analysts is highly visual. They work in a world of 3-D math models, constantly manipulating and working on them in various software programs (e.g., pre-processors, post-processors, and CrashLab). To augment notes taken during my observations of analysts, I also collected copies of the artifacts with which the analysts worked. Most often these artifacts were digital screen shots of the parts they were working on in the various computer applications on their workstations. I would routinely ask an informant to create a screen shot for me of the model in progress, or a

.AVI file of the crash-test video he or she was watching, and save it to a PowerPoint presentation. At the end of each session, the informant would email me a PowerPoint presentation containing all the images from that day's observation. I carried a large flash drive with me in the event that a file was too big to send via email. I also collected hard copies of other artifacts, including calendars, copies of pages from informants' notebooks, and meeting minutes. When I returned from the field, I scanned all the images and converted them into soft copies for easy storage. I then archived the relevant artifacts in a folder with the observation record for that session so that during analysis I could match my notes about how the informant used the artifact with the artifact itself. In the course of the study, I collected more than 649 artifacts that analysts either produced or used in the course of their normal work.

Interviews

To supplement the data I collected as I observed analysts at work, I conducted a number of interviews. In line with the principles and techniques for interviewing outlined above, the interviews were aimed at capturing analysts' explicit thoughts and ideas about CrashLab. I interviewed all but one of the analysts from the Piston Group and the Strut Group at two different times. In the first round of interviews, which took place before CrashLab was implemented (phase 2), I interviewed all 19 analysts from the Piston Group and all 17 from the Strut Group. During that round, I asked analysts what they had heard about CrashLab—specifically, what kind of technology CrashLab was, what it did, and how it would affect their work. I then asked informants to talk about any issues related to technological development or use at Autoworks of which they were aware. The second round of interviews took place during phase 3, after the analysts had been using CrashLab for more than six months. In that round, I again interviewed all 19 analysts from the Piston Group, and 16 from the Strut Group.[10] Hoping to uncover changes in perception of CrashLab after six months of use, I used the very same protocol I had used in the first round of interviews. I also asked the analysts to clarify any issues I uncovered through my observations. The interviews in both of these rounds lasted from 15 to 65 minutes. They were all audio recorded with the permission of the informants and later transcribed verbatim.

In addition to interviewing analysts, I conducted a number of interviews with design engineers and with managers in the Safety Division, and one with the vice-president of product development. The goal of these interviews was to obtain an outsider's perspective on analysts' work. The interviews were open-ended and didn't follow any protocol. Instead, they followed the taxonomic interviewing technique advocated by Spradley (1979), in which questions are raised that attempt to uncover informants' categories of thought about their work. All but two of these interviews were audio recorded with the permission of the informants, and later were transcribed verbatim.

Sociometric Surveys

Sociometric surveys are used to collect data on the patterns of social relations between actors. During my time in Autoworks' Safety Division, I observed analysts consulting their colleagues regularly about model setup and analysis. As will be explained in detail in chapter 7, all model setup requires knowledge of at least three activities: how to position a barrier, where to place accelerometers, and how to define sections. Likewise, to execute a useful analysis, every analyst has to make decisions on the basis of at least three factors that are necessary to improve crashworthiness: how to change the materials used to build parts, how to change the geometry of parts, and how to change the location of parts. Together, these six areas of expertise are the focus of the communication that constitutes the informal organization of work in the Safety Division. To determine whether these patterns of consultation—and therefore analysts' informal social structure—changed over the course of this study, all 19 analysts in the Piston Group and all 17 analysts in the Strut Group were given identical sociometric surveys in three waves.

The first wave of surveys were conducted in August of 2005, just before CrashLab was implemented in the Safety Division (phase 2). The second wave of surveys were conducted three months after implementation (also during phase 2). The final wave of surveys were conducted in August of 2006, after analysts in the Piston Group and the Strut Group had used CrashLab for 50 weeks (phase 4). The surveys employed a whole-network approach by utilizing a roster of all analysts in the Safety Division and asking informants to select as many names as they wished from the roster for each of the six questions. By including a complete roster for each question—what network researchers often term a "name-generator" instrument (see, for example, Marsden 2005)—I limited the possible universe of alters (that is, individuals with whom the focal actor communicates) that any one actor could select. This decision was made in part to provide a manageable dataset, but mainly because CrashLab was hypothesized to have caused things to change only in the Safety Division and not throughout the entire company. Thus, by limiting the potential universe of alters,

I was able to exploit one advantage of a name-generator instrument—namely that informants are more accurate in selecting alters since the names are given to them, which eliminates the risk of them forgetting. Ultimately, the instrument allowed me to increase the reliability of the results (Marsden 2005).

The sociometric survey was administered (in three waves, as has already been noted) via email. Informants were asked to select multiple names for each of the six questions, which asked them to indicate anyone they consulted about the specific issue indicated. The survey also offered participants the option to select the response "I do not talk with anyone about this" from a drop-down menu. At the conclusion of the survey, participants clicked a "submit" button that closed the email and sent the results, along with their identifying information, via the web to a researcher. After several reminder emails and some face-to-face visits, I received responses from 100 percent of the 19 analysts in the Piston Group and the 17 in the Strut Group in each of the three waves.

Tracking Logs

Tracking logs were the final method I used to collect data on the use of CrashLab at Autoworks. I was interested in understanding how analysts' use of CrashLab's features evolved over time. I was unable to continuously observe CrashLab's use. To overcome this shortcoming, I developed a system of tracking logs for informants to complete. Each Friday, I sent a tracking log to the informants in the Piston Group and the Strut Group via email. Each log contained a list of all of CrashLab's major features. (See table 7.1 in chapter 7.) The email asked analysts to select which features, if any, they had used during that particular week, and to click a "submit" button that closed the email and sent the results to the researcher via the web. Over the 50 weeks I sent these tracking logs to analysts in the Piston Group and the Strut Group, I averaged a response rate of 72 percent.

Some Notes on the Presentation of Data

To recount the processes of CrashLab's development, implementation, and use—which together spanned more than eleven years—necessitates some distortion and some truncation. To present the data within the pages of this book and achieve a readable and understandable narrative, I had to take a bit of liberty with the presentation of events in order to construct for the reader what Gary Allen Fine (1993, p. 273) called the "illusion of verisimilitude." Specifically, I had to relate some events out of sequence, positioning them in the story as though they had occurred at roughly the same time. In addition, I had to make deliberate choices about which parts of the story to tell and which parts to leave out. Thus, although I attempt to provide rich data, there is always more to the story than meets the eye (Golden-Biddle and Locke 1997).

On a more practical note, I made some alterations to the story and the data to maintain the anonymity of the research site and the people involved. This entailed changing names, dates, relationships between people and departments, and in some cases even descriptive statistics about the company or about the technology or the process of vehicle development. As Gideon Kunda (1992) suggests, I maintained relations between numbers to illustrate analytic points. To be completely explicit, I should note that I fabricated all the vehicle impact performance data that are presented in charts and figures throughout this book. I have maintained the original shape of the curves, or the magnitude of the results, in such cases, but the data are not by any means the real data with which informants were working. Most quotations from interviews and most excerpts from field notes are presented verbatim. However, to aid in readability, I often corrected grammar, added words, or truncated the original excerpt. In some quotations, I used brackets to indicate my changes. Other excerpts required more work and were completely rewritten.

4 Developing Problems and Solving Technologies

A growing number of methodologies for developing new technologies suggest that unless developers understand the needs of their users, they will generate products that have little impact on the organizations that use them and the markets that support them. Because most technology development efforts are considered successful only if the capabilities of the new technology fit the needs of the social context in which it is implemented (Leonard-Barton 1988; Tyre and Hauptman 1992), it seems essential to understand the problems a user community faces before selecting and developing a new technology's features. Indeed, research suggests that identifying a set of problems that could potentially be solved by a new technology is a crucial first step in any product development process (Henderson and Clark 1990; Krishnan and Ulrich 2001).

Many technology development methodologies suggest that developers should begin their development efforts by focusing on the problems specific to a community of users. Eric von Hippel's (1986, 1988) research on "lead users"—that is, users whose needs will become common in the marketplace in the coming months or years—represents one clear example of the benefits developers can reap when they ground the development of a new technology in the needs of a user community. Von Hippel shows that using a problem-identification strategy that treats users as a "needs-forecasting laboratory" can greatly enhance the probability that developers will create new technologies that will be accepted by users and, as a result, generate high demand. Kim Clark and Takahiro Fujimoto (1991) have made similar claims, arguing that effective product development concepts are born from a detailed understanding not only of current market conditions but also of the problems users encounter with the technologies currently available to them. In an in-depth case study of new-technology development, Andrew Hargadon and Robert Sutton (1997) found that developers at the highly regarded product development firm IDEO were most successful at developing new technologies that users really wanted and needed when they were able to connect the problems faced by individuals in one organization or industry with solutions already existing in another organization or industry. Thus, the insights offered by the last two decades of research tell us that a successful technology development process is one in which marketers, managers, engineers, and researchers actively identify problems that already exist within communities of users and develop technologies to remedy them.

This logic of problem identification and technology development is held in high esteem in multiple groups at Autoworks. During my first days at the company, a senior manager in the R&D Division told me that developing new technologies required identifying not only the problems that already existed but also those that would exist in the future:

R&D has several goals. We aim to develop new technologies for our vehicles and to develop new technologies for our engineers, so they can design vehicles better. To do this we identify the types of problems these communities face and we develop technologies that will solve those problems. That's the basic understanding. Sometimes, though, users—whether they're drivers of an Autoworks car or our own engineers—don't see something as a problem. I mean this in the sense that "X" doesn't seem to be a problem now, but because they can't see the bigger picture they don't think "X" will be a problem in the future. Our job is to be preemptive about identifying not only problems that are already out there, but problems that are likely to occur and to constantly work on developing the technologies to solve those problems even before they begin. That's the mission of an industrial research center.

It does seem pretty simple. Identify the problems that are out there waiting to be found, then develop a technology that can help solve those problems. But if it is so simple, why is it rarely done? As a manager in the Safety Division recounted, developers seem to take the time to ask users about the problems they experience in their work, but they continue to develop technologies that fail to address those problems:

Many of the new technologies we get from R&D, Techpro, or wherever don't quite meet our needs. It's not for lack of trying on their part. They come and ask us what issues we have, what sorts of events present problems in our work. They seem very interested and seem to care, they even take good notes. Then they go away for a few years and come back with a new technology that doesn't solve those problems. I'm not sure why this happens.

This concern about a mismatch between users' needs and the technology available to them is certainly not endemic to crashworthiness engineering or to Autoworks. Numerous studies show that firms often spend huge amounts of money and time developing a new technology only to find that, users reject the technology because it fails to meet their immediate needs (Markus 2004). Thus, from the outset, the relationship between problem identification and technology development appears a bit muddled. What happens between the time when a developer "identifies" a set of problems and the time when it "develops" a new technology? Is the problem forgotten? Does it cease to be important? Is the developer simply unable to build a technology that will address the problem at hand?

Our ability to answer these questions requires a shift in focus away from the traditional logic of problem identification and technology development. Rather than viewing problem identification as a straightforward process and technology development as a complex interaction between various group, organizational, and market influences, we might instead, as sociologists of science and technology, treat problems as "constructions" in their own right (Fujimura 1987; Pickering 1995). In this view, problems aren't floating around "out there" waiting to be identified; instead, members of invested organizations actively develop problems. As Joan Fujimura (1987) suggests, individuals within groups may engage with one another to focus on an important issue of common concern (e.g., how to investigate whether normal cellular genes transform into cancerous ones) while each developing his or her own individual sense of the particular problem that must be solved to resolve the issue. The process of problem development is further complicated by the fact that within a large company or organization it is typical for multiple groups to interact around such issues. Each of these groups is bound to develop problems that are, to borrow Fujimura's term, "do-able" within a group's particular frame of reference. The result is that what is considered a problem by members of one group may not appear to be a problem to members of another (see, e.g., Dougherty 1992), leaving each group with its own problem to be solved.

During the latter half of the 1990s, four distinct but interdependent groups at Autoworks—Safety, Techpro, Information Systems and Services, and R&D—expressed concern about crashworthiness analysts' ability to effectively use math-based technologies to reduce the number of simulations required to meet FMVSS regulations and garner high ratings in the NCAP and IIHS barrier tests. Each of these groups had its own reasons for being concerned about Autoworks' turn toward a math-based engineering workforce, and each subsequently developed its own understanding of the problem that had to be solved to help crashworthiness analysts more effectively build and analyze math models. The data presented in this chapter show that, despite a common focus, each of these four groups identified a different major problem that it felt had to be solved in order to improve math-based analysis in the Safety Division.

In the process of problem development, each group took three inter-related steps. First, each group delineated a strategic direction in which it wanted to move in the future, outlining the types of projects the group would have to undertake to establish a strong and distinct identity at Autoworks. Second, because the steps involved in building and analyzing math models are numerous and complex, each group analyzed the specific practices and processes used by crashworthiness analysts. Focusing attention on a small subset of practices rather than trying to understand the process of model building and analysis in its entirety allowed members of each group to gain a firm grasp of the types of constraints its own engineers faced. Third, a problem was considered fully developed only if members of the group had successfully identified a feasible technology to solve it.

These findings suggest that new technologies aren't born out of a simple stepwise progression in which developers identify a set of problems and subsequently develop a new technology to solve them. Instead, multiple groups in an organization actively identify problems that appear important and manageable to tackle while simultaneously identifying technologies that validate the existence of the problems by rendering them solvable. To explore how the problems that led to the eventual production and implementation of CrashLab were developed, let us begin by examining crashworthiness engineering at Autoworks in the mid 1990s.

Safety Division: The Accuracy Problem

The early 1990s marked a period of major organizational transformation at Autoworks. In 1992 the company reorganized its domestic and international engineering operations into two distinct groups. The Domestic Operations (DO) group—headquartered in Motorville, a short drive from Detroit—was now responsible for the engineering and manufacturing of all vehicles sold in North America. The International Operations group, headquartered in Switzerland, was responsible for all matters related to engineering and manufacturing for vehicles sold in the rest of the world. This plan to centralize operations consolidated a number of previously disparate divisions under a more streamlined management umbrella that could now take advantage of engineering and manufacturing resources across both domestic and international brands. Within the DO group, further organizational changes were taking place. Several of Autoworks' more prestigious brands were consolidated to form the Luxury Car Division, and several of the less prestigious but more profitable brands were consolidated into the Midsize Car Division. In 1993, Autoworks organized its North American truck and bus operations into the Autoworks Truck Department and moved its engineering and manufacturing operations to a large facility in nearby Truckville, Michigan.

Despite the formal designation of two distinct divisions imposed by the reorganization (one for luxury cars and one for mid-size cars), crashworthiness analysts who worked to build and analyze FE models of Autoworks' portfolio of cars were all grouped into one large Car Department. Members of the Car Department shared office space in large "cubicle farms" at Autoworks' technical center in Motorville. The analysts' close proximity to the design engineers signaled that one of the goals of the reorganization was to encourage a more symbiotic relationship between design and crashworthiness analysis than had existed before the reorganization. Similarly, in Truckville, analysts who worked in the Truck Department also sat in cubicles, just down the hall from the design engineers with whom they worked. In both the Car Department and the Truck Department, the DEs and the analysts are highly interdependent. The physical organization of work groups after the corporate restructuring made this interdependence between design and analysis a bit easier logistically, since now analysts and DEs could simply walk down the hall and talk to each other face to face. DEs are responsible for a particular vehicle part or assembly of parts (e.g., a brake booster or bumper assembly) from conception through manufacturing. DEs typically work in a world of CAD and are responsible for attending numerous meetings with specialists and management from all over Autoworks to determine the requirements for their parts. They then draft their parts in CAD, ensure that they are manufacturable, work with vendors to provide material specifications, and finally, vigorously test the parts to make sure they meet a number of performance requirements so that, ultimately, the vehicle can be sold in the United States.

A DE designs his or her part with a CAD software tool and assigns it vehicle coordinates (on a three-dimensional grid) that indicate where the part is located in the vehicle. Typically the schematics for these parts are updated in DataExchange, a central database located in the company's High Performance Computing Center in Motorville. Analysts access this centralized database, download part files, and, using the vehicle coordinates, assemble the parts they receive from DEs into a fully integrated model that contains all the parts of a vehicle. Analysts are the first engineers to see how all the parts of a vehicle fit together and behave with one another. Crashworthiness analysts benefited from their newfound proximity to DEs because they could meet with them face to face more frequently than was possible in the past. More meetings provided more opportunities for analysts to influence part design, and as a result it was more likely that DEs would create designs to favor crashworthiness performance requirements.

But crashworthiness analysts located in Motorville and Truckville still had to drive more than 30 miles to Testville to watch vehicle crash tests at the proving grounds. Depending on the stage of vehicle development, analysts might be at the proving grounds for up to four days a week waiting for crash tests (which are notoriously behind schedule), watching the tests, waiting for technicians to extract data from the sensors and record the results, and watching the vehicle tear-down procedure. In short, crashworthiness analysts at Autoworks in the mid 1990s were caught between worlds. In one world, they negotiated design and analysis, using their domain knowledge of crash energy management and a suite of FE tools to analyze the crashworthiness of a vehicle design and make suggestions for improving its structural response to loading conditions. In another world, they straddled physicality and virtuality, creating three-dimensional math models to simulate the deformation of physical parts and validate the robustness of those models by comparing the outputs to the results of physical crash tests.

Formulating a Strategic Direction

The year 1994 was both painful and strangely gratifying for crashworthiness analysts at Autoworks. That year, NHTSA commenced a new five-star rating system for evaluating the results of frontal impact tests performed with a rigid barrier for most consumer vehicles produced by Autoworks and its competitors and making the results available to consumers. On the horizon for 1995 was a new IIHS rating system that would also evaluate vehicles for frontal impact, but using an offset-deformable barrier rather than a rigid barrier. Autoworks' vehicles didn't fare well in either of the new rating systems. As a result, Autoworks' senior management decided to increase the number of crashworthiness analysts in the Car Department and the Truck Department. The poor (and, perhaps more important, public) ratings demonstrated the need for crashworthiness analysts to work more closely with other vehicle engineers to improve vehicle design. Guowei Tsu, a crashworthiness analyst who joined the Car Department in 1992, commented on this:

When the NCAP and IIHS ratings came out, we were sort of caught in between emotions. I mean, on one hand, our vehicles weren't doing so well, so there was that negative pressure on us. But on the other hand, the fact that our vehicles weren't doing so well gave us lots of attention and upper management started to give us more resources and we increased our staff by almost double. The reason was that we had to get good ratings on these tests is because if we didn't, consumers wouldn't buy our products. So suddenly everyone started to pay attention to safety again for the first time since the late sixties and early seventies, and we were told that we better be more involved with vehicle design.

Part of the reason the Safety Division had not been a more central player in vehicle design was because of the way CAE analyses, including finite element analysis, were used in the design process. At Autoworks, most of the engineering design work was done by design engineers, who used CAD tools. In most cases, CAE analyses were used only after the fact, to confirm decisions already made *a priori* by senior managers or decisions based on the results of physical tests.

Clearly, at Autoworks—and in the American automobile industry as a whole—CAE analyses weren't contributing meaningfully to the process of designing a vehicle in the mid 1990s. FEA technologies were primarily being used retrospectively to confirm the results of a physical crash test. FEA would have better been used prospectively to increase crashworthiness performance, but instead, more often than not, it occurred after the design of a particular part or assembly was already set in stone. This retrospective use of FEA posed many problems, because the types of structural members that most affected the crashworthiness of a vehicle were among those developed earliest in the design process. As figure 4.1 illustrates, the structural members of the vehicle with which crashworthiness analysts are most concerned are those that make up the vehicle's so-called body-in-white. The term "body-in-white" refers to the welded sheet metal components that form the vehicle's structure. Essentially, it is the load-bearing frame onto which the vehicle's other components, such as the engine, the transmission, and the exterior and interior trim, are affixed.[1] The body-in-white, which actually consists of numerous parts, is typically the first assembly to be designed and "frozen," or approved, because it serves as the base onto which all other components are assembled. Once the design of the body-in-white is frozen, dies for manufacturing are cast, parts such as brakes and transmission components are sized to fit it, and electrical systems are routed throughout the frame. In short, the body-in-white is the first and, many would argue, the most important assembly of a vehicle to be designed. Because it is the design upon which nearly everything else is based, the design of the body-in-white is not easily "unfrozen." In fact, as one informant somewhat jokingly noted, "even if you held a gun to the

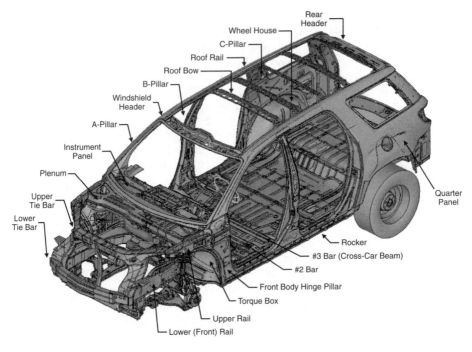

Figure 4.1
Structural members of a body-in-white most implicated in crashworthiness analysis.

president of Autoworks' head and told him he needed to make a major change to the body-in-white a few months before start of production, he'd probably laugh at you." Because the body-in-white is the vehicle's primary load-bearing structure, it is also the assembly of most concern to crashworthiness analysts. However, in the early to mid 1990s crashworthiness analysts' CAE analyses of the body-in-white often occurred only *after* it had been frozen. Consequently, analysts could do little to change a vehicle's design.

Gene Anderson, who moved up the ranks at Autoworks to become the director of crashworthiness for the Truck Department, joined Autoworks in the 1970s, when many analysts were still performing analysis using lumped-parameter models. He understood the crucial role CAE could play in improving vehicle design, and in 1994, given senior management's concern about the low ratings Autoworks vehicles were receiving in the consumer crash tests, he believed he might at last have the ability to bring simulation analyses to the center of the process of designing vehicles. Gene believed that producing a vehicle design that would optimize the crash-worthiness performance of the body-in-white and of other critical parts and assemblies would require that design and analysis not be done in isolation from one another. He felt that, instead, design and analysis should be synthesized into one fluid product development process:

What we would like to do is apply all the CAE work, not in even an analysis function, we want it to be in what we call the "synthesis" function, where right up front, before the design, as the design is being developed, we work with the design engineer and say, "This is how your part is going to work." "This is what it should be." "This is how it should be." So, before that design engineer gets a lot of inertia behind that particular design, we ought to be guiding through all of our CAE tools how that design should be. We should design it so, ideally, we never even need to run a test. We'll know, right out of the gate, that it will work. There's a lot of times when people say, "Well, let's treat analysis like a test, and we'll go ahead, we'll do all the design work, and then we'll subject it to some simulation. We'll take a passive role. We'll do an assessment at the end." Absolutely the wrong way to use CAE.

Gene's strategy was for analysts to conduct CAE analyses of the vehicle's structure before designs were frozen. At the very least, they should perform their preliminary analyses with FE models so as to lead the architecture of the vehicle in a direction that would generate better crashworthiness performance.

Gene realized that Autoworks would have to make an ideological shift if simulation work was to become more central in vehicle design. Many senior managers and design engineers simply didn't trust simulation and were therefore unwilling to make design revisions based on the recommendations of analysts who had yet to conduct a physical test. "I'm not going to bet my job, and the company's wallet, and someone's life, on a simulation," one design engineer commented. "I mean, how do I know it was done right? How do I know it really represents what's going on? You can do anything to make a simulation work—change a number here, another number there. Besides, I go to meetings and see some analyst say he ran the test three times and got three different results. Give me the hard data from the real test and then I'll consider making a change." The bias against simulation ran deep at Autoworks. Many of the design engineers had worked for the company in the 1970s and the 1980s. when simulations hadn't been routinely conducted within the engineering functions but rather had been seen as "prototype" technologies that engineers in the R&D Division were playing with, hoping that someday they would be used in regular production work.

Gene shared his concerns with Barry Glenn, the Car Department's director, with whom he met regularly. The two decided that they should put initiatives in place within the larger crashworthiness group to increase crashworthiness analysts' ability to initiate important changes in vehicle design. "We knew we had to do something to move us in a better direction," Gene recalled. "We needed a new strategy, but we weren't sure what it was. Taking small steps to make the results of our analyses more appealing and approachable seemed to be the clearest direction to march in." Gene and Barry set out to initiate a program of change in the Safety Division—one that would encourage analysts to build models that would correlate better with the results of physical crash tests performed at the proving grounds.

Targeting Specific Practices

To build models that accurately represented the behavior of a vehicle in a given loading condition, the results of physical tests conducted at the proving grounds and math-based simulations conducted in the Safety Division had to be strongly correlated. Figure 4.2 shows both strong and weak correlations between test results and simulation results for the performance of a lower front rail evaluated using the criteria outlined in an NCAP test. (Both curves in each panel of the figure represent deceleration after impact

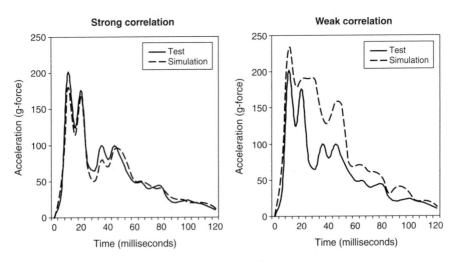

Figure 4.2
Strong vs. weak correlations between physical test and computer-based simulation. (One g is equivalent to 32.2 feet per second per second, the rate at which any object accelerates when dropped at sea level.)

and end when the vehicle comes to a rest.) To achieve tighter correlations between simulations and tests, the crashworthiness directors focused their attention on two model-building practices: meshing and assembly. To translate CAD geometry into data that could be used to run finite element analyses, analysts had to "mesh" the CAD parts. Meshing was not quite so simple a task as taking a vehicle's structural members (the B-pillar, for example) and filling them up with small boxes and triangles representing various elements. However tedious, building a high-quality mesh requires a great deal of knowledge about crash energy management. To understand why, we must consider the trade-off between mesh density and computer processing time. A mesh is considered "fine" when it has many nodes and elements (as opposed to few). Because FE solvers measure displacement at each node, the finer the mesh, the more locations at which displacement can be measured. A finer mesh produces a more accurate depiction of the deformation of a given part because there are more data for the solver to use to approximate displacements. A courser mesh does not as accurately capture part deformation, and its results don't correlate accurately with data from a physical crash.

Building a very fine mesh for the entire vehicle, though theoretically the best way to produce an accurate model, was not a feasible solution at the time with the computing resources available to analysts at Autoworks. The finer the mesh, the longer it takes the solver to generate the simulation. Because crashworthiness analysts shared supercomputing resources at Autoworks' High Performance Computing Center with other analysts in other engineering functions, computing capacity was at a premium. By 1994, even a model of modest size (containing 60,000–80,000 elements) would take more than 30 hours to process. One way to lessen the amount of time it takes to process a model without changing the density of the mesh is to adjust the sampling rate. When a solver simulates a vehicle crash, the solution is calculated at very small intervals—usually less than a millisecond. When an analyst submits a model to the solver, he or she typically indicates at what time step the model should record displacements of the various nodes. This method of outputting data at certain time steps is called *sampling*. For example, an analyst might output the results every 5 milliseconds. Most of the deformation that occurs in a crash event happens in the first 120 milliseconds of impact. If the solver measured displacements at each millisecond, it would be able to generate a constant curve of acceleration and thus able to produce a very accurate picture of the pattern of deformation. (See figure 4.2., which shows a sharp curve generated by multiple measurements). But time-step analysis also affect processing time. The smaller the sampling rate (interval between time steps at which the displacements are output), the longer it takes to process the model. However, building an FE mesh to more accurately understand the crash dynamics of a particular part or assembly but using a large time step to speed up the processing time would negate the precision of the finer mesh.

A more tenable way of striking a balance between model accuracy and processing time is to build a model that doesn't use meshes of uniform density—that is, to use a finer mesh on the areas of the vehicle that are of most interest and a courser mesh on parts that are of less interest. By using this differential strategy for mesh density, an analyst is able to produce a highly accurate model of a load case that takes far less time to process than would be required if the entire model were built with a fine mesh. Take, for example, the FE model illustrated in figure 4.3. This model was built to simulate a side impact. The areas of the body-in-white immediately adjacent to the barrier (at the bottom of the image) are meshed with an element size of 5 millimeters (ultra-fine mesh), whereas the surrounding areas are meshed with an element size of 10 millimeters (fine mesh). The areas of the body-in-white to which energy from the impact will not be dissipated are meshed with an element size of 20 millimeters (coarse mesh). Building a model in this way allowed the analyst to produce accurate

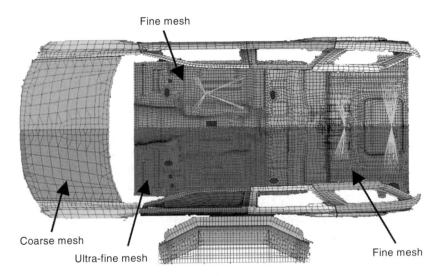

Figure 4.3
Using differential mesh sizes to balance accuracy and processing time.

energy and displacement curves while reducing the overall time needed to process the model.

The ability to produce a mesh with variable densities requires a tremendous knowledge of crash energy management and good engineering judgment. For example, an engineer who decided to mesh the front of a vehicle at an element size of 20 millimeters must be extremely confident that it isn't necessary to measure the forces in that particular area of the vehicle or to produce an accurate deformation curve. If forces were transferred to the front of the structure on impact, the coarse mesh might not capture the deformation accurately, and the model would be inaccurate. To an outsider, it might seem that simply knowing what kind of load case was to be analyzed would be sufficient to determine which parts of the model require a fine mesh and which require a course mesh, but crashworthiness analysts view this kind of knowledge as important. Despite the fact that learning how to build an FE model that strikes a balance between accuracy and efficiency requires substantial on-the-job experience, Gene and Barry both insisted that the senior managers in the Car Department and the Truck Department write preliminary guidelines for crashworthiness analysts to use when building meshes. The manual containing these basic and somewhat cryptic guidelines became known as the *Safety and Safety Manual*. It was distributed to all analysts.

Crashworthiness directors also focused their attention on model assembly with the hopes of helping analysts build FE models that more accurately represented physical crash tests. At Autoworks, design engineers are responsible for generating the architectural drawings for a few parts for which they are fully responsible, but crashworthiness analysts function in an integration capacity. When it comes time to test a vehicle's crashworthiness via simulation, an analyst accesses the DataExchange database, finds the CAD files for all the parts that are to be included in the model, then assembles the parts into a model representing the complete vehicle. This process of assembly presents many potential pitfalls, but during my period of study two problems were most common.

Design engineers drafted and updated parts at many junctures in the engineering process. The DE responsible for part A might change the shape of that part; another DE, responsible for part B, might not change the shape of that part. If the changes in the shape of part A made the part larger, it might then infringe on the space in which part B was located. If that happened, the DE responsible for part B would also to redesign that part to accommodate the changes in part A. In a perfect world, a change in part A's design would instantly trigger a series of changes to all the other affected parts. However, many times DEs didn't communicate with each other about changes in their parts, and often they weren't even aware that a change in one part would affect the design of another part. As a result, when analysts went to download parts from the DataExchange database, not all parts were in the same stage of development. One analyst explained:

A lot of times I get the parts ready to assemble, and I find out that they don't fit. Like two parts are occupying the same vehicle coordinates. That can't happen. Different matter can't occupy the same space. You know? So obviously something is wrong. One DE updated one part and, who knows why, but the other DEs didn't update their parts to match. So you have maybe two or three parts all intersecting and overlapping by maybe 10 or 20 millimeters. That's a problem that happens a lot.

In the math-based environment of simulation, two parts can occupy the same space in a coordinate system. If that happened, an analyst would discover, to his or her dismay, that the parts overlapped one other.

Many of the models analysts assembled using CAD files from DataExchange contained overlapping—or "penetrating"—parts, which significantly affected the solver's ability to predict the results of a particular test. If a penetration was substantial, the solver would return an error message indicating that it couldn't solve the model until the overlapping parts were fixed. If a penetration was minor (just a few millimeters), the solver probably would be unable to detect it, and the software would solve the model anyway. In that case, the simulation would produce results that couldn't be achieved in a real-world test scenario, because in the physical world, as the analyst quoted above observed, two parts can't occupy the same space. To ensure a high degree of correlation between simulations and tests, it was essential for analysts to fix any major penetrations in their models that would affect their results. Identifying and resolving overlapping parts entailed, as many other engineering practices do, a series of trade-offs. Fixing every penetration in a model could take an analyst more than a week—if he or she could identify them all. For most analysts, spending a week attempting to resolve penetration issues was not acceptable, because it would often mean missing important deadlines. Analysts had to make calculated choices, then, about which penetrations should be fixed and which could be overlooked. One analyst commented:

You don't want to and really there's no way you would have the time to fix all the penetrations in a model. So you have to choose. You have to think "What are the ones that are most important for the load case I'm evaluating?" If I'm doing an NCAP analysis and there is a penetration between the radiator and the tie-bar, I better fix it because that will give me bad results. But if there's a penetration between, I don't know, say the rear rocker and the C-pillar, then I probably won't worry about it because it's not likely to affect my results.

Like meshing a vehicle, resolving penetrations also involves sound engineering judgment and a substantial knowledge of crash energy management theories. Certainly the best strategy to employ would be to fix all the penetrations in each model. But such a strategy is not feasible for engineers who face strict deadlines.

The technology that Gene and Barry envisioned to solve this accuracy problem was one that would automatically create an FE mesh that was configured (by way of varying densities) to optimally balance mesh density and CPU time for the particular load-case analysis the analyst using the tool intended to run. In addition, the tool would provide model-checking capabilities that would flag engineers if the most up-to-date Unigraphics files had not been used to create a mesh, and would point out penetrations that would affect the accuracy of the model. As Gene suggested, identifying a potential technology that could help crashworthiness analysts achieve stronger correlations between their simulations and physical tests was an essential step in showing himself and others that a low level of accuracy in FE models was not just a matter of course—it was a problem that could be solved:

I think it is very feasible to think that you could develop a piece of software that would automatically scale your mesh in different spots to prepare the model for the kind of analysis you want to run. That same piece of software could also have a comprehensive model-checking capability that would let you know what penetrations existed and which ones need to be fixed. Then the engineers wouldn't have to spend so much time figuring these things out on their own.

If the accuracy problem could be solved with the help of a new technology that would automate meshing and assembly, the crashworthiness directors believed, CAE analyses could move from being used only for retrospective confirmation of physical tests to a more central role in the product design process—a role in which simulation would be used in the early stages of vehicle development.

Techpro: The Speed Problem

After work at Autoworks was reorganized into separate domestic and international operations groups in 1992, analysts in the Safety Division who worked in Motorville and in Truckville required little understanding of the work of their fellow crashworthiness analysts overseas. Despite this structural divide between domestic and international engineering efforts, Autoworks remained a global organization—one that licensed and implements tools for use by engineers all over the world. The Global Technology Production (Techpro) Department, located at the technical center in Motorville, was responsible for ensuring that Autoworks' engineers around the world had the best tools for math-based analyses and were well trained to use them. In a company increasingly fractionalized by geography, Techpro was truly a worldwide operation.

In addition to facilitating access to technology and related training, Techpro was also charged with working with vendors to ensure that the tools analysts used would have the technical features they needed. This responsibility required Techpro engineers to work closely with vendors in several capacities. First, when a vendor for a math-based analysis tool launched a new version of its pre-processing technology, Techpro engineers performed user-acceptance testing to ensure that the new version worked with other technologies already in use in engineering. Techpro engineers also worked with vendors to design new features for their software. For example, Techpro worked with the vendor of ElementMesh, the pre-processing tool most widely used by the Safety Division, to update the tool's capabilities for simulating spot-welds. Techpro also worked to identify prototype tools developed by engineers in Autoworks' R&D Division that seemed likely to improve efficiency in the various engineering divisions. When Techpro engineers identified a technology in development that looked promising, they would work with the Information Systems and Services (Infoserv) Division to negotiate contracts with vendors to build the technology. Techpro engineers acted as consultants during the development process, ensuring that the new technologies were built in a way consistent with R&D's vision.

Formulating a Strategic Direction

Though Techpro's focus was on the production and distribution of math-based tools for analysis, the group's explicit mission, according to Randy Johnson, vice-president for global engineering operations, was to help Autoworks move toward a completely virtual engineering environment:

We have spent years putting our vehicle development process together. We figured out how to measure our time to production, and along the way, we are shortening our vehicle cycle. Now, in doing that, we are eliminating hardware cycle, and we have to.[2] As a practical matter, Autoworks cannot afford the amount of hardware that we have in place right now. . . . We have to figure out how to do work differently than other manufacturers, and one of the ways is to leverage our CAE capability around the world to an even much greater extent then we have in the past. Very simply, we can't afford the extra time in the vehicle development process for hardware and we can't afford the cost of it. It's vitally important right now that we make the move to math, and we're going to continue to put tension in the company with less reliance on hardware and more reliance on our CAE skill set.

This concerted effort to move away from physical testing and toward math-based analysis was not just rhetoric spouted by Autoworks' senior management. Printouts of PowerPoint slides such as the one depicted in figure 4.4 hung on the walls of Techpro engineers' cubicles, reminding them that their primary goal was to help identify and "productionize" (as some informants put it) tools that would move Autoworks toward global math-based vehicle assessment. Of all the groups at Autoworks, Techpro was perhaps the most devoted to more broadly implementing math-based analysis. Unlike engineers in the product-engineering groups (such as the Safety Division), Techpro engineers weren't directly involved in vehicle development. Instead, their days were spent thinking about how to help product engineers improve their systems and processes. This separation

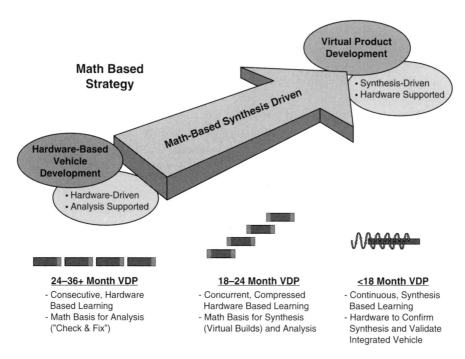

Figure 4.4
PowerPoint slide hung on Techpro cube walls as a reminder of the move to math.

from regular production work allowed Techpro engineers to think more strategically about the direction of engineering at Autoworks in a way that analysts—who had to meet day-to-day deadlines—could not.

In 1995, crashworthiness analysts at Autoworks conducted nearly 650 physical crash tests—more than had ever been conducted at the company in a one-year period since the very first crash tests were conducted at the Testville proving grounds in the late 1930s. This "milestone" was not celebrated by the engineers in Techpro, who were trying to move product engineering at Autoworks away from physical testing toward math-driven vehicle analysis. As one engineer noted, Techpro had to devise a practical plan for facilitating the move toward math—one that would enable analysts in various product groups to see the benefits of elevating their competencies with math-based simulation tools:

We had to reduce the number of tests; there was just no way around it. Some of the product groups got that, but others didn't. Our job in Techpro was to make sure that they saw the utility of it, that analysts would be easily able to build and analyze math models.

In order to convince the product-engineering groups that completely virtual vehicle assessment was indeed possible and to convince upper management that such a practice could drastically reduce the costs associated with vehicle testing, Mike Johansson and several other Techpro senior engineers identified what they called the "CAE Grand Challenges": identifiable projects that Techpro could complete in the coming years to promote use of math-based analysis in the product groups. As Mike commented, outlining the "Grand Challenges" not only helped promote an organization-wide focus on math-based analysis; it also identified specific projects that could be undertaken to make math-based analysis the standard:

You have to not only set the ideology of the organization that math is a good thing and a noble cause, but you have to also show them it can be done. The Grand Challenges were like saying "Okay, here are some small goals; these are the things we need to do to make math-based analysis a reality." If we could do these projects and meet some smaller goals, people would begin to believe in the promise of math. Also, the derivatives of these projects would be some real meat, some technology that could be used right away to increase the quality of the CAE process in the product groups.

Mike and his team went to work identifying several challenges that engineers in the Techpro group would have to meet in order for math-based analysis to be successful in crashworthiness analysis at Autoworks. The group came up with six challenges, and communicated them to each and every Techpro engineer via PowerPoint slides such as the one shown in figure 4.5 (a print of which hung on the walls in the Techpro offices for the next ten years). These "Grand Challenges" were all aimed at making the construction and analysis of FE models as smooth as possible for analysts. Although each of the six challenges represented different activities through which the process of math-based analysis could be improved, Techpro focused predominantly on the first challenge: to make it possible for analysts to build and analyze a functional FE model in two days. The remaining five challenges were seen as necessary to reaching this overarching goal. The two-day goal situated the work Techpro engineers had to do within a frame of reference in which speed of work was valued above all else. In the eyes of Techpro engineers, issues of accuracy (such as those that were of concern to Gene Anderson and Barry Glenn) took a back seat to the paramount goal of ensuring that FE models could be built quickly. One engineer in Techpro commented:

Everything here is about speed. Simulations are only helpful if they can be done quickly. The bottom line is that if a simulation takes longer to run than a hardware test, even though it costs more in the short term, management will always prefer the test. That's because where you really start losing your money is when you don't get the vehicle to market soon enough. If you didn't pay, say, $300,000 for another crash test, and instead you waited an extra month for the simulation to be done, and so you delayed product launch for 30 days, you would lose, say, something like $5,000 in profit per vehicle on like 10,000 vehicles. So that's, what, like $50,000,000 you just lost? No one would hesitate to do a $300,000 test to save $50,000,000. So the bottom line is that it's all about how fast you can do the math.

 CAE Grand Challenges

1. Build and analyze functional FE model in 2 days
2. Fast, upfront, CAE predictions that enable robust design solution
3. Early creation of parametric CAE "concept" models that enable up-front, multi-disciplinary optimization
4. First time quality body (fit, appearance)
5. Keep CAD/CAE in sync
6. Global Standard Work

Figure 4.5
Slide presented to Techpro engineers.

With the two-day FE-model-building challenge guiding their actions, Techpro engineers began to understand what was the problem with implementing FE simulations in vehicle development: speed. As Techpro engineers regularly commented, if analysts could only build their models faster, they would be able to focus more on vehicle design.

Focusing Attention on Specific Practices

To enable analysts to build and analyze a model in two days, Techpro had to drastically rethink the way analysis was conducted in product engineering. One variable that couldn't easily be changed was the time it took the solver to process a simulation. The time it takes to solve an FE model is dependent upon the number of elements in the model. Because displacements are calculated at each node, the more elements a model contains, the longer it takes to process. Within the Safety Division, the size of models (measured in elements) had been increasing steadily since the late 1980s. (See table 4.1.) By 1994, the average full-vehicle model took nearly 40 hours to process on a Cray C90 supercomputer. When the parallel processing capabilities of the High Performance Computing Center were used to distribute the model among six computers, the average time to process a model was just over 6½ hours. In terms of a two-day goal, this 6½-hour period represented a fixed constraint. Thus, Techpro engineers had to focus their efforts on speeding up other parts of the process—mainly those performed manually—with the use of new technology. With that in mind, the next step was for Techpro to take into its purview all the activities in which analysts engaged when building and analyzing an FE model, beginning the moment they downloaded CAD data from the DataExchange database.

Techpro engineers reasoned that if increasing the speed of model building and analysis was the ultimate goal, they had to identify the activities that took analysts the longest to complete and think of ways to expedite them. Techpro engineers asked their friends who worked as analysts in the

Table 4.1
Time required to solve FE models on supercomputers at Autoworks.

Year	Size of model (number of elements)	CPU time (Hours)	Computer
1988	8,000–10,000	5–10	Cray XMP
1990	15,000–20,000	10–20	Cray YMP
1992	30,000–40,000	20–30	Cray YMP
1994	60,000–80,000	30–40	Cray C90

various product-engineering groups to list the activities on which they were spending the bulk of their time. Although crashworthiness analysts told Techpro engineers that meshing and assembly were among the most cumbersome tasks, they didn't describe in detail the difficulties they were having with the specific activities. So while Gene and Barry focused on the particular nuances of meshing and assembly that reduced model accuracy (i.e., mesh density and penetrations),. A number of crashworthiness analysts recalled that the Techpro engineers were very straightforward about their goal of reducing the time needed to build and analyze an FE model, and the crashworthiness analysts were concerned that the quality of their models might suffer if the process were rushed. The crashworthiness analysts reasoned that, overall, decreased quality and accuracy would be more detrimental than models running behind schedule.

As members of the group responsible for the global "productionization and deployment" of CAE tools, Techpro engineers also had to pay attention to how analysts in the International Operations group were building and analyzing FE models. To do so, Techpro engineers focused on the two international engineering groups with which they had the most contact: Autoworks Germany and Autoworks Australia. The crashworthiness-engineering workforce at those two engineering locations was several orders of magnitude smaller than the engineering workforce at Autoworks' technical center in Motorville. Lacking the manpower to perform all aspects of model building and analysis "in house," the two engineering centers often outsourced crashworthiness-analysis work to local automotive supplier firms. Such outsourcing practices were troublesome to Autoworks managers for two main reasons. First, outsourcing increased the likelihood that proprietary information about vehicle design parameters could be leaked to competitors. Second, outsourcing analysis work is costly. Autoworks' overseas engineering centers had to pay a hefty price for supplier firms to translate their CAD geometry into FE data and assemble full-vehicle models. Not only were engineering hours more expensive when purchased through a third-party supplier; in addition, Autoworks had to maintain several external portals, such as FTP sites and VPN connections, so the supplier firms could access Autoworks data.

For management in Autoworks' German and Australian engineering centers, however, these two concerns were more than worth the risk in view of the time that was saved by outsourcing model building. One manager at the German engineering center commented:

Using supplier firms greatly enhances our ability to build FE models very quickly. If we did not utilize supplier firms as resources, it would take us much longer to build our models and our math analysis would be even further removed from the vehicle development process.

With Autoworks' global engineering centers eager to outsource their work, Techpro engineers faced a clear challenge: to implement technologies that would make model building go just as fast when done "in house" as it went when outsourced, so analysts in Germany and Australia wouldn't continue to use supplier firms to build models. Because Techpro aimed to productionize and globally distribute CAE technologies that would reduce the need for Autoworks' product-engineering groups to use external resources to conduct math-based analyses, developing technology to make in-house model preparation faster than outsourcing was a primary concern.

Focusing on the practices analysts used to build models both domestically and abroad, members of Techpro quickly reached consensus not only that math-based analysis could be performed in two days if the right technologies were in place, but also that the substantial amount of time required to run math-based analyses was problematic in and of itself. Techpro engineers soon realized that on the domestic front the speed problem prevented math-based analysis from taking a more central role in the process of designing vehicles, and that on the international front the speed problem was costing Autoworks millions of dollars each year as engineering centers outsourced their work to supplier firms so models could be built faster. It seemed that for product engineering solving the speed problem was essential to making the move from physical prototyping to a more comprehensive and robust virtual vehicle-assessment process.

Identifying a Feasible Technology
Working to meet the goals of the CAE Grand Challenges, and more specifically to achieve a two-day FE model, Techpro engineers developed a number of concepts to help speed up the model-building process. Ideas for three interrelated tools soon emerged.

The first, referred to as *rapid meshing assembly* (RMA), automatically translated CAD geometry into FE data. Using RMA seemed simple: open the tool, import the CAD file, select a number of basic parameters for mesh quality and density, and let RMA automatically mesh the parts. Using RMA would free engineers of having to spend so much time building FE models by hand.

After the CAD files were translated into mesh models, engineers would then apply a second tool: the *material model checker*. The MMC was used to ensure that all the correct material properties had been assigned to the parts that analysts would eventually assemble into a full-vehicle model. Mathematical representations of the behaviors of steel and those of various plastics and foams were stored in a central database. It was the job of one of the engineers in Techpro to work with vendors to ensure that the algorithms for properties of various materials were accurate and adequately reflected their behavior in physical loading conditions. Design engineers were responsible for associating the correct material properties with each of the parts in their drawings drafted in CAD. However, after numerous revisions of the parts, the material properties often became disassociated from the models. Then, when analysts went to set the models up for analysis, they were not sure what the material properties of certain parts should be. Not only would the MMC help analysts to determine whether or not material properties were associated with the parts; in the event that they weren't, the tool would help analysts determine which material properties were most accurate.

Next, analysts would use a third tool known as *vehicle model assembly.* VMA would gather all the parts associated with a particular model in one central location so they could be arranged into a full-vehicle model. The idea was to link VMA to particular DataExchange libraries (e.g., a powertrain library) so it could automatically pull the appropriate data into a model and check to make sure parts weren't penetrating one another and that all contacts (which indicate how parts are attached to one another) were properly specified. Using the VMA tool would reduce the amount of time analysts had to spend conducting tasks associated with routine assembly.

Techpro engineers were confident that if analysts used these three technologies in conjunction with one another the amount of time they spent setting up models would be reduced dramatically. Gene Anderson and Barry Glenn had mixed feelings about this new suite of technologies in the works in Techpro. Gene commented:

I was excited about the work being done by Johansson's group because it could mean that my engineers would be spending less time on routine tasks, but I was also concerned. I just wasn't confident that the tools could stand in for the judgment needed to build a good model. For example, with RMA, there's no way the tool could determine what areas needed to be meshed finer. An engineer needed to make that determination based on the sort of granularity he wanted in the analysis. That was somewhat done on a case-by-case basis—sort of idiosyncratic. And that's fine, especially if it helps the analyst get the results he needs.

Techpro engineers, however, didn't share Gene and Barry's concerns. Instead, as Jensen Lu suggested, the time-saving advantages afforded by this suite of tools would far outweigh any disadvantages brought about by a loss of accuracy:

> If you can do the model building faster and you don't like your result, you can just do it again with different parameters. Because the process is so quick, you could do it three times using RMA and VMA, and run your model, and still be done faster than if you spent only one time coming up with a very precise model. That is three times the data you can use to evaluate. And over time, after there is more data, the algorithms will only get more precise and then there will be no problems.

Techpro quickly went to work building RMA, MMC, and VMA. As pleased as they were with the suite of technologies under development, Techpro engineers still felt as if they were missing one final step in the process. With these tools, analysts could theoretically collect CAD data, mesh the parts, check their material properties, and assemble the meshed parts into a full-vehicle model in a relatively short amount of time—perhaps less than two days. However, to achieve a fully analyzable FE model in two days analysts still had to prepare the model for the specific load case they wished to evaluate by placing accelerometers on the model and positioning the model and the barrier in relationship to one another in accordance with NHTSA and IIHS specifications. This final process of model setup alone normally took analysts three or four days to complete. Thus, Techpro engineers still had to identify a technology that would ready FE models for analysis within two days.

By mid 1995, Techpro engineers knew that the technology they needed would have to work in tandem with RMA, MCC, and VMA to increase the speed of FE model setup. But, as Jensen suggested, exactly how that technology would look was still unknown:

> We knew we could make model building faster with a set of integrated tools. We had everything in the row except for one final technology that would automate load-case setup. We knew what the technology had to do in a general way, and we knew something could be built, but we weren't sure exactly what parts of the procedure should be automated and then exactly how you would develop an architecture to do that, because in some senses, it was the most complicated part since there were so many different variables to consider.

With plenty of other projects in the pipeline, all with lead times of at least five years, members of Techpro weren't too concerned with immediately identifying the technology that would complete the suite of math-based analysis tools they envisioned. Instead, they were confident that, if they continued to scout resources at Autoworks (including analysts and R&D people) and external resources (such as tool vendors), they would eventually find a technology that would help make the FE model-setup procedure far faster than the current mid-1990s standard.

Information Systems and Services: The Capacity Problem

Autoworks' Information Systems and Services (Infoserv) Division played a number of important roles in math-based analysis. Infoserv was responsible for basic information-technology (IT) support for users of all technologies at Autoworks. Infoserv was also responsible for managing the High Performance Computing Center and purchasing new supercomputers. Within Infoserv, a number of different departments catered to the specific needs of users across Autoworks' various specialties. Coinciding with the increased use of math-based tools for computer-aided analysis in the early 1990s, Infoserv established a CAE Department. The CAE Department consisted primarily of former product engineers who were interested in serving as advisors on matters of technology, including strategy and implementation. Its engineers were responsible for monitoring the number of simulations processed by computers at the High Performance Computing Center. As a corollary responsibility, the CAE Department established limitations on the number of jobs analysts in the various product groups could submit at a particular time and the amount of disk space allotted on shared drives. The CAE Department also rolled out major software updates to pre-processing and post-processing applications as they became available. Members of the CAE Department also served as points of contact for users who experienced problems with their software. For example, if a user found a bug in a pre-processor, or if a user's simulations were returned without having been solved, Infoserv would respond and would attempt to solve the problem in a timely manner.

Infoserv (more specific, its CAE Department) also served as Autoworks' primary interface with tool vendors. When the Techpro Division determined that one of the technologies being used in product engineering was in need of new features, the CAE Department worked with the tool vendor to negotiate a contract to update the source code and add new modules. In this capacity, the CAE Department made strategic decisions about which vendors it would award contracts to and which vendor agreements would be terminated. The CAE Department felt that having the final say about the technologies used in the product-engineering groups was paramount, because its members would be the ones who would have to implement, maintain, and troubleshoot the tools once they were in use.

When considering the many tools employed by Autoworks for math-based engineering, one cannot underestimate Infoserv's influence. As Kaleeb Azbad, an engineer in the CAE Department commented, nearly all aspects of computing that effect math-based analysis are regulated by Infoserv:

I came from the product engineering groups, working as a CAE engineer for many years. I know that you need powerful applications such as pre- and post-processors to do your performance analyses, and you also need powerful back-end support in terms of processing power to solve your models. All of those final decisions about what those technologies are that analysts are using are made in Infoserv. We don't work like a dictatorship. We rely on engineers in R&D and people from the Techpro Division to identify the technologies that are going to be most effective for engineers and to develop the concepts for new technologies. But we have the final stamp of approval. Ultimately, we pick the vendor and we do the contract, so it all passes through us in the end. That's a big responsibility. We have to do our homework to make sure we balance the needs of the user community with the strategic and financial goals of the company.

Clearly Infoserv plays a pivotal role in Autoworks' use of computer software tools for math-based analysis. By the mid 1990s, the new CAE Department was feeling pressure from upper management to help analysts run simulations and, consequently, to reduce the number of physical tests needed to validate vehicle performance. Responding to this pressure, the CAE Department began considering a long-term strategy for technology contracts with vendors that would ensure the department's ability to provide essential services to the CAE community.

Formulating a Strategic Direction

The CAE computing environment at Autoworks in the mid 1990s was quite eclectic. With more than twenty different technologies to choose from for pre-processing, post-processing, and solving math models, it was rare for two analysts to use the same tool for simulation work. This eclecticism of technology among the crashworthiness-analysis groups was left over from the days before Infoserv's CAE Department. Throughout the 1980s, the crashworthiness-analysis groups were largely responsible for purchasing their own tools on independent budgets. Salespeople from the tool vendors routinely attended crashworthiness-analysis staff meetings and attempted to convince directors and managers that the new features of their tools merited purchase by Autoworks. By the mid 1990s, the CAE Department found itself trying to clean up the mess that had been wrought by a highly decentralized structure for purchasing tools. Infoserv found it

too costly to maintain licenses for so many different tools and too labori-
ous to provide updates and guarantee service for multiple tools that performed the same task.

In 1995, engineers in the newly formed CAE Department formulated
a plan to reduce the number of tools used for math-based analysis in
the crashworthiness-analysis groups. The engineers worked with directors,
managers, and analysts to determine the advantages and drawbacks of
various technologies for crashworthiness analysis. The task was not easy,
though, because various crashworthiness-analysis groups had different
requirements for analysis. For example, the crashworthiness group had
long used a solver called DYNA because of its strengths in solving equations
of transient dynamic loading conditions, and the aero/thermal group used
another solver, ANSYS, because it was specifically geared toward solving
complex computational fluid dynamic algorithms. After much consideration, the CAE Department decided it would be best not to attempt to
consolidate tools across all the crashworthiness-analysis groups, but instead
consolidate within each group. Engineers in the department came up with
a tool-reduction plan that addressed specific functions of crashworthiness
analysis. The goal of the plan, which was slated to take effect in 1996, was
to cut the number of pre-processing and post-processing tools and the
number of solvers used in the department in half by the end of 1998.[3]

The tool-reduction plan began to shape Infoserv's actions in all its technology endeavors. As Kaleeb Azbad commented, senior managers and
directors in Infoserv adopted the view that the CAE Department's work in
the crashworthiness-analysis groups could be applied in areas other than
analysis. Their new goal was to create a trimmer and more efficient computing environment across all of Autoworks' departments. Guowei Tsu, an
analyst in the Safety Division, recalled his immediate concern that he
might lose some of the tools he had become comfortable using for math-
based analyses, and that he might be forced to learn how to use unfamiliar
and perhaps less intuitive tools:

There was a lot of talk from Infoserv about reducing our tools. They wanted less
technology overall. I was worried. I have built up competencies on some of these
tools, and then they would go away, so I didn't like that. And then I thought, what
if they made me use Taurus [a pre-processor] instead of ElementMesh? I tried that
once, and it was bad. That would not be so good, and the work quality would
go down.

To mitigate concerns voiced by analysts but continue to move forward
with their tool-reduction strategy, Infoserv engineers formed committees
of analysts from different crashworthiness-analysis groups to advise

Infoserv regarding which tools would be most beneficial to keep and which ones could be eliminated with the least disturbance to regular work.

As one engineer put it, when it came to math-based analysis in the mid 1990s, the major problem facing Infoserv was one of "capacity." Upper management at Autoworks was pushing Infoserv to enable engineers to conduct more math-based analyses so as to reduce the number of physical tests. But relative to its user community, the Infoserv Division was small. It lacked sufficient manpower to purchase, maintain, and troubleshoot all the tools the analysts wanted to use. Furthermore, the analysts' ability to perform analyses effectively and efficiently hinged on Infoserv's ability to support the tools on the front and back ends. For this reason, Infoserv had to carefully balance the analysts' desire to use the best tools for analysis and Infoserv's ability to maintain those tools. The tool-reduction strategy seemed the most prudent way to simultaneously satisfy these two demands. In terms of capacity, however, maintaining CAE tools was not the only concern. As Infoserv began reducing the number of tools used for math-based analysis, it focused on another capacity issue: the High Performance Computing Center's ability to process the increasing number of simulations submitted by analysts each day.

Focusing Attention on Specific Practices

By 1995, analysts in the Safety Division were collectively running nearly 3,500 simulations each year on the supercomputers in the High Performance Computing Center. At the time, the average computing cost of running one simulation, or job, was nearly $20,000. Crashworthiness analysts alone were responsible for more than $7 million in High Performance Computing Center costs per year. By 2005, the simulation cost per job had been reduced by nearly 99.5 percent, to roughly $100. In the mid 1990s, engineers in the Infoserv Division were painfully aware of the costs associated with processing simulations. Although they anticipated that the costs would be reduced with increased computing power in the coming years, few imagined that the cost reduction would be so dramatic. Martin Harris, an Infoserv director, commented:

In the mid 1990s, we were all real concerned about how much it cost to run a simulation. It was certainly cheaper than crashing a pre-production vehicle, which would cost you about $600,000 for one crash, but it was still real expensive. We anticipated that, based on past trends, we might get down by 2000 to maybe $2,000 a simulation as long as we could keep the element size down. But even that seemed optimistic. So we knew we were going to have to work when we thought about contracting with vendors to find some technologies that would keep this cost down.

Although Infoserv engineers expected costs per simulation to decrease, they also anticipated that advances in technology, coupled with senior management's urging for the crashworthiness-analysis divisions to reduce hardware testing, would beget an increase in the number of simulations conducted in the various crashworthiness-analysis groups. As figure 4.6 indicates, Harris was right about the trend, but he underestimated the quantity increase by nearly 100 percent. By 2000, analysts in the crashworthiness group were submitting 30,000 simulations a year to be solved by the DYNA software on the High Performance Computing Center's supercomputers. Only four years later, the number of simulations would exceed 50,000.

The steady increase in the number of simulations processed each year by the High Performance Computing Center's supercomputers was only one of Infoserv's concerns. In addition, the size of FE models (measured in elements) increased monotonically each year. As figure 4.7 illustrates, by 1994 the average-size model submitted to the High Performance Computing Center by the Safety Division contained more than 100,000 elements (a 400 percent increase in size from just eight years earlier), and by 2006 the number of elements would exceed 1.5 million. In view of the High Performance Computing Center's capacity at the time, Infoserv engineers' concerns were justified. If by the year 2000 the average model were to contain 300,000 elements, and if 30,000 models were to be submitted to the High Performance Computing Center in that year, the HPC center might not have enough capacity to solve all the models submitted.

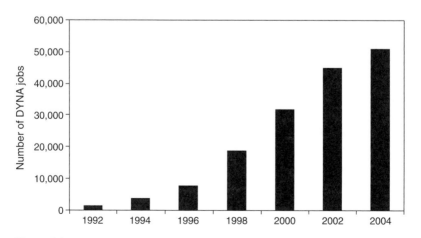

Figure 4.6
Number of DYNA Jobs submitted to the High Performance Computing Center by Safety.

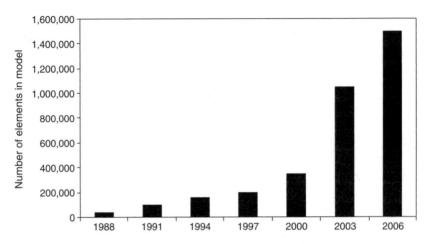

Figure 4.7
Growth in size of finite element models at Autoworks.

In the minds of Infoserv engineers, the two capacity problems—a dearth of engineers to support Autoworks' numerous technologies, and supercomputers' inability to process an increasing number of simulations—were inherently intertwined. As Kaleeb suggested, choosing which technologies to eliminate and which to add to the portfolio of CAE tools was largely dependent on the technology's processing speed:

The thing to consider was how the various CAE tools would deal with processing. I mean different solvers have different levels of efficiency, so we needed to use solvers that were as efficient as possible to keep run times down. And also, different pre-processors were different, meaning some wrote an input file that was cleaner with simpler instructions for the solver, while some were more complex. So it was a balance, you know, trying to make sure we weren't just narrowing to make it narrow, but we were narrowing strategically to think about processing needs.

Consequently, of the many features (e.g., user friendliness, mesh accuracy) on which Infoserv engineers could have chosen to focus their attention when selecting tools to keep in the CAE portfolio, they decided that they would be able to influence Autoworks' transition to math-based analysis most profoundly by selecting the tools with the fastest processing time. This would enable the High Performance Computing Center to process all the jobs analysts submitted and provide quick results that could be used to make suggestions for improved vehicle design.

Identifying a Feasible Technology

Although Infoserv engineers were looking to reduce the overall number of tools in the CAE portfolio, they were certainly not against considering new technologies, especially if one new tool could replace two or three less efficient ones. In fact, many engineers within the CAE Department were convinced that identifying a technology that could function as both a pre-processor and a post-processor might solve the capacity problem. As Bahrama Sadeek, an engineer in the CAE Department, commented, several members of the Infoserv community were actively looking for a technology to address this problem:

We had a problem that we had too many tools that were not efficient enough for our purposes. We wanted one tool that could do many functions and write an input deck that was clean and easy to process. I was looking for it, and many others were looking for it. We asked the vendors, and nothing. It was not very encouraging.

By 1995, engineers in the Infoserv Division had begun working in earnest with tool vendors and performance engineers to solve their dual capacity problem. Members of the CAE Department informally divided up the work to focus their efforts on the tools in specific crashworthiness-analysis groups. Kaleeb Azbad and Bahrama Sadeek were the primary engineers devoted to reducing the tool portfolio in the Safety Division. When they heard about Gene Anderson and Barry Glenn's initiative to increase analysts' use of math-based models, they grew concerned that they wouldn't be able to solve the capacity problem fast enough to meet the growing demand for computing resources.

Research and Development: The Credibility Problem

To most engineers working in the product groups at Autoworks, the Research and Development Division seemed simultaneously monolithic and mysterious. With nearly 300 engineers dedicated full-time to research activities, the R&D Division at Autoworks was certainly one of the largest industrial research centers in the United States. Few product engineers had a clear grasp of R&D's inner workings, despite the division's size. In view of the breadth of activities conducted by R&D, they were justifiably mystified.

Within the R&D Division, engineers were organized into a number of large laboratories. Though the names of the laboratories and their staff changed frequently, in general engineers focused on applied research in a variety of areas, including manufacturing process improvement, human factors, product improvement, alternative fuels, and engineering process improvement. In contrast with Autoworks' product-engineering groups, most of the engineers who worked in R&D had advanced degrees in a broad array of engineering specialties. From the inside, R&D seemed to function more like an academic institution than like a major industrial enterprise. Research engineers worked on multi-year projects, and they published their findings in academic journals, industry publications, and newspapers and magazines. Engineers who chose to climb the research ladder instead of the management one went through a series of reviews and promotions that resembled the academic tenure system in American universities. The top engineers were awarded the status of "technical fellow," a position equivalent in autonomy and prestige to an endowed chair at a major university.

Notwithstanding the similarities with academia, and despite the fact that one R&D engineer joked that he worked for the "University of Autoworks," the R&D Division adopted an explicit focus on application not shared by most academic research institutions. For more than two decades, R&D had not been able to decide exactly what conducting "applied research" meant. Did it mean that research engineers should be designing new technologies, on the order of antilock brakes or satellite navigation systems, that could be directly integrated into Autoworks' vehicles? Did it mean that research engineers should be designing technologies like finite element pre-processors to help product engineers work more effectively? Or did it mean both of these things? Autoworks' R&D Division had a number of different research departments, each with its own area of focus. Traditionally, the directors of these departments decided what "applied" would mean in the context of their respective departments' research. In the early 1990s, Jim Beamer became the director of the Engineering Mechanics Department and found himself confronted with this very question about what applied research would mean to his department. Jim's decision was among the earliest events that would influence R&D to help crashworthiness analysts more effectively build and analyze math models.

Formulating a Strategic Direction

As is the case for most R&D divisions, engineers were recruited R&D at Autoworks—more specifically, into the Engineering Mechanics Department—either straight out of advanced degree programs or from industrial research centers at other major companies. Most of the research engineers hadn't worked in product engineering at Autoworks before joining the

R&D Division. Thus, as one R&D manager suggested, their understanding of the work done by product engineers was always at least one step removed from practice:

Because most of the engineers and scientists here come from research backgrounds, they don't always have familiarity with how we build our products at Autoworks. They do know the products, though, and they learn quickly about the vehicle production process. I don't feel that an intimate knowledge of how engineering is done in the product organizations is essential to being a productive researcher here. Now that I've said that, let me say something that sounds quite contradictory. We do sometimes run into trouble when we don't have a clear understanding of the way people work. I think that is becoming more and more clear all the time, but we still have tended to make assumptions about the way our engineers work rather than find out directly for ourselves.

In addition to lacking people familiar with product engineering at Autoworks, one of the major reasons the R&D group had not developed a large knowledge base about the way engineers worked was that for many years the group had focused more on products than on processes. In other words, the Engineering Mechanics Department was more concerned with developing products that could be directly integrated into vehicles than with working to build technologies that would help engineers in the product-engineering groups build better vehicles. Throughout the 1980s and the early 1990s, engineers in the Engineering Mechanics Department brought a number of important inventions to Autoworks' vehicles, including advanced sensing airbags, antilock braking systems, and onboard computers.

When Jim Beamer became the director of the Engineering Mechanics Department, he sought to augment the department's product focus with a process focus. In one of his first attempts to move to a more process-based focus, Jim held meetings with a number of directors in various product-engineering divisions across Autoworks, including Gene Anderson in the Safety Division's Truck Department. During their meeting in the spring of 1994, Gene recounted some of the difficulties his engineers faced when building and assembling math models of vehicle impacts. Gene's story, though compelling, was not unique. Directors in other crashworthiness-analysis groups, including Noise and Vibration, Vehicle Dynamics, and Aero/Thermal, were also complaining of the difficulties they faced as their analysts increased simulations in order to reduce the number of physical tests required to evaluate vehicle performance. That same year, cooperating with directors in several of the other R&D departments, Jim Beamer launched an ambitious project called the "Next Generation Math-Based

Vehicle Development Process." The goal was to involve engineers in various departments within the R&D Division in creating technologies that would make math-based engineering more tractable and user-friendly for engineers in the product divisions. This process-based approach was the first in a series of projects that would begin to shift R&D's long-standing focus on products to one that addressed the need for company-wide process improvement.

One of the first major technologies developed under the Next Generation project was called the *integrated vehicle design analysis* (IVDA) tool. The idea behind IVDA was to integrate analysis into the early stages of vehicle design. Essentially, the team's goal was to build a technology that would combine the features of a CAD technology such as Unigraphics with the FEA capabilities of a tool such as ElementMesh. The project was ambitious and quite complex, and it was viewed by executives in the R&D group as R&D's version of a "concept car." A concept car is a vehicle built to showcase new designs and innovations and to solicit feedback from consumers at auto shows before a company commits itself to building a production version. Another purpose of a concept car is to generate new thinking and technologies that may not be feasible in their present form but that may inspire derivative products. Work on the IVDA tool began in this spirit. R&D engineers knew all too well the structural difficulties of truly integrating design and analysis at Autoworks, but they felt that, in the process of tinkering with ways to shorten the cycles between design and analysis, new innovations might surface that would begin to break down the artificial wall that existed between the functions. Work on the IVDA technology inspired a new way of thinking in R&D: Developing new process technologies wasn't simply about increasing technical complexity; it was also about helping Autoworks achieve important organizational changes that would increase the quality of its automobiles while simultaneously lowering production costs. One R&D director suggested that thinking of technological change as an initiator of organizational change would require R&D engineers to move away from a model of invention and toward a model of applied innovation:

Invention and innovation are not the same thing. Invention is having a new idea. Innovation is taking that idea and turning it into results. Our job is to innovate in R&D, and we innovate by initiating change in the organization. The problem is that organizations don't like to change. So we need to keep asking ourselves, "How can we make new technologies that will drive change here at Autoworks?" We're about technological change, because technological change brings about organizational change and produces results. That said, a good engineering group spends more time working on technologies for the future, technologies that . . . users don't even know that they need yet, and less time on remediation and release.

As these comments demonstrate, work on the IVDA technology initiated a shift in focus: R&D engineers began to realize the importance of thinking about technological change in relation to organizational change.

Jason Chan, an experienced engineer in the Engineering Mechanics Department, had been working on technologies related to safety and crashworthiness for several years. Just as IVDA began gaining momentum in the R&D Division, Jason completed a series of studies he had been conducting on improving sensing algorithms for air-bag deployment. Because of his expertise in the area, the leader of the IVDA project asked him to help design a set of modules for crashworthiness performance analysis to integrate into the tool. Jim Beamer, Jason's director, agreed that a set of math-based modules pertaining to vehicle crashworthiness analysis would be useful. But rather than have him begin blind, Jim suggested that, since Jason was between projects, he might benefit from taking a research sabbatical to spend a few months observing and working alongside analysts in the Safety Division to learn first-hand about the difficulties they faced moving toward a more effective math-based vehicle-assessment process. Jason agreed that it would be a unique opportunity not only to help one of the product-engineering divisions but also to improve his own crashworthiness-analysis skills. Jim contacted Gene Anderson, with whom he had met several months earlier, and arranged for Jason to be given a desk in the Truck Department in Truckville.

Focusing Attention on Specific Practices

Jason spent nearly all of the first two months of 1995 performing routine crashworthiness-engineering work with analysts in the Truck Department. Unlike most of the analysts in crashworthiness engineering, Jason worked in a group that focused on scientific research. The time lines for most projects in the R&D Division were much longer than those for projects in the product-engineering divisions, because R&D wasn't tied to the various stage gates outlined in Autoworks' formal vehicle development process. Similarly, because engineers in R&D published their work in journals and books and presented their findings at academic conferences, they were much more bound to the traditions of academic research, including the need to make their methods transparent and their findings reproducible. Jason had come to the Safety Division with an ideological orientation toward crashworthiness work as a scientific activity rather than a technical endeavor. This orientation wasn't shared by most analysts. Most of them thought it was far more important to make sure that a model correlated with the results of a test than to spend time making sure that the methods they used to correlate their models could be easily discerned by others. For example, note the ideological differences between Jason's explanation of what it means to be a crashworthiness engineer and the explanation of the same idea offered by Bridgett Misloslovich, an analyst in the Truck Department:

Jason   Crashworthiness work needs to be done logically. Everyone has to do it the same so you know you can trust the answers. It's about understanding, and you have to give credible results for people to understand and believe your results. Using methods people can trust is important. If you do something different than what is normal, you should be telling this to your people so they can consider it all when they evaluate your results.

Bridgett   Sometimes this is more art than science, especially when you get into the correlation part. If you standardize it and you get a model that doesn't correlate to a physical test, but you are the same as everybody, what good is that to you? You don't have a model that can predict results. You have a model that is consistent with everybody else's, but your vehicle might have quirks that you have to customize. That's where it's art, and that's more important than having everyone know what you did.

Though this difference in ideology regarding crashworthiness analysis didn't cause a rift between Jason and the analysts, it did focus Jason's attention on a different set of practices that could lead to more effective model building and analysis: pre-processing and post-processing mathematical models.

During his time with the Truck Department, Jason noticed that the steps analysts took in pre-processing their models (that is, preparing to submit them to the solver) were highly idiosyncratic. After analysts meshed their parts and assembled them into a complete vehicle model, they took a number of important steps to prepare the model for a particular analysis. Among these steps, three were absolutely essential. First, the analyst had to place accelerometers on the model to indicate where he or she wanted the computer to measure deceleration of the structure. Second, the analyst had to make section cuts in the model, which tell the computer where to measure the forces that are generated during impact. Third, the analyst had to position the barrier the vehicle would impact. In a physical test at the proving grounds, the vehicle is usually positioned in relation to a fixed barrier. In a math-based assessment, the barrier is positioned in relation to the vehicle, because all the parts in the vehicle are situated in a relative plane based on vehicle coordinates assigned by design engineers. Adjusting the position of a vehicle would necessitate changing the coordinates of several thousand parts. Thus, it was much easier and less time consuming to change the position of the barrier in relation to the vehicle. However, this modification became a bit complicated, because NHTSA and IIHS posted their guidelines in the form of measurements of the vehicle in relation to the barrier. For this reason, analysts had to translate the coordinates provided by the testing agencies in order to position the barrier in a math-based simulation. As Jason performed these three essential steps himself and watched analysts in the Truck Department pre-process their models, he learned that both NHTSA and IIHS had very strict guidelines for placing accelerometers and for positioning the vehicle in relation to the barrier. He observed, though, that interpreting these procedures was often difficult:

Let's say you are not the most familiar with them, or there's a new revision to [the NCAP or IIHS tests]. It's very complicated. And it takes a lot of time to read several times to understand what to do, what has been changed, and which will apply to what. But one way to do that is to try to sketch something to put on a big piece of paper to find the relationship; you know, if you are doing this, also, here is the impact speed, here is the occupant dummy, size you should use, here is the injury threshold. And I may understand it incorrectly; it's very possible.

As a result, analysts' placement of accelerometers was often inconsistent with accelerometer placement in NHTSA and IIHS tests. In addition, they often positioned the barrier incorrectly for the specific load case they aimed to evaluate. The engineers at the proving grounds in Testville, however, were responsible for setting vehicles up for physical tests exactly the same way they would be set up by NHTSA and IIHS, and since the test guidelines were written for physical testing, they were much easier to apply in a physical environment. Thus, if an analyst's placement of accelerometers and barrier position in a math model differed from the placement and position at the proving grounds (as, unfortunately, was often the case), a very poor correlation between simulation and test would result.

Deciding where section cuts should be made was an even more cumbersome process. Because forces were measured in the math only to provide a more complete picture of how the energy generated during a crash was dissipated throughout the vehicle's structure, NHTSA and IIHS didn't have procedures specifying where section cuts should be made. Instead, section cuts were often used more for informational purposes—that is, to give engineers a sense of the physics behind a model. Thus, analysts often placed section cuts in idiosyncratic locations. When Jason watched analysts determine where to make section cuts in their models, where to place accelerometers, and where to position barriers, he found that the steps they took were, in fact, far from arbitrary. Although the process one analyst used might be different from the process used by another, each analyst typically followed what he or she believed was a logical sequence. As Jason suggested, if analysts' work were standardized, perhaps the specific processes or the workflow could be made explicit and shared among engineers so that the procedures of pre-processing a model would not be idiosyncratic but instead would be replicable and credible:

My observation of a professional user of a pre-processor is you see he readily clicks different icons. He pokes here and pokes there, and then pokes somewhere else. And if you don't know what he's doing, you're totally lost, because there's no pattern that you can figure out for this. But, actually, he knows exactly; he has a flow, he has a sequence in his mind, a structure of how things should go. So it's already there. I thought we could try to capture that so it will become more explicit than implicit; so it's just not in one person's head, but everyone can know it.

A second practice that Jason identified as problematic during his time in the Truck Department was the way analysts post-processed their models. When analysts submitted their models to the solver, the software program (typically DYNA code) returned results in a text-based format. Analysts used a number of post-processing tools to visually render the text-based data in a three-dimensional format. Rendering the results in three dimensions allowed analysts to watch the crash in a movie format, just as if they were watching a physical test. However, because the movies were generated from math, analysts could manipulate them in ways they couldn't manipulate footage of physical tests. For example, they could rotate the vehicle in any direction and watch it crash, remove all the sheet metal or the power train and just watch the body-in-white deform during impact, or zoom in on particular areas of the vehicle to acquire an in-depth understanding of the deformation pattern. As useful as these visualizations were, they didn't allow analysts to compare data from simulations against data from physical tests. To do that, analysts had to export the data to a graphing program that would generate two-dimensional line images representing acceleration and displacement curves.

Regardless of whether crash data are obtained from actual accelerometers on test vehicles or from representations of accelerometers placed in math models, all data sources carry noise (distortion) along with signal. This noise might be from electrical interference, such as that from fluorescent lights or electric motors, or it might be caused by other factors, such as vibration. Because accelerometers are physically mounted to the vehicle, vibration from the impact is transmitted to the accelerometer and shows up as ambient noise. The extra noise in a signal can make the data difficult to interpret or (worse) inaccurate. To remove the noise from the data, the analyst had to use a filter. Filtering removes some of the noise frequency from a signal in order to generate a readable curve. In its crash-test guidelines, the SAE provides a number of different filters engineers can use to interpret test data. These same filters are built into the post-processing graphing software so analysts can filter the crash data generated by the solver. Although filtering may seem to be a relatively straightforward process, Jason quickly discovered that analysts in the Truck Department weren't all using the same filters to interpret their data. This lack of consistency was problematic, because a signal looks very different depending on the type of filter used to remove high-frequency and low-frequency noise. Jason observed that when an analyst used a filter different from the one used at the proving grounds, he or she was unable to make reliable comparisons between math and physical data. Moreover, differences in filtering practices made it nearly impossible for analysts to compare some of their math-based results with some of their other math-based results.

As Jason learned more about crashworthiness work, he formed an opinion that engineering managers could have little confidence in the credibility of the data they used to suggest expensive changes in vehicle design because their analysts used idiosyncratic processes to generate the results, and, as a consequence, managers had no way of knowing how those data were produced:

I was thinking that a reputable laboratory has to have a standard; people have to respect their work. In the computer simulation modeling area, it depends on who you talk to. There are still many people out there who don't believe you. And because whoever is doing the analysis, they basically didn't convince you that their result is reliable, people say, "You trick the model to get the result, to show it matched. So what?" And so, math modeling has that kind of reputation. And so, I think it . . . it's like you send some part to a lab. If you know this lab tends to fake results just try to please their customers, that would be awful, right? Then they won't be a credible laboratory. But you know if they're a good lab, if you can see their process, you know what happened to get the results. Our simulations, they have to be more credible like those of a good lab.

As Jason saw it, math-based analyses would have a chance of playing a more central role in the process of designing vehicles only if managers and decision makers within the company viewed simulation results as credible data with which to make programmatic decisions.

Identifying a Feasible Technology

When Jason returned from his research sabbatical in the Safety Division to his office in the R&D building in Motorville, many of his colleagues were still working on various modules for the IVDA tool. Jason began to think that perhaps R&D's goal of building technologies to integrate design and analysis and the issues circling around the credibility of math-based models he had observed over the past several weeks in the Safety Division might be interrelated. In other words, it might be possible to solve the credibility problem by building a technology that would automate some portion of analysis, thereby eliminating the inconsistencies in the process introduced by human error. Jason began envisioning a tool that would guide analysts through the pre-processing phase, showing them where to place accelerometers and section cuts and automatically positioning the barrier for them. He also saw the tool automatically selecting the appropriate filters and time steps for engineers to use when post-processing their data. Such a technology would ensure that all analysts were setting up and analyzing models in a consistent and reliable way, and would therefore bring much-needed credibility to math-based analysis—not only in the Safety Division, but across all of Autoworks. Jason explained:

I think many analysts, they know they should not just do things any old way, but it's always like, "It worked for me before," so they continue to work that way. Sometimes maybe they tried a few things before and it worked, and they continued to work that way. So in that view, engineering is not really science. You know, you learn a little bit of science, and you run with it. Engineering is just making it work—at least that's the way it seems people think about it mostly in the divisions. I thought, what if we can make them think of it as more scientific? What if they don't make decisions about models just because, but do it because it is proved the best way? Then doing a simulation would be like going to a laboratory. People in the laboratory are using scientific methods to make good recommendations. You can trust those—they are good results—and so we can have faith in math-based work. Management might actually make decisions on simulations at that point.

If technology were to be used to automate practices formerly performed in a highly individual and idiosyncratic fashion, Jason believed, math-based analysis could become more "scientific" and therefore more credible.

Over the next three months, Jason worked to develop a concept for a tool he called CrashLab. The name boldly implied that the technology would make math-based analysis as systematic and credible as analysis conducted by engineers and scientists in physical laboratories:

In a crash laboratory like the ones at the proving grounds in Testville, you have to follow a protocol and document the steps you took. You can't just say "I'll try this and see what happens." You have to follow a procedure and show that what you did could be replicated by others who followed the same steps. That is what we were trying to do with CrashLab. We wanted to build the rigor and credibility of a laboratory into virtual analysis. "Virtual" does not have to mean less real, but most people think of it that way. We hoped that CrashLab would change that by showing if you used the tool, no matter who you were, you'd get the same results just like if you followed the procedure in the lab. Anyone who brings one or the same model into CrashLab can get the same results.

Jason envisioned that the tool would work in conjunction with the pre-processors, post-processors, and solvers already being used in the Safety Division. An analyst would use a finite-element pre-processor such as ElementMesh to read in CAD files, and would mesh them. Analysts would also continue to use these pre-processing tools to assemble models, to define contacts between parts, and to add and subtract spot-welds. Once the model was completely meshed and assembled, the user would export the file and read it into CrashLab. In CrashLab, analysts would position the bumper in relationship to the vehicle depending on the type of analysis they were running, add accelerometers to the model, and make section cuts to indicate where they wanted to obtain information on load forces. After the model was ready, analysts would export the file and submit it to the solver at Autoworks' High Performance Computing Center. Once the model had been solved, the analyst would open it back up in CrashLab, filter the data, output results at appropriate time steps, and build a series of graphs to summarize the information. The engineer would then export the model from CrashLab and read it into one of the post-processing tools they already used, such as LSPOST, to render the model in three dimensions and visually discern how the simulated crash affected the vehicle's structure and occupants.

   Jason also began thinking about how the interface for such a technology might look. He envisioned clearly outlining and incorporating the steps he observed analysts following in their heads into the technology in a visual way. Along one side of the screen, a diagram of the workflow for model preparation would guide the user through a set of ordered process steps. As the analyst moved from one step to the next, a three-dimensional model of the vehicle would appear along the other side of the screen. CrashLab would indicate where an accelerometer or a section cut should be placed on the vehicle, and the engineer could use that information to perform the function manually. Jason drafted an image of how he thought

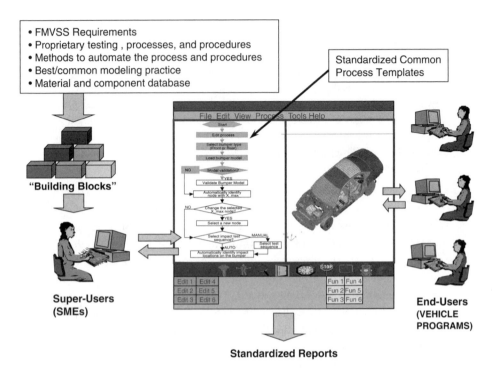

Figure 4.8
Slide from Jason Chan's first presentation of CrashLab to the R&D Division.

the interface would look and prepared a slide to present to his colleagues at an upcoming meeting of the Engineering Mechanics Department. Late in the spring of 1995, Jason presented the slide shown here in figure 4.8 for the first time. His colleagues found the project very interesting. Tai-Lap Leung, an engineer in the Engineering Mechanics Department who would later work with Jason on a CrashLab prototype, was struck by Jason's foresight:

I think the CrashLab was ahead of its time. This was a real good way to improve the quality of math-based analysis. Crash is the most knowledge-intense of most of the performance analysis, and there are more engineers with PhDs compared to the other divisions. These PhDs think they know how to do [analysis], and so everybody is doing [analysis] in their own ways and in their own time. So with [the CrashLab] concept we can standardize the process, then we should be able to have more credibility for the work.

Engineers in the Engineering Mechanics Department and across the R&D Division shared Tai-Lap's sentiment. If engineers in the product divisions could use a tool such as CrashLab to improve the credibility of their work, there was hope for more ambitious and highly integrated tools such as IVDA.

Emboldened by the positive feedback from his colleagues in R&D, Jason decided to present his proposal for CrashLab to the Crash Safety Focus Group. Each crashworthiness-analysis function at Autoworks maintained a "focus group" that was responsible for, among other things, endorsing and sanctioning all new technologies used by the analysts in the focus group's particular function. The Crash Safety Focus Group was no different. According to its formal mission statement, the group aimed to "commonize, improve and manage vehicle crashworthiness simulation tools and methodologies necessary to synthesize and validate Autoworks product designs to meet crash safety requirements." Put more plainly, the focus group worked actively with members of R&D, Techpro, and Infoserv to develop new technologies and methods that would aid math-based simulation. Most important, the focus group had the final say regarding tools implemented for the users in the Safety Division. If the focus group didn't deem a new technology sufficiently useful or appropriate for the work of its engineers, it would not endorse it, and ultimately, Infoserv couldn't install the software on analysts' machines.

The focus group's chair, Sunil Kitane, a senior manager in the Safety Division, had worked as an analyst in the crashworthiness-engineering organization for more than 15 years when the focus group was founded in the early 1990s. One of Sunil's first challenges as chair was to determine which engineers across the various groups at Autoworks were interested and/or involved in product engineering from a crashworthiness standpoint and make sure that these people became members of the focus group. The focus group also included Brad Bertallini and Barry Glenn from the Safety Division, Jensen Lu from Techpro, Kaleeb Azbad from the Infoserv Division, and Jason Chan from R&D, and there was *ad hoc* participation by senior managers from Autoworks' engineering centers in Germany, Australia, Canada, Mexico, and Brazil. These representatives from across the company met on the third Thursday of each month to review proposals from the R&D Division and from vendors for new technologies and to provide updates on projects currently in the works. The primary goal of the focus group was to ensure that crashworthiness analysts only had access to tools that the focus group felt would aid them in their work:

As a member of the focus group, Jason served both as an evaluator and as a presenter. It was in his role as a presenter that Jason proposed his concept for CrashLab to the focus group in June of 1995. In his presentation, Jason described the credibility problem that he believed was plaguing the Safety Division, and suggested that CrashLab, by automating many of the routine procedures associated with model setup and analysis (non-standardized procedures that were being performed inconsistently), would make simulation work more credible, more reliable, and therefore more useful. He presented four PowerPoint slides that outlined his ideas. His presentation did not meet with enthusiastic support. Though the other members of the focus group agreed with his assessment that crashworthiness engineering needed to move toward a completely virtual vehicle-assessment process, each of the members felt the technology was deficient in its ability to solve the problems he or she believed were most important. Because members of the Safety Division, the Techpro Division, and the Infoserv Division had all developed their own problems that had to be solved in order to integrate math-based analyses more meaningfully into the process of vehicle development, they expected CrashLab to have different features than the ones Jason proposed. Consider the following comments from members of the focus group:

Sunil   I remember CrashLab seemed like a good technology, but it wasn't ready for prime time. It did some important things, like provide set filtering algorithms, but that wasn't really the major problem. We needed a technology that would make the results our engineers gave more useful, more real; you know, more accurate. The early version of CrashLab didn't do that. It was like it ignored that problem altogether. Our needs were timelier than that.

Jensen   CrashLab had some issues because there was no immediate way to make the work faster, it didn't seem. We had all agreed to make the technology or to find a technology to work with the two-day FE model process. CrashLab was good in spirit, but not in practice, because many of the things it could do would make work slower.

Kaleeb   When Jason explained the architecture of CrashLab, I thought there was a problem, because if [analysts] used it they would generate more models with larger file sizes and they'd quickly exceed their dedicated space on the R-drive.[4] Also, it was another tool—and more tools, we were thinking, were bad, since we were trying to reduce our numbers [of tools] anyway.

Clearly, each member of the focus group expected CrashLab to be the technology he or she had identified to solve the particular problem developed in his or her respective group. Sunil was looking for a technology that would solve the accuracy problem by providing meshing and assembly capabilities. Jensen was looking for a technology that would solve the speed problem by making two-day FE models possible. Kaleeb was looking for a tool that would solve the capacity problem by creating smaller files—a tool made by a vendor with which Autoworks already had a relationship. It came as no surprise, then, that in its next monthly meeting the focus group voted not to approve Jason's concept for the CrashLab technology. Jason was frustrated with the decision:

I was not so sure why they would say no to CrashLab. I spent time in the [crash-worthiness] group, and I see directly the problems there. They say they want tools that immediately affect the production process. Well, CrashLab was that. But you know, sometimes the user, they don't know what they need. I think this was a case of that. It was sort of like their eyes were closed.

Perhaps the eyes of the other focus group members weren't closed, as Jason suggested, but rather were focused on something else—a different problem than the one Jason's structural position in the R&D Division had led him to develop.

5 Articulating Visions of Technology and Organization

By 1995, crashworthiness analysts were still playing a decidedly reactive role in the vehicle development process at Autoworks. Design engineers alerted analysts when CAD releases of parts or subassemblies were ready for testing, and analysts worked to validate the crashworthiness performance of the designs. Late that same year, Autoworks held its first annual CAE conference. The aim of the conference was to showcase the work engineers were doing in the domain of computer-aided engineering and to encourage more math-based analysis within the company. At the plenary session, Vice-President of Global Engineering Randy Johnson professed his belief that CAE work would have revolutionary effects on the product development process:

We are beginning to just unlock the potential of these new [CAE] technologies for engineering design. By the year 2000, we expect that design and analysis work will be so closely linked in our engineering functions that we will be able to reduce the necessary number of prototypes by more than 90 percent. We are investing heavily in the technology infrastructure to support CAE work, and no other automaker, not even Toyota, is being as aggressive as we are in this area. We at Autoworks believe CAE work will be an incredible source of competitive advantage moving forward.

As we saw in chapter 4, the development of problems associated with integrating the design and analysis functions at Autoworks belied such optimism. Although engineers in Safety, Techpro, Infoserv, and R&D all earnestly wanted CAE tools to blur the artificial distinction between design and analysis, the four groups couldn't seem to agree on the best way to make that happen. Because the various groups—influenced by Autoworks' operational structure, their own culture, and their own core competencies—had developed different problems and had identified different technologies as most likely to solve those problems, and because it was essential for the four groups to work collaboratively to design, develop, build, and implement new technology at Autoworks, the barriers to aligning design and analysis and achieving a more strategic position for math-based analysis seemed almost insurmountable. Gene Anderson commented:

We would hear the rhetoric from management saying that design and analysis work had to be integrated, but they were structurally different, and I agree they had to be. But to try to make analysis work more productive, we needed to solve some key problems in our work. But what happened was none of the other groups here would validate the existence of a mesh quality problem, for example, or at least even think it was important. Instead, you had Jason's group in R&D coming up and really trying to push a technology like CrashLab that didn't really meet our needs. Sure, it sounds easy to develop a new technology, but not if you can't agree on what it should be, and especially if that technology is necessary to fulfill the vision outlined by senior management.

Difficulty reconciling divergent interests across organizational boundaries is certainly not unique to Autoworks. For nearly half a century, researchers have shown that managing organizational interdependencies is crucial to the development of new technologies (Baron and Bielby 1982; Eisenhardt and Bhatia 2002). In fact, most technology development researchers argue that, because innovative ideas are formed at the intersections of divergent organizations, the organizations most successful at developing new technologies are those that use a cross-functional team structure to take advantage of the core competencies of different organizations, or groups, within them (e.g., sales, marketing, R&D, finance) and exploit the innovations that arise when they intersect (Jassawalla and Sashittal 1999; MacCormack, Verganti, and Iansiti 2001; Pinto, Pinto, and Prescott 1993). What most of this research has failed to consider, though, is how organizations' fundamental differences in methods of problem formation and problem solving—the very attributes that very well may make them ripe for cross-fertilization of ideas and knowledge (Hargadon and Sutton 1997) —can contribute to different meanings at the functional interface.

Since the early 1990s researchers have made a conservative move in this direction, calling attention to the functional, occupational, and ideological differences held by various groups involved in the production of new technology. Deborah Dougherty (1992), for example, has demonstrated empirically that "interpretive barriers" often exist between interdependent organizations involved in technological innovation. She suggests that because different functional organizations have unique relationships with the product market, members of the organizations are bound to hold dramatically different beliefs about how and why a particular product should be developed. Dougherty argues that although differences in interpretive schemes (as she calls them) might not seem, at the outset, to present insurmountable barriers to new technology development, organizational routines reinforce patterns of interaction that lead each organization to reinforce its own way of seeing the world. Dougherty suggests that many new technology development efforts fail because organizations are unable to bridge their differing interpretive schemes. Bucciarelli (1994, p. 62) similarly suggests that designing new technologies involves the coordination of organizations whose members occupy distinct "object worlds," which he defines as "the domains of thought, action, and artifact within which participants in engineering design move and live when working on any specific aspect of a project." For Bucciarelli, the interaction of individuals who occupy differing object worlds is fundamental to successful technical design precisely because distinct competencies are necessary for producing innovative products. Yet bridging object-world thinking is perhaps the activity that causes the most trouble for engineering design efforts.

Bijker (1993, 1995a) offers a similar assessment of the technology development process, holding that individuals from different social organizations each possess distinct ideological orientations toward the development process, which he terms "technological frames."[1] In Bijker's conceptualization, a technological frame "comprises all elements that influence the interactions within relevant social groups and lead to the attribution of meanings to technical artifacts—and thus to constituting technology" (1995a, p. 123) Bijker identifies a number of potential elements that may constitute an organization's technological frame, including the organization's goals, the problems the organization believes must be solved, the strategies the organization employs to solve the problems at hand, the requirements a particular solution to the problem must meet to be feasible, the current knowledge base possessed by the members of the organization, the type of technology the group believes will solve the problem at hand, and the function the new technology will replace once it is implemented.[2] For Bijker, technological frames structure the interaction among various organizations, producing problems of coordination and agreement when members who have been inculcated with different technological frames can't readily interpret and assimilate the suggestions made by collaborators who don't share their particular technological frame.

Using Bijker's framework, we can sketch a picture of the technological frames (or interpretive schemes or object worlds) of the four groups involved in math-based analysis at Autoworks. Table 5.1 lists the various elements of the technological frames of each of these groups. Although there were significant differences in the problems the various groups

Table 5.1
Technological frames of groups involved in math-based analysis at Autoworks

	Safety	Techpro	Infoserv	R&D
Goals	Move math-based analysis earlier in the vehicle-design process	Move math-based analysis earlier in the vehicle-design process	Move math-based analysis earlier in the vehicle-design process	Move math-based analysis earlier in the vehicle-design process
Major problems	Accuracy of math models	Speed of math-based analysis	Capacity of personnel and technical resources	Credibility of math-based simulations
Problem-solving strategies	Change the procedure engineers use to build models	Develop a suite of interdependent technologies to achieve two-day FE model analysis goal	Consider options for combining technologies and increasing computing resources	Identify discrepancies in process between math-based and physical test procedures
Requirements to Be Met by Problem Solutions	Engineers needed to build better mesh and reduce part penetrations.	Math models had to be built so they could run faster, and built in the same way in different parts of the world.	The number of different tools used to build and analyze models had to be reduced, and the size of FE models had to be compliant with CPU processing capabilities.	Engineers had to begin to pre-process and post-process their models in identical ways.
Current knowledge base	Product-engineering focus, knowledge of vehicle crashworthiness dynamics	Understanding of engineering operations in global context and vendor relations	Contractual obligations with vendors and costs of solving FE differential equations	Methodological orientation toward reproducibility and falsifiability of results
Exemplary artifacts	A technology that would automatically generate uniform mesh and detect penetrations	A technology that would fit into an already-envisioned suite of tools	A technology that would be more economical to maintain than current alternatives	A technology that allowed users minimal discretion in decision making
Perceived substitution function	Engineers working in an idiosyncratic manner	Engineers working in an idiosyncratic manner	Engineers working in an idiosyncratic manner	Engineers working in an idiosyncratic manner

believed had to be solved and the type of technology the various groups believed should be built to solve them, there were also important similarities among them. For example, all four groups shared a common goal: to move math-based analysis earlier in the process of designing a vehicle. And though each group identified a different type of technology to build to make this move happen, all four were also in agreement that what the technology should do, broadly, was remove the idiosyncrasies of individual crashworthiness analysts from the process of math-based analysis. This common goal served as an anchor for these four interdependent groups. Though Autoworks' organizational structure separated the four groups from one another in effect creating the mechanisms (outlined in chapter 4) that would produce distinct technological frames, the process of developing a new technology, which required them to coordinate their efforts, brought them together. But despite their common goal and their common belief that they could develop a new technology to reduce idiosyncratic engineering processes, by late June of 1995 the four groups were still unable to translate their own beliefs about what should be done to move math-based analysis to a more central role in the vehicle development process into terms understandable within the technological frames of the other groups at Autoworks.

Indeed, the four engineering groups at Autoworks seemed to be plagued by interpretive barriers in the technology development process. However, in contrast with the many examples recounted in the literature of development efforts that failed because of interpretive barriers (Cardinal 2001; DeLuca and Attuahene 2007; Vermeulen 2005), a new technology for crashworthiness-engineering analysis was developed at Autoworks. The main question this chapter explores is this: How do groups with differing technological frames eventually come to agreement about the type of new technology that is best for the company? To answer such a question, we need to understand not only why it is that groups within the same company would have distinct technological frames in the first place (the focus of chapter 4), but also how they overcome their seemingly irreconcilable differences so as to produce a new technology.

As an aid to an investigation in this direction, I adopt the concept of *articulation* as outlined by Anselm Strauss (1985, 1988; see also Strauss and Corbin 1993). Strauss suggests that as work in organizations becomes increasingly rationalized and fractionalized into small identifiable components and performed by individuals across a variety of functional groups, the "project" as a sociological concept takes on tremendous importance. Projects, he argues, involve a course of action which entails a division of labor—meaning not only of actors but of actions. It is useful to keep those analytic distinctions separate. In "work" terms, the project action is made up of many tasks done over time, and divided up according to various criteria among the actors (persons, classes of persons, departments or other organizational units). . . . Since the plurality of tasks making up their totality, as well as the relations of actors to tasks, are not automatically articulated, actors must do that too, and often in complex ways. (1985, p. 2)

In other words, any work that is artificially divided into structurally separate units must, at some point, be reintegrated or articulated into a complete whole. Although Strauss expounds the notion of articulation at the task level, the concept can be meaningfully extended to the co-orientation of groups involved in math-based analysis at Autoworks. Certainly the development of a new technology is a project in and of itself. The work undertaken to perform development in this capacity is reasonably dispersed across groups to take advantage of core competencies in the areas necessary to build a new technology—in this case, Safety, R&D, Techpro, and Information Systems and Services. In the way Strauss applies the concept, the tasks performed by each group have to be articulated in an anatomic sense (joined together) to generate a desired output. Hence, the term 'articulation' is best understood as referring to a union of distinct bodies. Just as two large freight cars can be articulated (that is, joined together with couplers) to temporarily take advantage of economy of motion, but can later be separated to be used in other ways, articulation takes advantage of the fact that organizations are separate and distinct (and thus able to develop their own competencies), but also interdependently fashioned.

At Autoworks, it didn't make sense from an economic, an organizational, or an occupational standpoint to combine all the resources necessary to develop a new technology in one organizational unit. In fact, separating skill sets such as meshing, contract negotiation, and algorithm development into separate groups allowed each functional organization to develop a more comprehensive set of skills than any one project organization ever could. (See Allen and Hauptman 1990.) In the context of cross-functional technology development, the downside of structuring a company this way is that each organization builds up a specific and unique technological frame. The primary consequence of these seemingly incompatible technological frames, as Jason Chan discovered, is that they make it difficult for organizations to coordinate their actions. In Jason's presentation, each group hoped to find even the suggestion of a solution to the specific problem developed within its particular technological frame, and, unfortunately, none found it. That they didn't find a technology they could assimilate within their respective technological frames should not be surprising, since Jason pitched CrashLab to the Focus Group as a solution to the credibility problem—a problem the three other organizations hadn't even considered.

Articulating four disparate organizations into a cross-functional project team required translating interests from one technological frame to other frames. Susan Leigh Star and her colleagues (Gerson and Star 1986; King and Star 1990; Star 1989) suggest that articulation in an anatomic sense is often accomplished through articulation in a semantic sense of technological frames through the production of boundary objects. As Gerson and Star's research suggests, semantic articulation resolves the inconsistencies produced by differing technological frames by "packaging a compromise that 'gets the job done,' that is, that closes the system locally and temporarily so that work can go on" (1986, p. 266). Star and colleagues observe that actors in a social system, in order to be able to frame an issue in a way that resonates within others' technological frames, often produce a number of boundary objects, which are only loose semantic articulations. The plasticity of such articulations, whether in the form of artifacts, words, or concepts, provides an ill-structured response to the exigencies of the situation that each other actor can then interpret as fulfilling his or her needs.

In this chapter, I propose that semantic articulation (the use of boundary objects), although necessary, is not enough to achieve the process of anatomic articulation (the joining together of organizations having disparate technological frames). The data presented herein suggest that articulation is accomplished through three sequential processes: *conceptual integration, organizational disengagement*, and *technical integration*. In order to reconcile the differences in technological frames, and eventually to build a technology to move math-based analysis earlier in the process of designing vehicles, both the organization of work at Autoworks and the material features of the new technology had to evolve in a way that would align the interests of Safety, Techpro, Infoserv, and R&D. The processes described in this chapter explain why such changes took place and offer a number of mechanisms that illustrate how the technology and the effort organized to develop it evolved over a period of nearly ten years.

Conceptual Integration

When representatives from the various groups invested in new-technology development at Autoworks came together at the Focus Group meeting in the summer of 1995, they faced a common problem. Although each group had identified a particular technology as likely to help move math-based analysis into a more central role in vehicle design, no single group could build the technology alone. Instead, members of each group had to convince the Focus Group (which was essentially an institutionalized cross-functional project team made up of members from each of the four organizations) that their technology was not only feasible but necessary. One of the main barriers to effective cross-functional collaboration was that each group had developed its own technological frame that structured its conceptualization of the relationship between crashworthiness work and the idea of a new technology.

Kaleeb Azbad, whose opinion was widely shared among the engineers who participated in the crash Focus Group, noted that differences in background and in goals produced problems of conceptual integration that threatened to thwart efforts to develop new technologies:

It happens fairly often that we all [meaning the Focus Group's members] have different concepts that we're working with, concepts that have to be integrated. This is a real problem because what it does is it blocks the new technology, it makes it so we can't move forward until we have, you know, consensus. That's the problem with having the Focus Group approve things like this. It makes them slower and it gets in the way of the real work, which is about designing new tools. If we could eliminate this problem, we'd probably be more effective, I think.

As Kaleeb and other members of the Focus Group noted, lack of consensus was a major barrier to new-technology development at Autoworks. Moreover, Focus Group members viewed the negotiation process as separate from and, by all accounts, somewhat ancillary to the design process, and certainly as an impediment to more streamlined technology development. Before a technology could be built to change the way crashworthiness analysts at Autoworks worked, members of the Focus Group somehow had to integrate their various conceptualizations of the problems crashworthiness analysts faced and articulate the kind of technology that should be built to solve those problems.

To achieve conceptual integration by resolving differences in technological frames, bridging object-world thinking, and removing interpretive barriers, members of Safety, Techpro, Infoserv, and R&D engaged in three important practices. First, they worked to develop a physical prototype that could be used as a platform for discussing the features that were needed to solve the problems identified by each group. Struggling to fit the functionality of the prototype into their own technological frames, Focus Group members were eventually able to craft a multivocal logic that allowed them to see the new technology as an appropriate solution to their particular problem. To revise the prototype to reflect this new, shared logic, they created a new transversal structure whose boundaries intersected perpendicularly with those of each of the four separate groups. Through these interdependent processes, the separate groups were able to articulate with one another to build what would eventually become CrashLab.

Developing a Prototype

Discouraged by his experience with the Focus Group in the summer of 1995, Jason Chan focused on other projects, temporarily putting his CrashLab idea on the back burner. Although Jason still believed that CrashLab could solve the credibility problem for math-based analysis, without support from the Focus Group there would be little chance that the technology would ever be implemented in the Safety Division. At the end of fiscal year 1995, Jason reviewed his project budgets and realized that he hadn't spent all of his funds. The money left in the budget could be used for discretionary spending on projects Jason felt were important but still too early in the conceptual stage to merit a full review for funding by R&D management. Jason decided CrashLab was a prime candidate for an exploratory project. If he could build a working prototype, there was a chance, he reasoned, that the Focus Group's members would come to see CrashLab's merit and decide to approve it for use in the Safety Division.

To build a working prototype on a small budget, Jason needed a project small enough to meet his resource constraints but complex enough to demonstrate an ability to reliably perform complex engineering operations. The FMVSS 581 standard for bumper tolerances, which specifies requirements to minimize damage to cars' front and rear ends in low-speed collisions, proved ideal. Essentially, the standard specifies the maximum amount of damage a bumper can sustain at speeds up to 10 miles per hour. The 581 standard comprises two tests: a pendulum test and a barrier test. In the pendulum test, a large steel frame supports a swinging mass via a parallelogram linkage. The mass frame supports contact planes and an impact ridge whose height can be adjusted using motor-driven screw jacks located at the corners of the support frame. Plates can be added or removed to adjust the mass of the pendulum between 1,200 and 4,500 pounds. The test simulates a vehicle hitting the bumper of the test vehicle at speeds up to 10 miles per hour by drawing the pendulum cable to an angle of up to 45 degrees and releasing the quick-disconnect holding latch. In the second test, a system made up of a 25-horsepower programmable acceleration motor and a winch cable propels the test vehicle along a guide rail at speeds of up to 10 miles per hour. The vehicle is then released and hits the load barrier. The purpose of the second test is to verify the crashworthiness of the bumper when the vehicle is involved in a second impact after initially being struck by a vehicle. (Although the standard requires that no visible damage occur, the bumper would presumably be weaker than it was originally, before the first collision.)

Scott Henderson, who worked with Jason on the early CrashLab prototype, commented that a project addressing the 581 standard was both manageable in scope and resources and complex in view of the numerous functions CrashLab could potentially automate for the operating engineer:

In 581, all of the residual effects of the pendulum impacts are there. If there's some material damage, it's still going to be there. So you have multiple DYNA runs, you have multiple simulations, one for each of these impacts, and then you have to carry information—it's not only that you have multiple impacts, but to do it right, you have to carry information from the previous impacts to the input files of the next impact—at least, for that last one you really kind of need that damage information, residual stresses, and strains and everything to go into that final impact with the wall, because it can make a big difference. So that one was kind of a nightmare for somebody to go through that whole process to set that up, so it was a perfect example or specimen to do a process like this to demonstrate how Crash-Lab could work.

As Jason and Scott were well aware, the 581 test involved a great deal of follow-up on the part of the engineer running the simulations. The analyst had to make sure that all the equations specified for the damage caused by the pendulum were integrated into the barrier-test model. In addition, the engineer had to specify the exact location where the pendulum would strike the bumper, and because of FMVSS standards the location was different for each vehicle, which meant the analyst couldn't simply memorize one set of generic requirements; the location and angle of impact and the mass of the pendulum had to be verified for each new simulation.

Jason's team in R&D was convinced that the Focus Group had rejected CrashLab because they didn't believe it could be built. What Jason and his colleagues didn't consider was that the Focus Group's members might have rejected CrashLab because it didn't solve the problems each member's group had identified. In fact, most of the Focus Group's members weren't confident that CrashLab could automate engineering work. The problem, as Sunil Kitane plainly stated, was that there seemed to be little point in talking about automation when there was no clear grasp of what should be automated in the first place:

Jason and the R&D guys were talking about automation. Automation's fine if you have something to automate. It presumes that you have some standards and you just want to execute on them automatically. Well, in 1995, we didn't have any standards, so what they were saying just didn't really make sense. In the crash groups, we were more concerned with making our models correlate better to the tests. That was mission number one. You know, put out the fire before you try to rebuild the house.

Unaware of the deep-rooted concerns of the other organizations represented in the Focus Group, Jason's team continued with the development of a working prototype, convinced that proof of concept would remove any doubt about CrashLab's potential to revolutionize math-based analysis at Autoworks.

In the summer of 1996, Jason contacted Joel Shannon, a professor of computer science at a technical university in central Michigan from which many of Autoworks' new engineers had graduated. Jason explained his interest in developing a prototype for CrashLab, noted that his R&D staff lacked the technical skills necessary to write code for the application, and asked if Joel and a graduate student would be interested in working on the project. In exchange for their help, the R&D Division would cover the tuition expenses for the student to work on the project. Joel agreed to take on the project, and he found a graduate student to write CrashLab's FORTRAN code for his master's thesis. In the request for funding he presented to the vice-president of R&D, Jason included a proposal outlining the goals of the CrashLab project:

CrashLab is a computational methodology with procedures and tools to take bumper model data through the complete analysis process. In doing this, the design time is reduced while minimizing error and increasing repeatability. When completed, this methodology, which is called a virtual bumper test laboratory (VBTL), will enable a design engineer to run a complete analysis on a bumper design overnight. This rapid analytical turnaround is accomplished by automating as much of the modeling as possible, and also by defining standard output.

With funding in place for Joel and his student, and with FMVSS 581 chosen as a test case, the first step toward building a workable prototype was to define an architecture and a file structure for the bumper-test module in CrashLab. Jason sketched out a rough computational flow chart for the bumper-test lab module in CrashLab. The architecture consisted of 17 files that were to be executed using CrashLab on a workstation (UNIX PC) command shell or on a Cray supercomputer. To accompany the flow chart, Jason wrote a structural-specifications document outlining the type of UNIX environment that was needed to support the bumper-test module. The document clearly laid out the functions for which Joel and his student would be responsible for writing FORTRAN code that would automate activities formerly performed manually by crashworthiness analysts.

In developing the guidelines for structural specifications, Jason had to be explicit about the types of activities he wanted to automate and those he wanted to leave open to the operating analyst's discretion. The choice seemed relatively simple. Jason decided that any process for which the FMVSS specifications outlined a specific test procedure enumerating the steps necessary for correct implementation should be automated. He and his team asked with safety engineers at the Testville proving grounds for the exact specifications for the 581 test. These procedures were incorporated into the design and, using the FORTRAN code, automated so the computer instead of the engineer would be responsible for routine setup and instrumentation practices. Similarly, for post-processing activities, the computer would follow the procedures outlined by the test engineers at the proving grounds to filter the data and sample the results at the appropriate time steps.

While specifications from the proving grounds took care of the micro-level procedural details for CrashLab, working in a math-based environment raised macro-level issues not addressed in the physical test procedures. For example, for math-based models, due to the constraints of a three-dimensional design coordinate system, analysts positioned the barrier in relation to the vehicle rather than positioning the vehicle in relation to the barrier. (This was explained earlier in the book.) In these types of setup procedures, analysts had much more flexibility with regard to order of operations than did test engineers at the proving grounds. However, altering the order of steps (e.g., choosing the J and K heights on the rocker[3] after identifying pendulum impact points) could reduce the fidelity of the model owing to mass scaling.[4] Hence, the macro-level issues concerning workflow still had to be sorted out. Jason felt that more experienced analysts in the crashworthiness group could offer valuable knowledge about the optimal order of procedures for math-based model building and analysis. During his sabbatical with the analysts, he had observed them performing operations in a specific order:

I'll never forget [the crashworthiness analysts] poking here and poking there. It was showing that there was an order to the operations that was locked in the engineer's head. That should not be put away in there. It should be out for all to follow so everyone does things the same.

Jason called several of his contacts in the Truck Department in Truckville and asked them to document the order in which they performed the various model-building and setup tasks. Over the next several months, while Joel and his graduate student diligently worked on the FORTRAN code, Jason struggled to determine how to arrange the various modules of code into a structured package.

By late 1997, the FORTRAN modules were complete and Jason had settled on a flow chart he would use to guide the order of operations for the VBTL procedure. The next step was to marry the work of the past year and a half to an intuitive graphical user interface (GUI) for analysts. After some deliberation, Jason and his team decided to contract with a supplier firm not far from the R&D Division in Motorville: a small startup, called Link Software, that built pre-processing and post-processing applications for crashworthiness engineering. A number of analysts in the Safety Division used the company's most popular software application, Link-Crash. Jason's team believed they could make use of Link Software's expertise in producing algorithms for pre-processing and post-processing FE models and developing intuitive GUIs. When R&D contracted with Link Software and began putting together documents outlining requirements for the user interface, Jason and his team were adamant about incorporating two important design features.

First, the interface had to include a flow chart along one side of the screen of the steps to pre-process and post-process an FE model. Constraints had to be built into the interface requiring the analyst to proceed through the steps in a sequential manner without skipping or repeating any step. By preventing analysts from subverting the process, Jason and his team hoped to reduce variation in simulation results between iterations and among engineers. After several months of coordination and discussion, Link Software presented a mockup of an interface that met Jason's requirements. The most important aspect of the design was the flow chart that appeared along the left-hand side of the screen. Not only would the flow chart "walk the analyst through" the appropriate steps; it would also help remind the analyst where he or she had been in the process if an interruption occurred.

Second, Link Software had to create a report that would display the simulation results in a concise format that could be easily understood by analysts, by managers, and by design engineers. Scott Henderson led the initiative to develop a report interface that met their needs.

And although CrashLab would tell an analyst where to place an accelerometer, where to make a section cut in the model, or what the preferred warpage or aspect ratio was for the formation of an element, Jason didn't want to limit analysts' ability to be creative. He felt that affording the analyst discretion to stray from "best practices" if the need arose was important:

In a good scientific laboratory, reports are standardized. If an individual modeler is too fancy or too sloppy, you should be able to tell that from his report—like when you run a physical crash test. They have to make clear documentation about what they did and if they did anything that violated the natural assumptions. . . . So in CrashLab, we provide a standard default value—we don't want to take away from the contributions of the modeler—so the best thing to do is to record anything that is changed from the default value and have it recorded in the simulation report. In a real lab, they report abnormalities.

To allow analysts the autonomy to use their judgment without sacrificing the integrity of the model, Jason engineered a report feature that would document when engineers deviated from the pre-processing and post-processing best practices embedded in CrashLab. The first column contained a description of the CrashLab best practice. The second column documented the parameter that was changed. A third column calculated the percentage by which the best practice was violated. The purpose of this was to give the reader of the report confidence in how close the model used to generate the results was to an ideal test case. Larger percentages of deviation might mean that the results wouldn't be reproducible or widely generalizable. What Jason was most concerned about, however, was not the inherent generalizability of the findings, but that the reviewer of the report would know exactly how the results could be used to make predictions about a vehicle's crashworthiness.

By mid 1998, the collaboration between Jason's team and the engineers at Link Software finally paid off in the form of a fully functional prototype of the virtual bumper module for CrashLab. The engineers in R&D were extremely enthusiastic about the results. They felt that they had succeeded in building a simple, intuitive technology that would help increase the credibility of math-based analysis at Autoworks. R&D tested the technology, using it to set up, run, and analyze a model for the 581 load case. The results were very promising. R&D managers were also quite pleased. Because CrashLab proved to be a workable module for the larger IVDA concept, management was eager to provide funding to bring the project to production if Jason could convince the Focus Group to adopt it. Jason was confident that, with a working prototype in hand, he could finally convince the Focus Group that the concept was viable. In the spring of 1998, emboldened by support from the R&D Division, Jason pitched the idea for CrashLab to the Crash Focus Group a second time. His presentation was quite similar to the one he had made almost three years earlier, but this time, at the end of his talk, Jason pulled out a secret weapon: a working prototype.

In attendance at the Focus Group meeting, as usual, were Sunil Kitane, Brad Bertallini, and Barry Glenn from the Safety Division, Jensen Lu from Techpro, and Kaleeb Azbad from Infoserv. Unfortunately, the Focus Group's members remained unimpressed by the new prototype. Reflecting on Jason's presentation some years later, Jensen Lu commented:

> I remember really liking CrashLab, and I was pleased but not surprised to see that Jason was able to execute on his proof of concept. But the problem that I had was that it seemed like it did just what he told us it would do the last time we discussed it at the Focus Group. I just couldn't see how it would fit into the two-day FE process. I know that sounds strange now, but at the time, it just didn't seem like it would fit. I'm not sure why I thought that, but everyone else there sort of agreed that it wasn't what they were looking for.

Other members of the Focus Group had similar reactions. Although they were pleased with the work Jason and his team had accomplished, Crash-Lab didn't seem align with the problems they had developed in each of their respective organizations. Thus, the prototype alone was insufficient, in Star's terms, as a boundary object: It didn't translate the R&D group's desire to solve the credibility problem into a logic that could be understood from the vantage point of the technological frames held by the other organizations. Much to Jason's dismay, the Focus Group again voted not to immediately endorse CrashLab for live production, and not to distribution it in the crashworthiness group.

Crafting a Multivocal Logic

Why was it that the members of the Focus Group couldn't see the potential utility of CrashLab? What blinded them from conceptualizing CrashLab as a tool that could "solve" the particular problems they had developed within each of their organizations? From an objective standpoint, Crash-Lab could be seen as a multifaceted solution to these problems. For the crashworthiness group, CrashLab had the potential to solve the accuracy problem by making sure that all models were set up precisely as physical prototypes were set up at the proving grounds. This concordance in procedure would lead to a better correlation between math-based models and physical tests. CrashLab did, however, lack the functionality to identify part penetrations and streamline the sizing of a mesh. In response to Techpro's speed problem, CrashLab promised to relieve analysts of the tedious tasks of model building and analysis. With the new technology, engineers would no longer have to search for FMVSS criteria when setting up a model, and automating procedures using scripts would ensure that models could be built faster than they could be by hand. However, the CrashLab prototype didn't provide a clear argument with which to convince engineers in the International Operations group to keep model building "in house," because a cost-saving ratio for the technology hadn't been clearly defined. In regard to the capacity problem developed by Infoserv, CrashLab had the potential to reduce the number of simulations necessary to evaluate a vehicle (thereby leading to shorter queues at the High Performance Computing Center), since more accurate procedures for setup and analysis would mean a higher degree of correlation between physical tests and virtual models. However, CrashLab wouldn't reduce the size of the models (that is, the number of elements) that had to be processed at the High Performance Computing Center. It also added yet another technology to a list of tools at Autoworks that was already too long.

Even though CrashLab promised a number of ways to overcome the separate problems developed by the Focus Group's members, individuals from the three other groups didn't see how CrashLab could solve their individual problems. If the members of these groups had weighed the technology's advantages and disadvantages and made a conscious decision that it just didn't have the capability to solve their problems, their decision to reject the new technology would be understandable. Instead, members of the Focus Group didn't—or perhaps couldn't—see CrashLab's potential for solving their problems. Sunil Kitane commented:

I wasn't alone, you know— not being sure of what CrashLab had to offer. I mean, I saw the prototype, and it looked good, but for some reason it didn't resonate with me that this could make the work more accurate. I think part of the problem was that maybe it was how Jason pitched it or something. It just didn't click. You know?

Why didn't CrashLab click? Jason clearly wanted it to succeed, and he was politically savvy enough to know that he had to sell his idea to the group in a way that would make them see the advantages of the new technology. In fact, Jason pitched CrashLab relying not on rhetoric but on faith that the technology would speak for itself. He was confident that once the members of the Focus Group saw CrashLab's features they would immediately recognize its utility. Without rhetoric aimed at convincing the Focus Group that CrashLab could fix the credibility problem, one would expect CrashLab to function rather well as a boundary object. In this sense, CrashLab was generic enough to allow each individual member of the Focus Group to interpret the technology from his or her own vantage point. SCOT researchers (Kline and Pinch 1996; Pinch and Bijker 1984) would argue that CrashLab was interpretatively flexible—plastic enough to contain multiple meanings for multiple audiences. But during Jason's presentation to the Focus Group, CrashLab was ineffective at serving as a boundary object, in large part, because it didn't seem to promote contextually specific interpretations of its functionality. As Thomas (1994, p. 207) suggests, when new technologies emerge as exogenous developments "they will attract attention only to the extent that they can be assimilated within an interpretive framework already resident in the organization."

Up until that point, what Jason had been unable to do successfully was semantically articulate his vision of CrashLab in a way that resonated within technological frames different from his own. That is, without positioning the perceived usefulness of CrashLab in alternative technological frames, he had been unable to help the members of the Focus Group overcome the interpretive barriers that conceptually separated them and promoted their differences. What Jason's prototype did do, though, was get them talking. When Jason presented the concept in 1995, it was easy for the Focus Group to dismiss his idea, which one focus member called "energetic but offering little utility," as little more than a figment of Jason's imagination. But by the spring of 1998, faced with a fully functional prototype, the Focus Group couldn't simply dismiss a concept; they had to dismiss a working piece of technology. This may seem a trivial point, but in practice the prototype had a permanence that Jason's conceptual explanation did not. Consequently, when the members of the Focus Group left the meeting, they took with them a mental image of the new technology and its functionality. Jensen Lu noted:

We said No to [CrashLab], but I would think about it. I watched Jason run through the 581 procedure, and it looked simple. It was a nice piece of software, and it could be useful, so I thought about it and what it did.

Kaleeb Azbad from Infoserv recounted a similar experience of thinking about the technology after leaving the meeting:

I remember even a few weeks later thinking what [Jason] did was pretty cool. I'd never seen anything like that before. It was something worth thinking about—how you could automate that work. Like I said, it was pretty cool and very innovative.

Very soon after Jason unveiled his prototype to the Focus Group, Infoserv hired a new senior manager to work in the CAE Department. Anthony Bernardo came to Autoworks in 1998 from another major auto company based in Michigan. Anthony's background was rare among members of the Infoserv group. He had spent more than fifteen years working as a CAE engineer before moving to the data-management and technological-infrastructure side of the business. His experience building and analyzing math models gave him a profound appreciation for the tedious task of model setup and analysis. He also knew that no matter how careful an engineer was, it was quite common to obtain simulation results one day and be unable to successfully reproduce them the next. Shortly after Anthony arrived in Infoserv, he took stock of the projects in development and the suite of tools currently in use in the CAE groups. During one of his early meetings with Kaleeb, he learned about R&D's prototype for CrashLab. Finding the concept interesting, he scheduled a meeting with Jason so as to see the tool for himself. As a newcomer to Infoserv, and to Autoworks in general, Anthony wasn't deeply inscribed in an institutionally defined technological frame. In Bijker's (1995a) terms, Anthony had a relatively low degree of inclusion in the technological frame that dominated the Infoserv Division. What Anthony saw in CrashLab wasn't necessarily a technology that could fix a problem, since as a newcomer he wasn't yet exactly aware of the problems that people believed existed. Instead, he saw CrashLab as a technology that could fill a larger void in the broader world of computer-aided engineering: the need for standardization. As Anthony commented, CrashLab held the promise of standardizing the work of disparate engineers with its capabilities for automation:

Well, I think [CrashLab] . . . is a way of capturing the standard. I mean, you know, if you look, go back in engineering organizations, the way they used to do it was the standards were in the standards book and they were on a shelf someplace; and so, you know, you can follow the standards. You have to go look them up, you have a complicated process. You're running maybe fifteen, twenty different safety load cases. You want to look it up or you just want to have the process basically in front of you. So, I think that it really helps get the standard work in front of the engineer on a daily basis.

At the Focus Group's next meeting, Anthony resurrected CrashLab. He told the group he believed the software could help "standardize" work at Autoworks, a term that was quite powerful largely because of its ambiguity. Standardization can simultaneously mean many things. From one perspective, it can be viewed as a means of increasing uniformity of action (e.g.. cars driving on the same side of the road). From another, it can be seen to increase speed (e.g., one doesn't have to look around for alternatives). From yet another perspective, standardization can be seen to reduce waste (e.g., common-size nuts and bolts save industries millions of dollars each year). The rhetoric of standardization is strong in many professions, from manufacturing (Walker and Guest 1952) and medicine (Bosk 1979) to laboratory science (Mukerji 1998) and engineering (Shapiro 1997). But the intended benefits of standardization depend on the needs of those who wish to employ them in the practice of their work (Lyytinen and King 2006). In this sense, the rhetoric of standardization can be seen to produce a multivocal logic. Padgett and Ansell (1993) describe multivocal logics as a singularly professed orientation that can be interpreted coherently from multiple perspectives simultaneously. In other words, two people who share the logic of standardization may very well agree that standardization is a desired goal—or even necessary—while holding very different ideas about what standardization actually means. As Padgett and Ansell describe, a multivocal logic typically arises when a few actors are able to express their interests in such a general and protean way that each community believes that the actors represent their interests almost exclusively. The authors describe Cosimo de' Medici, the notorious hub at the center of the budding Florentine Renaissance state in the fifteenth century, as the prime example of such an actor. Cosimo and his party sat at the nexus of a heterogeneous network of contradictory interests. He became the hero of the Florentine elite communities because he created a multivocal logic that led diverse groups of continuants to believe that he was on their side, and was therefore able to use his position to unite the disparate groups to create a great nation-state.

Anthony Bernardo was certainly no Cosimo de' Medici. But whether Anthony's rhetoric of standardization was a consequence of planning or fortuitousness, it resonated with members of Safety, Techpro, Infoserv, and R&D. Anthony's description of what it means to standardize work clearly exhibits this multivocal character:

Well, I've been involved in CAE for a long time, as a very heavy user myself at one point in time. And, you know, actually, kind of, I think probably my lifelong goal is to make CAE an important part of the vehicle development process, which I think it can greatly enhance and support the vehicle development process. And there were two things that I always felt held that up, one more than the other. The largest one was that it took too long to build models and get the analysis done, so the speed was a big issue, and the consistency of the results, you know, so that you could correlate it back to test. Because, you know, I mean, you can take a finite element model and I can find a way to make it match the test results, but it might not match the physics; it may be a mathematical match, but it's not capturing the physics properly. So, once you learn how to capture the physics properly, you get a good correlation. How do you ensure that everybody builds a model like that when you have 1,200 users spread out around the world? So, I viewed CrashLab as a way to help guide us down the direction of solving this problem of no standardization.

Because Anthony's rhetorical positioning of the idea of standardization was so vague, each of the organizations represented in the Focus Group was able to couch its specific problems in Anthony's terms. Thus, when he proposed that the Focus Group endorse CrashLab because it could make standardization a reality, each group began, for the first time, to see CrashLab as a potential solution to its problem. Consider the following reactions:

Sunil Kitane Anthony came sort of late to the process, but I think his contribution that was the best was to make clear that CrashLab could do more than what Jason said, because it could also standardize the work. That really was what we were after, you know, to create a parallel between physical test labs like the Testville proving grounds crash-test laboratory that we use and CrashLab. And in our minds at that time, we were saying a physical vehicle gets built somewhere and we ship it to the proving grounds, and after that, we do everything there: we set it up properly for the proper test that we need run on it; for the dummies, we use the right barrier, the right speed, the right instrumentation. And we run the test, we write a report, and the engineer walks away with a report and with a film now, digitally recorded information. . . . The parallel would be that, once you get the design information, rather than building it, you make a math model of it. Once that model is built, you bring all that into this CrashLab environment and then do everything—physical tests that we do—down to the point of writing a report, generating a report with a standard output format, so that the engineer can look at those results and not have to say "You know, I needed this information, that information." All that comes out as a standard template.

Jensen Lu Standardization and automation—so important; in a nutshell, because of consistency and speed. . . . When you run a test like frontal impact, it's not just you get a car and do whatever you want with it. There is a very rigorous step-by-step procedure that [an analyst] needs to follow to prepare the vehicle, to position the dummy, to instrument the dummy and the vehicle, to set up the test vehicle with some initial conditions. You want everyone to do the simulation in the same way, a standard way; that way the work happens faster. Then you can also talk about sending work abroad and doing work sharing with other engineering centers. If everybody does it in the same way, it doesn't matter who does it in which location. This way, you obviously do it faster; you eliminate the possibility of human variation. I think these are the main drivers.

Tai-Lap Leung   The idea was that if we can standardize the process, you don't have that many things you need to consider. So in a way, it depends on the technical difficulty. Everybody is [building and analyzing models] in their own way and in their own time. You don't have so-called standard procedures, and so sometimes some of the tasks are more difficult in the crash analysis, and people are not aware that you have this feature where you can do this. So we said "You can put the standard practice into the environment, because you are forced to use the CrashLab, so you'll follow the standard procedure, and whenever we know there's a better way of doing it, we update the CrashLab and you have standard practice in the organization and redo the learning curve for the engineers."

Standardization was powerful precisely because of its multivocality. Each member of the Focus Group could express the type of problem his or her group had developed in the logic the term created. Hence, Anthony's move to create a logic of standardization that enveloped everyone's understanding of what CrashLab could do allowed them to view the technology as a potential solution to their problems. The multivocality of the logic also made it possible for the groups to believe that they all shared a common problem CrashLab could solve. As Brad Bertallini commented, such recognition was prime motivation for wanting to bring CrashLab to the production environment:

We discovered that the lack of standardization was a problem that cut across functional areas at Autoworks, and what was better was that there was a tool that could potentially fix it. You see, standardization and automation go hand and hand. Once you automate something like CrashLab could do, it had to be standardized, and once you standardized something, you could easily automate it. So CrashLab showed some good promise as long as we could build some more functionality into it. It could solve the standardization problem.

The "standardization problem" was now defined as an issue common to many different groups at Autoworks. But no one ever sat down to discuss exactly what standardization meant. Instead, each group interpreted the idea in light of the particular problem it had developed, and each group believed that when other groups talked about standardization they were referring to the same problem. This is precisely why the multivocal logic proved so powerful. Each group felt that its needs would be met by a technology that would standardize and subsequently automate engineering work, yet each group had a different need. Had any one member of the

Focus Group probed deep enough to uncover what his colleagues meant when they talked about CrashLab fixing the "standardization problem," he would have quickly discovered that there was much less consensus of opinion than had previously been thought. But such probing didn't occur, and after a few weeks of email discussions, the Focus Group was abuzz with excitement about CrashLab's potential to solve a major problem for math-based analysis: standardization.

Generating a Transversal Structure

By the winter of 1998, the Focus Group had given Jason the green light to develop a second module for CrashLab: a virtual frontal-impact test laboratory to prepare and analyze a model for the FMVSS 208 standards. Although the Focus Group still hadn't officially endorsed the project, Jason was able to secure additional funds from R&D and Infoserv to continue exploration related to the development of the new module. Under the logic of standardization that now permeated the discourse of the Focus Group, Crash-Lab held great potential. Yet the Focus Group still wasn't ready to officially endorse the project, because, as Sunil pointed out, there was one crucial link missing. Before CrashLab could standardize the work, standards had to be created:

The problem that I and some others had with CrashLab was that, I mean, at that time, we didn't even have anything standardized. We didn't have standard practices. But we knew that they were important, and we wanted to get them standardized. And so, we felt early on that the biggest reason we wanted to do standard work was to minimize human error, it just had to be minimized. If we are ever going to have math lead the design and reduce our reliance on physical testing, we had to standardize the way we do the simulation work. So, that's where originally the idea was. How can we take physical testing out of our mix of work that we do? And, how can we be more accurate on the math? And the whole question of quality and accuracy of the results is what drove us to know that the engineers had to start doing the work the same way.

In short, before CrashLab could automate standard procedures, Autoworks had to define what those standard procedures were. Jason had been working with his team in R&D to define the standard work procedures on his own on the basis of his experience working with the Truck Department. But, as Ron Clark (an engineer in the Strut Group who worked with Jason during his sabbatical) noted, Jason wasn't the best person to be creating standards for crashworthiness analysts:

Don't get me wrong, Jason is a great guy, and he showed real promise when he was over here doing crash work. But he's not a crash engineer. I mean, his job is to advance the state of the art with the tools, but he definitely doesn't know what the latest practices and techniques are. He shouldn't. That's our job. He only did it for a bit, so whatever he comes up with is mostly just by following the requirements and then thinking about what the best thing to do is.

Logic would suggest that, if Jason wasn't a good candidate to define the standard procedures because he lacked experience doing the work himself, a well-respected senior engineer in the crashworthiness group would serve the role well. The problem with having an analyst write the standards was that it took time—one precious commodity the crashworthiness analysts didn't have. Analysts, who raced daily to meet hard-and-fast vehicle development deadlines, couldn't take time away from their regular work to document standards. Thus, to be able to create standard work practices, it would be necessary to institute organizational change.

In early 1999, on the Focus Group's recommendation, Gene Anderson and Barry Glenn, directors of the Car Department and the Truck Department, and Randy Johnson, vice-president for Global Engineering Process, approved the creation of a new engineering department at Autoworks called Best Practice Evaluation (Bestpra). The goal of this new department was to create and maintain standard procedures for crashworthiness analysis within the company. Structurally, the Bestpra group sat outside of regular engineering production work at Autoworks. On Autoworks' organization chart (figure 3.1), Bestpra fell under Autoworks' Structure Integration Department, which was responsible for developing concepts for future vehicles and performing initial feasibility studies for new products.

Because of this affiliation, Bestpra didn't face the time constraints that engineers in the Safety Division constantly battled. The new group instead functioned almost as a miniature R&D lab that was dedicated full-time to the study of crashworthiness work. Bestpra had a staff of six engineers, each of whom specialized in a different nonlinear loading condition: frontal impact, side impact, rear impact, occupant protection, pedestrian protection, and vehicle rollover. Gene Anderson and Barry Glenn selected all six of the analysts for Bestpra because, according to Gene, they were some of the brightest engineers, but they all had trouble meeting deadlines:

Why did we put those folks over there? Because they're good; they're brilliant, technically very apt. But they never got anything done on time, so we can't have them working on a program, or if we can give them longer-based development things, it may take six months or a year and they can handle one task at a time. They're very good engineers, but they just don't understand the urgency the user has to get this done in two days, two months, two weeks, whatever it is.

I call this new Bestpra Department a transversal structure because it perpendicularly intersected with the other four groups responsible for new-technology development at Autoworks. Unlike the Focus Group, which contained members from four different organizations at Autoworks, Bestpra didn't contain members from diverse corners of the company. But the kind of work Bestpra performed cut across all the other functions. In a sense, Bestpra interacted directly with members of all the other groups but didn't report directly to any of them. Their primary responsibility was to develop standard work practices and technologies to foster the efficiency and accuracy of crashworthiness engineering. Thanks to this structural arrangement, Bestpra was in a special position at Autoworks. It was the outgrowth of the Focus Group's decision to promote standardized work, yet Bestpra could influence the Focus Group's decisions about the kinds of practices undertaken in the Safety Division and could make or break a technology such as CrashLab depending on the robustness and efficaciousness of the work procedures it was able to create.

Each of Bestpra's six engineers was given the title of Subject-Matter Expert (SME). An SME's role was to collect information from Safety's analysts in order to determine the most appropriate and efficient standard procedures for a specific type of analysis related to the SME's area of expertise. The SMEs first attempted creating standardized guidelines with the help of an innovation from one of Autoworks' engineering centers in Germany. In early 1999, when SME Arnold Dong, a former crashworthiness engineer for the Piston Group, returned to the United States from assignment at the German engineering center, he brought with him an innovation used by the German crashworthiness analysts called a *virtual prototype chart*. The VP chart was a simple table that listed all the outputs that were essential for understanding the dynamics of a math-based simulation. More specifically, the chart listed the variables an analyst had to resolve during a test. Knowing the variables before beginning the analysis allowed analysts to work backward, setting up a model proactively to obtain the results they needed. As Arnold suggested, the VP chart was itself quite subjective—the product of an engineer's intuition and judgment—but it at least served as a codified representation of the type of information engineers, as a whole, believed was important to obtain in order to determine a vehicle's crashworthiness. Using the VP chart as a guide, SMEs in the Bestpra Department had a starting point from which to work to develop standards. Since they knew what kinds of outputs an analyst required, they could develop standard procedures to lead the analyst to generate those outputs. With the help of the VP chart, drawing on their experience as analysts in the Safety Division and on the experience of their friends who still worked as analysts, the SMEs slowly began documenting standard best practices for setting up and analyzing models for specific crash load cases.

A typical process document crafted by the SMEs consisted of nearly twenty pages instructing analysts on practices ranging from routine mesh generation to more detailed and load-case-specific practices, such as how to position the barrier in relation to the vehicle and how to write the appropriate contact cards (for the DYNA input deck) to specify how the solver should interpret this relationship. The procedures were outlined in great detail, and although the SMEs roughly translated the FMVSS guidelines, those guidelines specified only vehicle instrumentation and setup procedures for physical crash tests. Essentially, the SMEs were the first to document guidelines to "standardize" model building and analysis at Autoworks. Perhaps the most important conceptual move the SMEs made when they documented the standard procedures, at least as it pertains to the development of CrashLab, was creating a flow chart to outline the process for model building and analysis (figure 5.1).

In March of 1999, Bestpra published its first set of standard engineering procedures. The documentation applied to evaluating frontal load cases. Jason and his group used the best practices outlined in the document to determine how to automate the process of setting up and analyzing a math model to test FMVSS 208 specifications. Working with the engineers at Link Software, Autoworks' R&D Division implemented the new process in the virtual frontal-impact test module. By late 1999, the Focus Group was very happy with CrashLab's progress. As Jensen Lu observed, the Focus Group had come to an agreement that CrashLab would be very important to the work of crashworthiness analysts:

Once we had the 208 prototype under way, things were looking good. The problem was, before, we had a concept for a tool that would automate crash work. But we didn't have any standards, so we couldn't do automation. But that changed when Bestpra was created, because they came up with the standards CrashLab could automate. So everyone was pretty happy and liked what was happening. I think everyone was excited about the possibility of the two-day FE process that CrashLab could help achieve in combination with RMA and some other tools.

Although all of the Focus Group's members were now equally enthusiastic about CrashLab, and although they now saw it as a viable tool, each member of the group was excited for different reasons, as these comments by Senior Crashworthiness Engineering Manager Brad Bertallini suggest:

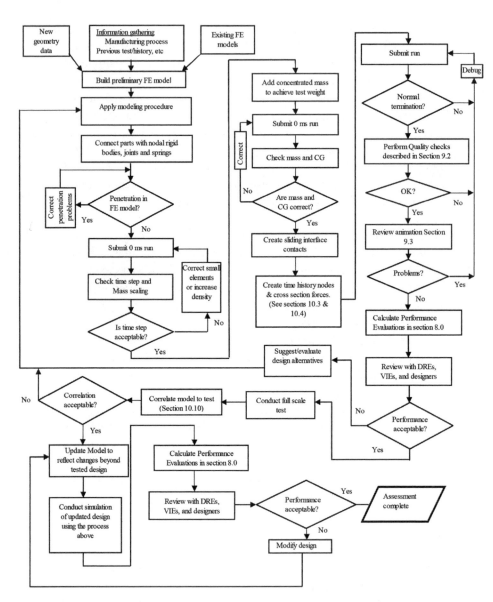

Figure 5.1

Flow chart of model building and analysis for frontal offset deformable barrier (ODB) test.

After Bestpra was formed and started churning out the standard work procedures, that's when CrashLab really took off. Everyone at the Focus Group made it a top priority, and it took up most of our discussion time. I think everyone was just really energized that it would make math-based work more accurate and help us get better correlations, and then make more of an impact in the design process.

Through the processes of developing a prototype, crafting a multivocal logic of standardization, and creating a transversal structure in Bestpra that could simultaneously meet the needs of all four organizations at Autoworks without reporting directly to any one of them, the Focus Group's members achieved conceptual integration. Eventually, they were able to come to an agreement: CrashLab would play a very important role in the transformation of crashworthiness-engineering work at Autoworks.

Organizational Disengagement

Although conceptual integration was necessary for Focus Group's members to align their technological frames, alone it wasn't enough to allow engineers at Autoworks to develop the technology that would eventually become CrashLab. Through the processes of developing a prototype, crafting a multivocal logic of standardization, and creating the transversal Bestpra organization, Safety, Techpro, Infoserv, and R&D were able to come to a conceptual agreement on the kind of technology that had to be developed to make math-based analysis more central to the process of designing vehicles. However, as communications researchers have long noted, conceptual agreement that is successfully sustained only through rhetoric often fails when it moves from a rhetorical space into one of practice (Bormann 1996; Deetz 1997). In other words, the Focus Group's members created a rhetorical blanket under which the idea of standardization was able to flourish; however, when it came time to actually build CrashLab, problems arose that revealed the existing but heretofore unacknowledged differences of opinion about what standardization actually meant.

As one example of this emerging conflict, Jensen Lu (who conceived of standardization as a way of increasing the speed of model setup and analysis) recalled a conversation he had had with Jason Chan (who saw standardization as a means to increase the credibility of math-based results) about the flow chart Jason had asked Link Software to incorporate into the prototype's GUI:

Jason and I would talk about the features we needed to work on for CrashLab, and I told him I was afraid the flowchart would take too much time for the users to go through and we should just think about getting rid of it. But he was all, you know, upset or not happy about that because he was saying that [not having the flow chart] would encourage analysts to do things all different from one another. But it's like, what is more important? We're standardizing [the work] so it goes faster, so it doesn't make sense to put in features that would detract from that goal.

Jason's opinion on the matter reflects a very different understanding of what it meant to standardize crashworthiness work:

Some people didn't get it. We say we are to standardize, and CrashLab does that to make the work more credible for engineers so everyone does the same thing and we don't have ten engineers doing the process ten ways. The flow chart was important, but I remember some people in Techpro didn't like it and didn't think it was helping and that it was a waste of resources or something. But [the flow chart] is essential to the process to standardize it. What is the point of speeding things up if we only speed up inconsistencies?

Clearly, when it came time to talk more specifically about CrashLab in order to determine what features were necessary to successfully standardize and automate model building and analysis, the collective facade of agreement that shrouded individual definitions of standardization began breaking down.

At this point, disagreement could have very easily led to CrashLab's being put on hold or discontinued. But, at least at a broad level, conceptual integration was maintained as organizations began disengaging from the development process. Through the practices of withholding information, redefining responsibilities, and reorganizing personnel, R&D and Safety's involvement in CrashLab's development quickly began to fade, thereby reducing the influence of their definitions of standardization on the selection of features for incorporation in the technology, and ultimately on the way work would be carried out within the Safety Division.

Withholding Information

In considering the way work is accomplished within organizations, Anselm Strauss (1978, 1988) suggests that manipulation—not revealing everything about one's goal or plan—is essential. If everyone in an organization knew one another's goals from the outset, and consequently knew the ways in which others' goals contradicted their own, too much opposition would exist for work to successfully continue. Strauss suggests that, for this reason, members of an organization must often be selective about the information they share about their goals, and about with whom they share it and when. Similarly, Eric Eisenberg (1984, 1987) has argued that successful organizational communication is often laced with a fair amount of strategic ambiguity. 'Strategic ambiguity' refers to instances in which members of an organization are purposely ambiguous about their goals. By selectively withholding some information about a particular topic, or by speaking in abstract terms that make it difficult for the listener to fully grasp the complexity of the message, organizational actors are often able to succeed in implementing programs of change that would otherwise be contentious or opposed. To preserve the conceptual integration that was achieved among members of the Focus Group during CrashLab's development while simultaneously moving forward with building the technology, the practice of withholding important information about a particular organization's goals or procedures became critical. During the development process, information about three important decisions was withheld from members of the other organizations: the decision to build more load-case modules into CrashLab, the decision to eliminate users' discretion, and the decision to integrate CrashLab into an existing third-party proprietary technology already in use at Autoworks.

From Techpro's standpoint, the demonstration of the virtual frontal-impact test lab module was proof that CrashLab could be used to automate nearly any crashworthiness load case. In fact, as Jensen Lu commented, the more load cases CrashLab automated, the more potential it possessed to increase the speed with which math models were built and analyzed:

If you think about CrashLab on the bigger scale, you need to think about analysts doing crash analysis on the entire vehicle. What good is a two-day FE process only for frontal impact? Not much. We need all the crash load cases to be automated to make this happen. So when we first took on the CrashLab project, my first goal was to think about implementing as many load cases as possible. That was the first priority. Implement the load case and make sure it works first, then you can go back and make them more accurate if you need to later. But we needed to just get them in there.

The goal of incorporating more load cases into CrashLab was supported by the work of Bestpra at the time. The SMEs, who had already developed the standard procedures for the 208 load case, were working on developing standard procedures for other load cases too. In fact, the group was organized so that each engineer focused on one particular set of load cases. Thus, from Techpro's perspective, not only was implementing more load cases into CrashLab feasible; it was warranted by the fact that Bestpra was diligently working to write the standards for them. At a Techpro staff meeting in late 1999, Jensen Lu presented the Focus Group's latest plans for CrashLab, which included completing a module for FMVSS 581 by January of 2000 and modules for FMVSS 201, 214, 216, and 301 by 2001. One of Jensen's slides illustrated his lofty goal of implementing all FMVSS regulations for frontal-impact and side-impact load cases as well as for IIHS and EuroNCAP tests for frontal and side impact. For Jensen and the rest of Techpro, extending CrashLab's reach to cover other load cases made good sense, since the goal of standardization was not only to speed up model building and analysis but also to ensure consistency of practice across all of Autoworks' global engineering centers. For example, Techpro hoped that incorporating EuroNCAP regulations would help convince Autoworks' German and Australian engineering centers to use the technology, subsequently reducing the cost of outsourcing model building and decreasing the cycle time for analysis.

At Focus Group meetings there was no mention of Techpro's work to increase the number of testable load cases with CrashLab. Jensen and Techpro knew full well that if they admitted to working with Bestpra to build more modules into CrashLab before refining and augmenting the algorithms for the existing modules, Jason and the R&D engineers wouldn't be happy. Thus, as the Bestpra SME Rob Hickland recalled, the updates Techpro gave the Focus Group seemed intentionally vague:

We were working closely with the people in Mike Johansson's group to implement more load cases in CrashLab, but that seemed to be kept quite. I mean, at the Focus Group meetings, Techpro would talk about working to develop new algorithms, but would sort of leave it at that. I think a lot of people knew that we were aggressively working to get the standard work for IIHS and EuroNCAP into CrashLab, too, but a lot of people didn't know it.

In hindsight, withholding information about implementing additional load cases proved wise. As Jason Chan commented some years later, he would have voiced opposition to the project had he known Techpro wasn't working to enhance the quality of the existing procedures:

The understanding was to make the quality improvements first and define the super users. But now, I look back, and you see the initial procedures are still there. They get into CrashLab once, and then, that's it, no more updates. That defeats the whole concept of a super user. Now what can I do? Nothing. But then, if I knew, I would have said no—that if they didn't take the role of super user seriously, they should not work on CrashLab.

A second area in which Techpro withheld information from R&D about their objectives was with regard to how much discretion an engineer should be afforded when building and analyzing a model in CrashLab. Though Jason originally conceived of automation as a way to ensure that each engineer followed standard practices, he was aware that there were certainly instances in which it was in the best interest not only of the engineer involved but also of the company for an analyst to stray from best practice. The point Jason hoped to make with the standard report format was that deviating from best practices was acceptable so long as it was documented. R&D's decision to allow analysts to override automated procedures embedded in the software was a sign of that group's belief that discretion was an asset rather than a liability, and that engineering institution and knowledge were of the utmost importance to good mathematical simulation. Engineers in Techpro didn't share the same view about allowing analysts a certain level of discretion in model building. As one Techpro engineer commented, allowing the engineer to exercise his or her discretion to deviate from a best practice undermined the very goal of instituting best practices and discounted the importance of SMEs in the Bestpra Department.

We don't want them to deviate. It's a standard procedure—why would you want people to do something different? It's structured that way because we feel that it's the best way to work. If someone has a different idea, they should suggest that to us. We don't want people doing things their own way because they feel their process is better. They should bring that forward so we can think about evaluating it.

By the summer of 2000, Techpro had made the decision to prevent analysts from deviating from Bestpra's best practices as they were embedded in CrashLab. When an analyst used CrashLab to position a barrier or a dummy or to place accelerometers or section cuts in a model, a series of pop-up windows would provide the engineer with exactly the information he needed to determine how to perform the desired operation, then would graphically indicate on the screen how the operation should be conducted. Since the engineers were constrained to best practices, there would no longer be a need for a separate column in the report describing best-practice violations. It would no longer be possible to violate a best practice. One Techpro engineer commented:

The goal was to take as much human involvement out of the process as possible. You still needed the analyst to tell you what the J and K height was, for example, so the software could make the calculation to position the barrier, but that was it. Other than that, we wanted the analyst to not be able to stray away from the procedure we identified from an institutional standpoint as the best practice.

From the perspective of the R&D Division, where standardization was viewed as a path to more credible math-based analysis, best-practice deviation wasn't problematic as long as it was consistently documented in a transparent manner. From the perspective of the Techpro Division, where standardization was viewed as a means to increase speed and consistency, it was a mystery why any automation software would ever allow its operator the discretion to diverge from a best practice. For this reason, Techpro didn't make public the fact that it was increasing Crash-Lab's automation capabilities and systematically changing the report format.

The prototype Jason developed with Link Software was a stand-alone application. This meant that analysts still had to use a pre-processor to translate the CAD geometry into an FE mesh. Once this was complete, the analyst would export the data from the pre-processor into a text file, and then read it into CrashLab. The analyst would set up the model to run in CrashLab, then export the data into a text file that could be read by the DYNA solver. By separating the platforms for pre-processing and CrashLab, Jason and his team in R&D aimed to signal to users that CrashLab performed an entirely different function than a pre-processor. From Infoserv's perspective, the advantages of what a stand-alone tool symbolized for the user didn't make a strong business case. What did make fiscal sense, however, was to use the existing code base of a pre-processing tool and integrate CrashLab as an additional module. That way, Autoworks could provide the vendor with the algorithms it had developed to automate model building and analysis, and Element Software—a new company that Infoserv had contracted—could combine those with its existing source code to take full advantage of ElementMesh's functionality. Thus, not only would integrating CrashLab into ElementMesh instead of building it as a stand-alone application allow Autoworks to take advantage of Element Software's experience pre-processing code; Autoworks also could take advantage of the ease of maintenance afforded by having the same company that updated the code also update CrashLab's functionality for code compatibility.

Though Infoserv had formally decided to drop Link Software as a vendor and migrate to Element Software's platform, the decision wasn't immediately communicated to the Focus Group's members. As Anthony Bernardo explained, the matter had to be dealt with more strategically:

Ultimately, it's our decision to assure that we get the best contract for the best price over the long haul. But people in the Focus Group had vested interests. So we made it clear that we were working to reduce the number of vendors, but we decided not to say explicitly that we were going to go with Element Software until the project had fully migrated over to us. The work Jason was doing with Link Software was still valuable, and we didn't want to make it seem as though we thought it wasn't important.

Fearing that Jason would be upset and might terminate his involvement in the development of the 208 module before it was complete, members of the Infoserv Division decided to sit on their decision to switch tool vendors until they had officially taken over the funding for the project.

Redefining Responsibilities

By April of 2000, responsibility for the production of CrashLab had been officially transferred to Techpro and Infoserv. As the project's owner, Infoserv could now officially announce its decision to contract with Element Software to build a production version of CrashLab. Much to Jason Chan's dismay, Infoserv severed its ties with Link Software. R&D's contract with Link Software had been written in such a way that Autoworks would retain the source code developed by Joel Shannon and his graduate student and any knowledge Autoworks obtained from Link Software about how to render the functions of a process automator software in a GUI format. Link Software could exploit any of the knowledge it had gained from its interaction with Autoworks to develop a technology of its own with a functionality similar to CrashLab's.[5]

The transfer of authority for the CrashLab project also underscored a shift in responsibility that had been in process for some time: With the approval of the Focus Group, Bestpra would now make the final determination regarding the exact order of procedures, or process, that would become CrashLab's foundation. Thus, the responsibilities once solely owned by R&D—to come up with a concept for the technology, to decide how to advance the state of the art, to develop standard procedures for engineers to follow, and to work to see the vision made manifest in a workable piece of software—were now distributed among three groups.

Much as R&D's role in the development of CrashLab had been redefined from that of a "key player" to that of a consultant, the Safety Division's role also began to change. In the organizational hierarchy, the Focus Group fell under Safety, which meant that it took most of its direction from Gene Anderson and Barry Glenn. However, after the Focus Group officially endorsed CrashLab, Techpro and Infoserv were able to assert much more influence in the actual development of the technology. The one remaining area in which the directors of the Safety Division could play a major role was in determining exactly what they wanted CrashLab to do for their department. For more than a year, the Focus Group had been discussing how, through its automation processes, CrashLab would help standardize the work of analysts. Gene Anderson in particular wanted to be sure that standardization was being implemented not just for the sake of standardization, but because it would change the way work was done in the Safety Division:

Sometimes R&D and the Techpro folks build technologies just to build them. But I'm a manager, and if I'm going to implement a new technology [and] disrupt the normal routines of my workers, I want to make sure that technology is going to bring about some change. I told those guys in Mike Johansson's group that the technology better be a change agent. It should help change the work of the crash engineers by making them have to spend less time building and setting up these models.

The idea that analysts should spend less time on routine model building and setup and more time on analysis was widely supported in the Safety Division. The Infoserv Division, too, understood the benefits of such an organizational change. As Anthony Bernardo commented, a new technology was only a means of instigating organizational change:

I mean, the tools should not be the focus of all of our effort. The output of the tool should be where we're working. But this—my reaction to this—this is exactly the root of our problem. Because the tool still does not yield a correlated model, and when the engineers are consulting with each other, they're not talking about how do you get this program to run, or what format do you put your data in, or what is the best time to submit the job. So what the engineers spend their time doing is trying to get models to correlate, and until your model is accurate, we're largely wasting our time.

By automating a large portion of the analysts' pre-processing and post-processing work, the Focus Group intended not only to help analysts work more efficiently but also to bring about significant change in the social organization of work in the crashworthiness group. Most modern engineering organizations make a sharp delineation between activities (such as model building or drafting) that require technical skill but don't require significant intuition and judgment and activities (such as analysis) that require engineers to apply in-depth knowledge of a specific discipline—for example, physics or thermodynamics—to the solving of complex mathematical problems (Brooks 1982; Vincenti 1990). In fact, the boundaries that demarcate most formal roles and responsibilities in engineering organizations—for example, those of design engineers and performance engineers—are drawn around activities related to model building and analysis (Suchman 2000; Vinck 2003). Participation in activities related to analysis places an engineering group at the center of important decisions about product architecture and design. Consequently, most modern engineering organizations seek to increase the amount of analysis they conduct and to reduce the amount of time they spend on routine model building.[6] Thus, shifting the focus from model building to analysis is a significant organizational change for an engineering firm—one that is of great importance and is highly desired (Collins 2003; Downey 1998).

Because such a shift would allow the Safety Division to contribute to design decisions in a more meaningful way, it would also win that division higher status and visibility within the company. Even Jensen Lu was certain that CrashLab would bring about important changes in the social organization of work within the Safety Division:

One of the objectives of automating engineering work is that we want our engineers to spend less time struggling to set up models. If engineers use this tool, they should not have to spend so much time consulting one another about how to set up a model and interpret load cases. CrashLab automates these procedures so engineers don't have to worry about them. We want them to spend more time actually engineering the vehicle, finding solutions to give us better performance and reduce cost and reduce weight, so if they're using the tool, consultation will hopefully happen in different areas. I hope the discussion among crashworthiness analysts will be in areas related to the analysis of their models. I'd rather see one engineer spend thirty minutes or an hour with another engineer saying "Based on your experience, how should I design this bracket?" or "How can I design the structure so it will give me maximum energy absorption?" You know, real engineering questions.

Thus, as the responsibilities of the five groups involved in CrashLab's development were redefined, making Techpro and Infoserv more central to the process and R&D and Safety more ancillary, the logic of standardization began to suggest that CrashLab could occasion an important organizational change that hadn't yet been considered by its developers.

Technical Integration

By the end of 2000, the two divisions most involved in CrashLab's development were Techpro and Information Systems and Services. The disengagement of R&D and Safety marked closure of conceptual agreement on CrashLab's proposed features and on how the technology would change the way analysts worked. With conceptual integration achieved, Techpro and Infoserv could now begin work with Element Software on the specific technical features that would define CrashLab. As Martin Yuen noted, conceptual integration and organizational disengagement had to happen before technical integration could occur:

If you think about the history of CrashLab, you have several organizations at Autoworks working together. Eventually we all sort of came to agreement on what we wanted. That was good, and it was hard work. But once we did it, then we needed to move from talk to action. If everyone stayed involved, it would be, you know, too many chefs in the kitchen, and everyone would have an opinion on how to chop the onions, so they would never get chopped. At least that's how it works at my house. So when R&D took a back seat, we [Techpro] could really sit down and say we're in charge of the technical development now, and here are the things we need to do to get our vision represented in technical form.

Although Techpro was successful in communicating its goals and in giving Element Software clear guidelines outlining the kinds of functions and features Techpro wanted CrashLab to have, Techpro wasn't entirely in charge of the technical integration process. CrashLab's features continued to evolve as Element Software and then Dynamic Software (the next tool vendor to work on the technology) transformed CrashLab's functionality to accommodate its own existing technological infrastructure. In addition, the ways in which Techpro and Infoserv tested the technology to ensure that it met their needs influenced the final configuration of its features.

Accommodating Technical Features

One of the primary reasons Infoserv decided to contract with Element Software to build the production version of CrashLab was because Infoserv wanted to use as much of Element Software's existing code as it could. Many of the basic computational functions needed to run CrashLab (e.g., rotating the model, zooming in, and selecting nodes) were functions that already existed in ElementMesh and could be migrated into a CrashLab module. Though the advantages of using the existing functionality of Element Software's software were obvious, several less obvious disadvantages didn't surface until Element Software coded the CrashLab module.

Element Software used Tcl/Tk programming language to script the commands for ElementMesh. Tcl (Tool Command Language) was originally developed as a reusable command language for experimental CAD tools. The interpreter was implemented as a C library that could be linked to any application. It was very easy to add new functions to the Tcl interpreter, so Tcl was an ideal reusable "macro language" that could be integrated into many applications. Tk is a GUI toolkit for Tcl that produces native applications that run unchanged on both Windows and UNIX platforms. Although Tcl/Tk provided the advantage of a dual common-language toolkit that was easy to learn and very easy to use to run programs, it had several notable disadvantages. Tcl/Tk's inability to handle large amounts of memory forced coders to alter several of the file structures in CrashLab. Techpro engineers envisioned that, as a user proceeded through Crash-

Lab's flow chart, the program would remember each of the actions the user took during each step. The idea was that an analyst could move through the flow chart to set CrashLab up to run a frontal NCAP test and then use the same file to run a frontal ODB (offset deformable barrier) test. However, because Tcl/TK's memory was limited, a new file would have to be created for each type of test. This meant that an engineer who was responsible for frontal-impact analysis and was running three different tests (e.g., FMVSS 208, IIHS ODB, and EuroNCAP) would have to go through the entire process of setting up a model for each test. Although this situation was less than ideal, it still marked a dramatic improvement over executing the process manually. However, for Techpro engineers, this was an unfortunate setback, because it meant that model setup wouldn't be as fast as it could have been.

An even more important change in CrashLab's functionality concerned the flow chart, a part of the GUI that Autoworks envisioned would serve as a visual guide for analysts. Jason had originally designed the concept of the flow chart (which was then developed by the SMEs in the Bestpra Department) to visually guide the user through the appropriate steps. However, ElementMesh was configured with a "wizard" structure. The wizard presented a window that would pop up to tell the user what activity should be performed. Once the user had performed that specific activity, he or she clicked the "next" button, and a new window popped up to indicate the next set of required operations. The wizard followed an embedded tree structure that wasn't made visually apparent to the user. In other words, the order of operations was embedded in ElementMesh's script but wasn't rendered as a graphical representation, or a flow chart, for the user to follow.

Element Software's wizard structure had two important implications for CrashLab.

First, it downplayed the symbolic importance of the workflow, or order of steps, which Jason had initially hoped to make visible for all engineers. Tai-Lap Leung, who worked with Element Software to build the interface for CrashLab, commented on his frustration with ElementMesh's wizard structure:

Working with Element Software, it was similar to the early part of the Link Software thing in that Element Software wanted to modify the way that it was done so that it fit into their framework of doing this kind of thing. So, whereas Link Software had kind of a JAVA-based visualization type of interface where they could bring things in like that, Element Software had a Windows wizard type of interface with the user. So they wanted to turn all of the things that we had into this wizard type of interface. All of the other products they were operating were more wizard-based things to give a common interface. You know, like I said, they wanted to do this wizard-based thing, and we would often say "I'm not sure if this is going to work with what we're trying to accomplish with this particular tool. Like the flow chart things, we want the users to be able to see a flow chart of the process, both the steps that are in the past and the steps that are in the future."

Despite Tai-Lap's exhortations to change the wizard structure because it lacked a visual representation of the process for the analyst (the "poking here and there," as Jason once called it), the wizard structure persisted—in large part, because it wasn't cost-effective for Element Software to change its process template for one tiny module in its large suite of tools.

The second consequence of the wizard structure was that it a user couldn't go back and redo one of the previous steps without undoing all the steps that followed it. For example, if an analyst positioned a barrier, placed accelerometers, and then took section cuts (in that order, following the ElementMesh wizard), then recognized that he had imported the wrong barrier for his analysis, he would have to undo the determination of section cuts and the placement of accelerometers. In a flow-chart format, such as the Link Software version of CrashLab had, the analyst could simply click on the step he or she wished to repeat without undoing any work. Both Tai-Lap and Martin feared that users would resist a technology that forced them to redo an entire process if they chose to fix one small decision. However, Element Software's wizard architecture wouldn't allow any changes to the operation of the module.

Although Element Software forced several major changes to Crash-Lab's functionality to accommodate ElementMesh's existing architecture, Techpro strategically chose to include a number of other features to meet its own goals. For example, as has already been mentioned, Techpro didn't agree with Jason that analysts should have the discretion to stray from the best practices outlined by Bestpra. When creating the requirement-specifications document for Element Software, Jensen Lu, working closely with Martin Yuen, specifically instructed Element Software to limit the user's ability to place accelerometers and make section cuts only at the locations outlined in the standard work documents. One of these specifications documents indicated that accelerometers and section cuts should be automatically "snapped" to predefined nodes, and that Element Software should include a model-checking function in its interface and automated job-submission and report-generation functions. Techpro insisted that the report CrashLab automatically generated should include all relevant information outlined in the VP chart.

The section cuts A,B,C,D are computed based on the logic given in URS. User can drag these section cuts along its normal direction. Confirm the section by clicking OK.

3.3.12   *Rocker Section Cut*

Step1:

Locate Rocker section cut by its standard group name
ROCKER_SECTION_CUT_GROUP, and highlight the parts connected to this group.

[handwritten: I thought we decided we needed to let the user change orientation of cross section]

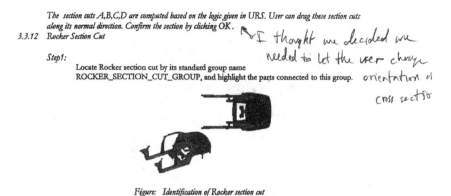

Figure: Identification of Rocker section cut

Step2:

At 20%,70% and 90% from Minimum X value of the Rocker cut 3 sections.

Step3:

Allow user to modify the sections.
All the selected section to contain all the parts that are used to define the Rocker

Figure 5.2
Tai-Lap's notation indicating his concern about constraints placed on locating section cuts.

At various points during the development process, Element Software provided periodic updates on its progress with CrashLab. On one occasion, Tai-Lap, who wasn't involved in creating the requirement specifications document, observed that Element Software had specified that users didn't have discretion to change the placement of an accelerometer or the locations of section cuts. Tai-Lap was confused. In his work with R&D over the previous several years, Jason always had emphasized that allowing the user discretion to change the placement of accelerometers and the locations of section cuts was an important aspect of the ideology behind CrashLab. Tai-Lap marked up the document with his question (figure 5.2) and sent it back to Element Software. A technician at Element Software informed him that the requirement-specifications document indicated that the location of section cuts should be determined by the procedures outlined in the standard work document provided by Bestpra, and that the user wasn't supposed to be able to make modifications to this procedure. Tai-Lap went to Jensen Lu and voiced his concern that removing users' discretion from the process violated one of the main principles of CrashLab. As Tai-Lap learned, however, Jensen and the other senior managers in Techpro didn't share his concern:

I remember talking about this to some people, and nobody cared. They were saying that the process would not be standard or as fast if users could modify it. But the whole reason we [in R&D] did this was because the transparency was important. Like we said, it didn't matter exactly what the user did as long as you know what he did. That is what gave the simulation credibility of the results. But they [in Techpro] weren't thinking about that. That wasn't their problem, they thought.

In the winter of 2001, Element Software delivered the completed Crash-Lab module to Autoworks. To access the module, a user had to open ElementMesh, then follow its menus. Then the wizard began running, and a window popped up in the middle of the screen, prompting the user to enter the information necessary for the particular step. The user could then take the math model he or she was working on in ElementMesh and use CrashLab to position the barrier and the occupant, to place accelerometers on the model, and to indicate section cuts. Following the standard work documents that the Focus Group had approved, the wizard menus told the user exactly where and how to execute those setup procedures, then prepared an input deck in the form of a text document that could be read by the solver. Once the solver had finished processing the simulation, the user would open the file in the CrashLab module and click through the wizard to produce a standard report in HTML format. The report used the filtering and sampling guidelines outlined in the standard work procedures to generate the important table of statistics delineated in the VP chart. Element Software's version of CrashLab contained modules for frontal-impact and side-impact load cases. In the last step before implementation, the software was loaded onto Infoserv's proprietary server in its computer lab for user-acceptance testing.

User Trials

Before implementation, all new software in the product-engineering groups at Autoworks was subject to user-acceptance testing (UAT) in Infoserv Division's computer lab. The products of tool vendors vying for contracts with Autoworks were subject to UAT, as was software developed in conjunction with Autoworks' engineers (such as CrashLab). The goal of UAT was to test the functionality of the new technology against the specifications outlined in the requirement documents used to build it. Because CrashLab had been developed at Autoworks, the review process for the requirement documents was somewhat loose. Jensen Lu asked the SMEs in the Bestpra Department to perform the UAT. He reasoned that because the engineers were most familiar with the standard work procedures (they wrote them, after all) they would be able to determine whether the procedures in Crash-Lab were indeed faithful to the process outlined in the standard work documents. When the SMEs encountered an inconsistency between the software and the standard procedures, they noted it in a log and communicated it to Element Software with a request to fix it. This testing process reinforced a self-referential loop. Because Techpro, in conjunction with Bestpra, had developed the requirement documents, they were essentially testing to make sure CrashLab lived up to their vision. Notably, users from Safety and engineers from R&D didn't test the beta version of CrashLab. The result was that UAT reinforced and promoted the work done by Techpro, further relegating the goals of the other two groups, which had been sidestepped along the way.

During this initial test phase, in early 2002, Anthony Bernardo was very eager to "go live" with CrashLab in the production environment. Despite the fact that a typical test phase for a new technology lasted four to five months, Anthony requested that the SMEs finish their UAT in two to three months. As Kaleeb Azbad noted, Anthony's sense of urgency was due in large part to the fact that he was eager to get his first major software development project at Autoworks into the production environment:

Anthony really wanted this all to happen fast. Once Element Software delivered the beta version, we tested it in about half the time we normally do. Anthony was new and eager to get his first product out to the engineers. At this point, if you go back to what Jason was doing, it had been almost six years since the CrashLab concept first came up, so spending a lot of time in UAT didn't seem that smart. We just wanted to get it out. Also, we have semi-annual product releases where we go through and implement the new tools on everybody's machines, and it was approaching that deadline, so time was short.

In September of 2002, CrashLab went live as a module in ElementMesh version 5.1. The update was loaded onto the workstations of all the analysts in the Safety Division who had licenses for the HyperWorks suite. Gene Anderson and Barry Glenn learned of CrashLab's implementation at a Focus Group meeting that same month and asked to have some of their more experienced analysts evaluate the software. They each chose one engineer from their respective groups. Bilal Mutyampeta, a respected senior engineer in the Piston Group, ran through several scenarios with CrashLab and returned with some very critical feedback on the software's "streamlined" wizard interface:

I don't know how they came up with this idea of CrashLab. I have no idea. Maybe they learned from ElementMesh. But the CrashLab initial idea was that we should be able to set up the models and crash, whether it's front or . . . and we should be able to set up the models within a reasonable amount of time—let's say one hour, one and a half hours. That was the whole idea of that. It was very good, but no one did realize what it takes to come up with that kind of software.

Bilal's concern was that, in the practice of setting up and analyzing a model, analysts often had to return to tasks they had completed earlier. The wizard interface made it difficult for analysts to do that without having to retrace all the steps they had already completed. Bilal was frustrated that CrashLab's developers lacked such a basic insight into the work of crashworthiness analysts. He sent an angry email voicing his concerns to Martin Yuen in the Techpro Department. Martin and Techpro framed Bilal's frustration as an acceptable response to a new technology—one that could be expected, even. Moreover, they positioned Bilal's comments about the wizard and its incompatibility with analysts' workflow as outside the scope of what they could reasonably fix.

After evaluating the software, Bilal and his colleague in the Truck Department made a recommendation to Gene and Barry to hold off implementation of CrashLab. In their opinion, it just wasn't ready for use in regular production work. Gene was very upset. After nearly seven years of development, three groups at Autoworks—R&D, Techpro, and Infoserv—had worked tirelessly to produce a technology that Gene believed contained flaws so great that he couldn't recommend it for use by his analysts in regular program-related engineering work. Gene commented on his frustration with the process. He was upset that much of the development had occurred without input from his analysts, the very engineers who would be using the technology once it was complete:

I am very bothered by this. You know, the developers don't know the users and vice versa. And I keep asking that question, because every time I do talk to someone who is doing tool development, I say "How do you know that this is what you should be doing?" And they talk in vague terms about some study that was done that I've never seen, and it doesn't make a difference what the topic is, but there's been a study, "We've looked at that," and no one ever has ever provided any of the data that is guiding whatever it is. I know when I've talked with Mike Johansson and Mike and I have this dialog and he has a manager and I have a manager and we have an engineer here and this is the user for apps and this is the developer. And I talked to Mike, and I said "Do these people talk?" No. This person is not allowed to talk to any user he thinks. Yeah, and the major problem here is that if you talk to many people in Johansson's group, they'll tell you "Well, our developer has talked with these users." And their justification is "Well, this person used to be over here working on program work, right now they're over here." Well, that's true, but not only was that eight years ago or whatever, but they are completely removed from program pressures.

Gene's understanding of the process used for testing CrashLab was accurate. Techpro had performed UAT testing with members of Bestpra—

analysts who were no longer involved in program-related work, who didn't deal with program-related deadlines, and whose understanding of crashworthiness-engineering work was at least several years old. More important, during its process of evaluation Techpro used only the engineers (SMEs) who were involved in the development of CrashLab to test the beta version. This insular testing community created a reinforcing loop in which testers looked only for the problems they anticipated the technology would have, and didn't consider that the technology could have been built differently. After much discussion, Gene and Barry told Sunil and the Focus Group that they weren't comfortable requiring their analysts to use CrashLab. After some negotiation, Techpro agreed to provide training and support for any analysts who wanted to use the new technology.

Without the support of the Safety Division's directors, CrashLab couldn't possibly succeed. Techpro took Gene and Barry's feedback seriously and decided to work to remedy as many of their concerns as was possible. Over the next several months, Jensen Lu and Martin Yuen worked closely with Element Software to revamp CrashLab so as to make the technology more attractive to the Safety Division. However, because Techpro was still convinced that many of the analysts' concerns about CrashLab were outside the scope of the technology, they felt that if they could implement more load cases the software would be attractive to a wider audience within the department and as a result would garner a larger user base.

By early 2003, frustration with Element Software had reached an all-time high. Several of Techpro's engineers recommended switching to Dynamic Software, a small company known for its flexibility and located only 40 miles from Motorville. At the time, Dynamic Software's main product—a pre-processor called DynamicMesh—was ElementMesh's primary competitor. Dynamic Software had developed an automator module for the Body Structure group at Autoworks, and it was getting rave reviews.

In October of 2003, Autoworks signed a contract under which Dynamic Software was to produce a process-automation tool for the Safety Division. The contract specified that Dynamic Software would pick up where Element Software had left off and would develop the technology on the basis of the existing concept of CrashLab. Owing to the frustrating delays of the previous year of working with Element Software, and to the fact that none of the analysts in the Safety Division were using the production version of CrashLab, Infoserv wanted a product from Dynamic Software as soon as possible. The contract specified that the software was to go live by April of 2004 and that it was to contain a frontal-impact module for FMVSS 208,

IIHS ODB, Sled, and US Frontal NCAP and a side-impact module for FMVSS 214, Dynamic Side Pole, IIHS Side, European Side, and US LINCAP.

Through the processes of conceptual integration, organizational disengagement, and technical integration, the technological goal had shifted from making math-based analysis more credible to speeding up the rate at which such work was carried out, and, in so doing, reducing human error. Alas, Dynamic Software's technicians began working to integrate the new CrashLab module into their existing pre-processor. Because Dynamic Software used the C++ language, the memory-management issues that had plagued Element Software's version were no longer of concern. Dynamic Software didn't use a Windows wizard interface, which in the past had posed many problems, and Techpro was excited about the prospect of reintroducing the flow chart to the GUI. Dynamic Software's underlying architecture couldn't support a visual flow chart such as the one Jason Chan originally envisioned, but it did support a tree structure that could be graphically displayed along the side of the screen. As the user moved through the steps for model setup and analysis, a yellow arrow would indicate where he or she was in the process. A user who wanted to go back and repeat a step could simply click on a higher branch of the tree and

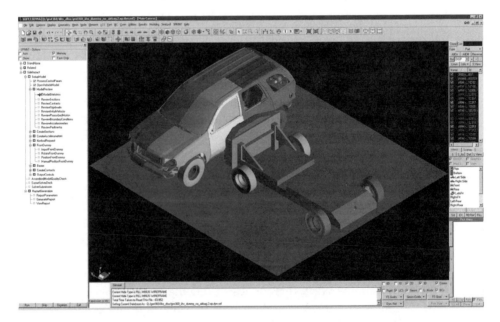

Figure 5.3
Screen shot of Dynamic Software's version of CrashLab.

redo the work without erasing all the steps that followed. This modification was a source of tremendous happiness for the members of Techpro, who now felt they had addressed the primary concerns raised by users in the Safety Division.

By July of 2004, Dynamic Software was able to deliver a working prototype of CrashLab. (See figure 5.3.) For several months, Techpro engineers had been working with Dynamic Software to develop a rear-impact module for CrashLab. Because the beta version was already three months behind schedule, Infoserv decided to allow Techpro to fully develop the rear-impact module before user-acceptance testing. The production release date for CrashLab was set for sometime in the summer of 2004. To avoid the user-acceptance problems that previously had plagued CrashLab, Infoserv and Techpro decided to launch a much broader implementation effort. The Focus Group would work with Dynamic Software technicians to create a training program for crashworthiness analysts, and Techpro would work with engineering managers in the Safety Division to pitch the advantages of CrashLab to the end users.

6 Interpreting Relationships between the Social and the Material

Researchers interested in understanding the organizational consequences of implementing new information technology have suggested that stasis or change in social structure can be traced to the ways users interpret the functionality of a new artifact (Boudreau and Robey 2005; Constantinides and Barrett 2006). Generally, studies that follow such a social constructivist framework contend that technological artifacts can simultaneously hold multiple meanings for diverse groups (Mackay et al. 2000; Prasad 1993). It is in clarifying those meanings—developing interpretations about what the technology is and how it should be used—that individuals construct the eventual effects the technology will have on the social organization of work. As Barley (1988b, p. 47) suggests, it is only when technology becomes "embedded in a matrix of interpretation" that it "acquires the status of a social object whose meaning and use are progressively uncoupled from its physical design."

Borrowing the concept of "interpretative flexibility" from the empirical program of relativism, Pinch and Bijker (1984) were among the first researchers to suggest that the developmental paths of a technology could be explained by attending to differences in interpretation of its meaning. Their framework posited that, because different groups associated with a technology's development had different goals, objectives, and social constraints, they would interpret the technology differently. The result of these differing interpretations was that the actual "working" of the technology— the criteria by which individuals determine what the technology is supposed to do and evaluate whether or not it does that—varies significantly among the diverse groups associated with it (Bijker 1995a; Pinch 1996). Thus, interpretative flexibility implies that the meaning of an artifact doesn't lie in the artifact itself, but is determined by the ways it is interpreted by relevant social groups. Weick (1990) argued that such a view of interpretation could be extended past explanations of technology development to account for the various ways in which a technology is used after it is implemented in organizations. Because they are embedded in social contexts, technologies can be and often are interpreted in a number of different ways. Therefore, Weick (ibid., p. 2) notes that technologies are best treated by researchers not as fixed and settled artifacts but as admitting several possible or plausible interpretations.

Building on this earlier work, recent research suggests that understanding the interpretations individuals make about a technology can help explain the contours of organizational transformation (Boudreau and Robey 2005; Orlikowski 2000; Walsham 2002). Orlikowski and Gash (1994, p. 175) drew on data about two occupational communities' interpretations of Lotus Notes to show that the meanings each group attributed to the technology conditioned their actual use of it:

> We argue that an understanding of people's interpretations of technology is critical to understanding their interaction with it. To interact with technology, people have to make sense of it, and in this sense-making process they develop particular assumptions, expectations, and knowledge of the technology, which then serve to shape subsequent actions toward it.

Indeed, the potential for a new technology to be interpreted in a number of distinct ways suggests that understanding how and why users make the interpretations they do should occupy a central role in theory and research regarding technology-induced organizational change.

In saying that the process of interpretation formation is socially constructed, researchers often treat technology interpretations solely as the product of people's interactions *with other people* (Arnold 2003; Walsham 2002). Such a perspective suggests that the functionality of a technology can't be separated from the context in which it is used, because membership in a community creates a system of knowledge that buffers understandings of a new technology (Jackson et al. 2002; Mackay et al. 2000). For this reason, Orlikowski (2000) has urged researchers not to study only artifacts but to also focus their attention on how a technology's material properties can reproduce, modify, and transform social structures as they are used in interaction with people. In response to such conceptualizations, most research about how interpretations of new technologies are formed has focused disproportionately on users' interactions with other people. As Bordereau and Robey's recent review demonstrates, "interest in explaining technology's organizational consequences has led increasingly to theoretical positions that privilege human agency over . . . technological features" (2005, p. 3). Researchers of technology and organizations have consistently shown that interpreting and using a new technology is an inherently social process, since users never encounter the technology in a vacuum—they are always exposed to others' opinions, beliefs, ideas, and stories about a technology.

When viewed together, studies of this flavor stop just short of suggesting that, if researchers or managers are attuned to the way a technology's users interact with other people, they will be able to predict the types of interpretations users will form. This view has certainly worked to establish the strength of the social constructivist position. However, when pushed to an extreme, this view can be taken to suggest that, for all intents and purposes, the material features of a technology don't "exist" apart from their engagement by users. But the material properties of a technology do persist outside a particular context of use. In fact, materiality's constancy across changes in social context is what makes technologies useful for coordinating work in organizations (Flores, Graves, Hartfield, and Winograd 1988). In addition, the stability of materiality is precisely what allows social constructivist researchers to show how people can use one technology in multiple ways. A conceptualization of materiality as something that doesn't exist outside its social context of use runs the risk of moving toward an ontology of social determinism in which the material agency of a technology is ignored.

If interpretations of a new technology do indeed arise out of the everyday interactions in which individuals engage, one way to move past the tendency to explain interpretations in purely social terms is to remember that, in the practice of their normal work, humans not only interact with other humans; they also interact with technological artifacts. As Pickering (1995, 2001) suggests, much of human life has the character of coping with the material agency of technological artifacts. Although those material properties were initially designed and created by humans, in the context of use they appear as real constraints on and affordances for the actions of users. In other words, material agencies "come at us from outside the human realm and . . . cannot be reduced to anything within that realm" (Pickering 1995, p. 6). In this view, the materiality of a technology has real consequences for the actions of users. Perceptual psychologists have made this claim for a number of years, suggesting that the material form of an object shapes one's perception about how the object should or even can be used (Gibson 1979; Wagman and Carello 2001). In fact, the materiality of a technology is often configured in specific ways to suggest certain uses and discourage others (Norman 1990).

The fact that in the context of their work individuals spend a significant amount of time alone interacting only with the material features of technology is often overlooked in empirical studies. Instead, interactions among individuals are highlighted in the foreground while the materiality of technology is seen as merely a backdrop to one's ability to engage in interactions with other people. In this view, materiality plays an ancillary role rather than a constitutive one in the formation of social systems. Indeed, even the most influential organizational studies are based on data collected on the interactions people have with others *around* a newly implemented technology, as opposed to data on the interactions people have *with* the material properties of the technology itself. Most studies document how and why people talk to one another about a technology but fail to document how a technology's material properties are actually used.[1]

In this chapter, I show that crashworthiness analysts' interpretations of CrashLab arose out of the confluence of users' interactions with one another and with artifacts during the course of their routine work. I begin by examining the final weeks of CrashLab's development in August of 2005, just before it was implemented in the Safety Division. During that time, Techpro worked closely with technicians at Dynamic Software to resolve some of the technology's remaining glitches. Training instructors from Dynamic Software were tasked with studying CrashLab's functionality so they could provide adequate training for crashworthiness analysts. As a result of their efforts, the trainers developed what they called a *Discourse of Efficiency*—essentially a script they would later use as a guide to help them emphasize the important features of the technology to users during training sessions. Autoworks also had its own trainers in the Technical and Computer Training (TCT) group; however, they didn't meet with Techpro or with technicians from Dynamic Software to develop a training plan. Instead, they devised their own framing techniques, which I refer to as the *Discourse of Inevitability*, in an effort to train CrashLab users. These alternative discourses helped to shape the way analysts thought about CrashLab and how they would eventually use the software in their work. Yet, as the findings reveal, these discourses alone don't explain why analysts developed the interpretations they did of CrashLab. However, it is clear that the discourses created a basis of understanding that analysts took to their everyday work. When they interacted with the material features of CrashLab and those of other technologies with which they routinely worked, they measured these interactions with artifacts against the discourse that told them what CrashLab should do for them. To the extent that their experiences with CrashLab's material features coincided with the discursive representations elucidated during training, analysts began forming favorable interpretations of CrashLab's role in their work. When misalignment occurred between the practice of technology use and the espoused discourse, analysts began to grow weary of CrashLab and to believe it was an inefficient technology.

Creating Discursive Realities

By August of 2005, CrashLab's development was nearing completion. In the ten years that had passed since Jason Chan's first days working on the prototype, the use of math-based simulations for prospective crashworthiness analysis had increased dramatically. As figure 6.1 shows, by 2005 analysts in the Safety Division were routinely submitting nearly 5,000 jobs a month to the High Performance Computing Center for processing on the DYNA solver—more than double the average number of jobs submitted only three years earlier. By 2005, there were 113 analysts performing math-based analysis, and on average each of them was submitting 44 simulations to the solver per month. This increase in math-based analysis at Autoworks was starting to yield results in the vehicle development process that couldn't go unnoticed. As figure 6.2 shows, although the

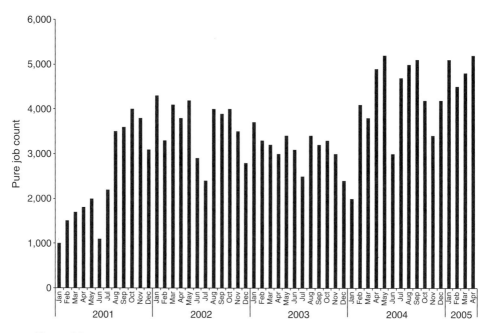

Figure 6.1
Total number of DYNA jobs submitted for crashworthiness analysis.

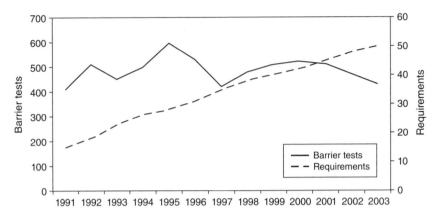

Figure 6.2
Number of physical tests vs. requirements.

number of crashworthiness requirements Autoworks had to meet in order to sell vehicles in the United States and global markets had grown steadily since the early 1990s, the increased use of math-based simulations for prospective analysis had decreased the number of physical (barrier) tests necessary to meet the requirements.

Ten years later, despite the increased use of math-based analysis in vehicle design, Gene Anderson was still unhappy about the role his organization was playing in the vehicle development process:

I've had people [at Autoworks] come to me and say "Your people must be happy. When you take your employee surveys, these anonymous enthusiasm surveys, people score very high, the department scores high—they like what they're doing." It has a lot to do with the fact that my engineers get involved in every part of the vehicle—you can't do seat belts without looking at the floors they attach to, you can't do the floors until you look at how the front crushes, and you can't do the analysis until you look at the test results. That, basically, people get a chance to work on every part of the vehicle, and it's not just like at the Lucy show, where the doughnuts are coming through, or whatever they're doing, they're wrapping chocolates, I guess it was—it's that they got it, they see how the program started and they see how the program finishes, and they get to work on the whole thing. So these guys know their stuff. They need to be sharing that knowledge more with each other. My engineers are at the center of all the action that goes on here because they know the whole damn vehicle, but still, their knowledge takes a back seat to some guys who just design radiators all day. That is not how you build a good product. We need to be more central in the design process.

This sentiment resounded among the engineers involved in the development of math-based tools for CAE analysis at Autoworks. As a result, everyone was anxious to give CrashLab to analysts. Fortunately, the Techpro engineers were quite happy with how their relationship with Dynamic Software had evolved. Dynamic Software had succeeded in meeting most of Techpro's expectations, and had done so within the budget provided by the Infoserv Division.

Thanks to the success of their collaboration, everything was on track for CrashLab to be installed on analysts' workstations early in September of 2005. Many Techpro engineers commented that the time spent working with Element Software, though it had delayed successful implementation (defined as a high level of use among analysts in the Safety Division), had helped them include the type of features that were most important to integrate. One such feature was the flow chart, which was often held up as an example of the type of feature that would be critical to CrashLab's success. As one engineer in the Techpro Department commented, "No one knew how important the flow chart was until it wasn't there anymore with Element Software." Many other engineers commented that the decision to work with Dynamic Software had allowed Autoworks to fulfill its original vision for CrashLab—a goal that had been subverted by Element Software's constraints.

In the month leading up to CrashLab's rollout, a group from Techpro— which included Jensen Lu and Martin Yuen, Sunil Kitane, Brad Bertallini, and several others from the Focus Group, and the subject-matter experts Rob Hickland and Arnold Dong—met twice a week with technicians and trainers from Dynamic Software to make sure that any loose ends were tied up before launch. The Dynamic Software project managers responsible for CrashLab encouraged two of the Dynamic Software trainers who would be conducting training at Autoworks to attend the meetings so they could learn about how CrashLab was built and what was most important to the Techpro Department. As one Dynamic Software trainer (Chowpa Maova) commented, sitting in on these pre-launch meetings was helpful in providing a context for the features he would be discussing in his training sessions:

One thing I like that Dynamic Software does is have use trainers come to these meetings. You learn more about things that are important to the customer. So when they say "We want this, or we want that," you know what they want. It gives good background so you know what they want, and then you can use this knowledge when you teach, which features to emphasize, and can answer questions if people ask why [those features] are there.

Although most of the conversations that took place at these meetings centered on clarifying the problems outlined in the bug tracking log and solving them, occasionally the SMEs found problems that resulted in a theoretical discussion about the overall purpose of CrashLab and the role of users' discretion in crashworthiness-engineering work.

One such issue concerned the placement of section cuts. The Bestpra Department had outlined in detail the best practices for locating section cuts in the standard work procedures. For frontal-impact analysis, for example, SMEs specified coordinates at which section forces should be measured along the vehicle's front rail, cradle, rocker, upper rail, A-pillar, and belt line. This is one practice Jason Chan also originally aimed to standardize (with CrashLab) to eliminate idiosyncratic practices among analysts. However, Jason recognized that there were times when analysts would be justified in straying from best-practice guidelines. To accommodate such exceptions and still achieve a higher level of credibility for simulation work, Jason devised a standard report format that allowed analysts to record deviations from standard practice, such as making a section cut in a location other than the one that was specified. After R&D disengaged from the development process, Techpro decided against allowing users to stray from best practices at any time, because the consensus was that such a departure from standards would lead to inconsistencies in the global execution of work at Autoworks and also would slow down the analysts' building and analyzing of math models. During UAT testing, SME Dennis Kwok discovered that when he attempted to insert a section cut in the model, the rectangular box used to mark the location at which a force would be measured would snap to an arbitrary point on the grid. Dennis was concerned that, owing to the algorithm used to place the section cut, the location of the force measurement wouldn't be the same each time. If that problem persisted, it could easily result in inaccurate readings of section forces. Dennis made a note about the bug in the tracking log and expected that the problem would be fixed in a timely manner. At one of the weekly staff meetings, however, Dynamic Software technician Chandra Mukesh raised the particular issue as one that wouldn't be as simple to fix as Dennis had anticipated. Chandra proposed that the easiest way to solve the problem would be to enable CrashLab to allow the user to enter the location of the section cut manually rather than have the software perform the operation automatically. Techpro engineers' immediate resistance to the idea was overwhelming:

Chandra We could probably fix this problem pretty easily if we didn't constrain the location where engineers put their section cuts. It doesn't look like much of a change, so I think we should be able to accommodate it easily and get it taken care of. Would that work for you guys?

Martin   There's no way we can change that. We have to define a process of making section cuts and where to take section forces. We want our engineers to use this tool often for this procedure, right? But this tool is about making sure everyone works the same way. That's not up to us; it's just what this tool is supposed to do. That's just the next logical step in the sequence. We can't argue with that. We'll just have to find another way around this issue, because that procedure will stay intact. That's just the way it is.

Jensen   If engineers are all doing things differently, we'll keep having speed differentials in the work, and we don't want that. Plus, no one can keep track of what they're doing that's different from what they're supposed to.

Martin   You see, that defeats the whole purpose of using automation to standardize the work. This was never the plan. We must keep that procedure automated.

Chandra   Okay, I'll work with it and see if I can come up with a solution. I think we might be able to fix that. . . .

Clearly the Techpro engineers were rattled by Dynamic Software's suggestion to leave the location of section cuts to the discretion of the user. To un-automate a feature such as this would directly contradict their understanding of the role CrashLab was to play in Safety: to standardize work. Because the Techpro engineers' definition of standardization emphasized speed and continuity, and not credibility or accuracy, the type of processes CrashLab should automate seemed clear to them. Moreover, through the process of organizational disengagement and technical integration, alternative visions of what CrashLab should do had been systematically removed from consideration; as a consequence, features that bolstered Techpro's goals had been selected. Thus, when Martin suggested that automating a feature such as section-cut placement was just the "next logical step in the process," it is not that he was waxing poetic, but that the articulation process had resulted in the production of an artifact that appeared as though it couldn't be any other way. Jason Chan had envisioned another way, and he had infused his vision into technical features such as the report that contained a column to indicate whether or not users strayed from best practice. Yet once those technical features were removed—even though Tai-Lap Leung tried to reinstitute them—alternative visions of what Crash-Lab could and should do were also eliminated. This resulted in comments such as the one made above by Jensen, who argued that if section cuts weren't standardized "no one" (presumably a manager or a design engineer) would be able to "keep track" of what analysts were doing "different from what they're supposed to."

Although the ensuing negotiations between Techpro engineers and Dynamic Software technicians were illustrative of the power the articulation process had to shut down alternative visions of the kind of technology CrashLab was supposed to be, they served a more immediate role in the context of user training. Chowpa Maova, the Dynamic Software trainer who heard the conversation about users' discretion reproduced above and others like it, felt that he was learning a lot about which features were most important to Techpro, and in the process was also learning a lot about the logic underlying CrashLab:

> When issues arise that need to be sorted out, it tells you about the character of the technology. So when the Autoworks engineers talk about automating work to speed it up, I understand that to be using a process automator technology is to make work faster.... So when I am doing the trainings and we are working with a generic model, I will show some of the features that will be faster with CrashLab than [analysts] can do without using [those features].

When Chowpa prepared for the training sessions he conducted with users in Safety, he went through the setup of a generic model and looked specifically for features that would help analysts work faster, such as automatic barrier positioning, model-checking capabilities, and accelerometer placement. What Chowpa didn't know, because it hadn't been discussed in the meetings Dynamic Software had had with Techpro, was what sort of change Autoworks expected CrashLab to bring about in the organization of work. One senior manager at Dynamic Software explained why such information was often unheard of by the technicians that worked on products such as CrashLab:

> When we take on a contract from a large vendor like Autoworks, our senior managers sit down with them and talk about strategic issues as to who will own the code and whether certain modules will be proprietary or whatever. We also try to find out at a lower level how the software will be used. It just gives us some context. But we rarely are interested in what they think the software will do for the company. That is more their concern. We believe that if we can implement their specifications on a micro level, we'll be able to give them what they need to make the transformations they deem necessary. All of that is their information systems planning, which I would imagine is proprietary to them. So unless they tell us, we don't normally ask or really even care.

Consequently, Chowpa's impressions of CrashLab's intended goal for engineering work at Autoworks came entirely from the last-minute meetings.

Chowpa wasn't the only individual leading CrashLab training sessions for the crashworthiness analysts. The corporate training center at Autoworks was staffed by a number of full-time employees who ran regular training sessions on new CAE software scheduled for release or software that had been recently implemented in the production environment. Eileen Gaffer was one such trainer. She had worked at Autoworks for nearly ten years creating and teaching various training modules on new CAE tools. Eileen worked with many of the integration groups, including crashworthiness, noise and vibration, and aero/thermal. Traditionally, Autoworks' process for training employees in a new technology was to have trainers come in from the vendor organization (such as Dynamic Software) and provide a series of intense (typically one-day) training sessions over a period of two or three weeks. Once these initial training sessions were complete, Autoworks trainers such as Eileen would step in to conduct additional sessions if the demand was high. Trainers such as Eileen were clearly not specialists in the technologies produced by any one company; they were CAE-tool generalists. As Eileen noted, this generalist position required her to take a more holistic approach to understanding a new technology before conducting a training session:

At any given time, I'm working on preparing or giving sessions for, like, five new technologies. So while I can have a good sense of what one does, I'll never get into all the details. My philosophy is that I should be able to show the general features, get people comfortable with using the tool, and then when an engineer actually starts to work with it on his own models, that's when he'll learn the details. At that point, if he has any questions, he can call me, and if I don't know the answer, I can quickly get that information from the vendor.

Clearly, Eileen's strategy of broad-based training was much different from Chowpa's strategy of identifying particular features of the tool that supported the goals of its designers. Eileen's strategy also put her in a position to learn about the technology in a very different way. She would typically spend a few days at the vendor's corporate training office taking an overview course on the technology. When she returned to Autoworks, she would run several training modules to familiarize herself with how the tool worked. For CrashLab, Eileen added an extra step to this process. Because the technology had been developed "in house", she scheduled a meeting with Martin Yuen to find out what he thought were the most important features of CrashLab and, as Eileen put it, get a feel for the way the technology was supposed to be used:

When I met with [Martin], I was just hoping to get the Autoworks perspective on things. You know, the vendor tells you something about how the tool works, but you want to know the motivation for why we actually paid money to build this thing in the first place.... The meeting was more or less helpful. What I walked away with was that they were hoping that CrashLab would really change the way crash engineers worked. I mean, the idea of automating seemed like the next logical step after standardizing work, which I understand the Focus Group has been doing over the last few years. So this was more or less an embodiment of that idea and was supposed to help engineers work differently than in the past by allowing them to do more analysis.

Eileen's understanding that the goal of CrashLab was to transform analysts' work was in line with the vision shared by the Techpro and Safety groups, both of which hoped that the automating of the routine tasks of setting up a model would mean that analysts would no longer have to consult one another as often about how to build models or how to set them up for various load-case analyses, and could instead spend more time discussing design solutions to the problems they identified during analysis. Yet, although Eileen grasped the transformational nature of CrashLab, she wasn't aware of exactly what Techpro expected to gain by its implementation. As we shall see, this ignorance led Eileen to construct a somewhat generic discourse framing the effects the technology would have on crashworthiness work when she introduced CrashLab to the analysts in her training sessions.

All engineers at Autoworks were required to take a certain number of hours of in-service training each year as part of the company's professional development program. The CrashLab training courses were specifically marketed (via email, flyers, voicemail, and personal visits) as among the few courses designed specifically for crashworthiness analysts. Because few professional development opportunities were specifically geared toward this group, the CrashLab trainings generated a very high turnout. A review of the course rosters indicated that of the 128 crashworthiness analysts who worked on CAE analysis in the Safety Division,[2] 113, or 88 percent (59 analysts from the Car Department and 54 from the Truck Department), enrolled in CrashLab training.

Before the launch, most of the information that analysts had about CrashLab cane from training sessions such as these, so trainers' explanations of CrashLab's functionality, its potential uses, and its advantages for crashworthiness-engineering work would be important in shaping analysts understanding of the new technology's place in their work. Certainly these trainers weren't the only individuals to provide a discursive explanation of CrashLab's benefits. Safety managers, Focus Group members, and even some Techpro engineers also actively attempted to demonstrate the virtues of the new technology for math-based simulation. Interestingly, the flavor of the discourse produced by any one of these parties was directly tied to the degree to which the individual was involved in CrashLab's development. Chowpa Maova, the Techpro engineers, and the Focus Group members were all well versed in CrashLab's features and the vision those features were meant to embody. By contrast, Eileen and many of the engineering managers who weren't members of the Focus Group had little inside knowledge of CrashLab's features and why they were organized in certain ways. This difference in knowledge about CrashLab led to the creation of two very distinct discourses—ideological narratives enacted through communicative practice[3]—that were used to frame the technology when it was introduced to the analysts. People who had been involved in CrashLab's development used a "discourse of efficiency" (as previously mentioned, also the name of an actual document created by Dynamic Software training instructors) to extol the particular features of CrashLab that would help engineers work more efficiently and consistently. People who hadn't been involved in CrashLab's development used a "discourse of inevitability" to let analysts know, in very general terms, that the new technology would change the way they worked.

The Discourse of Efficiency

Because people who had been at least peripherally involved in CrashLab's development had a detailed understanding of why certain features had been built into the technology, the discursive strategy used to introduce CrashLab to the user community was a focused on what its capabilities could do for crashworthiness work. The developers and the implementers were well aware that users wouldn't be willing to give up their current method of model building and learn an entirely new tool without perceiving some tremendous benefit. As Sunil Kitane commented, the act of technology implementation couldn't simply rely on a logic of new tools replacing old ones for novelty's sake. It was essential for implementers to choose the right means of persuasion:

People don't like to change things. We know that. And engineers really don't want to give up a way of doing things they're comfortable with. If you've got some guy who can build a model in, let's say, three hours, and then you tell him to use CrashLab, it will take him at least twice as long the first time he does it since he doesn't have it figured out yet. So that's motivation for him not to change, especially when that extra two hours could make him miss a deadline and make his [manager] unhappy. So we need to sell them CrashLab, they need to know exactly why these features are better than what they have now. That's key.

In an effort to "sell" CrashLab to the analysts, implementers used a number of framing strategies. I identified three framing strategies that, together, produced a discourse that suggested that using CrashLab would lead to increased organizational efficiency.

Frame 1: Time Is Lost in Tedium

The first frame that served to construct a discourse of efficiency suggested that a good portion of the time analysts spent on model building and analysis was lost as they performed tedious tasks that, in the grand scheme of things, added little value. Analysts certainly spent a lot of time performing tedious tasks, such as checking for model penetrations and checking the quality of the mesh. In fact, most analysts regularly complained that these parts of their jobs were "boring" or "dull," and felt that the most exciting of their activities were those that occurred during the analysis of a simulation. Well aware that analysts were often unhappy with the tedious parts of their work, Chowpa decided to open his training session with a statement he felt would resonate with them:

Today we're going to be talking about a new tool for crash analysis called CrashLab that was initially developed here at Autoworks. Basically, I think this is some software you're going to like, because it will automatically do a lot of the parts of the job you don't like and that are boring. This is going to give you more time since you won't be spending so much time doing the tedious activities.

Many of the analysts in attendance nodded their heads in agreement, confirming that they would indeed be thrilled if their jobs no longer entailed many of the more tedious aspects of crashworthiness engineering. After Chowpa provided a demonstration of CrashLab's features, an analyst asked how much time the technology was predicted to save:

Analyst You said CrashLab would reduce some of the routine activities, right? How much time do you think it will save for an average LINCAP type of analysis?

Chowpa From what I've seen, you should be able to take off at least one hour right up front using the model-checker function to identify any sort of problems that would be there in the model.

Analyst Okay. That's pretty good.

The prospect of using a technology to reduce or eliminate tedious tasks was certainly attractive to analysts who, when building a complete vehicle model from scratch, may easily have spent more than five hours searching for the correct parts and making sure they were all assigned the correct coordinates.

During training was not the only time analysts would hear that Crash-Lab would reduce the amount of time they spent on tedious tasks. In early

October 2005, Barry Glenn asked Sunil Kitane to give a short presentation at the Piston Group's monthly staff meeting to give the other managers in the group some insight into CrashLab. Sunil, who in addition to chairing the Focus Group managed one of the product platforms in the Piston Group, provided a brief demonstration of CrashLab's model-checker functions, then fielded several questions from managers. Here is an excerpt from the question-and-answer session:

Manager 1   So if I were to use CrashLab, I could rely on the software to specify the contacts?
Sunil   Yes, that's correct. What it will do is call the appropriate part and then create a contact algorithm. Overall, it's going to save you time from having to do this all manually.
Manager 1   Okay.
Manager 2   How reliable is the procedure?
Sunil   The SMEs in the Bestpra Department tested it just during UAT and didn't find any problems. So this will definitely save time that is normally lost on these activities.

The information the managers learned from Sunil was then passed along to the analysts who worked in the product groups they managed. During the first few staff meetings after CrashLab was released, most managers asked one or two analysts to "pilot test" the new technology to make sure it would be an effective, time-saving tool for model setup and analysis. At one such meeting, Don Kurtz, manager of a mid-size crossover vehicle, solicited volunteers:

Don   From what I understand, CrashLab will help us not to lose so much time in the more routine parts of our jobs. It's going to speed them up. So can I ask for a couple of folks to try this out just next time they're going to be doing some heavy modeling work?
Analyst   Sure, I'll try it. Is it already on our machines?
Don   Yeah, you go to DynamicMesh and then open it there.
Analyst   Is it on UNIX, or XP?
Don   It should be on both.

The power of this framing strategy lay in its appeal to eliminate some activities that analysts normally found boring and a waste of time. Yet, to make this framing strategy work, a bit of sugar coating had to be done on the part of the implementer. Many of the tasks associated with model building indeed were very tedious, but that didn't negate their importance. As was discussed in some length in chapter 4, building a high-quality mesh that balances granularity and processing power is a serious endeavor that requires intimate knowledge not only of theories of energy management but also of CPU processing constraints and the functionality of the solver. Thus, although analysts may have wanted to perform them as quickly as possible or avoid them altogether, these activities were necessary. Thus, when enacting a frame suggesting that CrashLab would help save analysts time in the tedious, everyday tasks of their work, implementers had to be careful not to overstep their bounds and suggest that CrashLab could do things it couldn't, such as make informed decisions about mesh size differentials.

Frame 2: Automation Increases the Speed of Work

A second frame enacted by many of CrashLab's implementers suggested that automation would increase the overall speed of crashworthiness work. Analysts involved in regular program-related work at Autoworks were under a tremendous amount of pressure to meet deadlines. Management constantly balked about the length of Autoworks' vehicle development process in relation to those of its Japanese competitors. Every year, senior vehicle architects set more ambitious goals for meeting vehicle development milestones. These shorter engineering cycles directly affected analysts, who were now tasked with producing vehicle-design evaluations that would guarantee increased crashworthiness performance and were expected to do so in less time than ever before. In theory, a number of CrashLab's automated features would remove the possibility of human error. Before CrashLab, an analyst setting up a model for a load case he or she hadn't worked on for some time would have to first locate the appropriate FMVSS or IIHS test guidelines and read them to determine how to position the barrier in relation to the model and where to place accelerometers on the model. Next, the analyst would have to open the model, find the locations outlined in the specifications, and perform the specified operations. Chowpa proclaimed in his training sessions that these time-consuming processes now were unnecessary thanks to CrashLab's capabilities for automation:

If you look at this slide [*he shows the first slide in a PowerPoint presentation on the wall behind him*], you see the objective of CrashLab is to automate testing procedures, like it says here, you know, where to put your measurement devices, accelerometers, and those things. What this is going to do is allow you to work faster since the program is doing a number of steps for you that were manually done before.

Thus, the automated routines embedded in the technology promised liberation from a number of second-order chores (e.g., looking for the document that specified how a barrier should be positioned) analysts had to perform in order to be able to carry out the first-order activities (e.g., positioning the barrier) that were crucial to accomplishing their work.

During regular staff meetings in the Safety Division, managers in the Car Department—who had been briefed on CrashLab by Sunil Kitane or by the SMEs (all of whom had previously worked in the Car Department and maintained personal relationships with their friends who still worked there)—talked about automation as a way of increasing the speed of model building. Even more so than the analysts, the managers felt the constant pressure of vehicle development deadlines. Because they oversaw the crash analyses for an entire vehicle platform, they constantly worried about completing all the different load cases that went into a vehicle analysis on time. Thus, managers were very keen on the idea that automation would reduce the amount of time it took their analysts to set up models. One manager expressed his excitement openly at a staff meeting:

Manager Apparently CrashLab is supposed to help us with an issue near and dear to my heart: making sure we stay ahead of the VDP [vehicle development process] curve. [*chuckles from the audience*] No, really, I talked with Sunil and some of the other Focus Group members about these automation functions, and it sounds like the barrier positioning and accelerometer placement functions actually work really well and will save you lots of time, so make sure to make use of them.
Analyst Do you know how the algorithm works behind that? I'm just curious.
Manager Behind what?
Analyst For the automation.
Manager I don't know, but do you remember Brett Pascal, who used to work in [another manager's group]? I think he was involved in it somehow, so you could ask him. Anyway, you should be able to figure it out with the training, and then we should see you guys work like lightning.
Analyst [*laughs*] You wish!
Manager You're right. I do.

The logic of automation was compelling when tied to a rationale of increased speed. Although most popular reports of "workforce automation" or "white-collar automation" paint a picture of helpless workers whose jobs are displaced by heartless machines, analysts at Autoworks were quite excited about the prospect that certain parts of their jobs would be automated.[4] In fact, many engineers who initially learned through this framing strategy that their jobs would be "sped up" by automation were interested. In staff meetings such as the one in which the conversation reproduced above took place, analysts would often ask one another and their managers why CrashLab didn't automate more aspects of their jobs. If automation could increase the speed of model building, it would prove superior to most of the technologies currently available in the crashworthiness portfolio. A few years before CrashLab was introduced, the Focus Group had taken out an evaluation license to test a new pre-processor called Edict. The analysts who evaluated Edict quickly voted to reject the it because, as one engineer estimated, "It probably took about 25 seconds to optimize an element when you clicked the button. That was way too slow." Thus, the idea of a tool that would use a different method—automation—to speed up model building and analysis was warmly welcomed.

Frame 3: Faster Product Development as a Competitive Advantage

Whereas the first two frames I have mentioned emphasized ways in which CrashLab would speed up crashworthiness-engineering work, a third frame attempted to justify why increased speed was important to Autoworks beyond an immediate improvement in task cycles. Since the early 1990s, almost every corporate-wide bulletin, speech, or announcement that came from Autoworks senior management contained an imperative to shorten the vehicle development process. Comparative studies such as Clark and Fujimoto's (1991) famous analysis of vehicle development lead time in the world auto industry estimated that, on average, American automakers took 60 months to develop a new vehicle, whereas Japanese automakers took just 46 months. At Autoworks, computer-aided analysis was seen as one of the primary ways to close this productivity gap.

Subject-matter experts from the Bestpra Department often came to monthly Quality Improvement Team meetings to update the Car Department on standard work processes. During the meetings that took place in September and October, the SMEs were accompanied by Ernesto Reyes, an engineer from another group in the Advanced Product Development Division who was in charge of competitive "benchmarking" (that is, assessing the degree to which Autoworks' vehicles were similar in form and function to the vehicles made by its competitors). At five different QIT meetings, Ernesto presented new information that his department had learned about the product development cycles of Autoworks' major competitors. Although the gap had gradually become smaller since the early 1990s, Ernesto estimated that Japanese automakers were still outpacing Autoworks by more than 13 months from concept release to the start of production. The SMEs used this opportunity to frame CrashLab as a technology that would help close the gap for good by speeding up simulation. At one QIT meeting, Arnold Dong discussed the advantages automation could bring to the product development process:

Arnold If you haven't had a chance to go to CrashLab training yet, you should. CrashLab will help us with closing this gap that Ernesto has been discussing, because it will automate a lot of your work to increase the speed. If we do this, we can use this tool to help close this gap more.
Ernesto Yeah, I've seen CrashLab, and it looks pretty good. This is definitely the kind of technology that will help to give us a competitive advantage by reducing our engineering time, so check it out.

Because most analysts were already aware that Japanese automakers were engineering and manufacturing vehicles faster than Autoworks (see, e.g., Womack, Jones, and Ross 1991), it was no stretch of the imagination to envision that increasing the speed of simulation with task automation might give Autoworks a much-needed boost in the product development race.

Managers in the Safety Division, who were also aware that CrashLab could help speed up simulation, also saw the technology's immediate potential for increasing Autoworks' competitive advantage in the global marketplace. Mid-level managers in the Safety Division and in other divisions typically felt the brunt of the pressure from upper management to reduce development time. It is no surprise, then, that managers readily adopted the frame that CrashLab was a technology that could speed up the vehicle development process and could thereby help Autoworks catch up with or perhaps even outpace its competitors. One manager told his analysts the following at a weekly staff meeting:

If you think about these features for model checking and barrier positioning and what not, the Techpro folks worked with Dynamic Software to design these algorithms to perform the tasks quickly and efficiently, and for a change, they did it with our input—at least by working with the SMEs. You might think that you already can do this quick, and probably you all do it fast, but CrashLab will make it faster, which should really cut down the amount of time it takes us to run a job, which means you can do more iterations in a shorter amount of time. So that seems like it will give us a great advantage not only at our level to really get at what's the best structural solution given the constraints from the body group, but also on a bigger scale to "out-engineer" [*makes "air quotes" with his fingers*] our competitors, if you will.

By framing CrashLab as a technology that would help Autoworks engineer products faster, implementers were able to tap into an underlying current of power in the company. Linking the micro-level practices of using CrashLab to a broader corporate goal helped analysts see the advantage of using such a technology. Perhaps, many analysts commented, the costs associated with revising their current work practices would be offset by the benefits they would gain from CrashLab's features. During training, at QIT meetings, in staff meetings, and in conversations with SMEs and Techpro engineers, analysts were inundated with a discourse of efficiency. Especially affected were those in the Car Department who had the strongest institutional ties to the individuals involved in CrashLab's development. In the first few weeks after CrashLab's launch, few engineers who were exposed to these framing practices were able to avoid hearing and thinking about the many ways CrashLab's specifically designed features would speed up their work.

The Discourse of Inevitability

Whereas trainers such as Chowpa Maova (who worked for the vendor that built CrashLab), members of the Focus Group (who also doubled as crashworthiness managers), and the subject-matter experts (all of whom had worked in the Car Department and had the added advantage of having tested CrashLab) were relatively well informed about CrashLab's features, functions, and goals, those responsible for implementing the technology knew next to nothing about CrashLab, its features, or why the features had been developed. Jeremy Dobbins, a crashworthiness manager in the Truck Department, noted that many of the new technologies implemented in the product-engineering groups seemed to have been launched with the assumption that managers would immediately understand their purpose—an assumption that Jeremy felt was misguided:

I know there is a fixed procedure where the Focus Group goes through some steps to make sure that whatever new technology we bring in is good. But that procedure's not really transparent for me. I mean, so we have CrashLab now, and Gene tells us that the Focus Group worked hard to get it here and that it will help to revolutionize crash simulation work, but I don't know anything about it. I mean, I think Element Software makes it, but I don't even really know that. So I'm not going to be much use to the analysts who will have to learn to use it. They'll probably take a bit of a productivity hit figuring it out, because I'm sure there'll be trainings and all, but they're never enough so you actually learn how to use it.

Even though many trainers and managers clearly weren't aware of how CrashLab worked or what Techpro hoped to achieve with the technology, their ignorance didn't prevent them from playing the role of framing agent. Lacking any concrete information about how CrashLab's specific features could be used to transform engineering work, these implementers adopted frames that tied the technology to general changes in the nature of work and to the betterment of Autoworks. I identified three frames that contributed to a discourse pronouncing that change in the way analysts worked was an inevitable outcome of using CrashLab.

Frame 1: New Technologies Require New Work Practices

The first frame that helped construct a discourse of inevitability about CrashLab reminded analysts that new technologies generally require users to either give up existing work practices in favor of new ones or else alter their existing work practices to conform to the demands placed upon their work by the new technology. Because licensing a new technology for more than a hundred engineers was costly and negotiating contracts with vendors was labor-intensive, the Focus Group and the Infoserv Division were reluctant to regularly advocate new technologies. This meant that when they did introduce a new tool in the user environment, more often than not it was a tool that made radical improvements rather than incremental ones. Eileen Gaffer commented that this was the case for most of the groups for which she provided training at Autoworks:

Managers often tell me that whatever the new technology is that I'm going to be training their engineers on is the newest and greatest. I don't mean that facetiously —I really think they're convinced that whatever the new tool is going to be important or they wouldn't spend all this money on it. So, it's one of these things where you've got these engineers that are required to go to a certain amount of training sessions per year for [in-service credit] but who don't want to change the way they work, that's very true. So we have to remind them that if they want to get whatever advantage they can out of whatever new technology they're learning, they're going to have to change the way they work.

Most of the managers in the Truck Department didn't have any useful knowledge about how CrashLab worked; however, they shared Eileen's understanding about why new technologies were implemented at Autoworks. As Francis Giordano (an engineering manager in the Truck Department) noted, new technologies were expected to bring about change in the way engineers worked:

We're not in the business of trying some new technology out because it looks good. We implement new technologies because we want to change the way people work. Sometimes we just want people to work faster. Lots of other times, we want them to work different; we want the organization to run differently. So we expect that if we spend the money to make or buy a new piece of software, we're going to see the changes we want, or else we'll save ourselves the money and headaches.

As Francis indicated, if new technologies didn't bring about desired change in the organization of work there would be little point in implementing them.

During the CrashLab training sessions she ran for analysts in the Safety Division, Eileen stuck to her script. Because she was not privy to specific details about CrashLab's purpose, she didn't preface her orientations with a vision of the future, as Chowpa did. However, when she was analysts asked her why CrashLab was configured as it was, Eileen relied on her broad understanding of technology and its ability to effect change in work practices when formulating a response.

Eileen   It will automatically find a node. I think it's at the center of your instrument panel on the top.

Analyst 1   Are these procedures required? That means you cannot skip any steps?

Eileen   No, you can't. You have to do it this way to make the IIHS reference plane. You need to set up this plane in order for you to do the calculation.

Analyst 2   That seems sort of annoying. That means we have to change the order of operations.

Eileen   Well, I know. New tools require changes to the work. I think to use CrashLab, well, you'll have to do things a bit differently. There's really no way around it.

Analyst 2   But, well, I guess that's right.

Eileen's response to the analyst's complaint about having to change the way he worked was as calculated as it was instinctive. She clearly believed that CrashLab was meant to transform the way analysts worked. Without any specific information about why certain features were built into the software (such as a flow chart of steps that couldn't be performed out of sequence), Eileen was unable to respond to analysts' concerns with a detailed explanation of the philosophy behind the technology. Instead, she was forced to rely on general abstractions about the relationship between technology and changes in work practice. Another reason why Eileen drew on such vague pronouncements was to avoid an exchange with an engineer who was obviously concerned about the notion of changing the way he worked. By providing the analyst with a vague but well-accepted causal argument, she was able to construct a general logic that the analyst couldn't refute.

Francis, who also knew very little about management's goals for Crash-Lab, experienced similar difficulties when he discussed the new technology with analysts at his weekly staff meeting. However, Francis decided the best approach would be a proactive one. When he introduced CrashLab to his staff for the first time, Francis openly admitted his ignorance about CrashLab's functionality, and instead framed the new technology as a generic yet decisive agent of change:

Francis   Okay, the next item on the agenda is CrashLab. Most of you have probably taken the training on this already; if you haven't, I'd like you to do it sometime before the end of the year. I don't really know much about this, but I know Sunil is pretty gung-ho on it and Gene and Barry are supporting it too. Basically, you're going to use it in conjunction with your pre-processor. So if you're using ElementMesh, I think you can just export the DYNA deck from there and read [it into DynamicMesh to run Crash-Lab. Or you can just use DynamicMesh for the pre-processing work if you want. Does that square with what you heard in training?

Analyst   Yeah, you can read it in without too much trouble, I think. We just read in some generic ODB model, and it worked fine.

Francis   I think when you use CrashLab you're going to have to make some changes to way you work. At least, I'm told that's what the goal is, but you know that's the case whenever you use a new technology—you've got to adapt to it.

Interestingly, Francis, like Eileen, suggested a linear causal relationship between CrashLab and changes in work practice without ever describing the changes. Thus, essentially, analysts were told that CrashLab would change their work but were given little information about *how* it would change their work.

Frame 2: Change Is a Technological Issue, Not a Managerial Issue

When analysts learned that CrashLab would change their work, they began questioning the need for change. Were they doing something wrong? Did something need to be fixed? Many implementation studies have shown that when users first experience a new technology, they attempt to use it in ways that allow them to maintain their current work practices. Such inertial tendencies reinforce the status quo and serve as a reminder that change is uncomfortable and often undesirable for the people who have spent months or even years developing and exploiting competencies using certain methods and technologies. When implementers framed CrashLab as an agent of change, analysts weren't afraid to ask questions. They wanted to know who wanted them to change the way they worked. When Jeremy Dobbins (a manager in the Truck Department) introduced CrashLab to his staff, a heated discussion ensued, and analysts asked a number of direct questions:

Analyst 1   Why do we need to change what's going on now if we're getting good results?

Analyst 2   Are you not happy with how we're doing things?

Jeremy   Whoa, hold on a minute. I don't want to change your work. I really don't care what you do as long as you generate the results you need to evaluate your load cases. As far as I'm concerned, you can use whatever software you want. Look, the Focus Group has decided that CrashLab is going to be the preferred technology, so I suggest you figure out how to use it, because I wouldn't imagine it will be long before some other tools like LinkMesh might disappear from your machines.

Analyst 3   They're not going to take away ElementMesh, are they?

Jeremy   No one has said anything about any software going away. I'm just saying—if the Focus Group is supporting CrashLab so strongly, no one knows what to expect. But as far as the changes go, those are driven by the technology, just improvements over older functions, so I'm sure it won't be a big deal, but it will require some adjusting. Come on, I'm not telling you anything you don't know.

By framing the impending change as being driven by technology rather than by management, Jeremy was able to dodge the accusation that he was dissatisfied with his analysts' performance or somehow wanted to change their work practices. By telling analysts that CrashLab required them to change the way they worked, Jeremy and other managers who used this framing tactic were able to signal that they were not agents of change. The rationale they presented was that even if management didn't want analysts to change their processes (of course, as we know, they certainly did), CrashLab necessitated change simply by virtue of its features.

Similar issues surfaced in the training sessions Eileen facilitated. For example, in one session, she was giving an overview of how CrashLab filtered the data returned from the solver when an analyst interrupted her and asked why management wanted the software to compute calculations pertaining to accelerative forces instead of allowing analysts to continue doing it manually:

Eileen   One is the bottom view; one is the, I think, isometric view. Then during the setup of your load case you will give all of your information. For example, how many dummies, what kind of dummy you use, is it belted or nonbelted, things like that. Okay, driver's side, passenger's side—this is the vehicle performance we see right here for this section. [points to a window that pops up in the bottom-right corner of the screen] It will give you all these numbers. Also, for the energy group you define, it will give you what is the energy at one millisecond after you reach the peak.

Analyst   Does it do all this automatically?

Eileen   Yes; it's the automated routine . . .

Analyst   That's different that it does that. I mean, now, that changes things a lot. If you wanted to check this information and do it yourself, you couldn't, it seems.

Eileen   Well, you can open your deck to check the parameters, but these changes are driven by the automation routines, if that's what you mean.

Analyst   So if you use that, you calculate your energy pulse here rather than in Hypergraph?

Eileen   That's right.

Analyst   Oh. Why are they making us change that?

Eileen   Well, it's a capability I think that CrashLab has that I haven't seen anywhere else, so it's the software that drives it. It's the innovation. So it's not as if managers are saying "We like this way better"; it's the latest evolution of the capability.

Analysts were skeptical about management's change programs largely because they felt management was too far removed from the work to discern what kind of change was warranted. And, as we have seen, the agenda of the managers and the technology developers at Autoworks did indeed include changing the way crashworthiness analysts worked. In fact, at one point there were as many as four such initiatives in the works. Through the articulation process, however, the four programs were consolidated into one, which was inscribed in CrashLab through the selection and survival of its particular features. Yet, by using this framing tactic, implementers who weren't aware that certain features embodied goals for change unwittingly separated management's intentions from the technology's functionality. That discursive move positioned CrashLab as a neutral technology—one that just did what it did—rather than as the sedimented remains of a contested process of negotiation. Such separation provided a rhetorical space in which users who were unhappy about the prospect of having to change the way they worked could blame the intrinsic properties of the technology rather than the imputed desires of Autoworks' management. This framing tactic hid the goals of a contextually specific process behind the shroud of a decontextualized artifact.

Frame 3: Today's Problems Lead to Tomorrow's Successes
As Sunil Kitane's comments above demonstrate, managers in the crashworthiness group knew that the transition from using multiple tools for model building and analysis to using a single tool would bring with it temporary problems of coordination and knowledge translation. Analysts had built skill sets using a wide variety of tools available in the CAE environment. With the implementation of CrashLab, the Focus Group was asking them to replace multiple technologies—tools with which they had considerable technical aptitude—with a single technology about which they knew nothing. What was certain, Jeremy Dobbins commented, was that analysts would see their initial difficulties with CrashLab as indicative of long-term difficulties:

Whenever you move to a new technology, there is a learning curve. When you buy a toaster, it takes you a bit to figure out how to set the dial so your toast is the right color, or toastiness, I guess you would say. Well, CAE tools are more complex, so it takes longer to adjust. One thing we talked about in our managerial meeting with Gene was that experienced analysts would migrate from other tools like Element-Mesh, and when they hit that learning curve, they would blame CrashLab. Really, it has nothing to do with CrashLab, but you don't normally get a guy whose been working in the CAE domain for five years saying "Oh, I'm just screwing up here, and the technology is fine." No. Instead, they say "I know what I'm doing, and if this tool is not super-intuitive or I can't figure out everything I need to know about it in five minutes." . . . They'll blame the tool. Then they won't want to use it.

To proactively mitigate the tendency to blame a new technology for losses in productivity, and to soften the inconvenience associated with learning a new set of skills, managers and QIT leaders used the framing tactic of reminding analysts that the troubles that they faced in the short term were necessary in order to reap CrashLab's long-term benefits.

Perhaps the most vivid example of management's use of this strategy occurred at a staff meeting during which one of the Truck Department's managers decided to give analysts a brief lesson on the history of technology. Anticipating his staff's reluctance to use CrashLab, the manager went through a list of successful technologies that had less-than-stellar beginnings:

Manager   I know what you're thinking about using CrashLab. Why should you use it when other things work fine and it's only going to slow you down? But remember that when the Duryea brothers were tooling around Springfield[5] people who rode horses said "How am I going to ever learn to change gears?" Or people said that about the PC—"This is so much harder than my typewriter." So, yeah, CrashLab might be a bear in the short run, but a short productivity loss is nothing compared to better benefits in the future.

Analyst 1   That's pretty dramatic, there!

Manager   [*laughs*] You're right, but I'm just saying . . .

Analyst 2   So no one will get on our case if things go a little slower for a while?

Manager   Just scale up to it. Figure out how to use it, and migrate your work over. Then it won't be such an impediment.

Without any specific knowledge of the reasons behind CrashLab's functionality, all that managers in the Truck Department and trainers such as Eileen could use to assuage analysts' fears were general abstractions about the benefits of technological change. An unintended consequence was that their generalizations allowed analysts to assimilate their own experiences into a web of popular knowledge about technology's deterministic effects on organizations, and even on society.

Distribution and Influence of Discursive Frames across the Piston Group and the Strut Group

From early September through late October of 2005, I observed 24 separate events—including training sessions, staff meetings, management meetings, QIT meetings, and formal and informal conferences—during which developers, trainers, implementers, and managers introduced CrashLab to analysts who were unfamiliar with the technology. In 98 hours of observation, two consistent trends emerged. The first trend was that those meetings in which a discourse of efficiency was expounded were run, either directly or indirectly, by individuals who had somehow been involved in or who were at least familiar with CrashLab's development process. By contrast, the meetings in which the discourse centered predominantly on the inevitability of technology-driven change were run by trainers, managers, and Quality Improvement Team presenters who hadn't been involved in CrashLab's development and who weren't aware of how its features had evolved. The second trend was that attendance at events rife with either one of the two discourses there seemed to be a divergence between attendance by in the Car Department analysts and attendance by Truck Department analysts. At events in which a discourse of efficiency was enacted, the majority of attendees were analysts from the Car Department; at events in which a discourse of inevitability was enacted, the majority of attendees were analysts from the Truck Department.

Though such a divide was certainly to some extent coincidental, there were several reasons to expect that differences in attendance might cleave along group lines. First, only members of one's vehicle platform group attended weekly staff meetings. Because work was organized in the Safety Division into either the Car Department or the Truck Department at a higher level, and then by vehicle platform group at a lower level, Piston Group analysts didn't attend Strut Group staff meetings, and vice versa. As was discussed earlier, managers from the Car Department were more intimately involved in CrashLab's development as members of the Focus Group and liaisons between Techpro and Infoserv. In addition, most of the subject-matter experts who worked on CrashLab came out of the Car Department, and when in their new roles they maintained close ties to former Car Department colleagues. As the director of the Truck Department, Gene Anderson was involved in the development of CrashLab from its earliest stages; however, none of his managers contributed to the development process in any significant way. Because Car Department managers were more heavily invested in CrashLab, they were more adamant about their analysts' attending the CrashLab training sessions, and in some cases they required attendance. For this reason, most of the analysts from the Car Department attended the first three training sessions, which happened to be taught by Chowpa Maova of Dynamic Software. Although the Truck Department managers heeded the Focus Group's recommendations and requested that all their analysts obtain CrashLab training, these managers weren't as optimistic about the new technology's prospects, so not until they felt pressure from the Focus Group did they began actively endorsing training sessions. Martin Yuen recalled:

We looked at the attendance rosters from the first couple training sessions and noticed that almost all of the people that were coming were from the Car Department. So the Focus Group had to tell the managers from the Truck Department to get their engineers to go to the trainings.

Eileen Gaffer, who hadn't been involved in CrashLab's development, taught the second set of training sessions, which was attended predominantly by analysts from the Truck Department. Thus, it appears that, through a combination of historical conditions and chance, Car Department members were exposed to a discourse of efficiency while Truck Department members were exposed to a discourse of inevitability about the changes CrashLab would bring to their work.

To determine whether these trends were present in the data, I turned to the observation records of the 24 events. From the records, I tabulated the number of analysts from each group who were in attendance and the number of framing tactics that were used during each event. The data, summarized in table 6.1, show that the assertion made above holds:

Table 6.1
Analysts' exposure to discursive frames.

Event		Number of Car Department analysts in attendance	Number of Truck Department analysts in attendance	Number of "efficiency" frames	Number of "Inevitability" Frames
1	Training session #1	17	2	14	2
2	Training session #2	14	0	17	3
3*	Training session #3	7	7	11	4
4	Managerial meeting	8	0	16	5
5	Car staff meeting	16	0	12	1
6	CAE Conference	24	5	21	2
7	CAE Conference	8	3	15	8
8	Training session #4	3	14	3	14
9	Truck staff meeting	0	21	0	17
10	Managerial meeting	0	7	2	13
11	Car staff meeting	20	0	15	0
12	Training session #5	7	13	1	13
13	Training session #6	3	10	2	17
14	Car staff meeting	9	0	11	7
15*	QIT meeting	1	5	9	2
16	Truck staff meeting	0	18	1	16
17	Truck staff meeting	0	12	0	9
18	Informal Conference	15	1	8	2
19	Car staff meeting	14	0	12	1
20*	Informal Conference	6	7	9	1
21	Strut staff meeting	0	14	3	12
22	QIT meeting	1	4	2	4
23	Truck staff meeting	0	14	1	9
24	QIT meeting	2	1	2	3

*In these events, members from the majority group in attendance were exposed to more of the opposite group's frames than to their own (e.g., Car Department members were exposed to more inevitability frames than efficiency frames).

Analysts from the Car Department were exposed to more "efficiency" frames than were analysts from the Truck Department, while more analysts from the Truck Department were exposed to "inevitability" frames than were analysts from the Car Department. In fact, the data strayed from this trend for only three of the 24 events (indicated in the table by asterisks). In these events, members from the majority group in attendance were exposed more to the opposite group's frames than to their own (e.g., Car Department members were exposed more to inevitability frames than to efficiency frames). This meant that in 88 percent of the events there was a direct mapping between the majority group in attendance and one of the two discursive frames. To determine whether this trend was prevalent at the individual level, I calculated the average number of frames to which an analyst in either the Car Department or the Truck Department was exposed by multiplying the number of analysts in each group who were present at a given event by the number of frames used during that event summed across all 24 events, then dividing by the total number of analysts in the group who were present at any of the events. The results, presented in table 6.2, indicate that the average analyst[6] in the Car Department was exposed to nearly four times as many efficiency frames as inevitability frames, while the average analyst in the Truck Department was exposed to more inevitability frames than efficiency frames at roughly the same ratio. Put more simply, 75 percent of all the frames to which analysts in the Car Department were exposed were efficiency frames, and 72 percent of the frames to which analysts in the Truck Department were exposed were inevitability frames.

These data suggest that from the earliest moments they learned about CrashLab, analysts in the Car Department and the Truck Department were presented with different information about how CrashLab would affect their work. Analysts in the Car Department were given very specific information about how CrashLab's features would allow them to work faster and would make model building and analysis more efficient. Analysts in

Table 6.2
Difference in exposure to discursive frames.

	Average number of frames to which analyst in Car Department was exposed	Average number of frames to which analyst in Truck Department was exposed
"Efficiency" frames	13.01	3.16
"Inevitability" frames	3.32	11.27

the Truck Department, by contrast, were given very generic information about how CrashLab would change their work—the message was that change was inevitable, and that learning to cope with it would not only benefit them individually but also serve as a boon to Autoworks over the long haul. The remaining sections of this chapter will explore how these initial discourses helped shape analysts' interpretations of CrashLab during the practice of their work.

From my very first observation in Autoworks' Safety Division, it became clear to me that analysts couldn't accomplish their work without simultaneously interacting with people and artifacts. In the practice of their everyday work, analysts regularly engaged in interaction with managers, co-workers, and customers (design engineers), as well as with CrashLab and other complementary technologies used to aid in crashworthiness-engineering analysis. The findings presented in the next section explore how, after exposure to differing discourses constructed by implementers, analysts developed different interpretations of CrashLab in the practice of their normal work. I separately examine the work conducted in one of the vehicle-program groups in each department—the "Piston Group" (a not-so-clever pseudonym) within the Car Department (consisting of 19 analysts) and the "Strut Group" within the Truck Department (17 analysts)—in order to understand the relationship between discursive constructions, interactions with co-workers, and interactions with the technology itself. I conducted 64 observations in the Piston Group and 60 observations in the Strut Group.

The Piston Group

Interactions with People
Scholars have long argued that, contrary to popular stereotypes, engineering is an inherently social activity that involves coordinating the interdependent actions of a number of parties to generate efficient and robust solutions to complicated problems (Bucciarelli 1994; Vincenti 1990). Crashworthiness engineering at Autoworks is the epitome of such claims. To effectively evaluate various load cases and make recommendations for improved vehicle performance, analysts regularly interacted with their managers, with their co-workers (analysts working on other load cases), and with design engineers. Upward information seeking, technological benchmarking, and technical teaching were three types of interpersonal interactions that led analysts to interpret CrashLab as a pre-processor.

Upward Information Seeking

The introduction of a new technology is always surrounded by discourse about what it will do and how it should be used. At Autoworks, discourse about CrashLab circulated at a number of levels, cascading down from tool developers to engineering managers and tool trainers and eventually to crashworthiness analysts. Crashworthiness managers were responsible for evaluating new technologies such as CrashLab and endorsing them as they saw fit. Without their approval, a new technology couldn't be implemented. However, managers didn't have the authority to require analysts to use a new technology. Thus, for developers, convincing managers of CrashLab's utility was a necessary step if they ever hoped to see CrashLab utilized in the user community.

As was discussed above, developers, implementers, and managers who were familiar with CrashLab's functionality—primarily those in the Piston Group—framed CrashLab in a way they felt would make it most attractive to analysts: by emphasizing the speed the engineers could gain if they used it to build and analyze their models. After analysts had had a chance to experiment with CrashLab, they sought information from their managers in weekly staff meetings to gain further clarification on CrashLab's purpose and to determine when and how the tool should be used. Piston Group managers' responses to these questions reinforced their initial framing practices:

Analyst I've tried out CrashLab, and it is a little confusing. Can you say more about what we're doing with it?
Manager Basically we've been asked to evaluate CrashLab and start using it in our program work. From what I know, the goal of this tool is to help us speed up the way we get models ready for analysis. That's something we all want, right?
Analyst Yeah, that's definitely the boring part.

'Speed' was a word that crashworthiness analysts associated with pre-processing rather than with post-processing—largely because most analysts considered model building a necessary but burdensome pre-condition for analysis, which, by contrast, required great care and precision. (For details, see chapter 4.) Thus, when exposed to this discourse of speed, analysts quickly likened CrashLab to other pre-processing applications, since pre-processing was the only part of the job an analyst would want to speed up. Such a comparison was problematic for two reasons. First, it caused analysts to overlook CrashLab's post-processing automation functions. Second, forcing an unwarranted comparison with tools designed for pre-processing was unfair—CrashLab would always lose, because it didn't have the capabilities of the pre-processing technologies analysts were using at the time, nor was it designed to have those capabilities. One analyst noted:

I keep hearing CrashLab is supposed to make setting up models faster. I think that's bullshit. I mean, I don't think it can do it faster than I can using the methods I use now with other pre-processors. I think that's true for 90 percent of the engineers here. Maybe for engineers who are just starting it would be faster. . . . I mean, I did a side-by-side comparison even. To get my model ready, it takes, like, maybe a half-hour with ElementMesh [a pre-processor]. When I sat down with CrashLab, even after I'd used it once or twice before, it still took more than an hour. Other people have told me the same thing.

Hence, through the discursive framing strategies that characterized their interactions with their managers and trainers, analysts began to interpret CrashLab as a pre-processing tool.

Technological Benchmarking

In the course of their everyday work, crashworthiness analysts regularly interacted with colleagues in order to construct vehicle designs to meet the demands of multiple load cases. During such interactions, it was common for analysts to ask questions about the functionality of a particular technology that was used for model building and analysis. This practice is understandable because once they completed training analysts typically didn't have access to the instructors who had trained them. Also, under normal circumstances, the engineers wouldn't know or have access to the developers who created the technology. To make matters worse, more often than not their managers hadn't been trained in how to use the technology. Thus, if an analyst wanted to learn about the features of a tool such as CrashLab, his or her only recourse was to ask another analyst who had some experience with it.

For analysts, relying on their co-workers to learn about a new technology was problematic in two ways. First, the analyst offering advice didn't have much more practical experience using the tool than the analyst seeking advice. Second, an analyst who had experience with a technology often felt that it was easier (in part because of his own limited knowledge) to explain its functionality not in technical terms but rather by likening it to other technologies already in the crashworthiness portfolio. Consequently, when one analyst explained to another how CrashLab worked, he or she often used other technologies as benchmarks with which to evaluate CrashLab's performance relative to the activity at hand. Other times, the analyst requesting help would benchmark CrashLab against other technologies to try to make sense out of what CrashLab did well and what it didn't do well. Consider, for example, the following exchange between two analysts, one of whom (analyst 2) had recently completed CrashLab training:

Analyst 1 When you pull in a vehicle model and CrashLab goes through the processes, does it generate a larger file than ElementMesh?
Analyst 2 I think so.
Analyst 1 Are you sure?
Analyst 2 I just took the training in October, and I think I remember that.
Analyst 1 Oh.
Analyst 2 Yeah, that's too bad. But ElementMesh or LinkMesh still generates smaller files?
Analyst 2 So it might be better to stick with that.
Analyst 1 Probably.

Objectively, one can see this was an incorrect characterization of Crash-Lab's functionality. CrashLab didn't generate larger files than the competing software (at least, not large enough to make any difference). Without any follow-up or ongoing access to developers or trainers, however, analysts were left to their own devices to learn about CrashLab's material features in the practice of use. When they engaged in interactions characterized by technological benchmarking, analysts turned to their peers, who weren't much more knowledgeable then they were, for guidance and advice. The result was that analysts often accepted another engineer's incorrect assessment without testing the technology themselves.

Instead of evaluating CrashLab on its own merits (as an automator of both pre-processing and post-processing functions), analysts explicitly compared CrashLab's features with those of existing pre-processors, and in so doing, began to interpret CrashLab itself as a pre-processor. The effect of this technological benchmarking was that analysts made determinations about whether or not to use CrashLab on the basis of what they learned it could or couldn't do compared to the pre-processing tools already available to them. When asked by a co-worker whether he should use CrashLab for an upcoming project, this was the advice one analyst offered:

Analyst 1 For me, CrashLab has to do more than ElementMesh for it to be useful. CrashLab is a good niche application, I think. It has some good potential to generate mesh for curvatures, but the reality is that it's just not as intuitive for me as ElementMesh. So, really, for me to use a new pre-processor, it would have to be significantly better and give me more of an advantage than ElementMesh. That's my benchmark. So I just don't think CrashLab is worth investing the time to learn.

Analyst 2   So it's essentially a pre-processor?

Analyst 1   Yup, that's right.

Notice that the analyst thinks of CrashLab as a "new pre-processor." The consequence is that this interpretation of CrashLab's utility is constructed through technological benchmarking. In the eyes of analysts, CrashLab became a "new pre-processor" for "niche applications" such as generating "mesh for curvatures" rather than an automator for more advanced pre-processing and post-processing functions.

Technical Teaching

Through their interactions with managers, trainers, and co-workers, crash-worthiness analysts began developing relatively robust interpretations of CrashLab as a pre-processing tool. Analysts' interactions with design engineers—their "customers"—gave further validation to their interpretations. Design engineers were responsible for drafting vehicle parts or subsystems in CAD software and then managing the performance and manufactur-ability of those parts until their designs were "frozen" by certain vehicle development stage gates. In a way, analysts worked for design engineers, conducting tests on their designs to ensure that they met certain perfor-mance requirements. To use Bucciarelli's (1994) term, design engineers and analysts occupied distinct "object worlds." Design engineers were charged with designing robust parts with as little mass as possible. Their object world conditioned them to think, as one DE said, that "parts should not break." "Even if I use inferior material," the DE continued, "I design it so it won't break." Crashworthiness analysts occupied a very different object world. They designed parts for failure. When a part or a vehicle subsystem deforms, it converts the kinetic energy of the colliding parts into internal work of those parts involved in the crash.[7] In other words, through defor-mation, the parts themselves absorb the energy of the collision so energy isn't passed on to the vehicle's occupant(s). This object-world thinking is, one analyst observed, quite different from the thinking of design engi-neers: "We design vehicles for failure. That's kind of a hard concept for a lot of people, because you normally think of engineering something so it won't fail."

Analysts and design engineers interacted regularly around the results of simulations of various loading conditions. Because they occupied different object worlds than design engineers, analysts were aware that, in order to convince a DE to make changes to the design of his or her part (which most were hesitant to do because one change quickly snowballed into many more), they had to teach their DE customers about the types of analysis they conducted so the DEs understood why it was necessary to redesign a part. To be effective in promoting a good design, analysts had to engage in a fair amount of technical teaching with DEs. Consider the following example of technical teaching, observed in a routine interaction between an analyst and his DE customer:

Analyst If we put the bracket there [points to the computer screen to an empty space next to the torque box], it will be in our crush space.[8]

DE Like I said before, due to our packaging constraints, I don't think we can put it anywhere else.[9] I can design it to break away if you need it to, so it won't be a problem. The bracket will still be intact, but it will just come loose.

Analyst The problem is that if it breaks away, the material will still be there and it will stack up.

DE Stack up?

Analyst It will stop us from getting a progressive crush.

DE Progressive?

Analyst Let me show you a picture of what it would look like. Do you have the PowerPoint I sent?

The design engineer opened the PowerPoint file the analyst had sent earlier that day, which contained a three-dimensional video rendering of the simulation captured in .AVI format in LS-POST software. The first video clip showed how a progressive crush (also called an axial crush[10]) looked on the front rail (upper panel of figure 6.3); the second video clip, from another iteration, showed how a bent rail—one that didn't crush axially— looked (lower panel of figure 6.3).

Clearly the design engineer, who had worked at Autoworks for many years, wasn't aware of the specific issues that were of concern to analysts. This is not because the DE was ignorant or incompetent; instead, as Bucciarelli suggests, the complexity of engineering design and analysis is so great that it is uncommon for a single engineer to be well versed in object worlds outside his or her own. Thus, in the practice of interaction, the analyst had to teach the DE about his analyses to convince the DE that the particular design change was necessary. Owing to the complexity of the analyses, the simplest way for an analyst to translate his needs into the DE's object-world understanding was through pictures. As the analyst did in the above example, most analysts brought images (typically screen shots or videos) of the problem areas they encountered in their simulations to their meetings with DEs. One analyst explained:

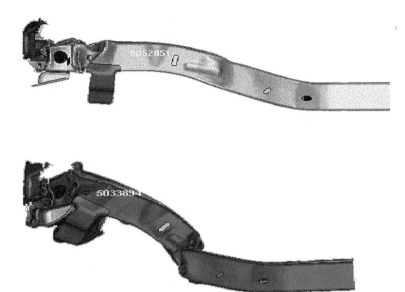

Figure 6.3
Visual depictions (still shots) of axial (progressive) and non-axial crush of front rail. Above: Axial crush in first video presented to design engineer. Below: Non-axial crush in second video presented to design engineer. In the upper image, the rail folds like an accordion at the front; in the lower image, the rails doesn't fold in the front and instead bends further down. Because energy is absorbed through the folding of steel, the rail in the upper image (which has more folds) provides better crashworthiness performance.

I don't always get what a DE does, and I know they don't get what we do. The best way is just to show them an image or video of what's going on. Then they can see what the problem is—they're smart—they see it—and then we can talk about the change. If I just brought in the results of my analysis, it wouldn't go anywhere. That stuff only means something to crash engineers.

When an analyst did use CrashLab to automate the post-processing of a simulation (a rare occasion), he or she received an HTML report that provided the same post-processing calculations as the other commercial post-processing technologies in Autoworks' Safety Division. The advantage of using CrashLab was that, because the software standardized the filters used to output the data and the time steps at which that filtered data was output, it produced a consistent and concise summary sheet for analysts to present to design engineers as evidence that change was necessary. As one developer commented:

My hope is that crash engineers will take the report that CrashLab generates to their meetings with their customers and use it to show what changes are required to the parts. I think this will be convincing for the DEs and managers, because they'll know that CrashLab used best practices to generate these results and they can have confidence in them, rather than having to trust that the crash engineer didn't fudge the model.

Despite such aims, the interaction presented above—which is typical of interactions between analysts and design engineers—demonstrates that such a report was insufficient in bridging object-world thinking. Since CrashLab didn't generate images or videos of deformed parts, an analyst who used the program for post-processing automation still had to open another post-processor and generate imagery to present to design engineers. Because CrashLab's post-processing functions were neither effective in generating a report that existing post-processors couldn't generate nor helpful to analysts for engaging in technical teaching with their customers, analysts continued to interpret CrashLab for what, in their eyes, it *could* do—pre-processing—and stopped using CrashLab's post-processing functions to aid them in their interactions with design engineers.

Interactions with Artifacts

Crashworthiness analysts work in a world in which nonlinear analysis is used to calculate the plastic deformation (permanent damage or change) of a structure. At Autoworks, calculations for nonlinear analysis were performed using finite element algorithms that solved a series of equations to approximate the stress and strain levels of a structure through successive iteration. The intense computational nature of nonlinear analysis required crashworthiness analysts to depend on a number of technologies to aid them in their work, including FE pre-processors and post-processors, solvers, data-storage systems, and high-performance computing resources. Consequently, in addition to using CrashLab, crashworthiness analysts spent a considerable amount of time interacting with a variety of technologies whose material properties either helped or hindered them from making predictions about vehicle performance for a specific load case. Preemptive debugging, iterative testing, and data dumping were three types of interactions through which analysts engaged the materiality of the technologies with which they routinely interacted.

Preemptive Debugging

When crashworthiness analysts used a pre-processor to convert CAD geometry into an FE model or to set up an FE model for submission to a solver, their primary objective was to write an input deck (a text file) that could be read by the solver. In effect, the graphical user interface of a pre-processing technology served only as a convenience to the user. Because analysts worked in a virtual world, the input decks that pre-processing technologies created sometimes contained arrangements that couldn't exist in the physical world. For example, a particular part in the input deck might not have a mass associated with it, or two parts might share the same physical space. Such errors in an input deck, if they were minor, would cause the solver to return inaccurate results. If the errors were large, though, the solver wouldn't be able to compute the particular load case, and the job would, as informants would say, "bomb out." Each input deck was so large that it was nearly impossible for an analyst to review an entire file looking for errors in a model. Therefore, analysts typically submitted each of their models to the solver for a so-called 0-millisecond run so that if the solver discovered any problems before the first time step the analyst could preemptively debug the input deck before submitting the model for a full run.

An analysis of my field notes indicated that analysts spent roughly 17 percent of their time debugging models that had bombed out after 0-millisecond runs. Again, preemptive debugging was not necessarily an indication that things could have been done better the first time—it was an expected part of the process, owing to the complexity of the models with which analysts worked. The trick to effectively debugging a model was to glean from the solver's error message where to look in the input deck to correct the problem. When using CrashLab to prepare a model for submission to the solver, analysts quickly discovered that the tool format-ted the input deck in a way that was different from what they were accus-tomed to seeing. In fact, because CrashLab was automating a number of model-setup processes, analysts were not sure how such modifications were displayed in the input deck. In effect, CrashLab "did things" that analysts couldn't control or completely understand; this frustrated them because if a job bombed out after a 0-millisecond run, they wouldn't know how to go back into the input deck and correct the problem. Since analysts spent, on average, 17 percent of their time debugging, their frustration that CrashLab produced an input deck they couldn't decipher seems quite warranted.

From the perspective of the developers, however, CrashLab was config-ured to generate an input deck that was virtually free from error; thus, analysts should have faith in the deck and shouldn't worry about its con-tents. Martin Yuen put it this way:

We hope that once you go through this, you should get a runnable deck, error free. You shouldn't have to spend so much time debugging it, so why would you do this? It's not necessary for you to know the deck inside and out, even though you may feel a little discomfort on your deck because you only spent two hours. But hopefully you can do all your engineering work with no problem.

But was hard for analysts to believe that CrashLab would generate an error-free deck. Even more problematic was their inability to read the contents of the input deck. They felt they were abdicating control to CrashLab—control which they believed was in their best interest to maintain, since it gave them confidence in their results:

When ElementMesh writes a deck, or any pre-processor, it puts all this extra junk in. So what you have to do is go through and clean it up before you submit it. The other issue is that let's say you use a tool like CrashLab and it automatically generates your deck for you. Well, you don't know how it's doing it or what it's putting in there. So I guess you've lost some control over the process. This becomes a real issue if you have to debug it because it bombed out. If you didn't know what was in the deck in the first place and didn't control your output yourself, you won't know where to begin debugging it, and it could take you forever. I don't have forever. I don't even have an hour.

Because the material features of CrashLab acted on the input deck in ways that analysts couldn't understand, analysts grew afraid that using the software would make preemptive debugging more complicated than it was with other pre-processing tools. Thus, analysts began to interpret CrashLab as an inefficient technology for pre-processing.

Iterative Testing
Crashworthiness analysts interactions with the steel used to build vehicles (or with mathematical representations of it) were among the most important interactions in their work. The goal of math-based analysis at Autoworks was to simulate the plastic deformation of vehicle components made of steel. What made this analysis so complicated was that the deformation of steel under nonlinear, dynamic conditions is difficult to predict (DiPaolo, Monteiro, Gronsky, Jones, and Brebbia 2000). If an analyst increased the gauge of a front rail by 0.2 millimeter, he or she couldn't simply write an equation to predict the difference in deformation linearly. Instead, the engineer had to run a new simulation to compute the new deformation pattern. Thus, when placed in a dynamic loading condition, steel acted in ways that analysts couldn't control.

Figure 6.4 shows how analysts managed the iterative testing of steel components. An analyst created this chart to track all of the iterative

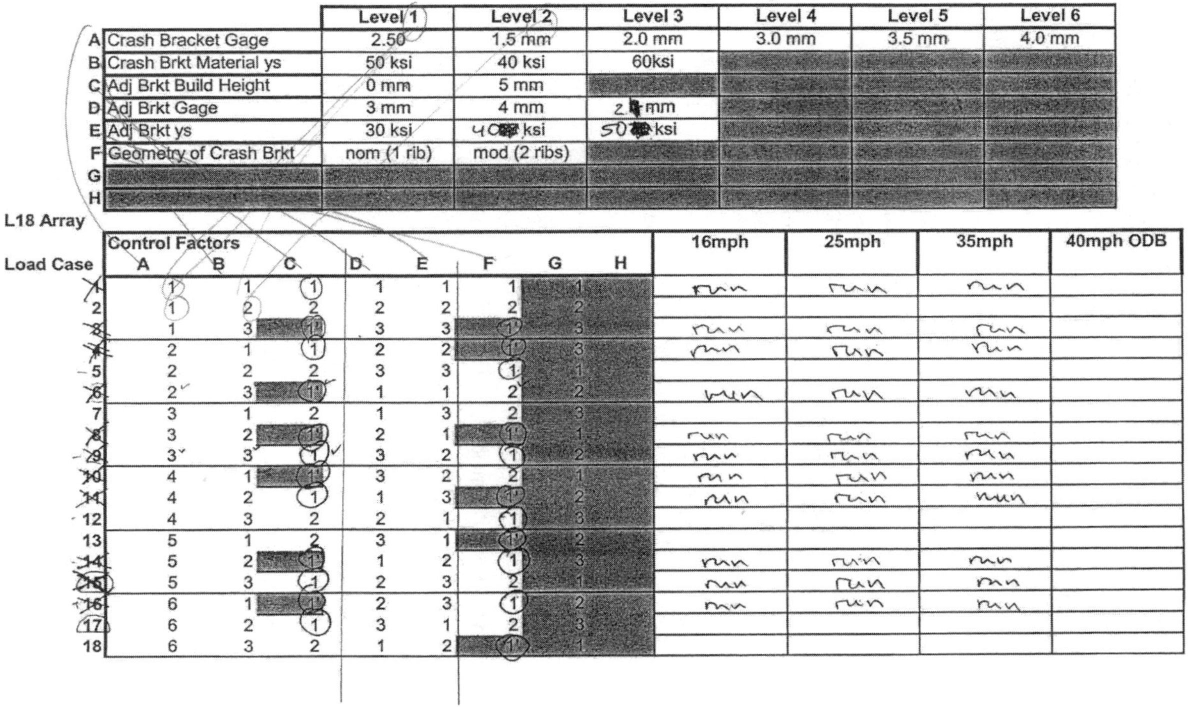

		Level 1	Level 2	Level 3	Level 4	Level 5	Level 6
A	Crash Bracket Gage	2.50	1.5 mm	2.0 mm	3.0 mm	3.5 mm	4.0 mm
B	Crash Brkt Material ys	50 ksi	40 ksi	60ksi			
C	Adj Brkt Build Height	0 mm	5 mm				
D	Adj Brkt Gage	3 mm	4 mm	2.[illegible] mm			
E	Adj Brkt ys	30 ksi	40[illegible] ksi	50[illegible] ksi			
F	Geometry of Crash Brkt	nom (1 rib)	mod (2 ribs)				
G							
H							

L18 Array

Load Case	Control Factors A	B	C	D	E	F	G	H	16mph	25mph	35mph	40mph ODB
1	1	1	1	1	1	1	1		run	run	run	
2	1	2	2	2	2	2	2					
3	1	3	1	3	3	1	3		run	run	run	
4	2	1	1	2	2	1	3		run	run	run	
5	2	2	2	3	3	1	1					
6	2	3	1	1	1	2	2		run	run	run	
7	3	1	2	1	3	2	3					
8	3	2	1	2	1	1	1		run	run	run	
9	3	3	1	3	2	1	2		run	run	run	
10	4	1	1	3	2	2	1		run	run	run	
11	4	2	1	1	3	1	2		run	run	run	
12	4	3	2	2	1	1	3					
13	5	1	2	3	1	1	2					
14	5	2	1	1	2	1	3		run	run	run	
15	5	3	1	2	3	2	1		run	run	run	
16	6	1	1	2	3	1	2		run	run	run	
17	6	2	1	3	1	2	3					
18	6	3	2	1	2	1	1					

Figure 6.4
A chart created by an analyst to track iterative testing.

testing she was performing on a bracket that held a steering column together. To meet an acceptable performance threshold, the engineer had to test six different criteria across six possible configurations at four different speeds. This matrix of operations resulted in 72 iterations (each requiring its own run) for one small bracket. Such iterative testing was quite common in crashworthiness-engineering work at Autoworks, and it happened on a much more dramatic scale as a part's location in a load path became more central. Iteratively testing the deformation of parts was an important component of crashworthiness-engineering analysis at Autoworks. In fact, it was common for analysts to run nearly 30 iterations for one part to verify that its virtual performance was representative of the way it would perform in a physical test, and to optimize a certain design with the goal of achieving the best performance possible given a set of initial constraints.

Using CrashLab to do multiple iterations posed several problems that led analysts to interpret it as an inefficient technology. Using a conventional method of making changes in a part, the engineer would open the input deck for the base-line run and would enter a new set of numbers. For example, if the difference between two iterations was only that the gauge of the rocker had been increased from 4.0 millimeters to 4.2 millimeters, the analyst would simply open the input file, find the line on which the gauge was specified, and change the number from 4.0 to 4.2. However, because analysts didn't feel comfortable navigating CrashLab's input deck, they often decided against making changes to it. Instead, they would use CrashLab's graphical user interface to make the changes, and then re-export the deck. As a result, running a new iteration took considerably more time than if the engineers had used another technology. One analyst explained:

Right now, this isn't so bad. I mean, most of the changes are small, and it's just a matter of opening [the input deck] and changing one or two numbers and submitting. But if I had to open up CrashLab every time and then go through the process, or even part of the process, and then submit, that would drive me crazy. Let me put this another way. If I did use it, I simply couldn't get my work done.

Like the other technologies analysts used, CrashLab didn't have optimization functions. In other words, an analyst who wanted to plot the results of successive iterations against one another still had to make changes manually to each input deck, submit each model individually, then take the results from each run and plot them against one another. Unlike the other technologies analysts used, however, CrashLab output its results in HTML format (so as to provide analysts with a "clean" document to present to their customers). However, the programs they used to plot the results (i.e., ElementMesh and Excel) were unable to read HTML data, so analysts had to manually search for the data generated in CrashLab's HTML report, then copy and enter those data into ElementMesh or Excel. This added yet another step to the process—a step that took time. In addition, manual data entry introduced more opportunities for error. "It [CrashLab] is just not an efficient way to work," said one analyst, "because you have to go through extra steps to get your results, and I'll probably screw it up." Consequently, analysts quickly began to see CrashLab as an inefficient technology for managing the iterative nature of their work.

Dumping Data

Crashworthiness analysts in the Piston Group typically used full-vehicle models (which represent almost every component in a vehicle) in their work. Since nearly every part in a vehicle is involved in an impact, it was necessary for them to work with a model that included all the parts and the connections between them in order to understand how a vehicle would perform under specific loading conditions. At the time of my study, the average full-vehicle model used for crashworthiness analysis at Autoworks had between 1.5 million and 2 million finite elements. Because, on average, analysts conducted more than 30 iterations on each of these models, space for storing data was a major concern for them.

Analysts had several options for storing their data. They could store files on their personal desktop computers; however, but since those computers weren't backed up, the analysts tried not to store anything important on them. They had storage space on a backed-up server, but that space was limited as a matter of procedure by the Infoserv Division. Finally, the High Performance Computing Center allotted each engineer a certain amount of space on another shared server, which was called the R-drive. The R-drive was used by the High Performance Computing Center to return models to analysts once they had been solved. If an engineer had used up his allotted space on the R-drive, his model wouldn't be returned. More important, if the combined size of the jobs submitted to the solver by an analyst was equal to that analyst's remaining space on the R-drive, the High Performance Computing Center wouldn't let the analyst submit additional jobs. In short, in order to submit new runs, an analyst had to make sure he had cleaned out his space on the R-drive and transferred the returned models to one of their other drives. On the basis of the average-size model, an analyst could store only about seven returned models on the R-drive. In effect, this limited an analyst to submitting seven iterations at a time. However, as has already been noted, the average analysis required nearly 30 iterations to optimize a design.

To deal with this problem, analysts looked for ways to subvert the system and submit more than their allotted number of jobs at once. The workaround they used most frequently was to borrow someone else's submission password so the High Performance Computing Center would return the model to that person's space on the R-drive. Analysts referred to this practice as "dumping data." The following exchange between two analysts illustrates the importance of data dumping in analysts' work:

Analyst 1   Are you running any jobs?
Analyst 2   Yes.
Analyst 1   How many?
Analyst 2   Two. Why?
Analyst 1   I'm just looking . . .
Analyst 2   Looking for someone to submit for you?
Analyst 1   Yes [*laughs*]; we submitted so many, we ran out of space. Even counting six at a time, we ran out of job spots.
Analyst 2   After 6 o'clock they'll probably go in.
Analyst 1   But what I'm saying is I've got more than 24.
Analyst 2   Oh, I see—you're looking for IDs to run stuff on. Now I see what you're asking for.
Analyst 1   Yeah.
Analyst 2   I borrowed Javier's password to do this the other day.
Analyst 1   Oh, you did?
Analyst 2   Yeah, but I don't remember it.
Analyst 1   Are you using Regina's?
Analyst 2   Am I using Regina's? No. I know Clark was using it, I'm pretty sure.

Data dumping was pervasive among crashworthiness analysts. Not only did they do it when they needed to submit jobs to the solver; they also did it when their other two drives were full and they needed to move data from the R-drive and temporarily store it somewhere else.

Not surprisingly, analysts expressed a great deal of concern about any technology or practice that would add extra data that then would have to be stored somewhere. As was noted earlier, analysts had good reason to think that CrashLab would add to their data-storage woes. Through technological benchmarking, analysts (inaccurately) learned that CrashLab generated larger files than pre-processing technologies such as Element-Mesh or LinkMesh generated, which suggesting that the models they would submit after using CrashLab would be larger than the models they had submitted in the past:

CrashLab generates bigger files, so basically, every job that comes back would be this huge file I'd have to put somewhere. I have so many space issues that I don't want to deal with that. I think it just helps to relieve my space woes to stick with the pre-processor I'm using now. At least I know how to manage these issues with it.

To add insult to injury, CrashLab's HTML report function produced a large report file for each run submitted to the solver. As one analyst observed, if a full report was generated for each iteration of a model, that report would have to be stored somewhere too, and the information the report contained might not even be completely relevant to the particular analysis the analyst was conducting:

I don't know what I'd do with all those reports. Those are big files. I don't have any place to store them, and I don't know if I'd need them. I think if I just use something like eCrush [a script for post-processing], I can find what I need and don't have to do something with a big report. It's just not very efficient to use it, I guess, over, like, ElementMesh, where you don't get those big files.

Because managing data was already a daily struggle for analysts, and because they had to "dump data" just to get their work done, they quickly came to view CrashLab as inefficient relative to the technologies they were currently using.

The Strut Group

Interactions with People
Analysts in the Strut Group also participated in upward information seeking, technological benchmarking, and technical teaching. However, because analysts in the Piston Group and the Strut Group were exposed to different frames about the role CrashLab would play in their work, these interactions meant something very different to them than what the interactions meant to members of the Piston Group. When Strut Group analysts first experimented with CrashLab, they knew it was supposed to change their work, but they had no idea how. Thus, as they engaged in interactions with people (and also with artifacts, as we will see later), analysts in the Strut Group didn't compare features of technologies within their existing context against features of CrashLab purported to improve speed. Instead, the ideas they formed about CrashLab emerged endogenously as they fitted the experiences gleaned from their interactions with people and artifacts

into a coherent framework that allowed them to start making sense of how CrashLab worked.

Upward Information Seeking

Once they had begun to use CrashLab, Strut Group analysts, like their counterparts in the Piston Group, had many questions for their managers. When the managers first introduced CrashLab to analysts in this group, using a discourse of inevitability, the analysts didn't have much practical experience with the technology. Since they weren't afforded the opportunity to test CrashLab's features on the job, they weren't prepared to ask detailed questions about how to use it. However, after several weeks of tinkering with the new technology, the analysts had a better understanding what kind of features the software possessed. This increased level of tool-based knowledge gave them a context in which to ask more pertinent questions about CrashLab.

For example, during one observation, an analyst who was working on occupant analysis approached his manager with a question about using CrashLab to route a seat belt around an anthropomorphic test device (i.e., a dummy):

Analyst I was looking at positioning the ATD with CrashLab, and I noticed that there's an automated routine for doing this. But I still need to enter the H-point[11] and other information in there. I mean, I get the H-point, but why didn't they just automate the whole thing?

Manager That's a good question. I'm not sure. Do you select the nodes for the IP [instrument panel] parts, and the knee bolster, and things like that to create a contact between your dummy and those IP parts?

Analyst Yeah, I did that, too.

Manager Hmm. I don't really know why that wasn't included in the routine. I guess they thought those things were important to do manually, or they couldn't figure out how to write a script for it.

Analyst Is that different than what I'm doing without CrashLab? How does that make what I do different?

Manager I'm not really sure.

Because he wasn't proficient in CrashLab and he didn't know why certain features were automated and others weren't, this manager could offer little help to the analysts who sought his advice. Managers in the Strut Group couldn't be expected to field questions about the new technology. They simply knew too little about it. In management's defense, it should be noted that analysts usually weren't so inquisitive about the features of a new technology purchased from a vendor. But word had spread in the Safety Division that CrashLab had been designed and developed at Autoworks, so analysts expected their managers to have more information about it than they would have had about a tool bought off the shelf.

Several analysts in the Strut Group developed scripts to perform simple tasks such as submitting jobs and calculating intrusion numbers. When these scripts were distributed in the crashworthiness group and analysts began using them, they attracted a lot of interest, and many engineers asked a lot of questions. As Andy Fong (an analyst who developed several scripts for the Strut Group) commented, information seeking was a common practice when it came to tools developed "in house":

When someone knows you wrote some script, they want to ask you all questions about it very often. It's like they want to know what you do and why you do it. It's like you're a little kid and you ask "Why? Why? Why?" I think it only happens because they can get the answer. If you can't get the answer, no one bothers to ask. But then, if you ask, you expect an answer. That happens to me a lot.

Analysts also enacted this norm when they sought information about CrashLab from their managers. Whenever they had difficulty running the software or it behaved in a way they didn't expect it to, analysts sent emails or went to management to try to gather as much information as they could. As analysts openly admitted, their managers weren't great sources of information about CrashLab—or about technology-related issues in general, for that matter. However, since the analysts didn't have any opportunity to speak of to people who *did* have valuable knowledge, their managers would have to suffice.

Technological Benchmarking

Interacting with colleagues was just as important to analysts' work in the Strut Group as it was in the Piston Group. To put it simply, analysts depended on one another. Each of Autoworks' vehicles, in order to be sold legally in the United States, had to meet basic crashworthiness requirements outlined by the FMVSS regulations. For any particular vehicle, the norm was for at least fifteen analysts to work together to evaluate a number of different load cases. Because most of the structural components that affect crashworthiness (e.g., the rails, the rocker, and the cradle) were involved in different load cases, if one analyst made a change to the front of a vehicle (for example) in order to meet a requirement, the change would be likely to affect another analyst's work on a different load case on the side or at the rear of the vehicle. Thus, analysts spent a great deal of time collaborating with one another to design structures that were mutually beneficial for their respective requirements.

As they worked together, analysts in the Strut Group talked about how CrashLab compared to other technologies in the organization. Whereas the analysts in the Piston Group had preconceived notions about what CrashLab was supposed to do, the analysts in the Strut Group had no such notions. Whereas analysts in the Piston Group were inundated with messages suggesting that CrashLab would speed up their work, analysts in the Strut Group were left to form such opinions on their own. And such opinions often arose when two analysts benchmarked it against different technologies. In these instances, analysts had to negotiate with one another about what CrashLab's purpose really was, as in this exchange:

Analyst 1   I couldn't figure out how to change the friction coefficient from inside CrashLab.
Analyst 2   Why are you trying to do that? Why don't you just do that in ElementMesh or even in DynamicMesh?
Analyst 1   Well, I wanted to see if it was easier to do it there rather than in ElementMesh, but I just couldn't find where it was.
Analyst 2   It's not supposed to be like ElementMesh. I think it's more just like a 3-D way to position the barrier. I've been using it instead of going just into the DYNA deck all the time.
Analyst 1   So, is it, like, taking the place of a text editor?
Analyst 2   Yeah, but I think it's better, because it gives you all the parameters and the friction coefficient, so you don't search for that stuff.
Analyst 1   Do you still edit the deck directly?
Analyst 2   No, you just click on the model, and it's all done in there.
Analyst 1   Oh, that's not too bad. Is it good?
Analyst 2   Yeah, it's easier to use the first time you set it up. After that, you just go into the deck.

When two analysts benchmarked CrashLab against different technologies, one analyst would usually end up convincing the other that his or her comparison point was more accurate. These interactions constituting the practice of benchmarking demonstrated that analysts didn't have a consistent understanding of how CrashLab should be used. Instead, CrashLab's functionality—what it was good for and how it should be used—was constructed through persuasive encounters of this sort. If one analyst was successful in convincing the other that there was a technology out there that was the proper benchmark for CrashLab, comparisons across the Strut Group continued as analysts engaged in further benchmarking interactions.

The technological benchmarking activities discussed above show that analysts in the Strut Group were often unsuccessful at likening CrashLab to any one other technology. In their interactions, CrashLab was seen as "sort of" a pre-processor and "sort of" an elaborate text editor, but in reality it was neither. In fact, analysts were unable to find any suitable benchmark in most of the technological benchmarking interactions that occurred in the Strut Group. Consider the following exchange between two analysts who had discovered features of CrashLab that appeared to be unique to it:

Analyst 1 When I read in my file, and it has a process file in it, and if I go through and I delete all the contacts, will that process file be written out again? You know, if I haven't used anything from my original process file and I've replaced it with . . .

Analyst 2 Okay, say you bring in file A, go through the process, then you write it out, and you got a process file.

Analyst 1 Yeah.

Analyst 2 Yes. CrashLab will create a process file, I think, so when you come back again, or during the process you do some changes, it will be right here.

Analyst 1 When CrashLab reads that in—when I read in my file, but if I go through and in CrashLab, if I delete all the contacts, will CrashLab break this out again?

Analyst 2 Oh, I understand.

Analyst 1 It will just have everything that is included in the CrashLab process file?

Analyst 2 Right.

Analyst 1 Oh, okay. Yeah, that's what I was wondering. Okay, that sounds like something totally different than any other software I know of.

Analyst 2 Yeah, me too.

Without a specific technology to measure CrashLab against, analysts had to develop their own descriptive categories in order to make sense of it. One analyst, whose view represented the majority, commented: "CrashLab doesn't seem exactly like a pre-processor or anything. It's kind of like a model-setup technology. It seems to be pretty unique for that." The analysts had never worked with a "setup technology" before, so they were interested in how it might affect their work. Strangely, the generic framing tactics that implementers used when presenting CrashLab to the Strut Group coincided with the analysts' emerging interpretations of CrashLab as a new and heretofore unavailable "setup technology." If CrashLab's capabilities were different than the capabilities of any technology they had used before, it was possible CrashLab could change their work in dramatic ways.

Technical Teaching

This emerging interpretation of CrashLab as a new kind of software for setting up models rather than for tasks such as mesh generation and optimization, welding, and material specification (activities indicative of pre-processing tools) was strongly reinforced as analysts in the Strut Group taught design engineers about the technical parameters of crashworthiness analysis. Analysts in the Strut Group also had difficulty bridging distinct object worlds in their interactions with design engineers. Like their counterparts in the Piston Group, analysts in the Strut Group knew that presenting data at the highest level of abstraction was often the most effective way to help design engineers understand the factors that influenced crashworthiness performance.

When analysts in the Strut Group began experimenting with CrashLab's reporting capabilities, they discovered a problem: The reports listed data on only a limited number of metrics. For example, the algorithms used to generate the HTML report would automatically select certain filters and a certain sampling rate. For other calculations, such as those for dashboard intrusion presented in figure 6.5, the report would generate information in numerical and graph form for only the nodes CrashLab required the user to choose during the setting up of a model. This was extremely problematic for analysts, who during meetings with design engineers and with other customers often needed to present a much more detailed analysis than a CrashLab report was capable of illustrating. Because many design engineers were unfamiliar with theories of crash energy management and with how structural members responded to dynamic loading, they often simply didn't believe that the analysts' recommendations were necessary to the success of the design. When that happened, the analyst would have to marshal a huge amount of data to convince the design engineer that the problems he or she had identified were real.

If an analyst used CrashLab to generate a standard report, any additional information the engineer needed to prove a problem existed would have to be compiled by hand. Thus, as one analyst commented, it seemed pretty pointless to take the time to generate a standard report in CrashLab in the first place:

I can see the utility of generating a report from CrashLab if you wanted just some quick information for yourself. But if you're trying to give that to a DE, it's not going to give you enough ammunition to make your case. You know before you

Vehicle Max. Dynamic Intrusion

Steering Column	unit	Max. disp (last time step)	@ms
X-displ	[mm]	14.68 (14.68)	104.11
Y-displ	[mm]	−34.31 (−21.89)	79.02
Z-displ	[mm]	43.71 (43.54)	102.63

Instrument Panel	unit	Max. disp (last time step)	@ms
IP Center	[mm]	11.76 (11.55)	103.79
IP Left	[mm]	−84.32 (−81.95)	102.86
IP Right	[mm]	91.97 (−91.97)	104.11

ToePan	unit	Max. disp (last time step)	@ms
Toepan Right	[mm]	179.71 (179.71)	104.11
Toepan Center	[mm]	182.27 (182.27)	104.11
Toepan Left	[mm]	172.73 (172.73)	104.11
Foot Rest	[mm]	123.08 (123.08)	104.11

Vehicle Dynamic Intrusion

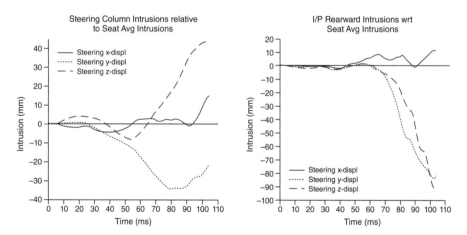

Figure 6.5

A page from a CrashLab report presented to a design engineer.

start how much data you'll need to be persuasive. One little report is not going to give that to you if the problem is complex or it's late in the program and changes are becoming more costly. I mean, once the change gets overly controversial, it's like "Give me all the data you have." And even though they don't know what it means, if this data is so voluminous and so far over their head they don't understand it, well, then they say "This person must be okay, because I've asked this question and they gave me a phone book of data to look at."

The analysts in the Strut Group and their Piston Group counterparts seemed to be disconcerted by CrashLab's report function for exactly oppo-site reasons. The Piston Group analysts were afraid that the report would be too complex for design engineers to understand, and therefore felt that a simple visual format—which CrashLab didn't offer—would be most effec-tive at bridging object-world thinking. The Strut Group analysts were afraid that the information in the report wouldn't be complex enough to con-vince design engineers that a problem was serious enough to warrant redesigning a part. In reality, analysts in both groups were concerned about the same thing: They and the design engineers didn't share the same object worlds, so they needed an effective means of persuasion that would gloss over the technical details and convince a DE that a revision was necessary. The strategy each group enacted to make this happen was different. Ana-lysts in the Piston Group tried to teach design engineers the basics of energy management using simplified representations, while analysts in the Strut Group tried to teach them by providing them with so much informa-tion in support of their position that the design engineers couldn't help but agree with them.

Through these technical teaching interactions with design engineers, analysts in the Strut Group came to the same basic conclusion as their counterparts in the Piston Group: that CrashLab was not a post-processing tool. This realization reinforced a notion that was already emerging as a result of the analysts' upward-information-seeking and technological-benchmarking interactions: CrashLab was a tool that should be used before analysis. In short, analysts increasingly grew to interpret CrashLab as soft-ware for setting up models.

Interactions with Artifacts

To successfully build, solve, and analyze a model, an analyst had to interact with CrashLab, with complementary technologies (ElementMesh, DYNA, LS POST, DataExchange, data-storage drives), and with the steel used to build vehicles. Because analysts in the Strut Group and analysts in the Piston Group worked with the exact same set of technologies, they engaged in similar interactions with artifacts. However, because their interactions differed in content from those of the Piston Group analysts, the Strut Group analysts drew on their interactions with artifacts to qualify their emerging interpretations of CrashLab as a tool to perform routine model setup. Thus, instead of painting CrashLab as an inefficient pre-processor, analysts' engagement in preemptive debugging and iterative testing reinforced their notion that CrashLab was an effective tool for performing such tasks. Because analysts in the Strut Group took a slightly different approach to model building than engineers in the Piston Group did, they didn't regularly dump data. As I will discuss, the absence of this interaction also helped bolster their interpretation of CrashLab as a technology for setting up models.

Preemptive Debugging

Like most engineers in the Piston Group, analysts in the Strut Group spent a considerable amount of time debugging their models. In fact, on average, they spent more time debugging than analysts in the Piston Group, since a standard truck platform had roughly three times as many variations in configurations as a car platform. For most of its car platforms, Autoworks offered a small number of configurations. Consumers could purchase either a two-door or a four-door model, with a choice of typically no more than three power-train options. Autoworks offered a lot more options with its trucks. At any given time, dealers had several different models in stock (multiple configurations of the same truck built on a single platform). For each truck, consumers could choose from a regular cab, an extended cab, or a super extended cab; more than five different power-train packages; at least two different bed lengths and types (straight or "flare-side"); and either two-wheel or four-wheel drive. And because each combination of options affected the structural components of the vehicle (including its weight and its length) differently, analysts working on any given platform were constantly testing multiple configurations of the same vehicle for NCAP, IIHS, and on occasion, EuroNCAP standards.

To handle this complex process of testing and model building, Strut Group analysts shared information with one another. For example, one analyst would build a finite element model of a truck with a bed of one length, another analyst would build a model of a truck with a bed of another length, and the analysts would then share their files with one another to test their respective configurations of components on the platform without having to duplicate efforts. Because pieces of the models were built by different engineers, naturally there were more problems with part penetrations and contacts. As a result, when analysts in the Strut Group submitted models for a 0-millisecond run, they often encountered more error messages than analysts in the Piston Group did. Thus, as the engineers frequently commented, model debugging was particularly painful for those who worked on trucks:

I think doing the truck work is a little harder up front than the car work, and I can say that because I've done both. The real difference is that your models sometimes have more problems at the beginning because you're dealing with more design variables. That means you really want to know your deck well so you can find those problems fast and fix them. Usually it's not too hard to do if you know where to look, and that just takes time to have that skill.

Although debugging was an equally if not more arduous task for engineers in the Strut Group, they didn't use CrashLab in a way that would lead them to see it as an impediment to effective preemptive debugging. Through their interactions with other engineers, the analysts began to view CrashLab as a technology for setting up models, so they didn't envision that they would ever get far enough in the process to write a DYNA input file. Most analysts felt that CrashLab was best used in the early stages of pre-processing. By using CrashLab in conjunction with ElementMesh or another pre-processor, analysts were able to avoid using the CrashLab code to submit jobs to the solver, and they were still able to specify the DYNA deck. As a result, they could take advantage of CrashLab's other features without forming the perception that they had to yield control of the deck to a strange new technology.

Iterative Testing

Analysts in the Strut Group also spent a great deal of time testing multiple iterations of their models. In many cases, the numerous platform configurations required Strut Group analysts to perform more iterations than Piston Group engineers had to perform. For example, even though one truck platform could be structurally configured in many different ways, the cost of casting the dies for manufacturing and the cost of physical testing necessitated different parts for each configuration. Design engineers worked to maximize the number of parts (such as rails and rockers) that could be used on multiple vehicles. If the acceleration of the rear rocker on a four-wheel drive vehicle with an extended cab and a short bed was acceptable in a frontal ODB test, but the acceleration of that same part on a two-wheel-drive vehicle with a regular cab and a long bed was not acceptable (perhaps because of differences in the vehicles' heights and weights), the analyst would have to make modifications to both vehicles so they could continue to share the same parts. Effectively optimizing so many different variations on a platform required an increased number of simulations. The analyst would have to run multiple iterations of the model for both the extended-cab truck and the regular-cab truck until he or she arrived at a design solution for acceptable levels of performance in both configurations.

Analysts who experimented with CrashLab drew heavily on their experiences conducting iterative testing to make sense of the new technology's functionality. When they tried to use CrashLab to post-process their jobs, analysts in the Strut Group, like their counterparts in the Piston Group, quickly found that CrashLab didn't allow them to compare multiple iterations, because the software didn't present the results together in one place. Instead, to use CrashLab to compare twelve different simulations, for example, the analyst would have to generate twelve separate CrashLab reports in HTML format, extract the relevant performance metrics, and then manually input those numbers into either Excel or Hypergraph to create charts for comparison. It didn't take long for analysts to become frustrated with CrashLab because it didn't automatically generate a summary comparing the results of multiple runs. The following excerpt from the observation records is an example of an analyst in the Strut Group, Prasad Vikane, encountering this deficiency in the software for the first time:

Prasad: [*He turns in his chair to look at me and points back to CrashLab, which is running on the computer behind him.*] Okay, so I've been just looking at this, and I can't figure out how to take the results of the base-line and the three tests I did and compare them in CrashLab. I thought there would just be some command here to compare, and then it would give me cross-plots. That's weird. I'm going to call Robin [another analyst in the Strut Group] to see if he knows about this. [*He turns to his phone and dials a phone number from memory.*] Hey, it's me. I'm messing around with CrashLab and trying to cross-plot results from some iterations. Do you know how to do that? [*He listens*] Oh. . . . Okay. I'll call him. Do you have his number? [*He repeats the number Robin gives him out loud while he writes it on the spiral note pad next to the phone.*] Thanks. [*He hangs up the phone and turns to me.*] He told me to call Arnold Dong in Bestpra. [*He turns back to his phone and dials.*] Hi, Arnold. This is Prasad Vikane in the crash group. I'm trying to use CrashLab, and I'm trying to do some post-processing, and I want to cross-plot the results but can't figure out how to do it in CrashLab. [*He listens*] I mean, I have a couple of different iterations, and I want them mapped on the same plot. [*He listens.*] It doesn't? [*He listens.*] Oh. [*He listens.*] Okay. [*He listens.*] Thanks. [*He hangs up the phone and turns to me.*] He said CrashLab won't do that. That's stupid. It seems like more work, then, to generate these reports and then still have to use Hypergraph. That's pretty stupid. Why didn't they put that in there?

When confronted with the knowledge that CrashLab couldn't help them evaluate more than one test of a design at a time, analysts in the Strut Group, just like their counterparts in the Piston Group, quickly became disillusioned with CrashLab's potential for post-processing results, and their interpretations of CrashLab as a technology for setting up models as opposed to one for analysis were further reinforced.

Absence of Data Dumping

The Strut Group was not plagued by data-storage troubles nearly as much as the Piston Group was. Although analysts in both groups were allocated approximately equivalent amounts of space on their desktop computers and on the R-drive, analysts in the Strut Group built their models in a different way: with what they called a "modular approach" to design. Because the truck platforms had so many different components, it made sense to share files so engineers weren't duplicating efforts when they built models. To facilitate this transfer of information, analysts in the Strut Group split a vehicle's structural components into a variety of different modules. Each module—many of which consisted of multiple parts designed in CAD by multiple design engineers—was saved as an individual FE file. These modules could then be shared among engineers working on various load cases. For example, an analyst performing a frontal-impact analysis might have to include the power-train, door, body-in-white, and suspension modules in the math model, but not the rear-axle module or the rear-door module, while an analyst performing a rear-impact analysis would need the latter modules but not the power-train module or the module for the front doors. Therefore, modules that were affected in multiple load cases had to be meshed finely enough to be used for multiple analyses. In most cases, this meant that the entire body-in-white was meshed with element sizes between 5 and 10 millimeters. Despite the fact that a higher mesh density was used for modeling common parts, overall the typical truck model was smaller than the average car model submitted to the solver since the Strut Group didn't build full-vehicle models. Since they adopted a modular approach, the only modules affected in the focal loading condition were the ones included in the model.

Each of these modules was saved on an analyst's personal computer. When an analyst needed to assemble the appropriate modules for an analysis, he or she would write an INCLUDE statement—a syntax in a text-editor file that would call modules from various places and integrate them into a full-vehicle model without ever physically moving them to one location. This distributed data storage prevented multiple analysts from hosting the same full-vehicle models on their personal computers, thereby reducing the amount of space occupied by FE models. Analysts often commented that they were very happy with using a modular approach to vehicle assembly—not only did it reduce the size of the files they stored, but, since the vehicle was assembled in smaller segments, there was a smaller chance of a model's bombing out when it was submitted to the solver:

If I get a crash model, well, I'd want one, at least I'd want one that's built in modules like this, because I don't think there's any other way to do it. If you want to do a full analysis—full system analysis from the standpoint of front, side, rear crash—you want modular, because you want all of the subsystems separate, as many as you can—so, as many different parts as possible. Um, so if you're making changes, say you're reducing the number of times and the number of files that you're making changes to—simple as that—and obviously if they care, if the person who develops the model takes care and does it properly, we find, at least I find, that the model will run every single time. So, a lot of people have complaints: "Oh, my model is going to take two or three weeks to debug so that it actually is able to run through the results." We rarely have that. I think that's important. Somebody asked you for a change, say "Can you validate this," and you say "Yeah. I'll give it to you in two days. It'll take me a day to put the change it, it'll take 24 hours to make the computer run, and it'll take me a day. . . . I'll give you the result." You don't want a model that sometimes runs, sometimes doesn't. I want something I'm sure will run.

Because the modular approach typically resulted in fewer bugs, analysts had fewer error files returned to them on the R-drive than analysts in the Piston Group did, so they had more free space on the R-drive. It became clear that analysts in the Strut Group were much less concerned than analysts in the Piston Group about having to dump data onto other people's drives. I observed analysts in the Strut Group asking to borrow passwords from their colleagues and looking for free space on other people's drives about half as often as analysts in the Piston Group. Because using modules tied together via INCLUDE statements meant that their drives were rarely ever pushing the storage limits enforced by Infoserv, Strut Group analysts weren't concerned that CrashLab would generate large files. After seeing analysts in the Piston Group struggle with the idea that Crash-Lab would add larger files to already maxed-out drives, I asked analysts in the Strut Group if they had similar concerns:

Researcher   Are you worried at all that CrashLab will generate larger files than ElementMesh?
Analyst   No. It's not like I have plenty of space, but I'm not hurting, either. No one really is. I think it's fine. Anyway, if you're just using it to set up

your models, all it's doing is throwing a few more command lines or just text that's commented out[12] into your deck, so that is not really going to make it bigger anyway. And I don't think I would do anything else with it, since you still have to map your iterations onto each other anyway. So it should be fine.

Such comments were evidence of the Strut Group analysts' relative lack of concern about file storage. Moreover, this example illustrates how the interpretations analysts developed of CrashLab through their interactions with people were reinforced by their interactions with artifacts.

7 Appropriating Material Features to Change Work

In October of 2005, Andrew Guizek, an analyst in the Strut Group, was attempting to use CrashLab to set up a model for an IIHS side-impact test. As he waited for his model to load, he made an interesting and rather colorful comment:

You know, I was talking to this guy I know who's also an analyst here at Autoworks and he told me that CrashLab was a piece of shit. I was like "Whoa, okay, that's weird to feel so strongly about software." But he was just saying that when he tries to use it, he has to ask more questions to people than if he did things by hand. I'm not sure why. I mean, I think, actually, I don't have to go and look up, like, the IIHS specifics if I use CrashLab like I would have to if I didn't. So for me, it makes me not have to ask so many questions. I wonder why that's different from what his experience was. Maybe it's just that he's not using it right. I don't know.

Was there a "right" way to use CrashLab? If so, was Andrew using it the "right" way, and was his colleague in the Piston Group using it the "wrong" way? Certainly the developers of any technology have intentions for how the technology "should" be used. Certain material properties are designed into technologies to suggest certain uses over others (Norman 1999), and trainers, managers, and other implementers provide explicit instructions for how they would like a technology to be used (Yates, Orlikowski, and Okamura 1999). These efforts notwithstanding, is there a way to use a technology correctly? How would we know a correct use if we saw one? When asked these questions, Jensen Lu provided a simple answer:

Yes. There is a way to use a technology right and a way to use it wrong. Basically, if you just use some of the capabilities of CrashLab and not all of them, you are not using it right. All those features are there so the users can use them together. They work together. If you don't use them for the reasons they're there, then you're not going to get the maximum utility out of the tool. I'm not saying you need to use them all at once. Like, you could set up a model initially, and then later, some things change, so you need a new section. Well you don't redo the barrier, because you already did that, but you redo the sections. But you should have used all the features at some point. If you just set up a model with it but don't do analysis, then you're not going to use it the way we intended. Setting up the model with CrashLab gives you a standard report. Ultimately, that's what the engineer needs—the report. So that's how to see if they're using it correctly. Did they set up the model, and then, did they get the report.

The technology developers at Autoworks, who were spread across different divisions of the company, did feel that there was a correct way to use CrashLab. Car Department managers, who had learned about CrashLab's goals and its many features in Focus Group meetings and through their interactions with Sunil Kitane, also felt that there was a right way to use the software. Those invested in the technology hoped that CrashLab would help to standardize work, thereby saving time and reducing inconsistencies in quality and performance. With these goals established, crashworthiness analysts could work in a new way, spending less time worrying about setting up models for analysis and more time analyzing the models and working with their colleagues to optimize designs for better vehicle performance in a crash. To achieve these goals, developers and implementers believed, analysts should utilize all of CrashLab's model-setup and model-analysis features.

Technology development researchers have suggested that one way to think about the relationship between a technology's built-in features and the kinds of changes its developers, managers, and implementers hope those features will bring is through the concept of *inscription*. This concept was first introduced in the sociological realm by Latour and Woolgar (1979), who drew on their studies in an endocrinology lab at the Salk Institute to show that scientists make a number of choices about how they will translate the practices of the material world into scientific findings. Specifically, Latour and Woolgar used Jacques Derrida's concept of inscription to suggest that scientists inscribe their findings by using of some kind of visual display (e.g., figures or diagrams) in a scientific text, which transforms the actions of the material world into written documents. Latour and Woolgar argue that inscriptions, which appear neat and tidy, actually cover up the messy processes by which they were produced. The concept of inscription has been used to explain technology development in roughly the same way, suggesting that the messy social processes that bring a technology into the world (for example, the articulation processes in which developers at Autoworks participated) are frozen in the new technology through the selection of its material features. Thus, a technology looks clean and tidy—as if it were the natural outgrowth of the artifact that preceded it—because the inscription process has hidden the contestation out of which the technology emerged. Technology development research-ers have gone even further to suggest that developers use specific material features to carefully script the actions of those who will eventually use the technology. Akrich (1992, p. 208) describes this as follows:

Designers thus define actors with specific tastes, competences, motives, aspirations, political prejudices, and the rest, and they assume that mortality, technology, science and economy will evolve in particular ways. . . . A large part of the work of innovators is that of "inscribing" this vision of (or prediction about) the world in the technical content of the new object. . . . Thus, like a film script, technical objects define a framework of action together with the actors and the space in which they are supposed to act.

This further appropriation of the concept of inscription suggests that developers of a new technology aim to take an active role not only in the development of a technology but also in the development of the social system the technology will help create or change with its implementation. Using the concept of inscription in this way, many authors have explored how developers of technologies actively work to promulgate their ideas for more effective actions and organizations in technical form. (See, e.g., Berg 1998; Holmström and Robey 2005.)

Poole and DeSanctis (1990, 1992) have suggested that technology devel-opers create a particular technological structure (a collection of material features) to lead a group of users to adopt a particular social structure (a set of interactions) through the technology's use. They assert that "advanced technologies bring social structures which enable and constrain interaction to the workplace" (DeSanctis and Poole 1994, p. 125). Within such a view, a new technology is described in terms of its structural features and the general spirit of those features. Structural features are a system's specific rules and resources, or capabilities. They are the vision of a specific social structure inscribed in material form. The spirit is "the 'official line' the technology presents to people regarding how to act when using it, how to interpret its features, and how to fill in gaps in procedure which are not explicitly specified" (ibid., p. 125). In the context of use, then, users can appropriate the features of a technology either in ways that are consistent with the spirit in which it was designed and implemented (what Poole and DeSanctis call a "faithful appropriation") or in ways that are inconsistent with the general spirit (an "ironic appropriation").

Other scholars, among them Orlikowski (2000, p. 406), have rebuffed such a view, claiming that once social structures (whether real or imagined) are inscribed in a technology's features they can't exert their force on users.

According to Orlikowski, this is so because "inscribed properties of a technology constitute neither rules nor resources, and thus cannot be seen to be structures." At a basic level, Orlikowski is at odds with a conceptualization of social structure as something that can exist outside the realm of practice (see Giddens 1984). Instead, Orlikowski suggests that, because users of a technology have human agency, they will, through their experience with a technology's features, "enact" a social structure that is contextually specific and embedded within the institutional constraints of their workplace. These finely cut philosophical discussions about what constitutes a social structure (whether social structures exist in material form, whether they have only a virtual existence) risk missing an important point: Everyday users engage with material features of a technology that were put there for a particular reason. As we have seen with the development of CrashLab, some features (such as algorithms to filter data) are created to reduce the amount of variability in performance of work. Other features (e.g., automated functions for setting up load cases) are created to speed up work. Still other features (such as the wizard window or the tree structure) are created to work in conjunction with features of other technologies. Thus, because the process of technology development *is* messy and contentious and involves the effort of numerous parties with diverse interests, features often become decoupled from the "spirit" in which a technology was designed. Perhaps more important, a technology's features may evince multiple "spirits" or agendas (e.g., bringing accuracy, speed, and credibility to crashworthiness-engineering work).

When we say that someone's vision for how a technology will be used and how it will change the way people work is inscribed into the technology, we may be well advised to return to the definition introduced by Latour and Woolgar. The material features of a technology represent the negotiations of a messy social process. Because they inscribe only the *resolution* of such negotiations, they don't tell users the whole story; how the technology should be used and what it is supposed to do are left open to interpretation. Such messages are carried from the land of developers to the land of users through the creation and promulgation of specific discourses. As we have seen, the actions of trainers such as Chowpa Maova and Eileen Gaffer and managers such as those in the Piston Group and those in the Strut Group provide users with frames with which they can begin to develop interpretations about how to use those inscribed features. In other words, a particular material feature, by virtue of its functional limits, will allow the user to do only so much. But even an immutable piece of hardware—for example, a hammer, which is given particular characteristics, such as a long handle, an oblong head, and an asymmetrical weight distribution, so as to suggest that it should be used to strike something—can be used to prop open a door. When the discourses created by trainers and implementers "key in on" the designers' intentions ("Why, then, put that long handle on the hammer?"), they can serve to make alternate and hence undesired uses of the technology appear objectionable, if not impossible.

As we have seen, though, messages intended to restrict a user's attention to a specific set of characteristics can be thwarted if the correct means of persuasion are not chosen. The discourse of efficiency, which was constructed to remind users that CrashLab would speed up their work, didn't align with analysts' work experiences. For this reason, analysts in the Piston Group began to interpret CrashLab as an inefficient technology for pre-processing activities. The discourse of inevitability was created and perpetuated because its implementers, who didn't have any knowledge of the developers' reasons for selecting specific features, created a generic discourse that didn't constrain analysts' interpretations of the new technology as narrowly. Through their social and material interactions, analysts in the Strut Group instead grew to see CrashLab as an efficient tool for setting up their models if they used other pre-processing technologies to prepare the models for analysis. The blanket discourse of inevitability allowed them to consider their experiences with CrashLab from within a loose structure. That is, because implementers told analysts in the Strut Group only that CrashLab would change the way they worked and not how its specific features would help them make certain changes, analysts were able to determine for themselves how they would use specific features and how they would allow such uses to instigate structural change.

So far, we have considered the concepts of inscription, interpretation, appropriation, and enactment. Alone, none of these concepts seems sufficient to explain whether and how CrashLab would help change the work of analysts in the Safety Division. As we saw in chapter 5, through the articulation process, the outcome of the primary players' (Safety, Techpro, Infoserv, and R&D) negotiations became inscribed in CrashLab as its material features. Through this inscription process, certain points of view and goals (such as those of Jason Chan and his colleagues in the R&D group) were either purposely or accidentally inhibited from being realized in material form. In chapter 6, we discovered that analysts based their interpretations of CrashLab—what kind of technology it was, and how it should be used in their work—only partially on their direct interactions with those inscribed features. Through their interactions with managers, co-workers, trainers, customers, and other complementary technologies, analysts in the Piston Group and the Strut Group began to develop distinct under-standings of the nature of the new technology. As we will see in this chapter, analysts in each group began using specific features of CrashLab in ways that aligned with their respective interpretations of its functional-ity. Could we call these uses appropriations? If so, what were analysts appropriating? For at least two reasons, it would be difficult to say that analysts were appropriating social structures that had been inscribed in the technology by its developers. First, as has become apparent, the features that eventually became CrashLab weren't all chosen intentionally—many were incorporated into the software because of exogenous constraints, such as the personnel who worked on the project and the choice of vendor firms that would code the tool. Second, we have seen little evidence that the analysts had any clear understanding of the social structure developers and managers aimed to impose on crashworthiness analysis work. Devel-opers, managers, and trainers associated with the Piston Group explicitly stated why CrashLab would be useful (it would speed up the work), but they didn't ever say—nor did they intuit—that if the analysts were able to complete their work faster they would be able to spend less time talking to their colleagues about setting up models and more time talking about how to build better vehicles.

However, analysts did appropriate CrashLab's specific material features. CrashLab had twelve concrete features (listed in table 7.1) that were immediately apparent and accessible to users. Although the features were presented in an order that suggested they should be used in a temporal sequence, users could, in practice, engage any of the features at any time and could choose to use only certain features as they saw fit. The English verb 'appropriate' comes from the Latin *appropriare*, which means "to make one's own." Thus, we can talk about the analysts' appropriating CrashLab's features not when they used them to set up and analyze models as developers hoped they would, but when they did so for their own purposes. Drawing on such a definition, I have suggested that users, by appropriating a technology's features (choosing to use some features and not others), actively aid in the social construction of a technology's functionality (Leonardi 2007). Therefore, studies of appropriation direct our attention in two directions. First, we must observe which combina-tion of a technology's features people use and in which order they use them. Second, we must observe how the features are used in the practice of regular work.

Table 7.1

CrashLab's twelve main material features.

Feature	Description
1. Check Model	Reviews assembled model to check for missing parts and part penetrations and to ensure material properties have been assigned to all parts.
2. Create Sections	Guides user through the process of making section cuts in predefined locations of a model so as to measure accelerative forces produced during impact.
3. Place Accelerometers	Guides user through the process of placing accelerometers in predefined areas of a model to conform to testing standards outlined by NHTSA and IIHS.
4. Create Energy Groups	Guides user through the process of creating energy groups (a collection of affiliated parts) to measure the balance of energy in a model before and after an impact condition.
5. Nodeout Request	Guides user through the process of selecting certain nodes at which measures of displacement will be taken after impact.
6. Position Barrier	Guides user through the process of selecting appropriate barrier for test and positioning the barrier using NHTSA and IIHS coordinates and user-generated calculations for J and K heights of loaded vehicle.
7. Define Initial Conditions	Guides user through the process of defining the initial or boundary conditions of the model, such as the angle of approach, friction coefficient at barrier face, velocity of impact, etc.
8. Create Contacts	Guides user through the process of selecting the appropriate means of creating contact algorithms between the vehicle and the barrier.
9. Position ATD	Guides user through the process of selecting appropriate ATD for load-case analysis and positioning dummy in vehicle in compliance with NHTSA and IIHS test requirements.
10. Route Seat Belts	Guides user through the process of routing seat belts around ATD in compliance with NHTSA and IIHS test requirements.
11. Write Input Deck	Converts the graphical representation of the model into a text-based input file that can be read by the DYNA solver.
12. Generate Report	Automatically generates, in HTML format, a report of the simulation containing data of interest (as specified in the VP charts) in tabular and chart format. Algorithms are used to sample and filter data per best-practice guidelines.

If users appropriate features—which are only the inscriptions of a nego-tiation process, not a template for a social structure intentionally built into a technology—how, then, do these appropriations lead to stasis or change in the social structures in which they are embedded? Orlikowski (2000), Boudreau and Robey (2005), and Vaast and Walsham (2005) suggest that, when using these features in their work, people enact—that is, constitute, actuate, perform—the social structures in which they participate. To buy into this view, one must subscribe to the performative theory of organizing outlined in chapter 1. From the vantage point of a performative perspective, organizational structures are enacted through people's interactions with one another. Thus, it seems safe to say that people's appropriations of a technology's features bring about stasis or change in the process of organiz-ing, since the features provide users with newfound capabilities they once lacked—capabilities they can exploit in the process of organizing.

In this chapter, I explore how the analysts appropriated CrashLab's features and how their appropriations led them to either maintain or change the informal organization of their work. These data suggest that while they were still exploring what CrashLab had to offer and forming their interpretations, analysts in both the Piston Group and the Strut Group made very different appropriations of CrashLab's features. Members of each of these groups used CrashLab in many different ways and for many different reasons. Eventually, however, analysts in the Strut Group began appropriating CrashLab's features in more convergent ways. Later in the chapter, I consider how the difference between convergent appro-priations and divergent appropriations can help account for the differences in informal organizational structure that I observed between the Piston Group and the Strut Group nearly a year after CrashLab was initially implemented.

Appropriating CrashLab's Features

By late October of 2005, analysts in both the Piston Group and the Strut Group were experimenting with CrashLab in their everyday work. In both groups, analysts' initial reactions to CrashLab ranged from positive and enthusiastic to annoyed. In both groups, many engineers felt it was too early for them to decide whether CrashLab was a valuable tool that should be used every day or was of little use to them. Consider these comments:

Piston Group analyst   My initial impression has not been too good. I mean, CrashLab seems okay, but I think other pre-processors are better. I've been just sort of messing around with some of its features to try them out. You know? It works okay.

Strut Group analyst   CrashLab seems fine so far. Last week I was playing around with it to do some model-setup work—early stuff like putting in the accelerometers—and it seemed to work pretty well. I need to just kind of test it out some more before I get totally comfortable with it.

Given that the analysts were up against tight deadlines and had no previous experience with CrashLab, one would not expect them to have been overjoyed about having to experiment with the new technology. To make matters worse, in order to use CrashLab analysts also had to also learn the basics of DynamicMesh, since CrashLab was embedded in that software and shared its user interface. By all accounts, the process of learning to use CrashLab was one of trial and error.

This early phase of CrashLab's use mirrors the experiences of users of many other types of technology, including computer messaging systems (Flores et al. 1988), email (Culnan and Markus 1987), group decision support systems (Scott, Quinn, Timmerman, and Garrett 1998), enterprise resource planning systems (Markus, Axline, Petrie, and Tanis 2000), and geographic information systems (Walsham 2002). Because of the startup costs associated with switching to a new technology, users are initially reluctant to changes technologies even if they perceive the new tool to be advantageous. And when users begin the transition from one set of tools to another, it is not always entirely clear to them how the new technology should be used. Tyre and Orlikowski's (1994) study of software and manufacturing technologies in three industries suggests that upon implementation there is a limited "window of opportunity" in which users can explore a new technology's features without fear of reproach or social sanction. New users can tinker with a technology and learn for themselves how its various features might prove useful or become an impediment to their work, but not for long. Why is the window of opportunity so small? Tyre and Orlikowski suggest that managers may initially expect users to take time to adjust to a new technology and (as analysts in the Safety Division commented) "mess around" with it, but eventually production pressures begin to impede experimentation and local improvisation. As one manager in the Piston Group commented, a period of adjustment for a new tool necessarily entails a temporary reduction in productivity:

When you move from doing things with one technology to a new one, you expect that people are going to be slow. It's like if you've gotten used to using ElementMesh for everything and now we say "Here. Use CrashLab." You don't know it as well as

ElementMesh, so you're going to be slower at it. Plus, I think most people learn better by tinkering with it. So you expect they'll try things out and just kind of test it out a bit to see how things work for a while. But while you can understand that productivity goes down for a while, it can't happen forever. We need to still meet our deadlines. So if after, like, four months some engineer is saying "Sorry. This model's late because I was working with it on CrashLab," you have to basically say "By now I expect you to be fluent with it already."

Tyre and Orlikowski suggest that this initial burst of experimenting with and acclimating to a new technology tends to last about two to three months after implementation, and that by seven months after implementation users no longer are experimenting with the features of the new technology; they are using some subset of the features in a consistent way. Other studies of technology implementation in different industries largely confirm that experimentation and innovation with a new technology seems to dissipate between two and four months after the technology is implemented (Leonardi 2007; Majchrzak, Rice, Malhotra, King, and Ba 2000).

Because CrashLab was launched at a crucial point in the vehicle development process,[1] there was another important reason to expect that experimentation with CrashLab's features would begin to diminish between two and four months after implementation. During the thirteenth week after implementation, both the Piston Group and the Strut Group approached a major development stage-gate: virtual mule-vehicle assessment (VMVA). The VMVA stage gate came only fourteen weeks after the vehicle's architecture was officially handed off to the product-engineering organizations ("vehicle product initiation"). At this critical juncture, Autoworks' management made a complete assessment of the feasibility of the vehicle platform by evaluating the results of performance tests on a virtual mule vehicle. In production terms, a mule vehicle (or test mule) is an operational vehicle with a newly constructed one-off chassis or body-in-white onto which assembled parts (e.g., seats and doors) from previous generations of the vehicle are mounted. In the virtual, math-based world in which analysts worked, a virtual mule had a similar structure. Analysts tested the performance of a math model of the body-in-white that was accompanied by math files from previous generations. Thus, as one senior analyst in the Piston Group noted, VMVA was one of the most crucial junctures in structural crashworthiness work:

Probably after VPI [vehicle product initiation], the next biggest hurdle for us is at VMVA. That is when all the higher-ups look over the performance and decide if we need to make any big change. By that point, we normally haven't cast any dies or anything, so the cost of changes at that point is not so bad. I mean, it's not good, but not like later. Once things go through VMVA and it gets approval, then we start working on solidifying the design and the program gets more inertia. . . . Probably, from a crash standpoint, most of our work happens before then. So between VPI and SVER [structure vehicle engineering release] is when we do most of our heavy lifting. If we haven't made the changes to the structure by SVER, then they get almost impossible to make and heads start rolling, because it gets too expensive and you have to start getting people all the way up to vice-presidents involved to put a little initiator in a rail.[2]

As many other analysts commented, work got more serious after VMVA, and deliverables were due to management on a more regular basis. Thus, one might expect that after VMVA analysts would have less of an incentive than before to "mess around" with CrashLab. Examining the number of features (0 through 12) analysts used after implementation and the number of analysts in the Piston Group (19) and the Strut Group (17) who could have used them reveals an interesting trend.

The graphs in figure 7.1 indicate that in both the Piston Group and the Strut Group the number of features analysts used dropped off dramatically around the thirteenth week after CrashLab was implemented, just at the time of the VMVA stage gate. Analysts from both groups were cognizant of this change:

Piston Group analyst Once we made it through VMVA, my deadlines started coming more frequently. I just needed to get things done quicker, so I went back to using ElementMesh more.

Strut Group analyst I think I didn't experiment with CrashLab so much after we started to get deeper in the program, since there wasn't so much time. You just do what works for those things that I wasn't too comfortable with it anyway.

As analysts moved into the portion of the vehicle development process in which deadlines occurred more frequently and they were expected to provide results in a timelier manner, they reduced their experimenting with CrashLab's features. Although VMVA appears to have been an important turning point for both the Piston Group and the Strut Group, the ways analysts in the two groups treated CrashLab's features after VMVA differed markedly. As the graphs in figure 7.1 illustrate, after week 13 analysts in the Piston Group used a much smaller set of CrashLab's features. In fact, by week 33 analysts in the Piston Group were either using just one of CrashLab's features or using none of them. By contrast, none of the analysts in the Strut Group abandoned CrashLab after week 13. Although the number of features they used routinely began declining after VMVA, by week 20 each of the analysts in the Strut Group was still consistently

Piston Group

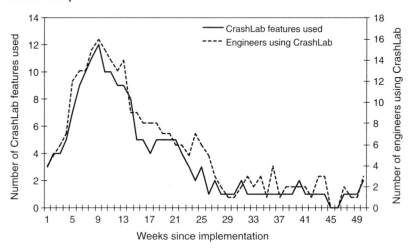

Strut Group

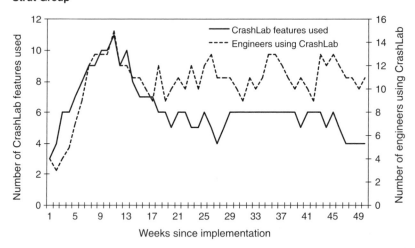

Figure 7.1
Number of CrashLab features used and number of analysts using them.

using about five of CrashLab's features regularly. This trend continued until observations ended, at week 50. By then, the average number of features used by analysts in the Strut Group had dropped only slightly, to four.

Because the VMVA stage gate was an important juncture in the crashworthiness-engineering process, I used that stage gate to demarcate two periods of CrashLab use after implementation. Period 1 begins with the implementation of CrashLab in both the Piston Group and the Strut Group and continues through week 13. Week 13 is a crucial break point for three reasons. First, this was the week in which the VMVA stage gate occurred. Second, the major inflection point in figure 7.1 occurred at week 13, marking a switch from analysts' using many of CrashLab's features to their using only some of its features. Finally, week 13 marked the end of my first period of observation of crashworthiness analysts. Thus, not only was that week important from the emic perspective of the analysts working with CrashLab; it was also important from the etic perspective of the researcher.

By dividing analysts' use of CrashLab into two periods, table 7.2 helps to explain the types of the change in CrashLab use captured in figure 7.1. The data in the table indicate that in period 1 analysts in both groups were using nearly the same number of CrashLab's features; analysts in both

Table 7.2

Number of analysts using CrashLab's features in each period (data from logs).

CrashLab feature used	Period 1[a]		Period 2[b]	
	Piston Group	Strut Group	Piston Group	Strut Group
1. Check Model	8	9	8	11
2. Create Sections	11	12	2	13
3. Place Accelerometers	13	8	—	13
4. Create Energy Groups	7	8	—	10
5. Nodeout Request	3	10	—	14
6. Position Barrier	7	12	1	13
7. Define Initial Conditions	2	—	—	—
8. Create Contacts	—	8	—	—
9. Position ATD	2	7	6	1
10. Route Seat Belts	3	8	3	—
11. Write Input Deck	4	10	—	—
12. Generate Report	8	7	—	—

a. weeks 1–13
b. weeks 14–50

groups had experimented with eleven of the twelve. Although the data indicate that analysts used multiple features in period 1, they show little depth of use. Fewer than half of the analysts in either group experimented with more than five of CrashLab's features. Period 1 is marked by a widely divergent pattern of use in which analysts were using CrashLab's features selectively, not as a bundled set. The data obtained from observations of analysts in the course of their everyday work explain these patterns of appropriation during the first period of use.

As was discussed in chapter 6, analysts in the Piston Group had begun to form interpretations of CrashLab as an inefficient pre-processor. Therefore, they were basing their decisions about whether or not to use the software on variables that were important to pre-processing tasks. In the following interaction, two analysts in the Piston Group discuss whether to use CrashLab or ElementMesh:

Analyst 1   Do you have time to run a LINCAP test for iteration 5?
Analyst 2   Are the changes to the cross-car beam done?
Analyst 1   No. You have to make them.
Analyst 2   When do we need to submit?
Analyst 1   Just to have the results by Thursday.
Analyst 2   Is it set up in ElementMesh, or CrashLab?
Analyst 1   ElementMesh. CrashLab doesn't seem to do as much for pre-processing.
Analyst 2   Yeah, that's why I asked.

Clearly, analysts were basing their decisions on whether the new technology could help them complete the tasks more quickly than they could with the other pre-processors they used. Because analysts had been told that CrashLab would "speed up" their work, they based most of their decisions about whether or not to use CrashLab, and most of their decisions about how to use it, on a criterion of speed. At times, though, analysts felt that they would be able to get their work done more quickly by using only certain features of CrashLab, not the entire package. On one such occasion, an analyst and his manager were reviewing some results of simulations the analyst had run on the configuration of a bracket when the manager unexpectedly requested more information for a meeting he would be attending the next day:

Manager   Did you run tests putting [the bracket] at the other angles?
Analyst   No, but you can see how the trend is looking.
Manager   Is it consistent?
Analyst   Yeah. It follows the trend, so it will just show that the offset gives you a worse pulse.

Manager   Can you give me just some numbers on that or some charts to show when I meet with [the design team] tomorrow? Because you know they'll ask.

Analyst   You just want the numbers?

Manager   Yeah, just to show them.

When the analyst returned to his desk, he commented that if he were to run the simulation overnight to come up with the extra iterations his manager had requested, he would not be able to organize all of the data into tables and charts in time for his manager's meeting. But then he thought of a quick fix:

> Well, tomorrow I can just open it up in CrashLab and it will give, I think, most of the numbers [the manager] wants in that report. I don't think it's enough to be conclusive, but it should be enough to show the trend, and it will be fast to do that. That will be good to see if it works for that or not.

Following the same logic, the analyst devised workarounds to accommodate his time constraints. He made the changes to the angle of the bracket in the text-editor file rather than in CrashLab, and then used a script he had borrowed from one of his colleagues to submit the job to the solver. The next day, when the solved model was returned to his R-drive, he used CrashLab to generate a report from the data he had submitted to his manager. The immediate demands of the situation and the analyst's understanding of CrashLab as a tool that would "speed up" work led him to use just one feature of the software to complete the task at hand instead of running the model through the program from start to finish. In cases such as these, CrashLab was appropriated as a report-generating tool, since that was its only function in the context of the analysts' work.

Analysts in the Strut Group also felt compelled to use CrashLab to meet the immediate demands of their work. However, their interpretations of CrashLab's utility weren't nearly as specific as those of their counterparts in the Piston Group. As they determined how best to utilize CrashLab in their work, analysts weren't looking for features that would speed up their work. In effect, an analysts in the Strut Group had one less interpretive filter than an analyst in the Piston Group did: When faced with a contextual demand, a Strut Group analyst didn't first have to determine whether using CrashLab would be faster than using another application; instead, he or she only had to decide whether CrashLab was appropriate for accomplishing the task. In many cases, analysts in the Strut Group decided to use one of CrashLab's features even though they knew full well that it would be faster to use another technology. In these situations, the demands of the task at hand helped analysts view CrashLab as the best choice for the job.

The following exchange, in which an analyst and a design engineer discuss the placement of a battery tray in an engine compartment, is representative of the contextual pressures that led analysts to choose CrashLab:

Analyst   If [the battery tray] could just be about four centimeters higher, I think that would take care of it.

Design engineer   I don't think we can move it higher without interfering with the reservoir. Could we move it back a few inches?

Analyst   Maybe. I'm not sure. I'll do some tests on it to see. How much room is there?

Design engineer   To move it back?

Analyst   Yeah.

Design engineer   We could probably go three inches or so.

When the analyst returned to her desk, she turned to me and said:

I think maybe what I'll do is create another energy group to see if we get a better pulse if we move it back like he said. I'm not sure exactly what to group, but . . . I think you can do that in CrashLab. I mean, it will select it for you. Maybe I'll explore that.

As this example illustrates, analysts in the Strut Group based their decisions about how to use CrashLab on the demands of their work, not just on the demands of impending deadlines. This particular analyst decided to use one of CrashLab's features specifically because its automated routines would perform a task that she didn't feel she had the knowledge to perform accurately on her own. In this instance, CrashLab was appropriated as a tool for specifying a section force. For this particular analyst—and for most analysts in the Strut Group—the calculus of decision making was divorced from any preconceived notions about how CrashLab should be used. Alternatively, whenever CrashLab's features were seen to confer some advantage on the user, those were the features the analysts used.

Although analysts were using CrashLab to respond to the immediate contextual demands of their work, they were still experimenting with the new technology. Comments such as "It will be good to see if it works" and "Maybe I'll explore that" indicated that analysts were still just "messing around" with CrashLab. After VMVA, however, they no longer had time to experiment. Under enormous pressure to produce results under deadline, they reverted to methods they knew would work. Figure 7.1 indicates that after VMVA there was a noticeable reduction in the number of CrashLab features analysts used in their everyday work. However, as the data in table 7.2 illustrate, the nature of the change in use differed between the two groups of engineers. In period 2, analysts in the Piston Group only used five of CrashLab's features, whereas in period 1 they had used eleven. Even though they were using fewer features, it didn't appear that the five features they were using were being used in any consistent way. Strut Group analysts were still using CrashLab's features in divergent ways, some appropriating CrashLab as a model-checking tool and others appropriating it as a seat-belt-routing tool. In period 2, however, analysts in the Strut Group exhibited a different pattern of use. They used six main features. In fact, upon closer examination of the engineers who were using these six features, it appears that analysts in the Strut Group didn't maintain a divergent pattern of use; instead, they converged on the use of a particular set of features. Taken together, the data presented in figure 7.1 and in table 7.2 seem to indicate that, over time, analysts in the Piston Group used CrashLab's features less often, while analysts in the Strut Group simply began using CrashLab differently than they had before. To confirm this assertion, I recorded the amount of time each analyst spent using CrashLab. If analysts in the Piston Group were in fact using fewer of CrashLab's features over time, and analysts in the Strut Group simply converged on the number of features they used, the mean duration of use in the first period should be higher than the mean duration of use in the second period for analysts in the Piston Group, and there should be no significant mean difference in the Strut Group.

A statistical comparison of data from observations of how much time analysts spent using CrashLab in two periods of use (shown in Table 7.3) confirmed that analysts in the Piston Group reduced their use of CrashLab dramatically between period 1 and period 2. By contrast, analysts in the Strut Group showed no significant difference in the amount of time they spent using CrashLab between the two periods. (See table 7.3.)

What accounts for this difference between the two groups? Why did Piston Group analysts' use of CrashLab drop off dramatically while Strut

Table 7.3

Comparison of time spent using CrashLab in two periods of use (data from observations).[a]

	Mean (period 1)[b]	Mean (period 2)[c]	Sum of squares	Mean square	d.f.	F
Piston Group	21.76	11.12	1790.01	1790.01	(1,62)	4.09*
Strut Group	19.84	22.68	120.02	120.02	(1,58)	0.422

*$p < .05$
a. measured in minutes
b. weeks 1–13
c. weeks 26–32, 46–50

Group analysts' use did not? To answer this question, we must revisit the different ways in which the engineers interpreted the new technology. Through their social and material interactions, analysts in the Piston Group had developed a view of CrashLab as an inefficient pre-processor. As the data in table 7.2 suggest, the only features the majority of analysts in the Piston Group experimented with were features (e.g., making section cuts, placing accelerometers) that could already be found in existing pre-processing tools (e.g., ElementMesh and LinkMesh). Analysts in the Piston Group gravitated toward using these features because they likened Crash-Lab to a pre-processor. As a consequence, most analysts didn't experiment with CrashLab's other features—new features that couldn't already be found in most pre-processing applications (e.g., seat-belt routing, report generation). Analysts continued to engage in their social and material interactions, and the opinion that CrashLab was an inefficient technology for pre-processing was reinforced; thus, over time, they used its features less often. Analysts in the Strut Group had developed very different interpretations of the software. Through their social and material interactions, they came to view CrashLab as a technology for early-stage model setup. Although analysts who experimented with CrashLab early in period 1 attempted to use its features for submitting jobs and for generating reports, their material interactions reinforced the notion that CrashLab was insufficient for those purposes. After VMVA, when analysts in the Strut Group came under more stringent time constraints, they reduced their experimentation with these other features and used only the features that aligned with their interpretations: those that allowed them to set up models.

Enrolling CrashLab in Interaction

More than 80 years ago, Chester Barnard drew on his experience as president of the New Jersey Bell Telephone Company to suggest that the managers who were most successful at initiating change in organizations were those who attended to the "informal" properties of organizing (Barnard 1938). Barnard differentiated the formal structure of an organization—the one codified into formal charts indicating the boundaries of different departments, who should be in those departments, and how those departments should interact with one another—from what he termed the organization's "internal economy," which, he suggested, was really just the informal communication among employees. Barnard argued that communication techniques "shape the form and internal economy of organization" and that "in an exhaustive theory of organization, communication would occupy a central place, because the structure, extensiveness, and scope of organization are almost entirely determined by communication techniques" (ibid., pp. 90–91). In short, the idea that members of an organizational could construct an informal network of meaning and authority directly challenged the assumption that changing the formal structure of an organization solves most management concerns and the assumption that by changing the formal structure of an organization managers are able to directly control the work of their subordinates. This early distinction between the formal and informal realms of organizing captured the attention of academics. Rothlisberger and Dickson (1939), Simon (1945), Blau (1955), and Dalton (1959) all soon suggested that the type of change that produces the most dramatic consequences for an organization is change in the informal realm of organizing—the realm of the actions and interactions through which workers accomplish routine tasks.

As Barley and Kunda (2001) suggest, researchers seeking to understand the nature of changes in the informal properties of organizing must look not only to the roles people play but also to the relationships between those roles. Drawing on the work of the structural anthropologist Siegfried Nadel (1957), Barley and Kunda argue that the "non-relational" and "relational" aspects of work roles are roughly equivalent to the notions of action and interaction, and that, in order to understand how changes in the way people work affect the process of informal organization, researchers must pay attention to this relationship:

Changes in the nonrelational aspect of a work role should be tightly coupled to changes in the role's relational elements—with whom one interacts and what those interactions involve. For example, altered tasks might narrow or expand role sets, shift dependencies, or change the frequency and content of encounters. In fact, since nonrelational roles largely comprise solitary actions, one cannot properly speak of social change until changes in work practices affect interactions. With such spillover one moves from an individual to a dyadic level of analysis, a position from which it is possible to explore whether role transformations confirm or alter forms of organizing. (Barley and Kunda 2001, p. 89)

Today, most researchers who adopt the view that organizing is a process accomplished through the daily interactions among individuals examine how patterns of communication construct status (Gould 2002), authority (Blau 1963), power (Deetz 1982), culture (Pacanowsky and O'Donnell-Trujillo 1983), and expertise (Barley 1986) in the informal social structure we call, for short, organizational structure. If communication is the mechanism through which the informal organization of work is constituted, one must ask, what types of communication encounters are most implicated in the process of organizing? Early work points in the direction of an answer. Rothlisberger and Dickson's (1939) famous "wiring" diagrams from their studies of Western Electric's Hawthorne plant, for example, depict a set of relationships based on patterns of advice seeking.[3] Rothlisberger and Dickson suggest that, even though the organization's formal structure left little unclear about who should ask whom for help on a problem, the organization's members often created their own consultation networks based on certain endogenous factors, such as who sat next to whom. Similarly, Blau (1955) studied agents in a federal department who weren't allowed to consult colleagues about special cases, only supervisors. Through the informal practices of consultation, however, communication structures were instantiated that gave rise to a system in which more experienced agents regularly told stories about "strange cases" and newer agents would troubleshoot them in order to learn. More recent studies that adopt a network analytic approach have suggested that analyzing a consultation network (or patterns of advice seeking) is one way to capture the informal properties of organizing and the types of interactions most implicated in organizational change programs. (See, e.g., Constant, Sproull, and Kiesler 1996; Gibbons 2004; Krackhardt 1992; Rice, Collins-Jarvis, and Zydney-Walker 1999.)

During my time in Autoworks' Safety Division, I observed analysts consulting their colleagues about model setup and model analysis regularly. Regardless of vehicle type or government test, each model setup required knowledge of at least three activities: how to position a barrier, where to place accelerometers, and how to define sections. Likewise, executing a useful analysis required an analyst to base his or her decisions on at least three factors that are essential to improving crashworthiness performance: how to change the materials used to build parts, how to change the geometry of parts, and how to change the location of parts. Together, these six areas of consultation signal the communicative exchanges constitutive of the informal organization of work in the Safety Division.

Jensen Lu and the other developers of CrashLab were excited about CrashLab's potential to change crashworthiness-engineering work at Autoworks. As we have seen, over a ten-year period of negotiation involving Safety, Techpro, Infoserv, and R&D, developers such as Jensen Lu, Martin Yuen, and Sunil Kitane—and even directors such as Gene Anderson—had come to an agreement that math-based analysis could not play a more central role in the vehicle design process because analysts spent far too much time performing wasteful model-setup activities. Developers hoped that automating routine tasks of model setup and evaluation would give analysts more time to do "real engineering" work—namely, to develop innovative solutions to improve vehicles' performance. Developers reasoned that including best-practice guidelines in CrashLab's automated routines would prevent analysts from "wasting" so much time consulting one another about how to perform routine tasks associated with setting up models. If analysts didn't have to interact with each other so often about how to set up their models, they could spend more time analyzing their models and developing robust solutions. Thus, the developers themselves operationalized the profound organizational changes they wanted to see in crashworthiness-engineering work as a decrease in consultation about setup activities and an increase in consultation related to model analysis.

If developers were correct that the Safety Division spent most of its time on activities related to setting up models rather than those related to model analysis, we would expect that in period 1, before CrashLab could have effected any change in the organization of crashworthiness work, the frequency with which analysts consulted one another about positioning barriers, placing accelerometers, and defining sections would be higher than the frequency with which they consulted one another about changing materials, gauge, geometry, and part locations. To determine whether this assertion was valid, I coded observations of analysts in period 1 in both the Piston Group and the Strut Group on the basis of the number of times the focal informant consulted a colleague about one of these six things. I then arrived at a sum of all of the model-setup consultations and a sum of all the model-analysis consultations that occurred in each observation record. A statistical analysis of these codes indicates that in both groups analysts consulted one another about model setup more than twice as often as they consulted each other about model analysis. (See table 7.4.)

Table 7.4
Comparison of consultations between the two periods of use (data from observations).[a]

	Mean (period 1)	Mean (period 2)	Sum of squares	Mean square	d.f.	F
Piston Group						
Model setup	1.94	1.50	3.36	3.36	(1,62)	2.93
Model analysis	.94	.91	.02	.02	(1,62)	.03
Strut Group						
Model setup	1.90	1.07	9.53	9.53	(1,58)	9.63**
Model analysis	.87	1.86	16.57	16.57	(1,58)	18.02***

a. number of consultations per observation
**$p < .01$
***$p < .001$

Thus, it appears that developers were correct in their assessment of the state of the informal organization of work in the Safety Division.

As we learned from looking at patterns of use, Piston Group analysts' use of CrashLab diminished in period 2, while many analysts in the Strut Group converged on a similar pattern of use and began appropriating CrashLab as a tool for setting up models. If analysts in the Piston Group were no longer using CrashLab in any meaningful way in period 2, there shouldn't be a noticeable difference from period 1 in the frequency with which analysts consulted their colleagues about model setup. Because analysts in the Piston Group were still consulting one another about model setup as frequently in period 2 as they had in period 1, we would also expect that they would have had little time to engage more frequently in consultations about model analysis. In short, the data from my observations suggest that CrashLab didn't bring about any change in the organization of work in the Piston Group.

Analysis of the data indicates that analysts who worked in the Strut Group did significantly (both practically and statistically) reduced the frequency with which they consulted their colleagues about model setup, while the number of consultations they engaged in about issues related to model analysis nearly doubled. Thus, it appears that CrashLab succeeded in bringing about important organizational change within the Strut Group. What accounts for this change? The data presented in table 7.2 show that in period 2 analysts in the Strut Group converged on a common use of CrashLab's features. Put simply, in period 2 most of the analysts were using CrashLab the same way, whereas in period 1 analysts had used CrashLab's features in divergent ways. Although using CrashLab's features to respond to the immediate demands of their work proved effective for analysts in both groups, this method of selective use resulted in an extreme amount of divergence in the way CrashLab was being used. For example, since analysts were using only certain features, one engineer might appropriate CrashLab as a barrier-positioning tool and another might see it as a job-submission tool. In order for the technology to be useful for crashworthiness-engineering work at Autoworks, all analysts had to use CrashLab in a consistent way. If some analysts were using it only to position the barrier and others were using it only to create sections, and both sets of engineers were using the features only sporadically as context demanded, CrashLab couldn't systematically reduce the amount of time the entire group of engineers spent on model setup. In order for the organization to change into one that spent more time discussing model analysis than model setup, *all* the engineers would have to have the time to discuss model analysis. If one analyst used CrashLab and had the time to discuss model analysis but the analyst he or she wanted to talk to did not (because he or she didn't use CrashLab), this important organizational change might fail to materialize.

This predicament is by no means unique to engineers at Autoworks. In her study of email use in a large organization, Lynne Markus (1990) describes the issue of "critical mass" in the early phases of new technology use. Markus suggested that users in the organization had little motivation to use a new, interactive communication technology if their colleagues weren't using it. The reason is plain. If one person has an email account and another doesn't, it makes no sense for the former to send email to the latter. Thus, as Markus suggests, organizations reap the benefits of the interactive technology systems they implement only when there are enough users to make others in the organization feel that the new technology is worth using. If one analyst at Autoworks had the time to discuss model analysis and another didn't, there was little motivation to continue using CrashLab. As we have seen, analysts in the Piston Group who appropriated CrashLab in divergent ways all but gave up using it in their work. However, in period 2, because analysts interpreted CrashLab as a tool for setting up models and then (after VMVA) no longer had the time to experiment with its other features, they began to converge on a common pattern of use. This convergence produced a "critical mass" of users who, by virtue of their shared appropriation of CrashLab's features, allowed the software to take care of model setup for them, leaving them more time to discuss model analysis.

Thus, when examining the way CrashLab was used in the Strut Group, we see an interdependent system such as the one depicted in figure 7.2. A convergence of appropriations of a technology's features seems necessary to produce a critical mass of users, but convergence can't occur without enough users (as was the case in the Piston Group, whose members stopped using CrashLab altogether). Similarly, it appears to be necessary for a sufficient number of users to use the technology in a consistent manner (convergence of appropriations) in order for change to occur in the patterns of interaction constitutive of organizing. Such a system would suggest that in order for a technology to bring about change in the organization of work, its users must first converge on a common pattern of use. To determine whether this is indeed the case, it is necessary to examine data on how frequently analysts consulted one another before CrashLab was implemented, since focusing only on post-implementation data allows for the possibility that the organization of work may have differed between

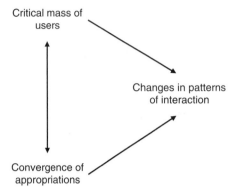

Figure 7.2
Relationship among appropriations, users, and changes in interaction.

the two groups to start with, and thus changes in the patterns of consultation among analysts couldn't be linked to appropriations of CrashLab's
features.

All 19 analysts in the Piston Group and all 17 analysts in the Strut Group
were surveyed in three waves. The first wave was conducted in August
of 2005, just before CrashLab was implemented in the Safety Division.
The second wave was conducted three months after implementation—
one week before the VMVA stage gate. The final wave was conducted in
August of 2006, nearly a year (50 weeks) after CrashLab was implemented
in the two engineering groups. The surveys asked analysts who they consulted regarding the six issues I identified during my observations: how to
position a barrier, where to place accelerometers, how to define sections,
how to change the materials used to build parts, how to change the geometry of parts, and how to change the location of parts. Their answers
revealed who they regularly consulted in the course of their work. With
these data, I constructed adjacency matrices for the Piston Group (59 × 59)
and the Strut Group (54 × 54), the rows indexing analysts who sought
consult from their colleagues and the columns indexing analysts whose
consultation was sought. An adjacency matrix is an $N \times N$ matrix in which
N equals the number of people in the network, the Nth row and the Nth
column identify the same individual, and the cells record whether person
i reported discussing the topic with person j. In other words, each time an
analyst consulted a colleague ("in-ties"), I recorded a 1 in the corresponding column. I populated these adjacency matrices with the sociometric
data I obtained from the 19 members of the Piston Group and the 17
members of the Strut Group. When the task was complete, I had 18 sepa-

rate matrices for each of the groups—three matrices for each of the model-setup and model-analysis issues in periods 1 and 2, before implementation of CrashLab.[4]

Together, these twelve matrices represent the social networks of analysts in the Piston Group and the Strut Group over a one-year period, from August 2005 to August 2006. The six consultation networks that make up the informal organizational structure of the Piston Group are illustrated as directed graphs ("digraphs") in figure 7.3. The digraphs for the Strut Group appear in figure 7.4.[5] Arrows pointing to a node show which analysts were consulted by other analysts in that particular time period. The perforated circle surrounding the core of each digraph encapsulates the particular vehicle platform observed in this study. Arcs extending outside the circle represent ties to analysts outside of this core work group.

If CrashLab did bring change in the patterns of consultation among analysts only after engineers converged on a common appropriation of the

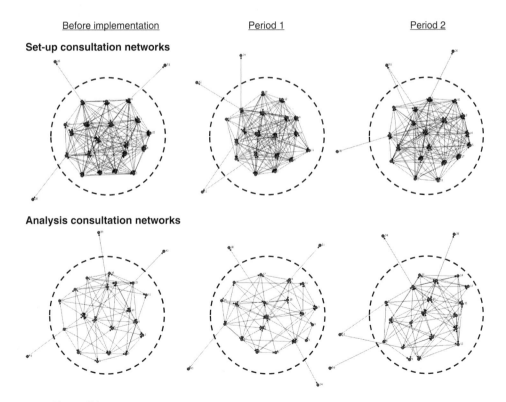

Figure 7.3
Consultation networks in Piston Group.

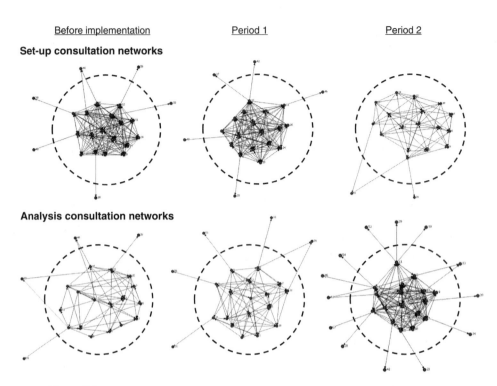

Figure 7.4
Consultation networks in Strut Group.

technology's features, the densities of the networks for both groups before implementation and in period 1 should be nearly identical for activities related to model setup and those related to model analysis. Between periods 1 and 2, however, network densities should change only for the Strut Group as analysts began to consult one another about model analysis on a more regular basis and discuss model setup less often. There should be no visible change in the Piston Group networks between periods. Inspection of the digraphs supports the findings of my observations of these work groups. Between August 2005 and August 2006, the Piston Group networks remained dense in terms of ties related to setting up models and sparse in terms of ties related to model analysis, and the Strut Group networks did, in fact, change during the second period. The model-setup networks became sparser, looking more like the model-analysis networks in previous periods, while the model-analysis networks became denser.

The digraphs in figures 7.3 and 7.4 show another surprising change. It appears that not only did analysts in the Strut Group consult co-workers within their respective vehicle platforms about model analysis more often than they had in the past in period 2; they also more frequently consulted analysts outside their vehicle platforms (indicated by arcs extending outside the perforated circle). Similarly, in period 2, Strut Group analysts consulted engineers outside their work group about setting up models less often than in period 1. By contrast, the digraphs in figure 7.3 show that analysts in the Piston Group consulted others outside their work group about model setup and model analysis with roughly the same frequency across the three time periods. Thus, not only did convergent appropriation of CrashLab's features change the Strut Group's internal patterns of consultation; it also changed the relationship this particular work group had with analysts performing similar tasks in other work groups in the Safety Division.

By triangulating these various data sources, we can see that CrashLab enabled a profound change in the organization of crashworthiness work in the Strut Group. I say "enabled" and not "caused" because, as we have seen, the new technology alone wasn't capable of bringing about change in the organization of work. In order for CrashLab to shift the patterns of communication constitutive of analysts' informal social structures, it had to be consistently enrolled in their routine interaction. However, to enroll CrashLab in their interaction, analysts had to converge upon a common use of the technology. Through their exposure to the discourse of inevitability produced and promulgated by trainers and managers at Autoworks, analysts in the Strut Group developed interpretive frames that led them to believe not only that CrashLab could change their work in profound ways but that it should. Yet this discourse of inevitability was generic enough to allow analysts the flexibility to fit any changes they saw happening in their work within its ideology. In other words, analysts in the Strut Group saw their use of CrashLab and the changes in their work as natural consequences of technological change. Consider these Strut Group analysts' comments on the topic in August of 2006, a year after they first learned about CrashLab in their training sessions and staff meetings, when simply asked "What is CrashLab?"

Analyst 1 Basically, CrashLab is a tool that you use to set up models. It's not like a pre-processor, really, but it's sort of. You do most of your pre-processing somewhere else, like ElementMesh, and then you just use CrashLab to set up your models, then you go back to the pre-processor. Really, that's the only way you can use it.

Analyst 2 CrashLab? You're supposed to use it to prepare your models for analysis. And it's pretty good for that. I mean, it can cut down on the time it takes to do that stuff. . . . I even noticed that I can do more thinking about design stuff now, or run more iterations to give me a better picture of what's going on. So I think it's been good, because CrashLab changed our work like it was supposed to. That's what they said it would do, and it did.

Analyst 3 Well, I'd say CrashLab is what it is. It's like a quasi-pre-processor that sets up your models for you. Sometimes it's got bugs, but it's actually pretty good for a new piece of software. I think what has been really good is that most people do a bit more in terms of thinking about changes in design and what not. But that's the natural outgrowth of using it, I think. I mean, that was basically what it made happen.

Two themes are apparent from the analysts' reflections. First, analysts unequivocally treated CrashLab as a tool for setting up models. In fact, they never even considered that CrashLab could have been used in any other way. Most analysts insisted that CrashLab "had to be used that way [i.e., for setting up models]." Second, analysts linked CrashLab causally to changes in the organization of their work. Analysts regularly commented that CrashLab "made" them "work somewhat differently." In line with the discourse under which they initially learned about CrashLab, analysts largely viewed the changes that resulted in the wake of its implementation as "inevitable" outcomes of technological change.

In sociological terms, analysts' use of CrashLab represents a self-fulfilling prophecy of sorts. According to Merton (1957, p. 423),

the self-fulfilling prophecy is, in the beginning, a "false" definition of the situation evoking a new behavior which makes the original false conception come "true." This specious validity of the self-fulfilling prophecy perpetuates a reign of error. For the prophet will cite the actual course of events as proof that he was right from the very beginning. Such are the perversities of social logic.

Perhaps the reason a discourse of inevitability was so effective in producing a self-fulfilling outcome was that this discourse socialized analysts into a way of understanding the relationship between the new technology and the organization of their work. Berger and Luckmann suggest that socialization processes are powerful precisely because they shape cognition in a way that allows individuals to internalize the reality they perceive as objective and immutable:

Primary socialization internalizes a reality apprehended as inevitable. This internalization may be deemed successful if the sense of inevitability is present most of the time, at least while the individual is active in the world of everyday life. (1967, p. 147)

More specifically, a discourse of inevitability successfully promulgates a perceived causal relationship by leading individuals to believe that their choices are predetermined by some exogenous force (in this case, a new technology), thereby systematically distorting other possible forces attributable to a given outcome. Giddens (1984, p. 178) writes:

> Why is it that some social forces have an apparently "inevitable" look to them? It is because in such instances there are few options open to the actors in question given that they behave rationally—"rationally" in this case meaning effectively aligning motives with the end-result of whatever conduct is involved. That is to say, the actors have "good reasons" for what they do, reasons which the structural sociologist is likely to assume implicitly rather than explicitly attributing those to actors. Since such good reasons involve a choice from very limited feasible alternative, their conduct may appear to be driven by some implacable force similar to a force of nature.

The discourse of efficiency strategically enacted by CrashLab's developers and by others who promoted its use to analysts in the Piston Group was not capable of producing such results. The discourse proved ineffective because developers and managers chose a framing technique that was out of alignment with analysts' work experiences. Sure, analysts in the Piston Group would have been happier with a technology that "sped up" their work, but their engagement in social and material interactions prohibited them from viewing CrashLab as such a technology. In other words, the discourse of efficiency was too strict; it didn't allow analysts to interpret their emerging experiences through the descriptive framework it promoted. We might speculate that, had analysts' engagement in social and material interactions prompted them to see CrashLab as a technology that could "speed up" their work, they might have used it in that way. But, of course, the opposite is true. If analysts in the Strut Group had been exposed to efficiency frames as opposed to inevitability frames, they too would have formed an unfavorable interpretation of CrashLab's performance, and as program-related pressures bore down upon them they would have had little motivation to use the technology's features in more convergent ways.

Taken together, these insights suggest that analysts, in order to enact change in the informal organization of their work, would have had to appropriate CrashLab's features in convergent ways. Their propensity to do so was influenced largely by the alignment between their existing work practices and the ways in which CrashLab was framed for them. Frames that allowed engineers to align their work experiences with the expected benefits of the new technology prompted them to use it, and, later, to attribute changes in the social organization of their work to it.

8 Organizing as a Process of Sociomaterial Imbrication

I began this book by suggesting that people who work with new technologies, whether they are developers, trainers, managers, or users, often come to a somewhat fatalistic understanding of technological change. Indeed, the results of numerous studies report that developers regularly adopt the view that the material features of a new technology "have to be" configured in a certain way, that managers who intend to implement new technologies in organizations often suggest that the work "cannot help but" change in certain ways as it is constrained by the demands of the new technical system, and that users who interact with the materiality of a newly implemented technology in the course of their normal work quickly come to believe that a new technology is "supposed to" be used for some tasks and not for others. Although they are typically involved in different sets of activities surrounding the artifact, developers, managers, and users all share in common the tendency to divest themselves of their own agency when working with a new technology. Since the early 1990s, a growing number of researchers have worked hard to show that developers and users have the agency to change the material features of a technology, thus physically constructing the artifact's form and function, as well as to change the way they use those features in the practice of their work, thus socially constructing the technology's effects on the organization of their work.

In this book, using these insights as a foundation, I have worked to construct a new understanding about the relationship between technological change and organizational change. Rather than continuing to assert that a technology's material features are generated out of contestation and negotiation among relevant social groups, or that users can and do often appropriate the features of a new technology, in the context of use, in unanticipated and novel ways, I have sought to uncover how certain understandings about what a new technology should do were formed, and what consequences those understandings had for the relationship between technological and organizational change. I have suggested that two alterations to extant theorizing are needed.

First, because a technology's materiality is that which is directly experienced at the confluence of communities (it is constructed by developers, rhetorically fashioned by implementers, and interacted with by users), any study attempting to uncover how people come to take technological change for granted as "the way things have to be" must cross the implementation line that has traditionally separated studies of technology development from studies of technology use. It must cross the implementation line because, as I have argued, materiality is shaped by the actions occurring around it. If developers believe that a technology "must have" certain material properties, they will design those properties into the artifact. It is those very properties that managers test and examine when deciding how the technology will affect the organization of work, and it is those same properties that users interact with when they come to believe that they should use the technology only for certain purposes. Thus, it stands to reason that appreciating how a technology became taken for granted as one set of activities occurred around it would effect how it was taken for granted when another set of activities began.

Second, when people interact with a technology, whether by physically modifying it or by enrolling in action, they always do so within the context of organizing. This point is subtle but important. The process of organizing is accomplished through action and interaction. When people base their interactions with each other on the actions that they normally perform in the context of their work, they informally structure their work. When a new technology becomes the focus of their actions, whether those actions are of production or consumption, people's interactions will feel this influence. Yet these ongoing interactions constitutive of social structure continually shape the kinds of actions people perform in the context of a technology. For this reason, I have proposed that technological and organizational change must be viewed as a mutually constitutive. That is, to uncover what consequences taken-for-granted assumptions about technological change can have for the process of organizing one must look at the relationship between the social and material changes occurring throughout technology-development, technology-implementation, and technology-use activities. To limit our attention to only one set of activities would be to miss the potentially important influences residing at the intersection of these loose boundaries of their temporal sequencing.

My investigation of CrashLab's development, implementation, and use at Autoworks over an 11-year period has been guided by these two theoretical insights. In this chapter I will summarize the main findings of this book and discuss how these findings may lead us to a new way of thinking about the process of organizing. Specifically, the ethnographic data presented herein suggest that organizing is not a process that is constrained and enabled by a technology's material features as organizations and technologies coevolve, as most social constructivist formulations would suggest. Instead, I argue, organizing is a process of sociomaterial imbrication. That is, like tiles on a roof, rocks in a riverbed, or bricks in a wall, social and material agencies activated in the practice of work overlap one another in regular patterns that we commonly refer to as the process organizing. Incidentally, how imbrication occurs at any moment is a consequence of previous imbrications and has consequences for those that follow. I will discuss how this emerging perspective on imbrication might help us to rethink the relationship between technology and organizing and how it might help us to resolve important inconsistencies in extant theories of change. I will end by discussing how a shift away from using the metaphor of impact to explain the relationship between technology and organizational change and toward the metaphor of imbrication may help developers, managers, and users to reclaim their agency in their interactions with technology and, consequently, to design better technologies and better organizations.

A More Nuanced Understanding of Change

The data presented in this book show, in detail, how people in organizations construct perceptions that technologies afford or constrain their ability to achieve their goals and then make decisions about how to change either the features of those technologies or the patterns of communication through which their work gets done so they can realize those goals. Figure 8.1 illustrates five such imbrications of social and material agencies in the course of CrashLab's development, implementation, and use. Of course, this figure idealizes cycles of imbrication in order to illustrate the usefulness of seeing organizing as a process of sociomaterial imbrication, and it should be read as such.

Drawing on figure 8.1, I will discuss five imbrications through which the human and material agencies of Autoworks' work system became interwoven. Three *social* → *material* imbrications (enclosed by perforated boxes in figure 8.1) produced changes in CrashLab's features as people

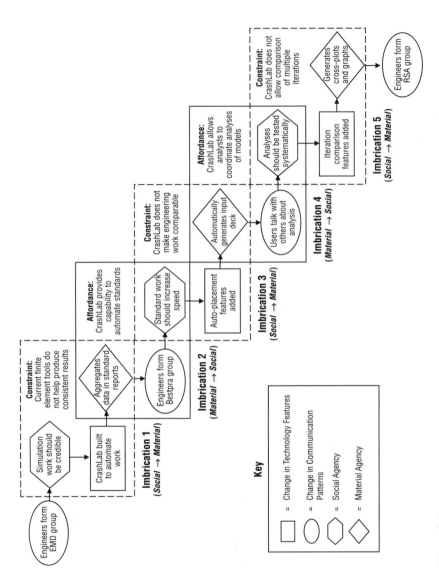

Figure 8.1

Imbrication of social and material agencies at Autoworks. Perforated boxes represent social → material imbrication; solid boxes represent material → social imbrication.

involved with the technology constructed the perception that it constrained their goals. The two *material → social* imbrications (enclosed by solid boxes in figure 8.1) produced changes in the way analysts at Autoworks interacted with one another as they began to construct the perception that CrashLab could afford them the possibility of changing the way they worked. As was mentioned above, these starting and stopping points are arbitrary. I intend to show why one type of imbrication led to another, and to use this understanding to explain how it is that the social and material agencies at Autoworks were interwoven and the consequent effects that these imbrications had on the process of organizing.

Imbrication 1 (*Social → Material*)

For many years, Autoworks' Research and Development Division had placed a dominant emphasis on the development of new technologies that could be used in production vehicles (air-bag sensors, anti-lock brakes, and so on) but had devoted few resources to developing technologies that would improve engineering processes within the company. In 1994, the newly formed Engineering Mechanics Department (EMD) within the Research and Development Division was charged with this new goal. To more fully understand how crashworthiness engineering was being conducted, and, by association, to develop ideas about what sorts of tools might help to improve it, developers in the EMD spent the first two months of 1995 working with crashworthiness analysts.

The EMD developers noticed that the steps analysts took to pre-process their models (that is, prepare to submit them to the solver) were highly idiosyncratic. Unlike most of the analysts in the Safety Division, these developers worked in an R&D Division that focused on scientific research. The time lines for most projects in the R&D Division were much longer than those for most projects in the Safety Division because R&D wasn't tied to the stage gates outlined in Autoworks' formal vehicle development process. Similarly, because analysts in the R&D Division published their work in journals and presented their findings at academic conferences, they were bound to the traditions of academic research, including the need to make their methods transparent and their findings reproducible. Both the institutional background of the R&D Division and the creation of the EMD, which brought together analysts who interacted around process-improvement methodologies, shaped the developers' goals of making crashworthiness simulation credible and reliable.

With these goals in mind, the EMD developers began to notice that the suite of finite element tools that analysts were using to build and analyze simulation models constrained their ability to produce consistent results. When current pre-processing and post-processing tools generated analysis results, analysts extracted from them only data on certain parameters, such as intrusion or energy dissipation. The results weren't presented in any systematic way, nor could they be stored or printed in a standard form. This constraint enforced by existing finite element tools was problematic for the EMD developers because, without standard results, the practices a analyst used to build and analyze a simulation model couldn't be verified to determine their robustness, nor could they be validated by an external reviewer. Thus, the EMD developers' perceived constraints imposed by the current finite element technologies that had to be overcome in order for them to realize their goal of making crashworthiness simulation more credible.

The EMD developers decided that they could develop a new technology that would work in conjunction with pre-processing and post-processing applications already used by crashworthiness analysts to increase the credibility of simulation work. They knew that they didn't have the structural authority within Autoworks to mandate that analysts create standard reports, but they did have the means to impose their goals technically. They recognized implicitly that their goal of making crashworthiness simulations more credible (social agency) might be fulfilled if they were to create code that would automatically aggregate simulation results into standard reports (material agency) by building CrashLab. To allow analysts discretion without sacrificing the credibility of their models, the EMD developers engineered a report format that would record any deviations analysts might make from the best practices embedded in CrashLab. In its visual layout, the report contained a table titled Best Practice Violation. In this table appeared any parameter in the pre- or post-processing of the model that diverged from the best practices. One column contained a description of the best practice embedded in CrashLab, and the column immediately to its right documented the parameter that was changed. A third column calculated the percentage that the best practice was violated. The purpose of the third column was to give the reader of the report confidence in how close the model that had been used to generate these results was to an ideal test case. Larger percentages of deviation might then mean that the results would not be repeatable or widely generalizable. What the EMD developers were most concerned about, however, was not the inherent generalizability of the findings, but that the reviewer of the report would know exactly how the results could be used to make predictions about a vehicle's crashworthiness.

Imbrication 2 (*Material → Social*)

As the EMD developers worked to refine CrashLab and to add more functionality to it, they began to share a fully functioning prototype across various engineering groups at Autoworks. By the winter of 1998, the Focus Group had tested CrashLab thoroughly. Whereas the EMD developers wanted to make crashworthiness simulations more credible, the members of the Focus Group were interested in standardizing the work of all analysts. Their desire to standardize was buttressed by the hope that standardization would remove human error from the process of designing vehicles. By interpreting CrashLab's material features through their own goals, members of the Focus Group began to agree that CrashLab could afford the automation of engineering standards. The problem for the Focus Group, however, was that although the current material features of CrashLab could afford the automation of engineering standards, there were no standards to automate. Before CrashLab could automate standard work procedures, Autoworks would have to define what those standard work procedures were.

In early 1999, with the recommendation of the Focus Group, Autoworks' vice-president for global engineering approved the creation of the Best Practice Evaluation Department ("Bestpra"), the task of which was to create and update standard work procedures for crashworthiness analysis. Structurally, Bestpra sat outside of regular engineering production work at Autoworks. Each of Bestpra's six analysts was given the title of Subject-Matter Expert (SME). Their role was to collect information from analysts in the Safety Division so as to determine what the standards would be for a particular type of analysis. On the basis of this information, the SMEs began to create documents outlining standards that all analysts should follow when setting up and analyzing models for specific crash load cases. In March of 1999, Bestpra published its first standard work guidelines, which were for frontal load cases. The EMD developers used the best practices identified in that document to determine how to automate the process of setting up and analyzing a simulation model to test FMVSS 208 specifications.

With the SMEs working to create guidelines that would standardize analysts' work, managers in the Safety Division began to develop a new set of goals (social agency). They were convinced that the automation of standardized work would lead to faster model building and model analysis because analysts no longer would have to take time to discern which practices were most appropriate or efficacious for the job at hand. Standard work guidelines would effectively replace this individual judgment and would lead to an increase in the speed with which analysts could do crash-worthiness work. Faster crashworthiness work was preferable because it meant that analysts would be able to conduct more simulations in a given time period than they could before. And the Safety Division would be able to move from using simulations to validate physical tests retrospectively to using simulations to prospectively predict the outcomes of physical crashes. Thus, the material agency of CrashLab was imbricated with the social agency of Safety's management through the creation of Bestpra, which began writing new standard work guidelines.

Imbrication 3 (*Social → Material*)

Safety managers, who took it as their new goal to speed up the work of analysts, began to search for clear and feasible ways to make simulation building and analysis more quickly without compromising the quality of the results. For many managers, CrashLab was an ideal application with which to carry out their goal because it was easy to envision how the technology could provide capabilities for automation. In view of the history of automation in industrial settings in general and in the automotive industry in particular, it is not surprising that managers looked to a tool such as CrashLab to make the work faster.

Although CrashLab automated reports of simulation results, it didn't automate the practices whereby analysts set up simulation models to be submitted to the solver. Even though SMEs rationalized crashworthiness tasks by writing standard work guidelines, managers believed that standardization could increase the speed of work only if paired with automation. When thinking about whether CrashLab could help them to achieve their goals managers began to perceive that the technology's features constrained analysts' ability to work faster than they could without the use of CrashLab. In many cases, analysts who were experienced at simulation work could build and analyze models faster by hand than they could if they used CrashLab. Thus, the constraints that managers perceived Crash-Lab as placing on analysts' abilities to work faster had to be overcome in order to realize the goal of reducing the time it took to build and analyze simulation models.

In particular, Crashworthiness managers told the EMD developers, CrashLab should automate the setting up of models. To respond to these concerns, the EMD developers built certain features into the tool. These features included scripts that would indicate to the analyst using them exactly where an accelerometer or a section cut, for example, should be placed according to the standard work guidelines. Engineers would then have only to execute a command indicating that they approved of these locations, and the software would automatically write the coordinates into the input deck (a text-based file that could be read by the solver). This automated procedure would eliminate the need for analysts to perform these tasks manually and thus would reduce the amount of time needed to set up a model for analysis.

By 2003, CrashLab had a new set of features. To use CrashLab, analysts now had to follow the automated flow of steps that the tool presented to them; they also had to abdicate to the technology the autonomy that they had had in creating their own input decks. CrashLab now automated these steps (material agency), and analysts who used it had no choice but to allow it to do so.

Imbrication 4 (*Material → Social*)

By the fall of 2005, all analysts who were involved with regular production related work at Autoworks felt tremendous time pressures. Management constantly complained about the length of the company's vehicle development process. Every year, senior vehicle architects set loftier goals for vehicle development stage gates. These shortened engineering cycles directly affected analysts, who were now tasked with producing evaluations of vehicle designs that would guarantee increases in crashworthiness performance in less time than they had been accustomed to taking. Despite these shorter design cycles, analysts weren't anxious to speed up all their tasks. Engineers consistently voiced a valued delineation between model building and drafting (which required technical skill but not detailed engineering intuition and judgment) and analysis activities (which required in-depth knowledge of physics, thermal dynamics, or some other domain). They hoped that by reducing the amount of time they spent on routine or "tedious" model-building tasks they could devote the bulk of their limited temporal resources to analyzing the results of their simulations. Such a desire was understandable, since participation in analysis activities placed analysts at the center of decisions about product architecture and design. Being at the center, analysts could play a primary role in the vehicle development process, which, in turn, would increase their status within Autoworks.

It was in this environment that analysts in the Piston Group, for reasons recounted in detail in chapter 6, rejected CrashLab, whereas analysts in the Strut Group began using it in regular production work. Engineers in the Strut Group interpreted CrashLab's ability to automatically generate an input deck (material agency) as affording them the opportunity to standardize their model-building activities, enabling them to compare their simulation results with the results produced by their colleagues who also used CrashLab. This increased standardization of outputs gave analysts opportunities to talk with colleagues about design solutions that had worked in the past and to work with them to troubleshoot simulations. Consequently, analysts began to consult one another about design solutions more often. Such new consultation routines occurred often during model-analysis activities in the Strut Group, signaling an important change in the focus of crashworthiness-engineering effort.

As analysts consulted one another about vehicle design, their goals began to shift. Because CrashLab's material agency gave them time to conduct more robust analyses, analysts had to be sure that they were armed with sufficient data to engage in helpful discussions. To generate more data, analysts had to run more iterations of their simulation models. Running multiple iterations was fast and easy to do. After analysts used CrashLab to set up a model for analysis, they had only to go into the input deck and change the parameters they wished to test in the new iteration. By following this practice, analysts took as their emergent goal (social agency) that analyses should be done systematically to provide as much information as possible for use in ongoing consultations with colleagues. CrashLab's material agency was imbricated with the social agency of the analysts through changes in their analysis activities.

Imbrication 5 (*Social → Material*)
To achieve the goal of increasing the production of systematic analyses, analysts increased the number of iterations they ran for a given crash-test simulation. As the number of simulations increased, analysts began to notice that it was very difficult to compare results among them. Crash-Lab generated a separate standard report for each iteration of a simulation test. By 2006, most analysts ran more than twenty simulations to test a given change made to the geometry of a part or the arrangement of parts in the vehicle, which meant that analysts had to deal with twenty reports generated by CrashLab. CrashLab didn't provide capabilities for systematically comparing the results of multiple iterations. To make such comparisons, analysts had to use CrashLab to generate a separate report for each iteration. Because the reports CrashLab produced were in HTML format, analysts had to manually copy the important data from each report into an Excel spreadsheet. Analysts could then use Excel to generate graphs and plots comparing the simulation results and take this information to their consultations with colleagues to indicate what

types of changes (e.g., to geometry or material properties) produced the "best" results.

It became clear to analysts that CrashLab's current material configuration constrained their ability to compare results from multiple iterations systematically. Specifically, CrashLab didn't enable the analysts to plot results from multiple iterations on a single chart for the sake of comparison—what analysts called "cross-plots." Analysts began to complain to their managers that CrashLab should have this capability. Crashworthiness managers who were keen on having analysts produce results more quickly were eager to champion new features that could speed up the work while simultaneously making analyses more robust. The EMD developers were receptive to the demands of the crashworthiness managers and began to develop new features for CrashLab that would make it easy for analysts to compare the results of multiple iterations. The developers wrote code that gathered performance metrics from multiple simulations into one common report and, further, enabled analysts to produce cross-plots and graphs of these data points. Consequently, when analysts began to use the newest version of CrashLab, they found that the tool automatically performed the comparison functions they desired without extra effort on their part. The goal of more systematic analyses characterizing analysts' social agency was imbricated with the material agency of automatic cross-plot formation through the addition of iteration comparison features to CrashLab.

Analysts brought comparisons of their simulations to consultations with colleagues. Slowly, they began to notice that the design changes that produced good performance for one vehicle were sometimes similar to the design changes that produced good performance for another vehicle. Although analysts could provide anecdotal examples of certain changes that produced good performance, they had no way of systematically comparing the findings generated by analysts across multiple vehicle platforms.

As crashworthiness managers came to understand that all of the new data generated through the use of CrashLab could be mined systematically to suggest general design trends for optimal crashworthiness performance, they worked with the Global Technology Production Division (Techpro), which specialized in the maintenance and deployment of finite element technologies, to put together a new group that could analyze performance data from across Autoworks. This new Robust Synthesis Analysis (RSA) group was made up of analysts who had backgrounds in optimization and in statistical analysis. These analysts created new routines for coding, analyzing, and comparing the data that analysts generated in their simulations. By the end of my study, in late 2006, the RSA group was planning to develop a new tool called CARDS (Computer-Aided Robust Design Solutions) to automatically analyze the vast amounts of data generated by analysts when they conducted simulation activities.

Implications of the Imbrication Framework for Organizational Analysis

As was illustrated above, when an existing material agency is imbricated with a new social agency (*material → social*) members of the organization may be likely to change their patterns of communication, and when an existing social agency is imbricated with a new material agency (*social → material*) a technology changes. Thus, communication patterns and technologies, though distinct empirical phenomena, are ontologically related in the sense that they are both constituted by imbrications of human and material agencies. The result is that a change in a technology's features is linked to the patterns of communication that came before it and will be linked to patterns of communication that come after it, just as a change in communication is linked to the technology features that preceded it and to those that will follow it. If we dispense with the language of communication patterns (or organizations) and technology features (or technological artifacts) and speak at the lowest level of abstraction, we can say that human and material agencies are constantly imbricated with one another and this chain of imbrications occurs in a path-dependent manner.

What keeps social and material agencies in a sequence of continued imbrication is that people draw on the infrastructure created out of past imbrications (realized as patterns of communication or technology features) to construct perceptions of affordances and constraints. The construction of these perceptions creates a space of opportunity or frustration in which people are motivated to act (Gaver 1996; Karat, Karat, and Ukelson 2000). To the extent that people are able to alter their goals (a presumption that has long undergirded discussions of human agency) and able to change a technology's features (a capability increasingly made common by flexible technologies), their perceptions of affordances and constraints may compel them to make new imbrications of human and material agencies, which then continue to produce changes in routines and technologies. This has at least two major implications for the study of technology and organizing.

The first major implication of the imbrication perspective is that it places technologies in a central role in the process of organizing. Organization scientists have been skeptical of talking about technologies' material agency because they haven't found a successful way of combining the important insights from social constructivist approaches to explicitly theorize the role of technologies in the production, maintenance, and change of the organizing process. The imbrication metaphor recognizes that human collectives have agency, and operationalizes social agency as peoples' ability to form and realize their goals. It also recognizes that technologies have agency, operationalizing material agency as a technology's ability to act on its own. For social and material agencies to become imbricated, someone has to arrange them in particular sequences. Thus, developers, implementers, and users of technologies, as they experience that material agency in real-time practice, actively imbricate their social agency with the material agency of the artifacts with which they work.

The ability to recognize the role of material agency within social constructivists' axiology means that the imbrication metaphor may help in specifying why people who can choose to change either their routines or their technologies to better execute their work make the choices they do. Because a technology's material agency is circumscribed by the set of features a technology possesses, a technology can only do so much. As Pentland and Feldman (2008, p. 243) observe, because a toaster's material agency is limited by its features set, a toaster simply can't be used as a cell phone, no matter how much someone wishes it could be. A technology can do only certain things. Of course, how people choose to interpret the things it does, or whether they recognize what those things are, is quite variable. For this reason, a technology's material agency can encourage people to perceive that the technology sometimes constrains their ability to achieve their goals and other times enables them to develop new ones. As the case illustrated in this book demonstrates, a group's perception of whether a technology constrains desired action or affords new action depends on earlier imbrications. Without perceptions of constraint or affordance, people probably would continue to use existing technologies and routines as they did before. As Orlikowski (2000) shows, to the extent that technologies and communication patterns allow people to accomplish their goals, no change in either takes place. Thus, it is important to recognize the role that changing material agencies can play in the ongoing process of organizing. Incorporating the notion of material agencies into a social constructivist approach helps to explain how people make choices about whether they will change their flexible routines or their flexible technologies. Moreover, whereas social constructivist approaches see material agency as a potential threat to human agency, the imbrication lens views material agency more neutrally: Its influence as either an affordance or a constraint depends on the perceptions people have about it.

The second major implication of the imbrication perspective is that it may help to realign our ontological specifications and empirical observations of the relationship between technologies and organizations. At the ontological level, scholars are beginning to suggest that communication patterns and technologies are indistinguishable (Baptista 2009; Constantinides and Barrett 2006; Davidson and Chismar 2007; Orlikowski and Scott 2008; Pinch 2008). Yet at the empirical level, technologies and routines are relatively easy to distinguish (Edmondson et al. 2001; Pentland and Feldman 2008). "If one were to ask individuals in actual organizations what technologies they use in their work," Barley (1988b, p. 46) writes, "the technology would have a name and the informant could, at least in principle, point to an instance of its use." Thus, our current understanding of the nature of the relationship between organizations and technologies evinces dissonance between our ontological specifications and our empirical observations.

The imbrication metaphor provides one way to reconcile this dissonance. If we recognize that organizations and technologies are figurations (Latour's [2005] term) or infrastructure (Star and Ruhleder's [1996] term) created from the imbrication of social and material agencies, it seems more appropriate to make both ontological and empirical claims about the relationship *between agencies* rather than about the relationship *between organizations and technologies*. In other words, the imbrication metaphor breaks down the walls between studies of organizations and studies of technology by suggesting that researchers who investigate them empirically are actually studying the same underlying process: the imbrication of social and material agencies. When we look at the theoretical string of agencies presented in figure 8.1, we don't naturally see any communication patterns or technology features; we just see agencies. Of course, our specification of some imbrication of agencies as either a communication pattern or a technology is a by-product of empirical operationalization. Thus, it might be more accurate to first conceptualize organizations as strings of human and material agencies and then ask how certain imbrications of these agencies produce particular figurations. Figure 8.1 performs this exercise by showing how certain social and material agencies were imbricated by strategic actors at Autoworks as they constructed perceptions of constraints and affordances in such a way that patterns of communication and the features of a technology were constituted and changed.

The benefit of talking about imbrications of social and material agencies is that the notion of imbrication emphasizes interweaving rather than impact. Many social scientists and even more organizational researchers have seemed hesitant to move technology into a more central role in their theories about organizational routines because they have been unable to speak of its role without resorting to deterministic thinking (Leonardi and Barley 2008). By suggesting that social and material agencies become interlocked in repeated patterns, rather than that patterns of communication and features of a technology impact each other at a particular point in time, the notion of imbrication recognizes that both social and material agencies are necessary if organizing is to occur; their imbrication is what produces complementary changes in technologies and in people's interactions.

From this vantage point, students of organizations and technology can begin to view organizational structuring (metaphorically and literally) as the product of imbrication. Currents in a river have a structure (a direction of flow) that is made visible through patterns of rock imbrication. By examining imbrication patterns in fluvial settlements, geologists can "see" how a river is flowing and how it flowed in the past, and in some cases they can predict how it will flow in the future. The structuring process is a lot like the flow of current in a river. While structuring is occurring, few visible traces of it can be observed. Firms often try to observe structuring by creating an "organization chart" that maps ideal flows of interaction between people of different hierarchical positions, and organizational researchers often use such charts to capture a glimpse of structure at a given point in time. Organization charts, however, capture only the social components of the organizing process. For example, if figure 8.1 consisted only of oval boxes (representing patterns of communication), the only other attribute we would be able to infer about the dynamics of the work system would be the hexagonal boxes (representing social agency). We would not know why, over time, the contents of the diamond-shaped boxes or of the square boxes changed. To know these reasons, we also must treat the square boxes (representing features of a technology) and the diamond-shaped boxes (representing material agency) as constitutive features of the structuring process. By focusing our efforts on how social and material agencies become imbricated, we can begin to visually conceive of how the structuring process looks. As the imbrication framework suggests, structuring involves simultaneous and interactive changes in the features of a technology and in people's communication. By mapping these changes over time, we may be able to gain new insights into the dynamics of sociomaterial change and into the role of such change in the constitution of organizations.

Recapturing Choice

It would be easy—too easy—to read the story of CrashLab through the lens of technological determinism. In a deterministic narrative, CrashLab would have arisen as the next "logical" technology in the evolution of pre-processors. In addition, a deterministic narrative would depict CrashLab's impacts as "natural" consequences of automation in the work of crashworthiness engineering. Although one could dismiss this deterministic narrative in light of the evidence presented in this book, to do so would be to overlook the very real fact that many developers at Autoworks, such as Jensen Lu, despite being instrumental in CrashLab's development and implementation process, believed it:

We had pre-processors for many years that took what we once did in hardware into math. Then as we built our math capabilities the next logical move was to standardize the work. That's what CrashLab did for us, but it did more because after standardization comes automation—once you standardized you can automate—so CrashLab helped with that too. And the it's clear that what automation does is free up people's time and I think we have some evidence that that did happen because people talk more to each other about analysis, which is what was naturally expected that they would do.

Jensen and his fellow developers weren't the only ones to construct and promote a deterministic version of CrashLab's development and use. Sunil Kitane also suggested that CrashLab's evolution was nothing more than a "natural progression":

CrashLab is a great technology to tell you about the natural progression of crash work over the last decade or so. It came out of other technologies in the sense that other technologies like pre-processors were needed first before you could say "Let's automate the work." And some groups are using it so that is what is supposed to happen and it is doing the things it is supposed to. But many others are not using it, and this has nothing to do with the technology but more to do with people not wanting to accept that natural progression, meaning they could now do new things.

Analysts from the Strut Group, who had appropriated CrashLab in ways not intended by Autoworks' developers and managers, also constructed their own narrative of CrashLab's use in a technologically deterministic way:

First you have the pre-processors, then you have CrashLab. That makes sense to me. And what does CrashLab do? It changes your work in some ways, meaning that you don't have to do those little things for setup so much. I think that's how it's supposed to be and you couldn't really use it any other way.

Even analysts from the Piston Group, who nearly completely rejected CrashLab after using its features in divergent ways for several months, were convinced that they played no substantial role in deciding whether or not to use CrashLab; instead, they believed that they were quiet observers of an evolutionary process wherein CrashLab was being selected against because it couldn't compete with other "similar" pre-processors:

I don't know that I really made any real like conscious decision not to use CrashLab. If CrashLab was the best pre-processor out there I would have naturally used it. But it's got to show that it's better than the other one's because it it's not, there is no strong pull to use it. So unless it can evolve better than its competitors it will go extinct, you know. Basically, that's just the way it is.

Most people who were involved with CrashLab, either as producers or as consumers, did seem to believe that CrashLab's evolution had played out "as it had to" and were blind to the fact that things could have been different. By contrast, the imbrication framework laid out in this book, and illustrated in figure 8.1, shows that developers, implementers, and users of CrashLab actively constructed constraints and affordances that led to changes in both the technology's features and the patterns of communication through which work was accomplished at Autoworks. Each of these imbrications occurred because members of the organization made choices about how they would imbricate social and material agencies. The question, then, is this: Despite the evidence that different choices about how to build, implement, or use CrashLab could have been made at many points, why, by August of 2006, did nearly everyone I talked to seem to act as if those choice points had never existed?

In chapter 4, I explained how each of the four organizations involved in technology development at Autoworks constructed its own problems that had to be solved before math-based analyses could play a proactive rather than a reactive role in the process of designing vehicles. Here we see the first important links between technology and organizing. At some point, well before my research was begin, Autoworks made a purposive decision to spread technology development efforts across multiple organizations. Perhaps this decision was made strategically by Autoworks' managers, or perhaps they were merely conforming to institutional forms of organizing within the industrial enterprise. Nevertheless, the activity of developing technologies was structurally separated from the community of people who would be using those technologies. In other words, development and use were institutionalized as two separate and analytically distinguishable activities.

Although this separation seems normal enough from within the industrial research enterprise, it looks rather strange from other vantage points. Take, for example, Thomke's (2003) discussion of Team New Zealand, according to which the same analysts who used finite element analysis to design *Black Magic* (the winner of the 1995 America's Cup race) were also users of the innovation, testing and sailing the yacht against competitors. Similarly, Lakhani and von Hippel (2003) report numerous cases of "open innovation" in which the boundary between users and developers of a technology are sometimes difficult and more often impossible to distinguish. One need not look to modern high-tech computing examples to see a blurring of the distinction between activities surrounding development and use. Farmers have long acted in the dual capacity of the primary developers and users of agricultural tools (Thomas 1985), and for many years photographers themselves produced most of the innovations in lens and lighting technologies that they would use in the practice of their work (Wade 1979). Perhaps, then the organizational separation of technology development is a vestige of the second industrial revolution, or perhaps it is required by the complexity of computationally intensive technologies. The reasons for such division are outside the scope of the present analysis. Nevertheless, the decision to structure the technology development process in such a way as to require (at least initially) the coordination of four separate organizations within Autoworks had important consequences. Each individual involved in this process was steeped in the goals, structures, and processes of his own organization. Thus, when confronted with the challenge of moving math-based analysis earlier in the vehicle-design process, each formulated a direction of inquiry that was viewed as strategic from his organizational vantage point, and each focused his or her attention on specific practices characteristic of the work of crashworthiness analysts. Thus, even before CrashLab was conceived, the way that the technology development process at Autoworks was organized locked its constituent members into object-world thinking—as Bucciarelli (1994) calls it—that was difficult for them to transcend.

With problems clearly developed, technological solutions were relatively easy to identify. Each organization envisioned a type of technology that would solve the particular problem that it thought plagued the work of crashworthiness analysts. We could say that technological solutions to these problems were taken for granted, in that anything that appeared to solve the problem at hand was not only a logical choice but also a rational one. The problem plaguing the development process was that the four hypothetical technologies were incommensurable within the technological frames that each organization had built up around the one it championed. For this reason, the technology Jason Chan's built to overcome the credibility problem seemed only to exacerbate the Information Systems and Services Division's capacity problem and did little to alleviate Techpro's speed problem.

The possibility of "developing" multiple technologies to "solve" multiple problems in crashworthiness engineering was perhaps the first point at which a different choice could have been made. From within their own technological frames they were unable to see that not only was a technology proposed by another organization feasible, it solved a real problem that existed in crashworthiness engineering. At issue was the fact that the organization of work at Autoworks precluded each organization from recognizing the validity of alternative problems. Instead of embracing the idea that multiple technologies could be built to respond to multiple demands, the decision-making process, institutionalized through the Focus Group, demanded convergence of opinions.

In chapter 5 I showed that to converge on an idea for one technology the Focus Group needed something on which to focus its attention. Jason Chan provided that in the form of a prototype of CrashLab. The construction of the CrashLab prototype was made possible by an important organizational change within the R&D Division's Research Mechanics Department: the shift from a focus on product innovation to a focus on process innovation. This shift not only gave Jason the research sabbatical that enabled him to develop the credibility problem; but it also provided funds and managerial support, under the auspices of the IVDA project, for Jason to work with Link Software to develop the code and a mockup of the interface. The CrashLab prototype allowed members of each organization to semantically articulate the problem they had developed in technical terms by comparing it against the prototype's functionality. Through the process of conceptual integration, members of each organization began to frame their own interests in terms of the multivocal logic of standardization. Here we arrive at a second important choice: What should be the goal of CrashLab? At least for a while, the multivocal character of the term 'standardization' allowed members of each organization to act as if they had convinced the others to construct CrashLab's features in such a way that the technology would solve that organization's own problem. Rather than truly coming to agreement on what the goal of the technology would be, members of each organization *acted* as if they had come to agreement. In acting in that way, they ceased to actively promote their own causes and lobby for changes to CrashLab. Thus, the possibilities of developing an alternate technology began to fade, and the emerging conceptual agreement prompted members of the Focus Group to believe that standardization was CrashLab's ultimate goal.

This emerging belief was institutionalized (in both the cognitive and the organizational sense of the word) through the creation of the Best Practice Evaluation Department ("Bestpra"), an organization founded solely to generate guidelines for "standardized" work. Owing to the multivocal logic under which the Focus Group's members were operating, the creation of Bestpra was inevitable. Yet had they been operating under a different logic, Bestpra may never have been created. But it was created, and that important organizational change not only legitimized the concept of standardization but also added a new formal organization to the development process. The idea of building a technology to "standardize" crashworthiness engineering (whatever that meant) was now widely accepted. For members of all the organizations involved, it now became difficult to think of moving along any other path. Because the logic of standardization guided the development process, and consequently each organization thought its interests were well represented, the R&D Division and the Safety Division began to disengage from the development process. Such disengagement freed the organizations that did remain involved (Techpro, Infoserv, and Bestpra) from having to actively compromise with the demands of the R&D Division and the Safety Division. Techpro began an aggressive effort to define standardization as a tool to "speed up" engineering work and began to develop more load cases for CrashLab and different algorithms to increase the speed of model setup. As a result, many of the R&D Division's goals (e.g., allowing users to deviate from standard practice and record deviations on the report form) and many of the Safety Division's goals (e.g., to have advanced welding and model-checking capabilities) fell by the wayside.

Infoserv also attempted to assert its own definition of the standardization process as one of tool consolidation. It pulled the contract from Link Software and awarded the development work to Element Software and then to Dynamic Software. These important organizational changes began to produce changes in the form and the function of CrashLab. The flow chart was lost, and other features (including constrained locations for section cuts) were added, as the development organizations within Autoworks directed the development process and the tool vendors attempted to develop CrashLab within their existing functionality. A third critical choice revolved around whether CrashLab should have integrated its functions with an existing pre-processing technology. This decision wasn't driven by any technical imperatives; it was a fully strategic choice made on the grounds of cost savings and justified by a rhetoric of economies of scale. After CrashLab was implemented, integrating the functionality of CrashLab into an existing pre-processor not only placed a limit on the way CrashLab's features worked but also made it difficult for analysts to conceptually distinguish CrashLab's purpose from the purposes of other pre-processors and thus led them to make unwarranted comparisons about its functionality. The decision to have the subject-matter experts in Bestpra (who were involved in this decision-making process in the first place) conduct the user-acceptance testing further reinforced the validity of this choice and marginalized the voices of the few practicing analysts who were asked to evaluate CrashLab and who gave it poor reviews. Through this process of articulation, developers fashioned a vision of what kind of technology CrashLab was supposed to be and what it should do to fulfill that role. These visions were instantiated as features in the technology, encouraging developers to take for granted that such was CrashLab, and that it should not be other than what it was. From the SCOT vantage point, CrashLab's technical functionality had stabilized and its form had reached closure. In the language of ANT, the goals of the organizations that had been involved in CrashLab's development were translated into a set of common understandings and inscribed into the technology. In the language of systems theory, CrashLab's functionality had acquired momentum.

But other choices could have been made that would have influenced CrashLab's effects on the organization of crashworthiness work differently. Although CrashLab's materiality was no longer changing, its influence on the practice of work had not. As I showed in chapter 6, the developing organizations still played important though more secondary roles during the period in which CrashLab was implemented in the Safety Division. Trainers such as Chowpa Maova from Dynamic Software, SMEs, and managers from the Piston Group were directly influenced by their affiliations with the developers, from whom they learned the specific ways in which CrashLab's features were designed to change engineering work. Trainers such as Eileen and managers from the Strut Group who didn't have a close affiliation with the developers didn't learn of such goals. A fourth choice, then, involved the framing of a new technology. One option, explicitly chosen by those who had knowledge of CrashLab's development process, was to provide specific direction to users about what features they should use, how they should use those features, and how such patterns of use would affect their work. Another option, chosen unwittingly by implementers who weren't familiar with CrashLab's development, was to make broad generalizations about the nature and effects of the new technology.

Although the choice of which framing strategy to use may seem small and inconsequential (and it certainly was viewed as such by implementers at Autoworks), the data presented in chapter 6 show that it had important consequences. Analysts drew on the discursive frames through which they learned about CrashLab to make sense of their social and material interactions. Analysts in the Piston Group who were exposed to a discourse of efficiency interpreted their interactions with colleagues and with technologies from within this frame. When talking with their co-workers, they compared CrashLab against other technologies that were supposed to "speed up" their work—pre-processors such as ElementMesh. Because their exposure to efficiency frames began to lead them to view CrashLab as just another pre-processor, they began to test its merits as a pre-processor through their material interactions. Piston Group analysts quickly discovered that CrashLab was inefficient compared to other pre-processors. Strut Group analysts who were exposed to a discourse of inevitability lacked the specific heuristics for deciding what sort of technology CrashLab was. Rather than start with a view of what CrashLab *should* do and seeing whether their experiences confirmed this view, analysts in the Strut Group started with their practices and then began to form opinions about what CrashLab *could* do. Because the inevitability frames were so broad, analysts were able to conceive of multiple uses of CrashLab and therefore didn't begin to make unwarranted comparisons to other technologies. Interpreting work practices by examining them through the lenses provide by discursive frames a fifth important choice point. Although analysts in the Piston Group were exposed to frames telling them that CrashLab should speed up their work, they could have chosen to ignore them. Alternatively, implementers could have more carefully chosen frames that aligned with analysts' own experiences of their work. Alignment of frames with work practices would have required little need for reconciliation, and analysts in the Piston Group might have interpreted CrashLab differently, as analysts in the Strut Group had.

As I showed in chapter 7, analysts began to appropriate CrashLab's features as they interpretations about what it was good for, whether they should use it in their work, and how they should use it. At first, analysts in both the Piston Group and the Strut Group appropriated CrashLab's features in wildly divergent ways, testing one feature at a time and rarely using the collection of features in any consistent manner. However, as time pressures exerted on them by the vehicle development stage gates increased, experimentation began to drop off. Analysts in the Piston Group who had developed an interpretation of CrashLab as an inefficient pre-processor couldn't afford to "waste their time" experimenting with a technology that wasn't a suitable replacement for their existing tools. Consequently, analysts in the Piston Group began to diminish their use of CrashLab. When time pressures began to bear down on analysts in the Strut Group, they drew on their emerging interpretations of CrashLab as a model-setup tool to converge on a common use of those features that would help them to set up rather than analyze models. In other words, analysts in the Strut Group converged on a common appropriation of CrashLab as a model-setup technology. The way in which a technology is actually used in the course of one's work is a sixth important choice. Analysts in the Piston Group didn't "have to" abandon their use of CrashLab, nor did analysts in the Strut Group "have to" appropriate CrashLab as a tool for setting up models. Instead, their choices were made at the confluence of endogenously formed interpretations of CrashLab's place in their work and exogenous time pressures dictated by the vehicle development process. Had the various groups of analysts developed interpretations of CrashLab different from the ones they did develop, they might have appropriated its features in distinct ways.

As the data showed, these differences in appropriation had consequences for the organization of analysts' work. By converging on a common use of CrashLab's features, analysts in the Strut Group produced a critical mass of individuals using CrashLab in a similar way, and were thereby able to shift the focus of their interactions with one another from conversations about setting up models to conversations about how to use analysis to optimize crashworthiness performance. Analysts in the Piston Group, never having converged on a common use of CrashLab's features, had little opportunity to shift their patterns of interaction, and their social networks remained much the same a year after CrashLab was implemented as they had been before it arrived. A seventh choice is evident here. Although analysts in the Strut Group did begin to communicate in different ways than they had before CrashLab was implemented, they didn't have to do so. Through its appropriation as a tool for setting up models, CrashLab *enabled* analysts to interact in different ways. The reason the Strut Group analysts believed that these new patterns of interaction were appropriate and expected was that the general frames with which they were still evaluating CrashLab's outcomes allowed them to view these changes in their work as direct outcomes of their use of CrashLab.

By nearly rejecting CrashLab (as analysts in the Piston Group did), or by appropriating it as a tool for setting up models (as analysts in the Strut Group did), Autoworks failed to take advantage of the organizational learning that could have occurred had simulations been post-processed in standardized ways. Based on my analysis of the data, I speculated that Autoworks would have faced another important choice if its analysts had used Crash-Lab to generate standard reports: whether to keep working as usual or to create a new organization that could perform analyses on results aggregated both within and across vehicle platforms. We might speculate further that creating such an organization would have generated yet another choice: whether or not to reconfigure CrashLab's material features so that it would allow analysts to cross-plot results, thus consolidating data for easy batch analysis.

As this summation shows, the development, implementation, and use of CrashLab can't be reduced to a deterministic explanation. Instead, we have seen that CrashLab's development, implementation, and use were fashioned from a series of choices by actors as to how to proceed with the new technology.

It is helpful to think about the life cycle of a new technology as a chain of decision points, as illustrated in figure 8.2. The ethnographic data presented throughout this book have shown that at each point actors had a number of options that they could have chosen instead of the one they did choose. However, each of the choices made at a given point influenced the choices that actors (either the same actors or different ones) made at the next point by narrowing the field of choices that could be made. For this reason, if we aim to generate a more complete understanding of why people take their encounters with technology for granted, and of how organizations and technologies mutually constitute one another, it seems important to consider the relationship between the choices made about technology development, technology implementation, and technology use throughout the life cycle of technological and organizational change.

As I discussed in some detail in chapter 2, our current theories of the social construction process are limited in their abilities to capture the dynamics of the organizing process because they end or being their modes of inquiry at seemingly arbitrary moments throughout the life cycle of technological and organizational change. As we have seen throughout this book, the choices that actors made during CrashLab's development heavily influenced the ways in which CrashLab was used in the Safety Division. Similarly, we generate only a limited and certainly incomplete picture of technological change if, by focusing on development activities, we fail to

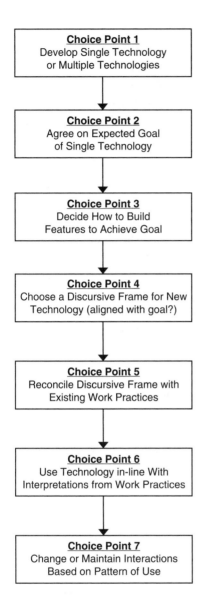

Figure 8.2
Choice points in the development, implementation, and use of CrashLab.

consider how users reconstitute the functionality of a technology and the organization of their work in the context of use. The data presented herein suggest a new way of looking at the mutually constitutive relationship between technological and organizational change, which treats organizing not as a process enabled or constrained by technology but as a process through which social and material changes become imbricated.

Conclusion

To bring the book to an end, I would like to return to my first days of field work. After a staff meeting at which I was introduced to the R&D Division as an "anthropologist" who would be studying "engineering innovations" at Autoworks, Felipe Hernandez, a senior director, called me into his office to give me, as he said, the "real story" on what it meant to develop new technologies in an industrial research center. His observation, I believe, underscores the thesis presented herein:

> When you have a new innovation it's not like it only affects the people who use it. It affects the people who develop it too. If you think about it, it has to. How can you develop something radical, something different than you ever have developed before if you're still doing the same kinds of things you always have. It's not possible. So in some senses you have to be smart and say "Is this the kind of technology we want to build?" Because if you say yes, you are going to get locked in a way of organizing your work and your time to make it happen.

As Felipe suggested, it wasn't possible to develop a new technology without simultaneously developing a new way of organizing work. In other words, the way in which one organization structured its work affected the development of the form and function of the very technology that was supposed to change the way another organization structured its work. Thus, that technology and work organization could exist independent of one another is a fabrication we keep alive to legitimize analytical categories that separate humans from their environments. In fact, we use terms such as "social system" to define cultures, organizations, or structures in ways that relegate materiality to an inferior position. Yet, as we have seen throughout this book, at every social turn there is a material one. In fact, it is impossible to conceive of technologies as "material systems" and organizations as "social systems." Instead, both technologies and organizations are imbrications of social and material agencies.

As the number of employable individuals with the technical acumen to design new technologies continues to rise, researchers predict that many firms, large and small, will begin to play a more active role in designing and developing the architecture of new artifacts than they have in the past (Markus 2004; O'Brien 2004; Tabrizi 2005). In some cases, firms will stop buying technologies "off the shelf" from suppliers and instead will build their own applications. In other cases, firms will continue to develop tighter inter-organizational relations with suppliers that contractually lock the firms and their suppliers into similar trajectories. In either case, the bond between technology development, technology implementation, and technology use grows much tighter in a pragmatic sense. Thus, in a conceptual sense, our tendency to use "impact" metaphors, which compel us to treat phases of development, implementation, and use as distinct categories of action and urge us to maintain artificial distinctions between technological and organizational change, may result in theories that are out of step with the new forms of work.

At a minimum, I hope to have shown in this book that organizing work is just as much a process of material change as it is a process of social change. People have choices as to how they imbricate the social and material elements of their work. To discount one element in favor of another is to resort to deterministic thinking, which is problematic not only for ontological reasons but also because it promotes a sense of hopelessness. When we think that technologies "have to" be built in certain ways, or that organizations "must change" as a result of new material capabilities, we divest ourselves of our own agency to build the kinds of organizations we want to work in and the kinds of technologies that make our lives better.

Glossary

Accelerometer An electromechanical device used to measure forces in a vehicle impact. An accelerometer contains microscopic crystal structures that are stressed by accelerative forces and generate an electrical current that can be read by a digital or an analog device. In a physical crash test, accelerometers are placed at various portions on the vehicle to measure forces. In a simulation, nodes are selected as accelerometers at which the solver will determine the accelerative forces in the model.

Aliasing Misinterpreting high-frequency data as low-frequency data due to sampling at a low rate.

Analysis Work on a model after it has been returned from the solver. The goal of analysis is to determine whether a vehicle meets criteria for crashworthiness set by the vehicle program and, if it doesn't, to determine how best to redesign the vehicle so that the criteria will be met.

Analyst An engineer responsible for validating and testing parts when they are assembled into complete vehicles. Using vehicle coordinates, analysts assemble the parts they receive from design engineers into a fully integrated model that contains all of a vehicle's parts (over 30,000 in most cases). Analysts are the first engineers to see how all the parts of a vehicle fit and act together. They are responsible for testing the performance of the complete vehicle on a number of different performance areas, including crashworthiness, noise and vibration, aerodynamics, heat transfer, and cooling. To complete these performance tests in a virtual environment, analysts use computer-aided engineering (CAE) tools.

Anthropomorphic test device (ATD) A full-scale replica of a human being, weighted and articulated to simulate the behavior of a human body and instrumented to record data on accident variables (such as speed of impact, crushing force, bending, folding, torque of the body, and deceleration rates) during a collision. Sometimes called *anthropomorphic test dummies*, *crash-test dummies*, or simply *dummies*.

Architecture A common set of subsystem and part components upon which different vehicle programs are set.

Assembly   Assembling the various math files of vehicle parts into a full-vehicle model.

Axial crush   A crush that moves in one direction only, without causing bending, thereby absorbing more of the energy generated during an impact. Also referred to as *progressive crush*.

Best Practice Evaluation Department ("Bestpra")   A department of Autoworks responsible for producing standard work procedures for crashworthiness analysis.

Barrier test   A physical crash test in which a vehicle (usually a prototype), aided by an electric linear motor, is crashed into a barrier.

Body-in-white   The welded sheet metal components that form the vehicle's structure—the load-bearing frame.

Chassis   A general term that refers to all of the mechanical parts of a car attached to a structural frame. In a car with unit-body construction, the chassis comprises everything but the vehicle's body.

Computer-aided drafting (CAD)   The use of computer database systems to design parts and systems, generate drawings, perform complex structural and design analyses, and directly program numerically controlled machines to produce parts.

Computer-aided engineering (CAE)   The use of computer database systems to perform complex computational and structural analyses on parts, systems, and the whole car.

Correlation   The degree to which the results of a simulation and a physical test match one another.

Crashworthiness   Refers to how well a vehicle protects its occupants in a crash.

DataExchange   A database of Unigraphics data files used for storing and managing version control of the large number of part files generated by various vehicle programs. Each Autoworks campus has a separate database requiring different access for design engineers or others looking for part files.

Debug   To investigate why the solver didn't solve a submitted job. To debug a model, an analyst usually reviews the input deck in a text editor to determine what has gone wrong.

Deflection   The degree to which a construction or structural element bends under a load.

Deformation   A change in shape due to an applied force.

Design engineer   An engineer responsible for the geometric design of a part of subsystem of parts, as well as the materials out of which the part will be constructed.

Director   One position higher than a manager in the Autoworks hierarchy. Normally, a director is in charge of an entire division.

Displacement   The vector that specifies the position of a point in reference to an origin or to a previous position. The vector directs from the reference point to the current position.

Domestic Operations Organization   Autoworks' Domestic Operations organization, headquartered a short distance from Detroit, is responsible for the engineering and manufacturing of all Autoworks vehicles sold in North America.

DYNA   A transient dynamic finite element solver for simulating complex real world problems. Produced by the Livermore Software Technology Corporation, it is used to predict the behavior of a vehicle in a collision and can report the impact of the collision on the vehicle occupants. DYNA is also used to predict the stresses and deformations experienced by sheet metal.

DynamicMesh   A finite-element pre- and post-processor, similar to ElementMesh, produced by Dynamic Software Technologies. It provides auto-meshing and geometry editing features. It offers superior capabilities for automatically generating and meshing design features such as holes in parts.

Element   Subregions of a computational model over which primary variables (displacements) are interpolated from nodal values.

ElementMesh   A finite element pre- and post-processor, produced by Element Software, that works in conjunction with a variety of finite element solvers, including Nastran, DYNA, and Abaqus. It enables the generation of finite element models for engineering simulation and analysis, providing geometry readers that allow CAE engineers to import Unigraphics data files into ElementMesh, where they create a mesh model and update various model parameters. After the model is exported and run through a solver, ElementMesh is used to view the results (including three-dimensional animation).

Energy   When a vehicle crashes into another object, the kinetic energy of the moving vehicle is partly consumed through friction and partly consumed through plastic (permanent) deformation. Energy is dissipated by the plastic deformation of a vehicle's structure as it is turned to heat. Because energy is a property of force applied over a certain distance, to control the energies present in a crash event it is necessary to control the forces generated between the vehicle and the object striking, or being struck by, the vehicle.

Finite element analysis (FEA)   A computational technique used to decompose an object into a large (though finite) number of much smaller objects known as *elements*. The word 'finite' refers both to the countable number of elements that are generated and to the separation of the technique from the infinitesimal elements used in calculus. The elements are considered connected at defined nodes (corner and mid-segment points), and the entire connected system constitutes a defined structure called a *mesh*. This mesh is programmed to contain the material and structural properties that define how the structure will react to certain loading conditions. These material and structural properties are normally related in a stiffness matrix, which defines the deformation patterns of the materials used to build automobiles (such as steel, plastic, and foam) in relation to the shape (normally called the "geometry") of the structure those materials constitute. The model is then populated with a separate series of equations representing boundary conditions. This entire system of equations is represented mathematically as a very large matrix, taking the form of complex differential equations or integral expressions, with the unknowns (in the case of crashworthiness analysis, usually displacements) solved at the nodes

Filtering A process that changes the frequency content of a signal. Filtering is often used in the analysis of test results to remove the "noise" or error in the signal and to analyze it more effectively.

Federal Motor Vehicle Safety Standards and Regulations (FMVSS) Under Title 49 of the United States Code (chapter 301, Motor Vehicle Safety), the National Highway Traffic Safety Administration has a legislative mandate to issue Federal Motor Vehicle Safety Standards (FMVSS) and Regulations, compliance with which the manufacturers of motor vehicles and of related equipment must certify. FMVSS 209 was the first standard to become effective (on March 1, 1967). A number of FMVSS became effective for vehicles manufactured on and after January 1, 1968. Other FMVSS have been issued since then. New standards and amendments to existing standards are published in the *Federal Register*.

Focus Group A group responsible for, among other things, endorsing and sanctioning the use of all new technologies used by Autoworks' analysts in a particular function.

Friction coefficient A dimensionless quantity used to calculate the force of friction that is generated as a vehicle crashes into a barrier.

Gauge The thickness of a piece of material used in a vehicle, now typically given in millimeters.

Geometry The physical shape of a part, represented by its bounded dimensions.

Global Technology Production Division ("Techpro") An organization responsible for ensuring that all Autoworks engineers all over the world had access to, and training on, tools for math-based analyses. In a company increasingly fractionalized into geographic subunits, Techpro was truly multinational. It was also responsible for working with tool vendors to ensure that the tools Analysts used had the technical features they needed to complete their work. This responsibility meant that engineers in the Techpro organization worked closely with tool vendors.

High Performance Computing Center   A centralized division in which Autoworks maintains supercomputers.

H-point   The point where a person's hip sits in a car seat—a location used to position dummies in a vehicle.

Include file (or include statement)   A syntax in a text-editor file that would call modules from various directories and integrate them together into a full-vehicle model without ever physically moving them into one location.

Information Systems and Services Division ("Infoserv")   A division responsible for providing basic information-technology support to users of all technologies at Autoworks. Also responsible for managing the High Performance Computing Center and purchasing new supercomputers.

Insurance Institute for Highway Safety (IIHS)   A nonprofit research and communications organization funded by auto insurers. Its research focuses on countermeasures aimed at all three factors in motor-vehicle crashes (human, vehicular, and environmental) and on interventions that can occur before, during, and after crashes to reduce losses. In 1992 the Vehicle Research Center (VRC) was opened. This center, which includes a state-of-the-art crash-test facility, is the focus of most of the IIHS's vehicle-related research. The IIHS's affiliate organization, the Highway Loss Data Institute, gathers, processes, and publishes data on the ways in which insurance losses vary among different kinds of vehicles.

Intrusion   The distance a certain point identified on a vehicle moves toward the occupant compartment during an impact.

Job   A term informants used to refer to a simulation that was to be submitted to the solver for analysis. See also *Run, Simulation, Math-model, Test)*

Lateral Impact New Car Assessment Program (LINCAP)   A component of the New Car Assessment Program in which lateral (side) impacts are tested.

Linear and nonlinear analysis   Structural analysis consists of linear and nonlinear models. Linear models use simple parameters and assume that the material is not plastically deformed. Nonlinear models consist of stressing the material past its elastic capabilities, to the point of plastic deformation. The stresses in the material then vary with the amount of deformation. Safety engineers typically work in a world of nonlinear analysis, since the idea behind crashworthiness is to have the vehicle's structure deform in a collision.

LinkMesh   A pre-processing tool produced by Link Software

Load cases   Conditions under which loads, in the form of energy from an impact, are applied to a vehicle's frame.

Load path   The directions in which loads are transferred (move) through the structure of the vehicle.

LS Post A post-processing tool produced by Livermore Software Corporation to work in conjunction with results produced from the DYNA solver

Manager A direct supervisor of an engineer. In the Safety Division of Autoworks, a manager is in charge of the crashworthiness analysis for a specific vehicle platform.

Material model checker (MMC) A technology, under development by Autoworks' Techpro Division, for ascertaining whether parts have the appropriate material properties assigned to them.

Material properties A mathematical representation of the behavior of certain physical materials (e.g. steel or plastic) used in the construction of vehicles.

Math A term used to refer to any computational simulation of a vehicle. FE models are considered math at Autoworks; CAD is not.

Math-model (or model, or math-based model) See *Simulation*.

Mesh A collection of elements used to discretize a region—that is, to break the geometry of a shape into a series of smaller elements. The functions used to interpolate the primary variable between the nodes is usually defined over the elements.

Modular design An approach toward model building in which the vehicle's structural components are split into modules. Each module (many of which consist of multiple parts designed in CAD by multiple design engineers) is saved as an individual FE file. These modules can then be shared among engineers working on various load cases.

Mule vehicle (or test mule) An operational vehicle with a newly constructed one-off chassis or body-in-white onto which parts (e.g., seats, doors) from previous generations of the vehicle are installed.

National Highway Traffic Safety Administration (NHTSA) The NHTSA, under the U.S. Department of Transportation, was established by the Highway Safety Act of 1970 as the successor to the National Highway Safety Bureau, to carry out safety programs under the National Traffic and Motor Vehicle Safety Act of 1966 and the Highway Safety Act of 1966. The Vehicle Safety Act has subsequently been recodified under Title 49 of the U. S. Code in chapter 301, Motor Vehicle Safety. NHTSA also carries out consumer programs established by the Motor Vehicle Information and Cost Savings Act of 1972, which has been recodified in various chapters under Title 49.

New Car Assessment Program (NCAP) A program, begun by NHTSA, that crash tests vehicles in frontal impacts and rates the performance on a scale of five stars. NCAP testing was begun for vehicles in the 1979–1980 model year.

Node A location at which primary variables are computed. Each element is defined by the nodes to which it is connected.

Occupant   A passenger or a dummy sitting in a vehicle during an impact.

Offset deformable barrier (ODB)   A frontal-impact test administered by the IIHS. The barrier is meant to simulate a vehicle crashing into the front bumper of a full-size pickup truck. Only one side of the vehicle's front end hits the barrier, which deforms slightly upon impact.

Parallel processing (or parallel computing)   Simultaneously executing the same task (split up and specially adapted) on multiple processors in order to obtain results faster. The idea is based on the fact that the process of solving a problem usually can be divided into smaller tasks.

Penetration   When the mathematical representations of two parts intersect one another—that is, occupy overlapping vehicle coordinates.

Piston Group   A vehicle program group within Autoworks' Car Department, which, in turn, was located within the Safety Division.

Plastic deformation   Permanent, non-recoverable deformation. When a vehicle crashes into another object, the kinetic energy of the moving vehicle is partly consumed through friction and partly consumed through plastic deformation. Energy is dissipated by the plastic deformation of a vehicle's structure as it is turned to heat.

Platform   See *Architecture*.

Post-processor   Since the grown calculation capacity of computers makes it possible to make more and more detailed finite element models, the file output of these programs can be enormous. It can be so large that you need to post process this data. Post-processing may be defined as the "art of results representation".

Power train   Engine and transmission.

Pre-processor   A software program that processes its input data to produce output that is used as input to another program. The output is said to be a pre-processed form of the input data, which is often used by some subsequent programs such as a solver.

Product   A vehicle that is in a production cycle.

Program   A vehicle program is roughly analogous to a consumer model. To use a Japanese example, Toyota (which also makes Lexus) has several models (what engineers would call programs) such as the Toyota Camry, the Toyota Highlander, the Lexus ES and the Lexus RX, which all share a common platform.

Progressive crush   See *Axial crush*.

Proving ground   A location at which physical crash tests are conducted.

Quality Improvement Team (QIT)   A monthly meeting held for engineers working on a common load case across various vehicle platforms so they can share insights into model building and analysis and communicate information about new procedures and tools under development.

Rapid Meshing Assembly (RMA) A tool that automatically translates CAD data into a finite element mesh.

Research and Development Division ("R&D") A division responsible for investigating new processes and products for Autoworks' engineering and manufacturing operations.

Rigid body displacement A rigid body such as an engine doesn't deform easily when forces are applied to it. Instead, forces displace (move) the rigid body.

Run See *Simulation, Test, Math-model, Job.*

Safety Division A division of Autoworks in which performance engineers use math-based models to evaluate the crashworthiness of vehicles' structures. The Safety Division comprised a Car Department and a Truck Department, which housed, respectively, the Piston Group and the Strut Group.

Sampling Recording data in digital form at discrete time intervals and discarding the remaining data

Section cut A plane through a vehicle member that is used to measure the force in that particular member (section)

Section force The force going through the vehicle member (the section) under measurement.

Simulation A symbolic device (a computer model) used to represent certain aspects of a real object. The model attempts to mimic a real-life situation so that it can be studied to see how the system works. By changing variables, predictions may be made about the behavior of the system. Informants at Autoworks used the 'simulation' and 'math-model' as synonyms.

Subject-matter expert (SME) An engineer responsible for writing standard work procedures for analysts in Autoworks' Safety Division

Solver A code that performs computational analyses on finite element models, applying equilibrium equations to each element and constructing a system of simultaneous equations that are solved for unknown values using linear or nonlinear numerical schemes.

Stage gate A project is divided into stages (or phases) separated by gates. At each gate, the continuation of the process is decided by (typically) a manager or a steering committee.

Strain The geometrical expression of deformation caused by the action of stress on a physical body.

Stress   The internal distribution of force per unit area that balances and reacts to external loads applied to a body

Strut Group   A vehicle program group within Autoworks' Truck Department, which, in turn, was located within the Safety Division.

Submit a job   To send a simulation (also called a *math-model*, a *run*, or a *test*) to the solver.

Supercomputer   A computer that leads the world in processing capacity, particularly speed of calculation, at the time of its introduction. Usually several orders of magnitude more powerful than a personal computer.

Supplier   An external firm (sometimes called a *vendor*) that produces either vehicle parts or computational software for an automaker. Occasionally supplier firms are contracted to build math models or to run simple analyses.

Test   See *Simulation, Run, Math-model, Job.*

Unigraphics   A general-purpose feature-based CAD system, capable of creating parametric solid models and wire-frame models of mechanical components, that allows conceptual design and visualization, product design, engineering, quality management, and product manufacturing. Its feature-based nature allows users to create and modify parts by manipulating (adding, subtracting, etc.) two- and three-dimensional features, rather than building parts up from lines or from simpler objects..

Validation   A process of checking that a model represents the aspects of the reality that is the scope of the model—that is, checking that the correct equations are solved.

Vehicle Model Assembly (VMA)   A technology, under development by Autoworks' Techpro Division, for automatically assembling math-models.

Vendor   See *Supplier.*

Notes

Chapter 1

1. All names used in this book—names of companies, departments, and individuals—are pseudonyms.

2. A number of studies have documented that when people fail to understand the technical complexity of the technologies with which they work they often justify their lack of knowledge by linking new technologies to complex advances in science that are beyond the understanding of normal users (Staudenmaier 1994). Another tactic is to frame the "mysterious" inner workings of a technology that aren't readily understandable to normal users as magic (Kaarst-Brown and Robey 1999). Barley (1988a) reports that even technology-savvy radiology technicians resorted to magical thinking about the operation of a new computerized tomography scanner when their traditional means of explanation for how such a machine should work failed.

3. Indeed, social choices delimiting their functions are embedded even in the seemingly mundane technologies we use every day. Schwartz Cowan (1983) suggests that the fan over the stove could indeed have worked differently—there could have been a fan speed in between high and low—had the negotiations among its developers proceeded along different tracks. Similarly, within the context of use there is always the possibility that users will do things with the technology that to others appear impossible. Orlikowski and Gash (1994), for example, show that email programs can be, and regularly are, used for electronic conferencing.

4. The difficulty of incorporating the notion of material agency into a human-agency framework is perhaps most clearly seen in discussions of structuration theory. Agency is, of course, given a central role in structuration theory, which either implicitly or explicitly has shaped the writings of many constructivist authors. Giddens (1984) defines agency, in general, as the "capacity for action." At first glance it may seem that such a definition extends agency to humans and technologies alike. But Giddens makes an important qualification. He suggests that all action involves motivation, rationalization, and reflexive monitoring (p. 5). These cognitive processes are linked to human intention. People have goals that

motivate them. Given a set of circumstances, they can rationalize their goals as acceptable, and they can continuously monitor their environment to determine whether or not the goal is being achieved. For this reason, Giddens notes that "agency concerns events of which an *individual* is the perpetrator" (p. 9). In view of Giddens' explicit bestowal of agency upon humans, Rose et al. (2005) observe that the idea that technologies could be seen to have material agency is problematic within constructivist approaches to technology development and use because such approaches treat "agency as a uniquely human property" (p. 133) and "technology as having no agency of its own" (p. 137). Orlikowski (2005, p. 184) concurs that "structurational treatments . . . privilege human agency and (inappropriately) discount technological agency" and has suggested that structuration theory may not be able to fully account for the fluid and flexible interchange between the material agency of technologies and the human agency of those who produce and use them because "structurational perspectives reflect the humanist tradition of making the human subject the center of the action."

5. This observation is similar to Collins and Kusch's (1998) claim that researchers (and lay observers) often attribute agency to machines when the "vantage point is low in the action tree" (p. 124). In other words, the analyst looks at the technology without recognizing that it is embedded in a web of human agency. Collins and Kusch don't discount that technologies can act on their own; however, they caution researchers to keep in mind, as Taylor and his colleagues do, that it is always humans that are configuring material agency and deciding how it will become interwoven with their goals.

6. Clearly, the imagery of imbrices and tegulae has its shortcomings. Both tiles are made of "material" in the sense that they are physical creations of clay. The struggle to find a suitable image with which to describe the imbrication of human and material agencies points to the conceptual difficulty of integrating these phenomena. Thus, the analogy is meant to be illustrative rather than to be read literally.

7. More details on the slowdown in auto sales in 2008 can be found at the website of the Alliance of Automobile Manufacturers (http://www.autoalliance.org/).

8. For details on this statistic, see Hill 2007.

9. The SAE is an independent professional association established in 1905 to promote the use of standards in the fledgling American automobile industry. Today it sets most of the standards for the testing, measuring, and designing of automobiles and their components.

10. See Miel 2008.

11. For similar ideas in other sociological traditions, readers should consult Anthony Giddens' theory of "structuration" (1979, 1984), Anselm Strauss' perspective on "negotiations" (1978), and Howard Garfinkel's "ethnomethodology" (1967).

Chapter 2

1. Predicting this shift was the primary focus of McLuhan's work. More recently, this claim was made by Michael Heim (1987). Heim suggested that the shift from a print culture to a culture of electronic word processing is bringing about fundamental changes in the way people think and relate to the world.

2. Many macrosocial theorists and historians do recognize the inherent indeterminacy of technological change at the microsocial level. In his fascinating discussion of the evolution of the modern business enterprise and the creation of the multidivisional or M-form corporation, Alfred Chandler cautions readers not to fall into the trap of conflating technological change with organizational changes: "Although technological change has often been defined to include organizational change, it does seem useful to distinguish between them. Technological change in production and distribution refers, for the purposes of this study, to innovations in materials, power sources, machinery and other artifacts. Organizational change refers to innovation in the way such artifacts are arranged and the ways in which the movement and activities of workers and managers are coordinated and controlled." (1977, p. 240) But without microsocial data with which to trace variations in social practice over time, such a venerable position becomes difficulty to maintain. Throughout his treatise, Chandler himself falls victim numerous times to technologically deterministic explanations about the organizational change to M-form arrangements. For example: "As long as the process of production remained powered by humans, animals, wind, and water, the volume of outputs was rarely enough to require the creation of subunits within the enterprise or to call for the services of salaried manager to coordinate and monitor the work of these subunits." (ibid., pp. 50–51)

3. Among the most commonly used perspectives are Social Shaping of Technology (SST), Science and Technology Studies (S&TS), Science, Technology, and Society (STS), and Sociology of Technology. For reviews of these different perspectives, in particular their commonalities and differences, see Bijker, Hughes, and Pinch 1987b; Bijker and Law 1992; Williams and Edge 1996.

4. For a detailed review of such studies and the structural relationship between technology and society they promoted, see Bijker 1995a.

5. A common error is that all theories in this program are called *social construction of technology* (SCOT). This is not the case. Pinch and Bijker's initial formulation of SCOT was programmatic in the sense that it attempted to draw attention to the inner workings of technological artifacts as a focus of sociological inquiry. (For details see Bijker and Pinch 2002.) Accordingly, the program they helped to establish is populated by several distinct but interrelated theories about the relationship between the technical and the social. Not surprisingly, the theories in this program that arose in response to SCOT influenced later developments of the theory.

Although Actor-Network Theory and Systems Theory both focus on the processes whereby the social and technical are integrated, they differ from the SCOT, and from each other, in the mechanisms they use to explain this process.

6. In fact, Perrow (1967, p. 195) suggests that "by technology is meant the actions that an individual performs upon an object with or without the aid of tools or mechanical devices, in order to make some change in that object." This seems to be commonly overlooked in many studies of technological artifacts that draw on contingency theorists' views of process technologies as evidence that previous theories have held deterministic notions about physical artifacts. Though many of contingency theory's insights into process technologies would certainly apply to discussions of technological artifacts, the former are best understood as ways to organize work to deal with environmental uncertainty about resource allocation (Thompson 1967) and thus are amenable to very different sorts of discussions about the relationship between the material and the social than those studies that look empirically at how people use hardware and software as they work. However, organizational researchers didn't focus on technological artifacts before the 1980s. It was not until the arrival of personal computerized technology that such researchers began to take interest in an artifact's implications for organizing. Be that as it may, the ontology of determinism promoted by contingency theorists is rightfully criticized by these newer studies.

7. Orlikowski (2000) proposes a distinction between the terms 'appropriation' and 'enactment'. She argues that uses of 'appropriation' in the literature often suggest that technology structures exist before a technology is used, and that such a perspective is theoretically inconsistent with the premises of structuration theory. Orlikowski's distaste for 'appropriation' may be a reaction to the normative value that DeSanctis and Poole (1994) seem to place on it in their writings: that "faithful" appropriations are better than "unfaithful" ones. If we remove this normative bias, 'appropriation' can be used as a neutral term for the actions people take with a technology's material features. In this sense, 'appropriation' is better suited than 'enactment' to capture an individual's interaction with a technology. This is because technology's features aren't enacted—they are there regardless of whether someone uses them or not—but their consequences are.

8. For this reason we say that technology use is "socially constructed" rather than "physically constructed."

9. This definition is taken from the *American Heritage Dictionary of the English Language*, published in 2000.

10. This is the primary point of the cybernetic theory of communication, outlined in most detail by Norbert Wiener (1966).

11. As a notable exception, the SCOT perspective is one of a small number of perspectives that do attempt to show how the processes by which a technology reaches

a state of "stabilization and closure." As critics have pointed out, however, SCOT generally tends to be more concerned with opening up the black box of technology —and providing a method to do so—than with showing how the box is closed.

12. The vast majority of studies of the social construction of technology development do take a historical perspective. This should come as no surprise, since the program of research originally grew out of the union of the work of historians of technology and sociologists (Bijker, Hughes, and Pinch 1987a). Thus, following the historian's methodology means beginning where we are today and working backward to understand how we got there. Shifting methodologies to follow the sociologist's approach would entail combining this historical focus with real-time observations and empirical data that could then help to demonstrate those specific practices through which black boxes get closed. Pinch's recent work on the development of the Moog Synthesizer (Pinch 2003; Pinch and Trocco 2002) has attempted to move this program in such a direction.

13. Research on technology use is also influenced to a major degree by its methodological toolkit. Most constructivist studies of technologically induced organizational change tend to utilize ethnographic rather than historical methods (Robey and Boudreau 1999). As a consequence, researchers typically begin an investigation when a technology is newly introduced and thus watch in real time as the organization responds to its constraints and affordances.

14. 'Cobble' is a geological term for a rock or rock fragment with a particle size between 64 and 256 millimeters (between 2½ and 10 inches).

15. Brick walls that provide structural support for a roof, as opposed to walls that are simply facades, normally use this alternating pattern of header and stretcher bricks in two rows (called *courses*). This particular type of bond is normally referred to as a Flemish or an English bond.

16. This view coincides with the recent tendency to call into question the distinction between routines and technologies. This tendency is based on ontological claims such as that routines are patterns of social action that are often mediated by technology (Pentland and Feldman 2007) and that a technology's material form is shaped to a significant degree by the routines of product development (Dougherty 1992; Garud and Rappa 1994), and that a technology can affect the way people work only if it becomes a technology-in-practice; that is, if it is incorporated in people's existing work routines (Orlikowski 2000; Vaast and Walsham 2005).

17. This is akin to saying (as chemists do) that our theories of physical chemistry should treat diamond and graphite as equivalent because they are both made of carbon, but that empirically we must distinguish between them because they have different crystal structures by virtue of the ways in which carbon's atoms have interlocked.

18. For a more detailed discussion of this point, see Latour's example of the relationship between a person and a gun (1994, pp. 30–33).

19. Note that a constraint, as the term is used here, is not the property of the technology. Rather, a technology that was once everything users wanted or needed is now perceived by them as a constraint to achieving their new goal. This perception of constraint arises because their goal has shifted and because they can't figure out how to achieve their goal with the features of the existing technology.

Chapter 3

1. Most of this is done virtually, and Autoworks' management wants it to be done virtually to reduce costs.

2. For an overview of testing procedures used to determine the "collision sequence," see Lundstrom 1967.

3. The first known description of FEA appeared in a paper by an applied mathematician named Richard Courant (1943). It was mostly ignored because of the high computational requirements of the technique, since at that time all calculations would have to have been performed by hand. The concept re-emerged separately in the 1950s with practical applications in aeronautics; the first paper using the technique modeled an airplane wing by decomposing it into three separate elements. The idea caught on fairly quickly, although the number of elements that could be managed without computing support was very small. The name "finite element analysis" was coined in 1960.

4. Kythe and Wei (2004) note that in mathematical theory the 1960s marked a dramatic transition from earlier research into the finite-element method. During this period, development of mathematical theories provided a rigorous and firm foundation for application of the finite-element method in fields other than structural analysis.

5. The 1964 annual review of NASA's research program in structural dynamics revealed that the research centers were separately developing structural-analysis software that was specific to their own needs. The review recommended that a single generic software program be used instead. In response, an *ad hoc* committee was formed. The committee determined that no existing software could meet their requirements, suggested that a cooperative project be established to develop the software, and created a specification document that outlined the software's capabilities. The committee later developed NASTRAN, which is written primarily in FORTRAN and contains more than a million lines of code.

6. Structural analysis consists of linear and nonlinear models. Linear models use simple parameters and assume that the material is not plastically deformed. Nonlinear models stress the material past its elastic capabilities, to the point of plastic

deformation. The stresses in the material then vary with the amount of deformation. Since the whole idea behind crashworthiness is for the vehicle to deform in a collision, safety engineers typically work in a world of nonlinear analysis.

7. In the auto industry, 'load case' refers simply to the way in which a load (a force resulting from a collision) is applied to a vehicle's structure.

8. By July of 2005, the Car Department had increased its workforce by one engineer to a total of 67 analysts performing CAE work; the Truck Department had increased its workforce to 61.

9. Vehicle teardowns are performed after physical crash tests at the proving ground. Technicians take the crashed vehicle apart piece by piece and in most cases make measurements and take photographs of the damage. Engineers who work on math-based analyses often attend the teardowns to visually inspect whether the vehicle deformed in the test as it did in their simulations.

10. Despite my best attempts, I was not able to conduct second interviews with these informants; our schedules kept crossing.

Chapter 4

1. Folk history suggests that the term 'body-in-white' originated in the days when coachbuilders delivered bodies to automakers painted only with a white primer. Today, many automotive engineers suggest that the name comes from the appearance of a car's body after it is dipped into a white primer. However, usually the initial primer used on the steel is medium gray.

2. This informant uses the term 'hardware' to refer to the vehicles that are destroyed during physical crash tests at the proving grounds.

3. In reality, Infoserv far exceeded its immediate goal. In concert with the crashworthiness organization, Infoserv also took control of the dummy models used by the analysts and attempted to consolidate the use of those too. By 2003, Infoserv had reduced the number of tools by more than 80 percent.

4. The so-called R-Drive was a disk on the HPC server on which analysts were allotted a certain amount of space to store their models. If there wasn't enough free space on the R-Drive, the HPC wouldn't allow the model to be submitted to the solver. The size of the R-Drive allotted to analysts was decided on by the ISS organization on the basis of considerations of computing capacity and space.

Chapter 5

1. Note that Orlikowski and Gash (1994) use the term 'technological frame' to refer to something much more psychological than ideological.

2. This is not a complete list of all the elements of a technological frame presented by Bijker. Bijker does note, however, that there are many possible elements, and that not all elements apply in every case. I have chosen to present here the elements of a technological frame that surfaced through my coding of the data.

3. "J and K heights" refer to the height of a vehicle's rockers measured from the ground. J is the height of the rocker in the front of the vehicle, and K is the height of the rocker in the rear of the vehicle. J and K heights are used to set the position of the vehicle and the barrier.

4. Mass scaling is a technique whereby nonphysical mass is added to a structure in order to achieve a larger explicit time step. Typically, mass scaling is achieved by adding a "mass node," a command that tells the solver to solve the differential equations with the indicated amount of mass.

5. Using what it learned in the course of its work with Autoworks, Link Software produces a version of CrashLab under another name, and sells it to supplier firms that work on tasks outsourced by Chrysler, Ford, and General Motors. The functionality of this product is similar to that of early CrashLab, but there are many new features.

6. This shift is often reflected most prominently in an organization's decision to outsource model-building or drafting work, thereby freeing up more in-house resources for engineers.

Chapter 6

1. In a review of all articles appearing in a major journal dedicated to research on technology and organization, Orlikowski and Iacono (2001) found that in 25 percent of the reported research studies technology was an "omitted variable"; that is, its form or function was never even described or explored.

2. There were 137 analysts in the Safety Division. Nine of these worked primarily with the Safety Engineers at the proving grounds and didn't do CAE simulation work.

3. Here I use the term 'discourse' as it is used by communication theorists: to represent an ideology that is created through talk. Many communication researchers (e.g., Alvesson and Kärreman 2000; Fairhurst and Putnam 2004) refer to discourse (not capitalized) as the everyday talk of members of a social group and to Discourse as the ideology that is created through discourse. Here, I dispense with this distinction and simply use 'discourse' to mean a type of ideology constructed out of frames produced in talk.

4. Mine is not the only study to reveal that white-collar workers were excited at the prospect that some portion of their job could be automated. Zuboff's (1988) analysis of pulp paper engineers, consultants, and bankers was perhaps the first study to

show in depth that many white-collar workers were bored by certain parts of their jobs and saw new automation technologies as a way to relieve them from the tedium of their work and to provide them with the opportunity to engage in new work tasks.

5. The brothers Charles and Frank Duryea are recognized as the manufactures of America's first gasoline-powered commercial automobile. Bicycle makers who became interested in gasoline engines and automobiles, they manufactured their first vehicle on September 20, 1893. The car was tested on the public streets of Springfield, Massachusetts. In 1896 Charles Duryea founded the Duryea Motor Wagon Company, the first company in the United States to manufacture and sell gasoline-powered vehicles.

6. Note that the total number of analysts exposed to a particular frame is not the same as the total number of analysts in each group. Some analysts were exposed to frames in more than one event (e.g., a training session and a staff meeting); others didn't participate in any of the events. In addition, because of time constraints, I didn't observe every staff meeting for every vehicle platform in both the Piston Group and the Strut Group. Thus, the numbers in tables 6.1 and 6.2 are suggestive only of the number of frames to which the *average* analyst in either the Piston Group or the Strut Group was exposed.

7. Here the word 'work' is used as it is defined in physics: as the line integral of a scalar product of force and displacement vectors: $W = \int_C \vec{F} \cdot d\vec{s}$.

8. The term 'crush space' refers to an empty space in a vehicle's load path into which the vehicle's structure can deform. A torque box is a structural feature located between the engine and the firewall.

9. The term 'packaging constraint' is used to refer to the available space to locate a part in a vehicle. All vehicle parts must "fit" within the vehicle's architecture and are thus "packaged" according to a master blueprint specified by a vehicle's lead program manager.

10. Informants used the terms 'progressive crush' and 'axial crush' in the same way. In geometric terms, 'axial' refers to movement along one axis. Thus an axial crush moves in one direction only, without causing bending, thereby absorbing more energy generated during impact. 'Progressive' simply implies that the crush continues to produce bending in the vehicle's structure (in an axial manner) that isn't impeded by bending.

11. The H-point—the position of a person's hips relative to a car seat—is a primary location used to position dummies in a vehicle.

12. When generating a text-editor file that will be used as an input deck to the solver, an analyst might wish to add notation about the work she has done. These notations, because they are for the analyst and not the solver, would confuse the

solver. Thus, the analyst has the option to "comment out" the text—that is, to place certain symbols before and after it that tell the solver that the text inside those symbols is not to be solved.

Chapter 7

1. As was noted in chapter 3, I happened to pick two vehicle programs that weren't yet in the SVER phase of development.

2. An initiator is a small divot, placed in a strategic spot on the vehicle's frame, that weakens the structure just enough to initiate a fold in the frame. Sometimes a frame is too thick and will not crush at low speeds. In these cases, the energy of the impact is not absorbed in the folding of the frame and is passed to the occupant. An initiator ensures that the frame will fold, thereby absorbing energy.

3. Rothlisberger and Dickson studied patterns of informal communication in Western Electric's wiring rooms. To visually depict the relationship between informants, the authors drew the network diagrams as if they were wiring diagrams for electrical circuitry.

4. Because the analysts within each of the groups needed to work together so closely to accomplish their goals, they regularly interacted with each other face to face. However, as Barley (1990a) has suggested, evidence of a strong collegial bond between workers exists when they discuss not just one, but a variety of work-related matters. To determine where ties among analysts were the strongest, I combined all three of the matrices for model-setup consultations and model-analysis consultations in a given period into one valued adjacency matrix to represent all of the analysts' consultations during that time period. The matrices were dichotomized (converted to binary relations) by setting each cell equal to 1 if its value was greater than or equal to the average number of consultations sought by any one analyst in the group during that time period ($a_{ij} \geq \bar{n}$). Otherwise, the cell was set to 0. This transformational process produced one directional dichotomized matrix for consultations related to model setup and one for consultations related to model analysis representing each of the three time periods for both groups.

5. The digraphs were generated using spring embedding algorithms, which sort nodes into a desirable layout that satisfies the aesthetics for visual presentation (symmetry, non-overlapping, etc.). Spring embedding algorithms treat nodes as physical bodies and edges as springs connected to the nodes providing forces between them. Nodes move according to the forces placed on them until a local energy minimum is achieved (Battista, Eades, Tamassia, and Tollis 1994). The algorithms used to generate these digraphs can be found in version 6 of UCINET (Borgatti, Everett, and Freeman 2002).

References

Akrich, M. 1992. The de-scription of technical objects. In *Shaping Technology/Building Society: Studies in Sociotechnical Change*, ed. W. Bijker and J. Law. MIT Press.

Allen, T. J., and O. Hauptman. 1990. The substitution of communication technologies for organizational structure in research and development. In *Organizations and Communication Technologies*, ed. J. Fulk and C. Steinfield. Sage.

Alvesson, M. 1998. The business concept as a symbol. *International Studies of Management and Organization* 28 (3): 86–108.

Alvesson, M., and D. Kärreman. 2000. Varieties of discourse: On the study of organizations through discursive analysis. *Human Relations* 53: 1125–1149.

Anderson, P., and M. L. Tushman. 1990. Technological discontinuities and dominant designs: A cyclical model of technological change. *Administrative Science Quarterly* 35: 604–633.

Arnold, M. 2003. On the phenomenology of technology: The Janus-faces of mobile phones. *Information and Organization* 13 (4): 231–256.

Bailey, D. E., P. M. Leonardi, and S. R. Barley. 2012. The lure of the virtual. *Organization Science*, in press.

Baptista, J. 2009. Institutionalisation as a process of interplay between technology and its organisational context of use. *Journal of Information Technology* 24: 305–319.

Barley, S. R. 1986. Technology as an occasion for structuring: Evidence from observations of CT scanners and the social order of radiology departments. *Administrative Science Quarterly* 31 (1): 78–108.

Barley, S. R. 1988a. The social construction of a machine: Ritual, superstition, magical thinking and other pragmatic responses to running a CT scanner. In *Biomedicine Examined*, ed. M. Lock and D. Gordon. Kluwer.

Barley, S. R. 1988b. Technology, power, and the social organization of work: Towards a pragmatic theory of skilling and deskilling. *Research in the Sociology of Organizations* 6: 33–80.

Barley, S. R. 1990a. The alignment of technology and structure through roles and networks. *Administrative Science Quarterly* 35 (1): 61–103.

Barley, S. R. 1990b. Images of imaging: Notes on doing longitudinal field work. *Organization Science* 1 (3): 220–247.

Barley, S. R., and G. Kunda. 2001. Bringing work back in. *Organization Science* 12 (1): 76–95.

Barnard, C. I. 1938. *The Functions of the Executive*. Harvard University Press.

Baron, J. N., and W. T. Bielby. 1982. Workers and machines: Dimensions and determinants of technical relations in the workplace. *American Sociological Review* 47 (2): 175–188.

Battista, G., P. Eades, R. Tamassia, and I. G. Tollis. 1994. Algorithms for drawing graphs: An annotated bibliography. *Computational Geometry: Theory and Applications* 4 (5): 235–282.

Ben-Joseph, E., H. Ishii, J. Underkoffler, B. Piper, and L. Yeung. 2001. Urban simulation and the luminous planning table bridging the gap between the digital and the tangible. *Journal of Planning Education and Research* 21: 196–203.

Berg, M. 1998. The politics of technology: On bringing social theory into technological design. *Science, Technology & Human Values* 23 (4): 456–490.

Berger, P. L., and T. Luckmann. 1967. *The Social Construction of Reality: A Treatise in the Sociology of Knowledge*. Anchor.

Bijker, W. E. 1993. Do not despair: There is life after constructivism. *Science, Technology & Human Values* 18 (1): 113–138.

Bijker, W. E. 1995a. *Of Bicycles, Bakelites, and Bulbs: Toward a Theory of Sociotechnical Change*. MIT Press.

Bijker, W. E. 1995b. Sociohistorical technology studies. In *The Handbook of Science and Technology Studies*, ed. S. Jasanoff, G. Markle, J. Peterson, and T. Pinch. Sage.

Bijker, W. E., T. P. Hughes, and T. J. Pinch. 1987a. Common themes in sociological and historical studies of technology: Introduction. In *The Social Construction of Technological Systems: New Directions in the Sociology and History of Technology*, ed. W. Bijker, T. Hughes, and T. Pinch. MIT Press.

Bijker, W. E., T. P. Hughes, and T. J. Pinch. 1987b. The social construction of technological systems: Introduction. In *The Social Construction of Technological Systems: New Directions in the Sociology and History of Technology*, ed. W. Bijker, T. Hughes, and T. Pinch. MIT Press.

Bijker, W. E., and J. Law. 1992. Shaping technology/ building society: General introduction. In *Shaping Technology/Building Society: Studies in Sociotechnical Change*, ed. W. Bijker and J. Law. MIT Press.

Bijker, W. E., and T. J. Pinch. 2002. SCOT answers, other questions. *Technology and Culture* 43: 361–369.

Billari, F. C., and A. Prskawetz, eds. 2003. *Agent-Based Computational Demography: Using Simulation to Improve Our Understanding of Demographic Behaviour*. Physica-Verlag HD.

Bimber, B. 1990. Karl Marx and the three faces of technological determinism. *Social Studies of Science* 20 (2): 333–351.

Bimber, B. 1994. Three faces of technological determinism. In *Does Technology Drive History? The Dilemma of Technological Determinism*, ed. M. Smith and L. Marx. MIT Press.

Black, L. J., P. R. Carlile, and N. R. Repenning. 2004. A dynamic theory of expertise and occupational boundaries in new technology implementation: Building on Barley's study of CT scanning. *Administrative Science Quarterly* 49: 572–607.

Blau, P. M. 1955. *Dynamics of Bureaucracy*. University of Chicago Press.

Blau, P. M. 1963. Critical remarks on Weber's theory of authority. *American Political Science Review* 57 (2): 305–316.

Blau, P. M., C. M. Falbe, W. McKinley, and P. K. Tracy. 1976. Technology and organization in manufacturing. *Administrative Science Quarterly* 21 (1): 20–40.

Bloor, D. 1973. Wittgenstein and Mannheim on the sociology of mathematics. *Studies in History and Philosophy of Science* 4: 173–191.

Boland, R. J., K. Lyytinen, and Y. Yoo. 2007. Wakes of innovation in project networks: The case of digital 3-D representations in architecture, engineering, and construction. *Organization Science* 18 (4): 631–647.

Borgatti, S. P., M. G. Everett, and L. C. Freeman. 2002. *UCINET for Windows: Software for Social Network Analysis*. Analytic Technologies.

Bormann, E. G. 1996. Symbolic convergence theory and communication in group decision making. In *Communication and Group Decision Making*, second edition, ed. R. Hirokawa and M. Poole. Sage.

Bosk, C. L. 1979. *Forgive and Remember: Managing Medical Failure*. University of Chicago Press.

Boudreau, M.-C., and D. Robey. 2005. Enacting integrated information technology: A human agency perspective. *Organization Science* 16 (1): 3–18.

Bourgeois, L. J. 1984. Strategic management and determinism. *Academy of Management Review* 9 (4): 586–596.

Brooks, F. P. 1982. *The Mythical Man-Month: Essays on Software Engineering*. Addison-Wesley.

Bucciarelli, L. L. 1994. *Designing Engineers*. MIT Press.

Burkhardt, M. E., and D. J. Brass. 1990. Changing patterns or patterns of change: The effects of a change in technology on social network structure and power. *Administrative Science Quarterly* 35: 104–127.

Callon, M. 1986. Some elements of a sociology of translation: Domestication of the scallops and the fisherman of St. Brieuc Bay. In *Power, Action, and Belief: A New Sociology of Knowledge*, ed. J. Law. Routledge.

Cardinal, L. B. 2001. Technological innovation in the pharmaceutical industry: The use of organizational control in managing research and development. *Organization Science* 12 (1): 19–36.

Carl, E. J., and W. C. Hamaan. 1974. How finite element methods are introduced in large and small organizations. *SAE Transactions* 83: 10–22.

Chandler, A. D. 1977. *The Visible Hand: The Managerial Revolution in American Business*. Harvard University Press.

Ciborra, C. 2006. Imbrication of representations: Risk and digital technologies. *Journal of Management Studies* 43 (6): 1339–1356.

Clark, K. B., and T. Fujimoto. 1991. *Product Development Performance*. Harvard Business School Press.

Collins, H. M. 1974. The TEA set: Tacit knowledge and scientific networks. *Science Studies* 4: 165–186.

Collins, H. M., and M. Kusch. 1998. *The Shape of Actions: What Humans and Machines Can Do*. MIT Press.

Collins, S. T. 2003. Using ethnography to identify cultural domains within a systems engineering organization. *Bulletin of Science, Technology & Society* 23 (4): 246–255.

Constant, D., L. Sproull, and S. Kiesler. 1996. The kindness of strangers: The usefulness of electronic weak ties for technical advice. *Organization Science* 7 (2): 119–135.

Constantinides, P., and M. Barrett. 2006. Negotiating ICT development and use: The case of telemedicine system in the healthcare region of Crete. *Information and Organization* 16: 27–55.

Cooren, F. 2004. Textual agency: How texts do things in organizational settings. *Organization* 11 (3): 373–393.

Courant, R. 1943. Variational methods for the solution of problems of equilibrium and vibrations. *Bulletin of the American Mathematical Society* 49: 1–23.

Culnan, M. J., and M. L. Markus. 1987. Information technologies: Electronic media and intraorganizational communication. In *Handbook of Organizational Communication*, ed. F. Jablin, L. Putnam, K. Roberts, and L. Porter. Sage.

Daft, R. L., and K. E. Weick. 1984. Toward a model of organizations as interpretation systems. *Academy of Management Review* 9 (2): 284–295.

Dalton, M. 1959. *Men Who Manage*. Wiley.

Davidson, E. 2006. A technological frames perspective on information technology and organizational change. *Journal of Applied Behavioral Science* 42 (1): 23–39.

Davidson, E. J., and W. G. Chismar. 2007. The interaction of institutionally triggered and technology-triggered social structure change: An investigation of computerized physician order entry. *Management Information Systems Quarterly* 31 (4): 739–758.

Davis, R. L. 1974. How finite element methods improve the design cycle. *SAE Transactions* 83: 1–3.

Deetz, S. 1982. Critical-interpretive research in organizational communication. *Western Journal of Speech Communication* 46 (2): 131–149.

Deetz, S. 1997. The business concept and managerial control in a knowledge-intensive organization: A case study of discursive power. In *Case Studies in Organizational Communication*, second edition, ed. B. Sypher. Guilford.

DeLuca, L. M., and K. G. Attuahene. 2007. Market knowledge dimensions and cross-functional collaboration: Examining the different routes to product innovation performance. *Journal of Marketing* 71 (1): 95–112.

DeSanctis, G., and M. S. Poole. 1994. Capturing the complexity in advanced technology use: Adaptive structuration theory. *Organization Science* 5 (2): 121–147.

Dewett, T., and G. R. Jones. 2001. The role of information technology in the organization: A review, model and assessment. *Journal of Management* 27: 313–346.

DiPaolo, B. P., J. M. Monteiro, R. Gronsky, N. Jones, and C. A. Brebbia. 2000. An experimental investigation on the axial crush of a stainless steel box component. *Structures and Materials* 8: 397–406.

Dodgson, M., D. M. Gann, and A. Salter. 2007. "In case of fire, please use the elevator": Simulation technology and organization in fire engineering. *Organization Science* 18: 849–864.

Dougherty, D. J. 1992. Interpretive barriers to successful product innovation in large firms. *Organization Science* 3 (2): 179–202.

Downey, G. L. 1998. *The Machine in Me: An Anthropologist Sits among Computer Engineers*. Routledge.

Dreyfus, H. L., and S. E. Dreyfus. 1986. *Mind over Machine: The Power of Human Expertise and Intuition in the Era of the Computer*. Free Press.

Dutton, W., and K. L. Kraemer. 1985. *Modeling as Negotiating: The Political Dynamics of Computer Models in the Policy Process*. Ablex.

Edmondson, A. C., R. M. Bohmer, and G. P. Pisano. 2001. Disrupted routines: Team learning and new technology implementation in hospitals. *Administrative Science Quarterly* 46 (4): 685–716.

Eisenberg, E. M. 1984. Ambiguity as strategy in organizational communication. *Communication Monographs* 51: 227–242.

Eisenberg, E. M., and M. G. Witten. 1987. Reconsidering openness in organizational communication. *Academy of Management Review* 12 (3): 418–426.

Eisenhardt, K. M., and M. M. Bhatia. 2002. Organizational complexity and computation. In *Companion to Organizations*, ed. J. Baum. Blackwell.

Emirbayer, M., and A. Mische. 1998. What is agency? *American Journal of Sociology* 103 (4): 962–1023.

Fairhurst, G. T., and L. Putnam. 2004. Organizations as discursive constructions. *Communication Theory* 14 (1): 5–26.

Fayard, A.-L., and J. Weeks. 2007. Photocopiers and water-coolers: The affordances of informal interaction. *Organization Studies* 28 (5): 605–634.

Feldman, M. S., and J. G. March. 1981. Information in organizations as signal and symbol. *Administrative Science Quarterly* 26: 171–186.

Fine, G. A. 1993. Ten lies of ethnography: Moral dilemmas of field research. *Journal of Contemporary Ethnography* 22 (3): 267–294.

Flores, F., M. Graves, B. Hartfield, and T. Winograd. 1988. Computer systems and the design of organizational interaction. *AMC Transactions on Office Information Systems* 6 (2): 153–172.

Francoeur, E., and J. Segal. 2004. From model kits to interactive computer graphics. In *Models: The Third Dimension of Science*, ed. S. de Chadarevian and N. Hopwood. Stanford University Press.

Fujimura, J. H. 1987. Constructing 'do-able' problems in cancer research: Articulating alignment. *Social Studies of Science* 17: 257–293.

Fulk, J., C. W. Steinfield, J. Schmitz, and G. J. Power. 1987. A social influence model of media use in organizations. *Communication Research* 14 (5): 529–552.

Galbraith, J. 1973. *Designing Complex Organizations*. Addison-Wesley.

Gale, N. 2005. Road-to-lab-to-math: A new path to improved product. *Automotive Engineering International*, May: 78–79.

Garfinkel, H. 1967. *Studies in Ethnomethodology*. Prentice-Hall.

Garud, R., and M. A. Rappa. 1994. A socio-cognitive model of technology evolution: The case of cochlear implants. *Organization Science* 5 (3): 344–362.

Gaver, W. 1996. Affordances for interaction: The social is material for design. *Ecological Psychology* 8 (2): 111–129.

Gerson, E. M., and S. L. Star. 1986. Analyzing due process in the workplace. *ACM Transactions on Office Information Systems* 4 (3): 257–270.

Gibbons, D. E. 2004. Friendship and advice networks in the context of changing professional values. *Administrative Science Quarterly* 49 (2): 238–262.

Gibson, J. J. 1979. *The Ecological Approach to Visual Perception.* Houghton Mifflin.

Gibson, J. J. 1986. *The Ecological Approach to Visual Perception.* Erlbaum.

Giddens, A. 1979. *Central Problems in Social Theory.* University of California Press.

Giddens, A. 1984. *The Constitution of Society.* University of California Press.

Golden-Biddle, K., and K. D. Locke. 1997. *Composing Qualitative Research.* Sage.

Gopal, A., and P. Prasad. 2000. Understanding GDSS in symbolic context: Shifting the focus from technology to interaction. *Management Information Systems Quarterly* 24 (3): 509–512, 539.

Gould, R. V. 2002. The origins of status hierarchies: A formal theory and empirical test. *American Journal of Sociology* 107 (5): 1143–1178.

Hargadon, A. B., and R. I. Sutton. 1997. Technology brokering and innovation in a product development firm. *Administrative Science Quarterly* 42 (4): 716–749.

Heidegger, M. 1959. *An Introduction to Metaphysics.* Yale University Press.

Heilbroner, R. L. 1967. Do machines make history? *Technology and Culture* 8: 335–345.

Heim, M. 1987. *Electric Language: A Philosophical Study of Word Processing.* Yale University Press.

Henderson, K. 1999. *On Line and on Paper: Visual Representations, Visual Culture, and Computer Graphics in Design Engineering.* MIT Press.

Henderson, R. M., and K. B. Clark. 1990. Architectural innovation: The reconfiguration of existing product technologies and the failure of established firms. *Administrative Science Quarterly* 35 (1): 9–30.

Hickson, D. J., D. S. Pugh, and D. C. Pheysey. 1969. Operations technology and organizational structure: An empirical reappraisal. *Administrative Science Quarterly* 14 (3): 378–397.

Hill, K. 2007. *Contribution of the Motor Vehicle Supplier Sector to the Economies of the United States and Its 50 States.* Motor & Equipment Manufacturers Association.

Holmström, J., and D. Robey. 2005. Inscribing organizational change with information technology. In *Actor-Network Theory and Organizing*, ed. B. Czarniawska and T. Hernes. Liber.

Homer, J. B., and G. B. Hirsch. 2006. System dynamics modeling for public health: Background and opportunities. *American Journal of Public Health* 96 (3): 452–458.

Hubert, L. J., and J. Schultz. 1976. Quadratic assignment as a general data analysis strategy. *British Journal of Mathematical and Statistical Psychology* 29: 190–241.

Hughes, T. J. R. 2000. *The Finite Element Method*. Dover.

Hughes, T. P. 1983. *Networks of Power: Electrification in Western Society*. Johns Hopkins University Press.

Hughes, T. P. 1986. The seamless web: Technology, science, etcetera, etcetera. *Social Studies of Science* 16: 281–292.

Hughes, T. P. 1987. The evolution of large technological systems. In *The Social Construction of Technological Systems: New Directions in the Sociology and History of Technology*, ed. W. Bijker, T. Hughes, and T. Pinch. MIT Press.

Hughes, T. P. 1994. Technological momentum. In *Does Technology Drive History? The Dilemma of Technological Determinism*, ed. M. Smith and L. Marx. MIT Press.

Hutchby, I. 2001. Technologies, texts and affordances. *Sociology* 35 (2): 441–456.

Innis, H. A. 1951. *The Bias of Communication*. University of Toronto Press.

Jackson, M. H. 1996. The meaning of "communication technology": The technology-context scheme. In *Communication Yearbook*, volume 19, ed. B. Burleson. Sage.

Jackson, M. H., M. S. Poole, and T. Kuhn. 2002. The social construction of technology in studies of the workplace. In *Handbook of New Media: Social Shaping and Consequences of ICTs*, ed. L. Lievrouw and S. Livingstone. Sage.

Jassawalla, A. R., and H. C. Sashittal. 1999. Building collaborative cross-functional new product teams. *Academy of Management Executive* 13 (3): 50–63.

Kaarst-Brown, M. L., and D. Robey. 1999. More on myth, magic and metaphor: Cultural insights into the management of information technology in organizations. *Information Technology & People* 12 (2): 192–217.

Kaghan, W. N., and G. C. Bowker. 2001. Out of machine age? Complexity, sociotechnical systems and actor network theory. *Journal of Engineering and Technology Management* 18: 253–269.

Karat, J., C.-M. Karat, and J. Ukelson. 2000. Affordances, motivation and the design of user interfaces. *Communications of the ACM* 43 (8): 49–51.

Kauffman, M. E., and D. F. Ritter. 1981. Cobble imbrication as a sensitive indicator of subtle local changes in river flow direction. *Geology* 9: 299–302.

King, J. L., and S. L. Star. 1990. Conceptual foundations for the development of organizational decision support systems. *System Sciences* 3 (3): 143–151.

Kline, R., and T. J. Pinch. 1996. Users as agents of technological change: The social construction of the automobile in the rural United States. *Technology and Culture* 37 (4): 763–795.

Knorr Cetina, K. 1981. *The Manufacture of Knowledge: An Essay on the Constructivist and Contextual Nature of Science.* Pergamon.

Krackhardt, D. 1992. The strength of strong ties: The importance of *Philos* in organizations. In *Networks and Organizations: Structure, Form, and Action,* ed. N. Nohria and R. Eccles. Harvard Business School Press.

Kranakis, E. 2004. Fixing the blame: Organizational culture and the Quebec bridge collapse. *Technology and Culture* 45 (3): 487–518.

Krishnan, V., and K. T. Ulrich. 2001. Product development decisions: A review of the literature. *Management Science* 47 (1): 1–21.

Kunda, G. 1992. *Engineering Culture: Control and Commitment in a High-Tech Corporation.* Temple University Press.

Kythe, P. M., and D. Wei. 2004. *An Introduction to Linear and Nonlinear Finite Element Analysis: A Computational Approach.* Birkhauser.

Lahsen, M. 2005. Seductive simulations? Uncertainty distribution around climate models. *Social Studies of Science* 35: 895–922.

Lakhani, K. R., and E. von Hippel. 2003. How open source software works: "Free" user-to-user assistance. *Research Policy* 32 (6): 923–943.

Latour, B. 1987. *Science in Action: How to Follow Scientists and Engineers through Society.* Harvard University Press.

Latour, B. 1993. *We Have Never Been Modern.* Harvard University Press.

Latour, B. 1994. On technical mediation: Philosophy, sociology, geneaology. *Common Knowledge* 3: 29–64.

Latour, B. 1999. *Pandora's Hope.* Harvard University Press.

Latour, B. 2005. *Reassembling the Social: An Introduction to Actor-Network Theory.* Oxford University Press.

Latour, B., and S. Woolgar. 1979. *Laboratory Life: The Social Construction of Scientific Facts.* Sage.

Law, J. 1987. Technology and heterogeneous engineering: The case of the Portuguese expansion. In *The Social Construction of Technological Systems: New Directions in the Sociology and History of Technology,* ed. W. Bijker, T. Hughes, and T. Pinch. MIT Press.

Lawrence, P., and J. Lorsch. 1969. *Developing Organizations: Diagnosis and Action.* Addison-Wesley.

Leitner, P. M. 2002. Teaching science and technology principles to non-technologists—lessons learned. *International Journal of Public Administration* 25 (9–10): 1155–1170.

Leonard-Barton, D. 1988. Implementation as mutual adaptation of technology and organization. *Research Policy* 17: 251–267.

Leonardi, P. M. 2007. Activating the informational capabilities of information technology for organizational change. *Organization Science* 18 (5): 813–831.

Leonardi, P. M. 2008. Indeterminacy and the discourse of inevitability in international technology management. *Academy of Management Review* 33 (4): 975–984.

Leonardi, P. M., and S. R. Barley. 2008. Materiality and change: Challenges to building better theory about technology and organizing. *Information and Organization* 18: 159–176.

Leonardi, P. M., and S. R. Barley. 2010. What's under construction here? Social action, materiality, and power in constructivist studies of technology and organizing. *Academy of Management Annals* 4: 1–51.

Leonardi, P. M., and M. H. Jackson. 2004. Technological determinism and discursive closure in organizational mergers. *Journal of Organizational Change Management* 17 (6): 615–631.

Leonardi, P. M., and M. H. Jackson. 2009. Technological grounding: Enrolling technology as a discursive resource to justify cultural change in organizations. *Science, Technology & Human Values* 34 (3): 393–418.

Lewis, W., R. Agarwal, and V. Sambamurthy. 2003. Sources of influence on beliefs about information technology use: An empirical study of knowledge workers. *Management Information Systems Quarterly* 27 (4): 657–678.

Lindlof, T. R. 1995. *Qualitative Communication Research Methods.* Sage.

Lundstrom, L. C. 1967. The safety factor in automotive design. *SAE Transactions* 75: 57–62.

Lyytinen, K., and J. L. King. 2006. Standard making: A critical research frontier for information systems research. *Management Information Systems Quarterly* 30: 405–411.

MacCormack, A., R. Verganti, and M. Iansiti. 2001. Developing products on "internet time": The autonomy of a flexible development process. *Management Science* 47 (1): 133–150.

Mackay, H., C. Carne, P. Beynon-Davies, and D. Tudhope. 2000. Reconfiguring the user: Using rapid application development. *Social Studies of Science* 30 (5): 737–757.

MacKenzie, D. 2006. *An Engine, Not a Camera: How Financial Models Shape Markets.* MIT Press.

MacKenzie, D., and J. Wajcman. 1985. The social shaping of technology. In *The Social Shaping of Technology: How the Refrigerator Got Its Hum*, ed. D. MacKenzie and J. Wajcman. Open University Press.

Majchrzak, A., R. E. Rice, A. Malhotra, N. King, and S. L. Ba. 2000. Technology adaptation: The case of a computer-supported inter-organizational virtual team. *Management Information Systems Quarterly* 24 (4): 569–600.

Markus, M. L. 1990. Toward a "critical mass" theory of interactive media. In *Organizations and Communication Technology*, ed. J. Fulk and C. Steinfield. Sage.

Markus, M. L. 2004. Technochange management: Using it to drive organizational change. *Journal of Information Technology* 19: 4–20.

Markus, M. L., S. Axline, D. Petrie, and C. Tanis. 2000. Learning from adopters' experiences with erp: Problems encountered and success achieved. *Journal of Information Technology* 15: 245–265.

Markus, M. L., and M. S. Silver. 2008. A foundation for the study of IT effects: A new look at Desanctis and Poole's concepts of structural features and spirit. *Journal of the Association for Information Systems* 9 (10/11): 609–632.

Marsden, P. V. 2005. Recent developments in network measurement. In *Models and Methods in Social Network Analysis*, ed. P. Carrington, J. Scott, and S. Wasserman. Cambridge University Press.

Mashaw, J. L., and D. L. Harfst. 1990. *The Struggle for Auto Safety*. Harvard University Press.

McLuhan, M. 1964. *Understanding Media: The Extensions of Man*. Routledge.

Merton, R. K. 1957. *Social Theory and Social Structure*. Free Press.

Miel, R. 2008. Auto suppliers seek edge with automation. *Plastics News*, August: 23.

Millane, R. P., M. I. Weri, and G. M. Smart. 2006. Automated analysis of imbrication and flow direction in alluvial sediments using laser-scan data. *Journal of Sedimentary Research* 76: 1049–1055.

Misa, T. J. 1994. Retrieving sociotechnical change from technological determinism. In *Does Technology Drive History? The Dilemma of Technological Determinism*, ed. M. Smith and L. Marx. MIT Press.

Misa, T. J. 2003. The compelling tangle of modernity and technology. In *Modernity and Technology*, ed. T. Misa, P. Brey, and A. Feenberg. MIT Press.

Mukerji, C. 1998. The collective construction of scientific genius. In *Cognition and Communication at Work*, ed. Y. Engstrom and D. Middleton. Cambridge University Press.

Nadel, S. F. 1957. *The Theory of Social Structure*. Cohen and West.

Nardi, B. A., and V. L. O'Day. 1999. *Information Ecologies: Using Technology with Heart*. MIT Press.

Norman, D. A. 1990. *The Design of Everyday Things*. Doubleday.

Norman, D. A. 1999. Affordance, conventions, and design. *Interaction* 6 (3): 38–43.

O'Brien, J. A. 2004. *Management Information Systems: Managing Information Technology in the E-Business Enterprise*. McGraw-Hill.

Ong, W. J. 1982. *Orality and Literacy: The Technologizing of the World*. Routledge.

Orlikowski, W. J. 1992. The duality of technology: Rethinking the concept of technology in organizations. *Organization Science* 3 (3): 398–427.

Orlikowski, W. J. 1996. Improvising organizational transformation over time: A situated change perspective. *Information Systems Research* 7 (1): 63–92.

Orlikowski, W. J. 2000. Using technology and constituting structures: A practice lens for studying technology in organizations. *Organization Science* 11 (4): 404–428.

Orlikowski, W. J. 2005. Material works: Exploring the situated entanglement of technological performativity and human agency. *Scandinavian Journal of Information Systems* 17 (1): 183–186.

Orlikowski, W. J. 2007. Sociomaterial practices: Exploring technology at work. *Organization Studies* 28 (9): 1435–1448.

Orlikowski, W. J., and D. C. Gash. 1994. Technological frames: Making sense of information technology in organizations. *ACM Transactions on Information Systems* 12: 174–207.

Orlikowski, W. J., and C. S. Iacono. 2001. Research commentary: Desperately seeking the "IT" in IT research—a call to theorizing the IT artifact. *Information Systems Research* 12 (2): 121–134.

Orlikowski, W. J., and S. V. Scott. 2008. Sociomateriality: Challenging the separation of technology, work and organization. *Academy of Management Annals* 2 (1): 433–474.

Orr, J. E. 1996. *Talking about Machines: An Ethnography of a Modern Job*. ILR Press.

Pacanowsky, M., and N. O'Donnell-Trujillo. 1983. Organizational communication as cultural performance. *Communication Monographs* 50: 126–147.

Padgett, J. F., and C. K. Ansell. 1993. Robust action and the rise of the Medici, 1400–1434. *American Journal of Sociology* 98 (6): 1259–1319.

Peirce, C. S., ed. 1932. *Elements of Logic*, volume 2. Harvard University Press.

Pentland, B. T., and M. S. Feldman. 2007. Narrative networks: Patterns of technology and organization. *Organization Science* 18 (5): 781–795.

Pentland, B. T., and M. S. Feldman. 2008. Designing routines: On the folly of designing artifacts, while hoping for patterns of action. *Information and Organization* 18 (4): 235–250.

Perrow, C. 1967. A framework for the comparative analysis of organizations. *American Sociological Review* 32: 194–208.

Perrow, C. 1970. *Organizational Analysis: A Sociological View.* Wadsworth.

Peterson, W. 1971. Application of finite element method to predict static response of automotive body structures. *SAE Transactions* 80: 1056–1072.

Pickering, A. 1995. *The Mangle of Practice: Time, Agency, and Science.* University of Chicago Press.

Pickering, A. 2001. Practice and posthumanism: Social theory and a history of agency. In *The Practice Turn in Contemporary Theory*, ed. T. Schatzki, K. Knorr Cetina, and E. von Savigny. Routledge.

Pinch, T. 2008. Technology and institutions: Living in a material world. *Theory and Society* 37: 461–483.

Pinch, T. J. 1996. The social construction of technology: A review. In *Technological Change: Methods and Themes in the History of Technology*, ed. R. Fox. Harwood.

Pinch, T. J. 2003. Giving birth to new users: How the minimoog was sold to rock and roll. In *How Users Matter: The Co-Construction of Users and Technology*, ed. N. Oudshoorn and T. Pinch. MIT Press.

Pinch, T. J., and W. E. Bijker. 1984. The social construction of facts and artifacts: Or how the sociology of science and the sociology of technology might benefit each other. *Social Studies of Science* 14: 399–441.

Pinch, T. J., and F. Trocco. 2002. *Analog Days: The Invention and Impact of the Moog Synthesizer.* Harvard University Press.

Pinto, M. B., J. K. Pinto, and J. E. Prescott. 1993. Antecedents and consequences of project team cross-functional cooperation. *Management Science* 39 (10): 1281–1297.

Pollock, N. 2005. When is a work-around? Conflict and negotiation in computer systems development. *Science, Technology & Human Values* 30 (4): 496–514.

Poole, M. S., and G. DeSanctis. 1990. Understanding the use of group decision support systems: The theory of adaptive structuration. In *Organizations and Communication Technology*, ed. J. Fulk and C. Steinfield. Sage.

Poole, M. S., and G. DeSanctis. 1992. Microlevel structuration in computer-supported group decision making. *Human Communication Research* 19 (1): 5–49.

Poole, M. S., and G. DeSanctis. 2004. Structuration theory in information systems research: Methods and controversies. In *Handbook of Information Systems Research*, ed. M. Whitman and A. Woszczynski. Idea Group.

Prasad, P. 1993. Symbolic processes in the implementation of technological change: A symbolic interactionist study of work computerization. *Academy of Management Journal* 36 (6): 1400–1429.

Ramos Alvarez, M. 1999. Modern technology and technological determinism: The empire strikes again. *Bulletin of Science, Technology & Society* 19 (5): 403–410.

Rice, R. E., L. Collins-Jarvis, and S. Zydney-Walker. 1999. Individual and structural influences on information technology helping relationships. *Journal of Applied Communication Research* 27 (4): 285–309.

Rice, R. E., and U. Gattiker. 2001. New media and organizational structuring. In *The New Handbook of Organizational Communication: Advances in Theory, Research, and Methods*, ed. F. Jablin and L. Putnam. Sage.

Rice, R. E., and E. M. Rogers. 1980. Reinvention in the innovation process. *Knowledge* 1: 499–514.

Robey, D., and M.-C. Boudreau. 1999. Accounting for the contradictory organizational consequences of information technology: Theoretical directions and methodological implications. *Information Systems Research* 10 (2): 167–185.

Robey, D., and S. Sahay. 1996. Transforming work through information technology: A comparative case study of geographic information systems in county government. *Information Systems Research* 7 (1): 93–110.

Rodgers, K. E. 1996. Multiple meanings of alar after the scare: Implications for closure. *Science, Technology & Human Values* 21 (2): 177–197.

Rohrer, M. W. 2000. Seeing is believing: The importance of visualization in manufacturing simulation. In *Proceedings of the 2000 Winter Simulation Conference*, ed. R. Joines, K. Kang, and P. Fishwick. Institute of Electrical and Electronics Engineers.

Rose, J., M. R. Jones, and D. Truex. 2005. Socio-theoretic accounts of IS: The problem of agency. *Scandinavian Journal of Information Systems* 17 (1): 133–152.

Rosenkopf, L., and M. L. Tushman. 1994. The coevolution of technology and organization. In *Evolutionary Dynamics of Organizations*, ed. J. Baum and J. Singh. Oxford University Press.

Rothlisberger, R. F., and W. J. Dickson. 1939. *Management and the Worker*. Harvard University Press.

Rust, B. R. 1972. Pebble orientation in fluvial sediments. *Journal of Sedimentary Petrology* 42 (2): 384–388.

Sassen, S. 2002. Towards a sociology of information technology. *Current Sociology* 50 (3): 365–388.

Schwartz Cowan, R. 1983. *More Work for Mother: The Ironies of Household Technology from the Open Hearth to the Microwave.* Basic Books.

Scott, C. R., L. Quinn, C. E. Timmerman, and D. M. Garrett. 1998. Ironic uses of group communication technology: Evidence from meeting transcripts and interviews with group decision support system users. *Communication Quarterly* 46 (3): 353–374.

Shane, S. 2000. Prior knowledge and the discovery of entrepreneurial opportunities. *Organization Science* 11 (4): 448–469.

Shapiro, S. 1997. Degrees of freedom: The interaction of standards of practice and engineering judgment. *Science, Technology & Human Values* 22 (3): 286–316.

Sheppard, S. R. J. 2005. Landscape visualisation and climate change: The potential for influencing perceptions and beaviour. *Environmental Science & Policy* 8: 637–654.

Simon, H. A. 1945. *Administrative Behavior: A Study of Decision-Making Processes in Administrative Organization.* Free Press.

Sims, B. 1999. Concrete practices: Testing in an earthquake-engineering laboratory. *Social Studies of Science* 29 (4): 483–518.

Smith, M. L. 1994a. Recourse of empire: Landscapes of progress in technological America. In *Does Technology Drive History? The Dilemma of Technological Determinism,* ed. M. Smith and L. Marx. MIT Press.

Smith, M. R. 1994b. Technological determinism in American culture. In *Does Technology Drive History? The Dilemma of Technological Determinism,* ed. M. Smith and L. Marx. MIT Press.

Snijders, T. A., and S. P. Borgatti. 1999. Non-parametric standard errors and tests for network statistics. *Connections* 22 (2): 1–11.

Spradley, J. P. 1979. *The Ethnographic Interview.* Holt, Rinehart and Winston.

Star, S. L. 1989. The structure of ill-structured solutions: Boundary objects and heterogeneous distributed problem solving. In *Distributed Artificial Intelligence,* ed. L. Gasser and M. Huhns. Morgan Kaufmann.

Star, S. L., and K. Ruhleder. 1996. Steps toward an ecology of infrastructure: Design and access for large information spaces. *Information Systems Research* 7 (1): 111–134.

Staudenmaier, J. M. 1994. Rationality versus contingency in the history of technology. In *Does Technology Drive History? The Dilemma of Technological Determinism,* ed. M. Smith and L. Marx. MIT Press.

Strauss, A. 1978. *Negotiations.* Jossey-Bass.

Strauss, A. 1985. Work and the division of labor. *Sociological Quarterly* 26 (1): 1–19.

Strauss, A. 1988. The articulation of project work: An organizational process. *Sociological Quarterly* 29: 163–178.

Strauss, A., and J. Corbin. 1993. The articulation of work through interaction. *Sociological Quarterly* 34 (1): 71–83.

Suchman, L. 2000. Organizing alignment: A case of bridge-building. *Organization* 7 (2): 311–327.

Sundberg, M. 2009. The everyday world of simulation modeling: The development of parameterizations in meteorology. *Science, Technology & Human Values* 34 (2): 162–181.

Tabrizi, B. N. 2005. *Accelerating Transformation: Process Innovation in the Global Information Technology Industry.* Universal.

Taylor, J. R. 2001. Toward a theory of imbrication and organizational communication. *American Journal of Semiotics* 17 (2): 269–298.

Taylor, J. R., C. Groleau, L. Heaton, and E. Van Every. 2001. *The Computerization of Work: A Communication Perspective.* Sage.

Thomas, R. J. 1985. *Citizenship, Gender, and Work: Social Organization of Industrial Agriculture.* University of California Press.

Thomas, R. J. 1992. Organizational politics and technological change. *Journal of Contemporary Ethnography* 20 (4): 442–477.

Thomas, R. J. 1994. *What Machines Can't Do: Politics and Technology in the Industrial Enterprise.* University of California Press.

Thomke, S. H. 1998. Simulation, learning and R&D performance: Evidence from automotive development. *Research Policy* 27: 55–74.

Thomke, S. H. 2003. *Experimentation Matters: Unlocking the Potential of New Technologies for Innovation.* Harvard Business School Press.

Thompson, J. D. 1967. *Organizations in Action: Social Science Bases of Administrative Theory.* McGraw-Hill.

Tushman, M. L., and P. Anderson. 1986. Technological discontinuities and organizational environments. *Administrative Science Quarterly* 31: 439–465.

Tushman, M. L., and D. A. Nadler. 1978. Information processing as an integrating concept in organizational design. *Academy of Management Review* 3: 613–624.

Tyre, M. J., and O. Hauptman. 1992. Effectiveness of organizational responses to technological change in the production process. *Organization Science* 3 (3): 301–320.

Tyre, M. J., and W. J. Orlikowski. 1994. Windows of opportunity: Temporal patterns of technological adaptation in organizations. *Organization Science* 5 (1): 98–118.

Vaast, E., and G. Walsham. 2005. Representations and actions: The transformation of work practices with IT use. *Information and Organization* 15: 65–89.

Van de Ven, A. H., and E. M. Rogers. 1988. Innovations and organizations: Critical perspectives. *Communication Research* 15 (5): 632–651.

Vermeulen, P. 2005. Uncovering barriers to complex incremental product innovation in small and medium-sized financial services firms. *Journal of Small Business Management* 43 (4): 432–452.

Vincenti, W. G. 1990. *What Engineers Know and How They Know It: Analytical Studies from Aeronautical History.* Johns Hopkins University Press.

Vinck, D., ed. 2003. *Everyday Engineering: An Ethnography of Design and Innovation.* MIT Press.

Volkoff, O., D. M. Strong, and M. B. Elmes. 2007. Technological embeddedness and organizational change. *Organization Science* 18 (5): 832–848.

von Hippel, E. 1986. Lead users: A source of novel product concepts. *Management Science* 32 (7): 791–805.

von Hippel, E. 1988. *The Sources of Innovation.* Oxford University Press.

Wade, J. 1979. *A Short History of the Camera.* Fountain.

Wagman, J. B., and C. Carello. 2001. Affordances and intertial constraints on tool use. *Ecological Psychology* 13 (3): 173–195.

Wajcman, J. 1995. Feminist theories of technology. In *The Handbook of Science and Technology Studies*, ed. S. Jasanoff, G. Markle, J. Peterson, and T. Pinch. Sage.

Walker, C. R., and R. H. Guest. 1952. *The Man on the Assembly Line.* Harvard University Press.

Walsham, G. 2002. Cross-cultural software production and use: A structuration analysis. *Management Information Systems Quarterly* 26 (4): 359–380.

Wasserman, N., and K. Faust. 1994. *Social Network Analysis: Methods and Applications.* Cambridge University Press.

Weick, K. E. 1979. *The Social Psychology of Organizing*, second edition McGraw-Hill.

Weick, K. E. 1990. Technology as equivoque: Sensemaking in new technologies. In *Technology and Organizations*, ed. P. Goodman, L. Sproull, and Associates. Jossey-Bass.

White, L. A. 1949. *The Science of Culture.* Farrar, Straus & Giroux.

White, W. S. 1952. Imbrication and initial dip in Kweenawan conglomerate bed. *Journal of Sedimentary Petrology* 22 (4): 189–199.

Wiener, N. 1966. Cybernetics. In *Communication and Culture: Readings in the Codes of Human Interaction*, ed. A. Smith. Holt, Rinehart, and Winston.

Williams, R., and D. Edge. 1996. The social shaping of technology. *Research Policy* 25: 865–899.

Winner, L. 1977. *Autonomous Technology: Technics-out-of-Control as a Theme in Political Thought*. MIT Press.

Winner, L. 1993. Upon opening the black box and finding it empty: Social constructivism and the philosophy of technology. *Science, Technology & Human Values* 18 (3): 362–378.

Womack, J. P., D. T. Jones, and D. Ross. 1991. *The Machine That Changed the World*. HarperPerennial.

Woodward, J. 1958. *Management and Technology*. HSMO.

Wotiz, A. 1974. Finite element model data checkout with interactive graphics. *SAE Transactions* 83: 1523–1531.

Wyatt, S. 2008. Technological determinism is dead: Long live technological determinism. In *New Handbook of Science, Technology and Society*, ed. E. Hackett, O. Amsterdamska, M. Lynch, and J. Wajcman. MIT Press.

Yates, J. 2005. *Structuring the Information Age: Life Insurance and Technology in the Twentieth Century*. Johns Hopkins University Press.

Yates, J., W. J. Orlikowski, and K. Okamura. 1999. Explicit and implicit structuring of genres in electronic communication: Reinforcement and change of social interaction. *Organization Science* 10 (1): 83–103.

Yearly, S. 1999. Computer models and the public's understanding of science: A case-study analysis. *Social Studies of Science* 29 (6): 845–866.

Zammutto, R. G., T. L. Griffith, A. Majchrzak, D. J. Dougherty, and S. Faraj. 2007. Information technology and the changing fabric of organization. *Organization Science* 18 (5): 749–762.

Zuboff, S. 1988. *In the Age of the Smart Machine: The Future of Work and Power*. Basic Books.

Index